D1596981

Shetland Life and Trade
1550-1914

Shetland Life and Trade
1550-1914

HANCE D. SMITH

Department of Maritime Studies
University of Wales Institute of Science and Technology

JOHN DONALD PUBLISHERS LTD
EDINBURGH

ISBN 0 85976 103 7

The publishers acknowledge the financial assistance of the Scottish Arts Council in the publication of this volume.

Exclusive distribution in the United States of America and Canada by Humanities Press Inc., Atlantic Highlands, NJ 07716, USA.

Phototypesetting by Burns & Harris Limited, Dundee.
Printed in Great Britain by Bell & Bain Ltd., Glasgow.

Acknowledgements

The research behind this book began as a Ph.D. thesis. I am indebted to the late Professor Kenneth Walton, and to Dr. J. R. Coull, both of the Department of Geography, University of Aberdeen, who between them provided many hours of constructive criticism through discussion and reading sections of my writings. Much inspiration and practical assistance then and now has been given by Brian Smith, Shetland's archivist, in discussion of the themes and problems of Shetland history, and in the provision of innumerable references based upon his extensive archival work over many years.

For hours of helpful discussion, provision of literature, documentary material and interchange of ideas and information over the years I am especially grateful to Dr. Frances J. Shaw, Professor K. Friedland, Mr. John J. Graham, the late Mr. Tom Henderson, the late Mr. G. M. Nelson, Mr. Walter Scott, Mr. William P. L. Thomson and Mr. Jonathan Wills.

Helpful interchange of ideas and information was provided by Dr. Ian Adams, Mr. John Baldwin, Mr. F. Bastian, Professor Gordon Donaldson, Dr. C. A. Goodlad, Mr. Malcolm Gray, Mr. Johannes Heggland, Professor Knut Helle, Professor H. H. Lamb, Mr. Evan MacGillivray, Dr. Ronald Mooney and Professor T. C. Smout.

For access to manuscript sources I would like to thank Professor and Mrs. S. G. Checkland (Letter Books of John Gladstone, University of Glasgow MSS, now in Clwyd Record Office); Mr. F. Garriock, formerly Managing Director, Hay & Company (Lerwick) Limited (Hay & Co. MSS); Mr. J. Gray (the former Zetland County Council Roads Department maps); the late Mr. R. A. Johnson, Sheriff Clerk (Records of Lerwick Sheriff Court, now in the Shetland Archives); Mr. A. Laurenson, Secretary, Lerwick Harbour Trust (Lerwick Harbour Trust plans and photographs); Mr. Lewis, formerly Commercial Manager of the former North of Scotland, Orkney and Shetland Shipping Company Limited (North Company records); Mr. David MacDonald, when Executive Assistant, Head Office, Royal Bank of Scotland (Records of the Royal Bank of Scotland); Mr. Mitchell, formerly Lerwick Fishery Office (for Records of Lerwick Fishery Office, now in the Scottish Record Office); Mr. A. G. Ockendon, formerly Custom House, Lerwick (for Lerwick Custom House MSS, now in the Shetland Archives); Mr. John H.

Scott, Gardie House (Gardie Papers); the late Sir Basil Neven Spence, D.L. (Neven of Windhouse papers in Busta House) and Mr. and Mrs. Bertley for assisting in my consultation of these papers — now in the Shetland Archives.

I wish to thank the staffs of the following for provision of much help in extensive documentary searching: Shetland County Library, Library of the University of Aberdeen, Scottish Record Office and the National Register of Archives (Scotland), Library of the Society of Antiquaries of Scotland, Library of the University of Edinburgh, Meteorological Office Library — Edinburgh, the British Museum, Public Record Office, H.M. Customs and Excise Library, London.

I wish to thank the following European institutions for the provision of helpful information: Universitetesbiblioteket i Bergen; Universitetets-biblioteket i Oslo; Riksarkivet, Oslo; Statsarkivet i Bergen; Fiskerimuseet i Bergen; Rigsarkivet, København; Det Kongelige Bibliotek, København; Staatsarchiv Bremen; Senat der Freien und Hansestadt Hamburg; Museum voor de Nederlandse Zeevisserij; the Spanish Embassy in London; El Director del Archivo de la Corona de Aragon; El Ingeniero Director del Puerto de Barcelona; Salinas de Torrevieja, S.A.; Biblioteca Central, Barcelona; the Portuguese Embassy in London.

For the provision of practical assistance during the later stages of the work I am grateful to Professor A. D. Couper, Department of Maritime Studies, University of Wales Institute of Science and Technology, and to the staff of the Cartographic Unit in the Department of Maritime Studies, and especially to Alun Rogers, who completed the cartography despite difficult circum-stances. I wish to thank Mrs. Joyce Suthers for arranging typing, and Mrs. Vivien Jordan who typed the manuscript.

Last, but by no means least, I thank my father and mother who provided much help and encouragement throughout the early phase of the work, and my wife, who saw it to completion!

Hance D. Smith

Contents

Introduction

Shetland, Ultima Thule, the land of the simmer dim, a focal point of European fisheries and Britain's oil resources, the Old Rock — the images are many and vivid, almost as kaleidoscopic as the changing patterns of light and shade and colour of a Shetland sunset. The writings on Shetland are correspondingly varied, and a reason perhaps ought to be given for yet more.

In his monumental work on the Mediterranean, the great French historian Fernand Braudel drew attention to three kinds of time, geographical, social, and individual. This book is primarily concerned with the social dimension, the time scales of distinctive social change related to economic development, itself a central theme in modern European history and still central to life today. It is not, however, a social history, or 'structural' history, though it may cast further light on aspects of Shetland social history. Rather, the primary focus is upon the preoccupation of successive social groups with material betterment, which is an important distinguishing feature of the modern European historical period, and which may even have something to do with the characterisation of the thrust of my research preceding this book as constituting a 'Whig interpretation of history'!

On the longer time scales of geographical time, the period roughly spans the climatic deterioration known as the 'Little Ice Age', a circumstance of substantial significance for a group of islands on the edge of the European world, dependent upon land and sea, and frequently afflicted by the repeated and often coincidental harvest and fishing failures which threatened to undo the work of those aiming at material improvement. The southward movement of cold ocean surface waters from the north, the easterly gales and frost, the fluctuation of fish abundance and harvests from year to year, and the thankfulness experienced every year when the corn was safe in the yard are constant themes.

The relatively short time scales of individual time also receive considerable attention, focusing upon those individuals and families who appear from the standpoint of today to have exerted a guiding and at times decisive influence upon the course of events, a history perhaps more akin to that of contemporary Britain and Europe than is fully realised, to be set against an ever stronger sense of identity among the Shetlanders themselves as well as for many from across the sea.

This sense of identity undoubtedly has much to do with the great weight today put upon shaping the future, especially in matters of economic life, such as regional planning, the management of natural resources, and the contribution of material things to the quality of life, itself an ill-defined concept which is, among other things, concerned with regional culture or 'ways of life'. The idea, expressed by Geoffrey Barraclough, that the past and future are less different, that 'a sense of history implies a sense of the future' is arguably implicit in planning. A proper interest in Shetland's past may indeed inform decisions taken for the future. It is upon the past that awareness of Shetland's separate identity in large measure depends, for Shetlanders — and others — past and present, wherever they may be.

Hance D. Smith
University of Wales

1

The Legacy of Time

To many in Shetland and beyond, Shetland's past has a timeless quality. This was especially the case for the late nineteenth and early twentieth-century romantics who looked back to the 'golden age' of Viking times built upon the Scandinavian settlement, which laid the foundation of the medieval period in Shetland history. Although in the historical record Shetland is eclipsed by Orkney, centre of the sea-based sphere of influence of the Orkney earldom, it too was at the centre of the North Atlantic world of the Norsemen, a world of great men and great deeds, immortalised in the Icelandic sagas, and an inspiration for the nineteenth-century founders of Up-Helly-Aa, not to mention the members of the new Zetland County Council of 1890.[1] Despite its Scottish, and British, recent history Shetland seemed to be looking for its identity to the long-lost world of the tings, recreated with some imagination by nineteenth-century intellectuals.[2] 'Med logum skal land byggia' read the motto on the windows of the new Lerwick Town Hall. It is still there to guide the re-organised Shetland Islands Council of the 1980s.

Thus, central to the Shetland identity by 1914 was this world of the imagination, made use of in the creation of an identity perhaps as much for the outsiders as for the Shetlanders themselves. It was a fitting image of the past for a part of a Britain at the height of its imperial powers. But it was buttressed by a real Norse inheritance in the place-names of the unchanging land and sea itself, and in the fast-disappearing vocabulary of the Norn, salvaged for posterity in the nick of time by that great, and appropriately Faroese, philologist, Jakob Jakobsen.[3] One of the main reasons for the decline of the vocabulary in Jakobsen's time was the gradual disappearance of the tangible aspects of the old culture, material and otherwise, upon which it was based. This book is about the people and ideas contributing to this change, as well as about the nature of the change itself, particularly those aspects relating to the economy based on land and sea, and its links from the edge of the European world to the lands beyond that sea. These changes span much of the 'modern' period of European history, which has been dominated among other things by a preoccupation with material betterment — the 'development' of academic and political jargon; and by the

1

strengthening of regional cultural and political entities, above all the nations of Europe.[4] At the centre of all this in Shetland's case were those who developed the economy and who gave shape to a constantly evolving society, which in turn gave form to a distinctive series of economies, which left a now fast disappearing imprint upon land and sea. Most of all, this modern period has been associated with the emergence of a regional consciousness, highlighted by the characteristic but deceptive isolation of all islands, and yet which may be almost as tangible as the very patterns of land and sea.

Land and Sea

At the centre of human activity were the townships (Fig. 1a) which dated from Scandinavian times,[5] and with their associated hill pastures and near-shore fishing grounds were the geographical units not only of settlement, but also of subsistence and commercial production upon which the economy was based. Although the world of the medieval township must remain to some extent speculative, in being based on painstaking reconstruction by research in several disciplines,[6] by the early nineteenth century agriculture was still being organised on the basis of runrig. There was still a timeless quality about the nature of production.

The fields produced oats and bere from which came the staple item of diet — meal. The small enclosures of yards and plantie-crubs were used to produce mainly cabbages, and later also potatoes and other vegetables. Meadowland produced hay, and the animals were kept on the township land in the winter, being put to the hill in summer. Cattle provided milk, made into butter, blaand* and cheese, and meat for the winter with tallow for a source of light and hides for the making of footwear known as rivlins*. These hides were often exported along with the surplus butter. Sheep provided wool, the basis of domestic clothing manufacture, 'wadmel'* cloth for the payment of rent, with surpluses going into the making of woollen stockings, an export item of great importance until the end of the eighteenth century (Chapters 2, 3). Local outcrops of stone and stones gathered from fields, and probably sometimes beaches also, provided building materials, although imported wood was also used in homebuilding down to perhaps the seventeenth century.[7] Coarse hill grasses along with straw provided roofing, and the means of making kishies* to carry the almost ubiquitous peat, which was the staple source of fuel for heating and cooking. Nearshore fishing in the voes and sounds was an important supplement to the diet, and also provided large quantities of oil made from coalfish livers which, along with butter production, entered commerce largely via the rental system. Thus a very large proportion of the material needs of the community were served without the need to enter trade.

Footnote: Asterisked words are defined in the Glossary.

A:The Landscape Basis

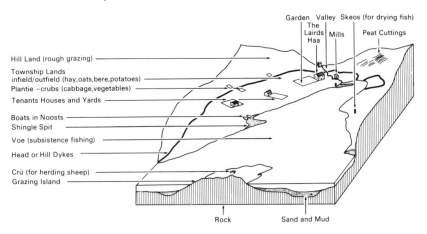

B:The Seasonal Cycle of Activity

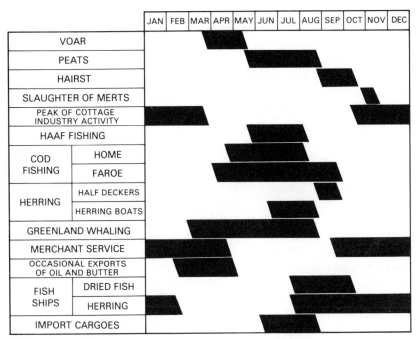

Note: Subsistence fishing was carried out all year round.

Figure 1. A: Production from land and sea   B: The round of the seasons

The round of the seasons (Fig. 1b) began with the spring or 'voar'* round the end of March or first week of April, when the land was delved* (sometimes ploughed in the flatter fertile lowlands), seaweed manure often being used. This season lasted until the end of April and was followed in May or June by the cutting ('casting')* and drying ('raising')* of the peats, which were normally brought home in July or August. The period from the end of August until mid-October was occupied by the harvest, the timing and length of which depended on the weather. Meanwhile, from May to mid-August the commercial haaf* fishery, which lasted until the end of the nineteenth century, was carried on by the majority of the men, while the women and children tended the farmland. Once the corn was stacked* in the yard, the round of summer and harvest-time activity was at an end, and the winter routine was entered. The young cattle ('marts')* were slaughtered and salted down about the beginning of November, and the ensuing winter season was the peak time for domestic manufactures, including the knitting of goods for export.

This seasonal rhythm of production determined much of the character of trade which was based to a large extent on its extension into commerce, especially before 1800. This character of the system and the balance between subsistence and commerce determined the export and import commodity types and quantities respectively (Chapter 2). Variations in the timing of the seasons caused similar variations in the operation of trade, such as ship sailing times (Chapter 6). Perhaps most important of all, the division of labour both seasonally and occupationally was conducive to the expansion of new types of summer fishing including cod and herring fishing.

The aggregate of townships which made up the settlement pattern was probably the primary influence in determination of patterns of production and trade in an era when a subsistence economy tied closely to land and sea was typical of the islands as a whole. This pattern was, and remained, closely adjusted to the seemingly unchanging elements of land and sea and historically was a major determinant of the spatial organisation of production and hence of internal trade. The most evident influence on the settlement pattern is the threefold division of geological structure (Fig. 2).[8] Thus the metamorphic central area is typified by long, narrow townships clinging to valley sides, notably in the limestone valleys which possess good quality soil, and along long stretches of relatively sheltered coast, as in the central Mainland area. The outlying western sedimentary districts and the crystalline complex of Unst and Fetlar are associated with townships of various irregular shapes of which a considerable number are inland. Both these areas tend to have townships scattered individually on favourable sites and a dispersed pattern of steadings within each township, in contrast to the south-east sandstone lowlands with their large number of clustered townships and steadings frequently grouped in a cluster at the centre of each township. The dependence on the sea highlighted the contrast between exposed cliff coasts of the periphery, and the central sheltered voes with

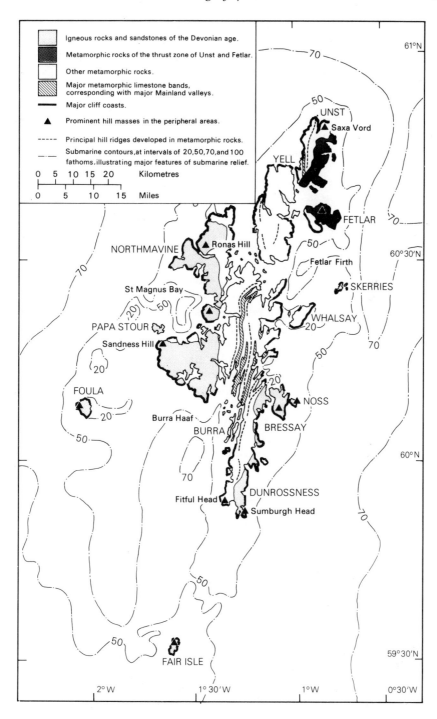

Figure 2. Features of land and sea

their numerous beaches and bay-head barriers.

It seems likely, particularly from place-name and other evidence, that most of the readily cultivable land was occupied in the Scandinavian period,[9] when the population may have been higher than during the later Middle Ages. Although a considerable proportion of land was ley* in the seventeenth and eighteenth centuries, especially in the more fertile areas of Unst, Fetlar and Dunrossness, it occurred largely within the area of settled ground. Large nucleations were non-existent, the only possible exception being Scalloway, which was the centre of government and may have had a few houses in early times. Certainly by the beginning of the seventeenth century a few traders had settled, and it became the site of a castle. In addition, merchants' booths were scattered among some of the more important harbours (Chapter 2).

The essentials of the land production system, including a constancy in agricultural technology, probably remained unchanged during the whole period of the Scandinavian settlement and after. But it was not a static world. There was probably a gradual deterioration in climate, which may have affected production through being cooler, wetter and more stormy than the Middle Ages.[10] While fragmentation of the landholding structure under the influence of the udal system of land tenure tended to detract from agricultural improvement of any kind, not only because of the fragmentation of land into small units of ownership, but also because of the disputes over tenure which were likely to arise, nonetheless there were large estates before the coming of Scottish settlers and influence in the fifteenth century.[11]

A further element of change was the population. Due to the subsistence character of the economy, large shifts in population would have implied correspondingly large changes in the levels of production. The level of population cannot be measured at all accurately before the middle of the eighteenth century; the estimate of around 20,000 for the Scandinavian period[12] is based unreliably on the high density of Scandinavian place-names as reflecting a correspondingly high density of settlement. There is practically no information at all for the intervening period. The prevalence of smallpox epidemics in the first half of the eighteenth century is strongly suggestive of a level of population at least no higher than Webster's count of just over 15,000 in 1755, and it is probable that the population in the seventeenth century was in the order of 10,000 to 12,000, or even less.[13] Unfortunately there is little specific evidence in a Shetland context relating to recurrent disease and famine, which were among the most potent influences on subsistence populations, although famine was practically endemic in Scotland in the period 1550-1600.[14] It is likely that the Black Death produced a steep decline[15] which, if losses in population following this epidemic in 1349 were as high as in Norway and the British Isles,[16] would have reduced the population by one-third to one-half. Such a change would have contributed to the depression of Shetland-Norway trade which appears to have taken place between 1350 and 1500.[17]

There is no reason to suppose that there were any major technological changes in the fisheries either.[18] The predominantly commercially oriented inshore open boat fishery appears to have been maintained until the early eighteenth century (Chapter 3). Subsistence probably took up a greater share of productive effort than subsequently, although the expansion of the German merchants' trade in the fifteenth century suggests that the fisheries were becoming more commercially oriented.[19] It is unlikely that there was any great specialisation in fishery areas such as developed in the eighteenth century. The only probable change of far-reaching consequences was in the distribution of herring stocks in the North Sea/Baltic area[20] linked to a relatively greater abundance and exploitation of herring in Shetland waters by European fleets during the late fifteenth and sixteenth centuries.

The Edge of the European World

By the end of the Middle Ages, trade was arguably the main means of contact with the lands beyond the sea. Before the early fifteenth century, trade was probably mainly with Norway and controlled by Norwegians and Shetlanders. In 1186, traders from Shetland were mentioned by King Sverre as coming to Norway with necessary supplies.[21] The islands came under the direct rule of Norway in 1195,[22] and thus the Crown Rents* were payable direct to Norway, as in the case of the other 'scatlands'* of Faroe and Iceland. Norwegians owned land in Shetland — as did the Norwegian Church.[23] There was a Shetland burgess in Bergen in 1316,[24] and during the later Middle Ages, Shetland fish were much thought of in Bergen and indeed throughout the Hanseatic world.[25]

The second component was the dominant role of the Hanseatic League, which was perhaps the most important single feature of trade in Europe north of the Alps in the Middle Ages[26] — especially the later Middle Ages in Shetland's case. The Hanseatic domination of Norway rose as the power of the Norwegian Crown declined, the first trade treaty being signed with Lübeck in 1250,[27] and German power had become an important influence in Bergen in the 1290s.[28] The Bergen kontor*, under the direct control of Lübeck, was established in 1343,[29] though the northern Norwegian fish supplies continued to be shipped by local people,[30] and the same may have occurred in Shetland. The Bergen kontor monopolised Norwegian trade to a very large extent until around 1500,[31] and it is significant that this period 1343-1500 tallies almost exactly with the trade depression between Shetland and Norway already referred to.

There were two important reasons contributing to this depression. First was the virtual extinction of Norwegian (and probably Shetland) business entrepreneurs in the face of competition from the Germans, aggravated by the effects of the Black Death, which in Norway certainly disrupted the economy sufficiently to cause decline in Norwegian trading interests.[32] The second factor, which had the greatest long-term consequences for

Shetland trade, was the increasing degree to which the Bergen kontor was bypassed by Hamburg and Bremen merchants, who acted independently of the edicts of the Wendish cities (especially Lübeck, which maintained its hold over Norwegian trade through the Bergen kontor).[33] Accompanied by advances in shipping technology which, by the fifteenth century, enabled long open-sea voyages to be undertaken with a degree of confidence,[34] it resulted in the diversion of most of the fish trade directly to Germany by the beginning of the sixteenth century, when the split between the western and eastern cities of the League occurred.[35] The first recorded direct voyage between Hamburg and Shetland took place around 1415 and, by 1434, there had been three prohibitions of trade between the 'scatlands' and northern Germany by the Bergen kontor.[36] Also, from 1397 onwards, Norway came under the political domination of Denmark, whose aspirations to power resulted in war with the Hanseatic League between 1438 and 1441 and consequent weakening of the Bergen kontor for a time, which was an added advantage to the western cities of the League in developing their trade with Shetland.

However, the various wars in which Denmark became involved during the fifteenth century led to her general weakening and to financial difficulties which contributed to the pledging of Orkney and Shetland in 1469.[37] Whereas in Orkney's case much Scottish influence, including the development of trade links, was already evident,[38] Shetland was much more closely linked to Norway and north Germany. It is also likely that the English were present as traders in the Shetland area, though not to the same extent as in Iceland in the fifteenth century.[39] Certainly English merchants and fishermen continued to operate on an appreciable scale in the Shetland area in the first half of the sixteenth century and on a reduced scale until after the beginning of the seventeenth century.

The important trade links and landowning connections of Shetland with Norway and of Orkney with Scotland were not immediately affected by these political changes. The influence of Scotland was but gradually exerted through the administrative structure and only became very powerful in Shetland's case when the Scottish immigration began in the latter half of the sixteenth century.[40] Meanwhile, by around 1540, immigrant Scots, English and Dutch merchants together with local Bergen merchants had established a foothold in Bergen trade once more,[41] and it was from about this time that Shetland trade with Norway began to expand again. The decline in the power of the Bergen kontor was not the only reason; another was the rise of the Scottish landowners in the Shetland area. Thus although political factors in a direct sense were unimportant until the middle of the sixteenth century, the power struggles of Denmark with her neighbours were instrumental in causing Shetland to come within the political ambit of Scotland, and ultimately made Scotland's impact on Shetland that much more decisive. When the expansion of the Scottish economy and strengthening of Scottish political structure got under way, she could revolutionise much of Shetland's way of life, including domination of the socio-economic structure by the immigration of a landowning class.

Perhaps the outstanding feature of the historical background of the later Middle Ages is the relatively slow rate of change of trade characteristics, although of course there were events such as the Black Death of 1349 which must have produced sudden far-reaching change in the volume of trade.[42] At the local level, the probable significance of the slow deterioration of climate, between the Little Climatic Optimum and the Little Ice Age, and the changes in distribution of herring stocks have already been referred to.

In the context of external factors, the decline of Norway as a great power in northern Europe occurred slowly in the thirteenth and fourteenth centuries,[43] as did the decline of Denmark in the fifteenth. The depression in trade between Shetland and Norway lasted a century and a half, and recovery in the first half of the sixteenth century was exceptionally slow by the standards of even the second half of the same century, let alone later times. Meanwhile, the slow upward trend of prices in the fifteenth and early sixteenth centuries was subjected to a sharp upturn in the mid-sixteenth century.[44]

Most important in the long term for Shetland as a whole was the decline of the Hanseatic League in the fifteenth and sixteenth centuries, an affair which must have been almost imperceptible at the time as year succeeded year in the islands. The divergence of interests between Lübeck and Hamburg took a century and more, from 1415 until 1530, to fully emerge, and signalled the formal end of the Hanseatic League insofar as Shetland trade was concerned. It had taken seventy years after the Bergen kontor was established for direct trading with north Germany to develop significantly, and a similar time elapsed between the initial development of the Dutch fisheries in Shetland waters around 1500[45] and the beginning of their great expansion in the 1580s.[46] Clearly it was an era not notable for great development in trade.

By the middle of the sixteenth century, therefore, a new and uncertain phase was being entered in which these slow changes were combining to produce a relatively sudden cumulative effect, creating an 'early modern' world which was very different from that of the Middle Ages. There was a relatively free and unhindered trade with north Germany in the hands of north German merchants; a less important but developing link with Scotland and, to some extent, England, partly of a similar nature to the north German trade, but partly composed of the immigrant landowners' transactions with their homeland; an expanding Norway trade in the control of the immigrant Scottish landowners; and a definite expansion in foreign fishery activity led by the Dutch, and to a lesser extent the Scots, combined with a decline of the English fisheries in the area. It is on these four components of external origin that the external relations of Shetland for a century and a half were to be based — a trade system of itinerant 'ship' merchants.

2

The Ship Merchants, 1550-1710

The chief aspect of Shetland's society and economy as Europe emerged from the Middle Ages was of a world of divided initiatives and spheres of influence. At the centre of the stage were the German merchants, mainly from Hamburg and Bremen, their ships plying on an annual summer round to Shetland and carrying away most of the commercial surplus. They had some competitors, from the emerging commercial powers of Holland and England, and also from Scotland. Also, from the southern shores of the North Sea came the fishermen of Holland, their industry expanding greatly with the relative stability provided by the United Provinces after 1581. They too had competitors from Scotland and England. Shetland was a land of landowners and tenants, and the local role involved maintaining some of the medieval links with Norway, but by the end of the seventeenth century there existed the local initiative crucial to sustain the island economy after the Union of Parliaments of Scotland and England in 1707. It was a world in which the mass of the population lived out their lives in the same place, often in the same township, and in which merchants, great and small, travelled to the source of production and dared not trust even a part of their transactions to any but themselves. By the middle of the sixteenth century these spheres of influence were firmly established to form a distinctive geography both within Shetland and through its maritime links to the lands beyond.

The German Merchants

The first references to direct trading with north Germany date from the 1410s, and there are scattered references in the better-documented German sources throughout the fifteenth century.[1] The earliest references from British sources relate to the beginning of the sixteenth century. In a complaint by certain Bremen merchants made to the Privy Council of Scotland in 1567, some of the complainers were alleged to have commenced business in Shetland 66 years previously,[2] that is, around 1500, and there are indications in this case that these merchants were carrying on the trade as had been done by previous generations. The tombstone of Segebad Detken of

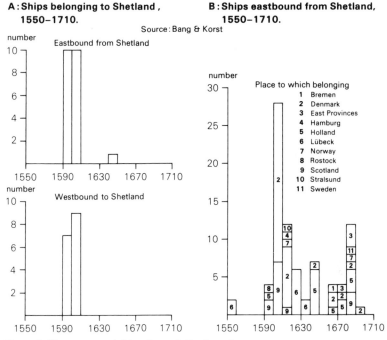

Figure 3. The passage of ships through the Sound

Bremen, who died in 1573, states that he had traded in Shetland for 52 years, i.e. since 1521.[3] Even as late as the 1520s the Hansetag were reiterating their prohibition of direct trade with Shetland.[4] The first frequent allusions to the merchants occur in the account of charges against Laurence Bruce of Cultmalindie in the 1570s.[5] Whilst there are normally no references to individual merchants in this account, Buchanan in 1582[6] mentions a Bremen merchant resident at Burravoe in Yell. Thereafter, records become more abundant, principally through the Court Books[7] and Register of Testaments[8] (1602-1649), both of which list large numbers of individual names and, from the 1650s to the 1680s, in the accounts of the Earldom rents[9] and customs returns.[10] On the whole it seems likely that the trade expanded in parallel with the similar Iceland trade in the latter half of the fifteenth century,[11] and its demise is recorded as being round 1707 — the last Bremen merchant is referred to as being in the islands in 1711.[12]

The origin of the merchants is notable in that, during the whole period, only three north German towns are mentioned in Scottish and English sources, viz. Hamburg, Bremen and Lübeck. The town of Lübeck is only mentioned in the literature and in Hamburg and Bremen records,[13] especially in the first half of the century, but the passage of ships from Shetland through the Sound[14] suggests that a small trade may have been based on that town at that period (Fig. 3). Unfortunately, although the number of merchants mentioned in the first part of the century is considerable, very few have their city of origin referred to — four from Bremen and two from Hamburg in 1602-1604, for example.[15] Hamburg sent one or two ships per annum until 1600, and from two to nine per annum between 1600 and 1633, when continuous records cease,[16] although there were a record number of fourteen Hamburg ships in 1647, and as many as twenty-six in 1679.[17] In the customs accounts of 1669-1673, seven of the ships are designated as belonging to Hamburg and two to Bremen, which is in contrast to the list of merchants in 1683-1684,[18] where nine of the merchants are from Bremen and two from Hamburg. The Baltic towns of Danzig, Rostock and Stralsund, and also Kampen and Deventer, were also involved at various times,[19] probably before the seventeenth century.

In the absence of other statistics, such as those relating to imports and exports, the number of merchants is of particular importance in gauging the scale of the trade. The earliest information relates to the period 1602-1604, when fifteen separate merchants are mentioned, generally organised into companies of some sort ('moscopes,' 'Maschup', Danish, 'maskepi'),[20] thus making it impossible to state exactly how many merchants there were in any given year, as few names are mentioned as belonging to companies. A family tradition of carrying on the business was not uncommon — Herman Dicken had a son Magnus in the trade, and Yaine Martfield was the son of Hetman Detmure.[21] The greatest number of merchants at any one location in Shetland was four — at Laxfirth (Fig. 4).[22]

The Register of Testaments containing the personal estates and liabilities of local people at the time of their deaths provides further information for the period 1604-1648.[23] At least 36 separate merchants are named, including 10 in the period 1604-1619; 16 in the period 1620-1629; and 12 in the period 1630-1648.

The principal sources of information regarding the remainder of the century are the Lordship rentals with their associated accounts, and the customs records. Thus in each of the years 1656 and 1657 there were 12 merchants paying tolls to the superior, of whom 10 were 'Dutchmen' (13 different names), the word 'Dutch' signifying German (i.e. 'Deutsch') origin, thus distinguishing them from the two 'Hollanders' (3 different names) from the Holland area of the Low Countries.[24] In the customs account of 1669-1673 there are 17 names in all, including 11 entries in each of the years 1669 and 1672 and 10 entries in 1673.[25] Finally, in the year 1683 a total of 11 merchants were granted bonds for butter and oil exports.[26] In all there are at least 46 individual merchants' names from the above sources in the period 1656-1683. A few of these men can be traced over considerable periods of time — thus Otte Meyer ('Otta Macke' in the record) was operating in Shetland in 1653[27] and 1673;[28] Adolph Westermann, from as early as 1669[29] until as late as 1684, was succeeded by his son Daniel.[30] As in the early part of the century there was a company association among the merchants. In the period 1669-1673, for example, there were not more than 9 ships among the 17 merchants,[31] and there were from 7 to 9 ships operating in 1700.[32]

Plate 1. Busta House and Farm: This was the seat of the Giffords of Busta, the leading eighteenth-century landowning family. The oldest part of the house dates from 1714 and was built by Thomas Gifford, who also started the garden. The oldest part of the dock is of eighteenth-century date, though this was probably a site for the operations of the German merchants before that. Beyond is Busta Voe, where Thomas Gifford's four remaining sons and their cousin were drowned on the night of 14th May, 1748, while crossing over from Brae (off to the left of the picture) to Busta House. The interlocking pattern of land and sea, and the low, cliffed coast are typical of Shetland's 'inner coast', sheltered from the open sea. Copyright: Shetland Museum and Library.

Plate 2. The haaf station, Stenness: (c. 1880). Stenness was one of the leading haaf stations in Shetland. Note the sloping stony beach, the fishermen's lodges in the background, and the boats hauled up on the beach. The fishermen stayed in the lodges when ashore during the week, and walked home at weekends. Copyright: Shetland Museum and Library.

Plate 3. The South End of Lerwick: Most of the buildings along the shore beyond the breakwater date from the late eighteenth century, and consist of former lodberries built out into the sea, together with former merchants' houses. Immediately to the rear of these buildings was the southern stretch of Commercial Street, to which the houses had access. The breakwater enclosing the Small Boat Harbour in the foreground was completed in 1915. It was designed primarily to provide shelter for the Lerwick haddock boats and pleasure craft. This picture was taken c. 1930s. Copyright: Shetland Museum and Library.

Plate 4. Kergord, Upper Weisdale: This shows part of Upper Weisdale, cleared in the 1840s. The estate subsequently became famous as the location of the only extensive tree plantations in Shetland. The first plantations were established in the 1860s as a trail experiment, but were unsuccessful. The present trees were planted between 1908 and 1921, and more recent plantings have been undertaken by the Forestry Commission. The principal types of trees are Japanese larch and sitka spruce, of little economic value as growth is restricted by climatic conditions. Copyright: Shetland Museum and Library.

Plate 5. Garthspool and the North Ness: Although taken c. 1928, by which time the herring drifters were supreme, the picture shows the layout of the docks area at a stage it had reached by 1914, with Garthspool and the West Dock (extreme right, foreground), Hay's Dock (near centre, behind, largely obscured by buildings), and the North Ness (left, middle distance). Note the drifters anchored in Bressay Sound with mizzen sails set, and the large quantities of herring barrels on the stations. Beginning with the construction of Hay's Dock in the early 1820s by William Hay of Laxfirth, soon to be followed by Garthspool at the instigation of the Mouats of Gardie (Gardie House is on the Bressay shore, just off the picture to the left), this area was the centre of Shetland's trade development throughout much of the nineteenth century. Copyright: Shetland Museum and Library.

Plate 6. Hauling a shot of herring aboard the *Queen Adelaide,* c. 1922. Note the capstan and the wheel. Copyright: Shetland Museum and Library.

Plate 7. John Brown's Station, Garthspool, 1905: Gutting herring at the farlins. Copyright: Shetland Museum and Library.

Plate 8. Hamnavoe, Burra: (late 1890s): In the foreground is Cooper's herring station, with the village beyond. The only true fishing village in Shetland, Hamnavoe owed its origins to the combination of herring and haddock fishing which permitted specialisation in fishing all year round. The large building in the background, left of centre, is the shop. From left to right, the clusters of houses are Highmount, Gleburn, Dukestreet and Roadside. Note the English names. Copyright: Shetland Museum and Library.

Plate 9. A motor haddock boat: The *Homeland,* shown here, was one of the largest of her class, and was notable in being the only straight-stemmed modified Shetland model type built by Walter Duncan, Hamnavoe, Burra. Fully decked, generally with a raked stem, these boats were a great improvement on the open haddock boats which had been the basis of the winter haddock fishing until that time. She was built in 1919 and sometimes used in the herring fishing as well as for haddock fishing. In the background (right) is Nicolson & Co's shop, at Scalloway, established by Charles Nicolson, pioneer of the cod fishing, in 1820. Photograph: Harry Jamieson, Collector, Lerwick.

Plate 10. Building a corn 'skroo': Benigarth, North Roe, c. 1920. Bringing the corn into the relatively sheltered, enclosed croft yard remained central to the crofting year until the inter-war period, although the growing of oats and barley was in decline from around 1870. Copyright: Shetland Museum and Library.

Plate 11. Bringing home the peats: These ponies are walking across the beach at Tresta in Fetlar with peats from the 'hill' of Lamb Hoga in the background. Ponies were commonly used in this way until the end of the nineteenth century. Fetlar and Unst, along with Bressay, were major sources of breeding stock for the export trade. Peats were also exported from time to time in the nineteenth century for use in the distilleries of Scotland, although the main use was for domestic fuel. Copyright: Shetland Museum and Library.

Plate 12. A Shetland schooner: This is a drawing of the topsail clipper schooner *Matchless*, built by Hall's of Aberdeen in 1846 for the mail run between Lerwick and Leith. She remained on this route until 1881, by which time competition from North Company steamers was proving too much for her operators, the Zetland New Shipping Company. She was 89 feet long and 107 tons register. Copyright: Shetland Museum and Library.

Plate 13.   Neutral Shipping, 1916: This photograph shows shipping brought into Lerwick for examination during the First World War. Lying in Breiwick, the vessels demonstrate clearly both the variety of shipping and the mix between sail and steam at the close of the period discussed in this book. Note (foreground) the Faroese smack, with a schooner immediately behind and steam drifter to the immediate left. There are two barques (right) and a full-rigged ship (left) as well as a number of large steamers. Note, also, the sheep grazing in the foreground. By this time the name 'Shetland' was perhaps as well, if not better, known worldwide for knitwear, wool and ponies than for fishing and shipping interests. Copyright: Shetland Museum and Library.

Plate 14.   Dale o Waas: Note the compact nature of the group, enclosed by the yard dyke, and the mixture of tarred felt and thatched roofs; also the roofless steading, extreme right. In the background is Foula, used for the filming of 'The Edge of the World' in 1936, inspired by the story of the evacuation of St. Kilda in 1930. This film was evocative of the early twentieth-century view of such places as remote and, perhaps fairly realistically, of a way of life rapidly passing away. Copyright: Shetland Museum and Library.

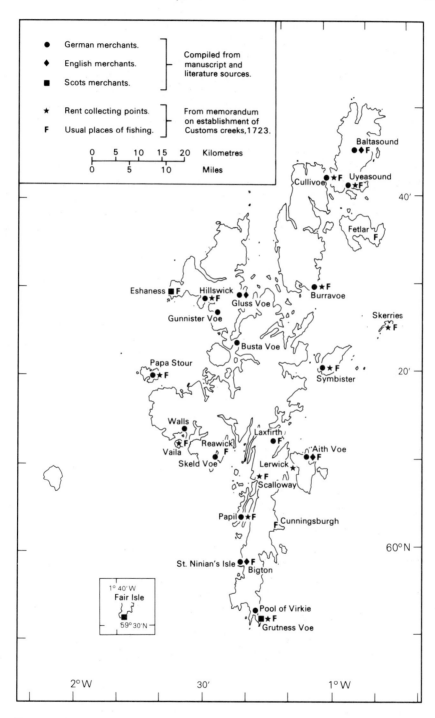

Figure 4. The ship merchants

In summary it would appear that there were about 10 to 12 merchants trading in Shetland in normal years, and that this figure remained relatively constant from the mid-seventeenth century onwards. It may have been somewhat higher in the early part of the century, since even as late as 1647 there were 14 ships in that one year.[33] There may have been too many merchants for the volume of the import trade in particular[34] towards the end of the period, which supports other evidence for a decline of the export trade.

There were trade points in Shetland, which tended to be more or less permanently recognised. Identification of these locations from the records is fraught with a considerable degree of uncertainty, arising partly from the incompleteness of the information given, and partly from the factors influencing the location and the mode in which trade was carried on. Those places which were certainly occupied at some time during the period are recorded in Fig. 4. The only reasonably comprehensive lists of locations relate to the 1560s and early 1600s. In 1602-1604,[35] of 12 merchants, one was based at Uyeasound; one each in Cullivoe and Burravoe; one in Gluss and one in Gunnister Voe; four in Laxfirth; and two in Dunrossness — most probably at the 'Dutch Pool' (Pool of Virkie — Fig. 4). In addition there are references to 'the Duchemen of Papa' and 'the Duchemen of Skeldevo'[36] (Papa Stour and Skeld Voe respectively — Fig. 4). In the period from the late 1620s to the early 1650s there was one in Burra (near Papil).[37] The locations of the remainder of the merchants before 1650 can only be inferred from references to the tenants who owed them debts,[38] from which it appears that there were spheres of influence round these centres determined largely by the degree of accessibility by sea. Combining these sources, it seems likely that certain areas were of greater importance than others in trade activities, although the statistics are by no means reliable enough to be certain. Unst and Fetlar loom particularly large in respect of the number of foreign merchants. For example, out of a list of 96 seventeenth-century merchants, 12 — or one-eighth — are associated with these two islands; this represents one-fifth of the 60 in this list specifically located, tending to lend weight to independent evidence that they had a monopoly of trade in the North Isles in the mid-sixteenth century.[39]

Information is even more sparse in the second half of the century. From the 1656 Rental it is evident that there were German merchants at Bigton and Papa Stour, and from the perambulations of the customs officer in 1669-1673[40] it can be demonstrated that Whalsay, Burravoe, Uyeasound, Hillswick, Papa Stour, Walls, Burra, Bigton and Dunrossness were definite sites, and also Lerwick and Scalloway on odd occasions, at least for entry of goods. From the sheriff court records it emerges that there were merchants situated in Northmavine, Unst (including Balta and Uyea), Walls, Burravoe, Laxfirth and Whalsay in 1681.[41]

Location was also determined by the mode of operation of the merchants — either by ship, booth or permanent residence. Of these three, permanent residence was least common, though merchants sometimes stayed over the winter.[42] Probably the most pressing requirement and therefore the most reliable indication of location were the harbours in which the ships were based. Suitable harbours depended on the physical suitability of the anchorage and relationships with the local landowners, and the established rent-collecting points may also have tended to stabilise locations. The locations of booths, on the other hand, were necessarily related directly to the requirements of individual fishing areas, and are thus a less reliable guide to merchants' locations. For example, round 1700 there were said to be six booths in Unst,[43] yet Uyeasound, and sometimes Baltasound, are the only two places generally mentioned as being the bases of German merchants — thus Uyea and Balta referred to in the above may have been booth sites only in 1681.[44] In 1709 the merchants were said to have operated 18 booths at the time of their expulsion from trade,[45] suggesting that there were not many outside the locations on the map (Fig. 4). Of course the major centres had their booths on shore in addition to ships moored nearby, notably at Laxfirth and Whalsay for example, and the scattered nature of the inshore fishery areas sometimes rendered it necessary for the merchant to build or acquire interests in booths at places other than his main 'ship' base — a process simplified by operation in companies. Thus, for example, in 1603 two merchants in Dunrossness contracted to have a booth built at Aithsvoe in Bressay.[46]

The trade was a summer phenomenon geared to the fisheries. The merchants arrived about the end of May or the beginning of June to coincide with the commencement of the summer ling fishery, and remained until its close, returning in August or September.[47] There is nothing to suggest that there were any variations in this routine during the period, though it is possible that there might have been more than one voyage by individual ships in any given season in spite of the fact that the number of ships in relation to production capacity does not suggest a large number of additional voyages.

The arrival of a ship was of course a major event, its importance measurable by the fact that non-arrival might signify local dearth,[48] and for some considerable time before the commencement of the period under review until the changing of the old order which came about in the years immediately following the demise of the Stewart Earls, the whole operation was carefully regulated according to recognised rules, as is apparent from evidence in the 1570s[49] and 1600s.[50] Thus the location of the ship was regulated by the Foud (chief administrator), notwithstanding the other influences on location enumerated above, as were the dues which were paid by the merchants to the owner of the adjacent shores used for fish-drying purposes.

Disagreements on occasions reveal how these rules might bring about changes in location in order to preserve small-scale district monopolies around specific harbours. Thus when Simon Harriestede in Gunnister Voe was ordered by the Foud to remove in 1603 at the instance of the protests of Otte Meyer in Gluss (Fig. 4), the former represented unsuccessfully that he had been granted this privilege of location in 1582 by the Earl himself. He had to remove to Papa Stour,[51] where he appears still to have been in business in the early 1620s.[52] Similarly, the foud of each parish, with the assistance of a few local men of standing, met the merchants in each case at a 'coupsetting' after the ship arrived, when the prices of the merchant's and the locals' goods were agreed. The owner of the land received a barrel of beer or meal by way of rent, and the tenants (at least prior to 1570) received 'ane coup barrell of beir (beer) at the said coupsetting'.[53]

The relationship of the landowners and the merchants in the sixteenth century was thus a quite highly formalised one, notably with regard to location. After the demise of the Earl and the old legal system in the second decade of the seventeenth century,[54] however, the relation of merchants and landowners is much less clear until the latter part of the seventeenth century, though no doubt the courts would have settled disputes. By the end of the period, the relationship appears to have been more highly commercialised, and the landowners were building the booths at their own expense — Stewart of Bigton built the booth for the merchants at Bigton,[55] and Sinclair of Quendale did likewise on Fair Isle.[56] Landowners could recover the cost of a booth in three years or so through rents charged for it.[57]

The toll formerly paid by the Earl continued to be paid to the owner or tacksman of that estate in addition to the landowner's exactions, and formed part of the superior rental account amounting to almost £800 Scots by mid-century.[58] From the 1650s to the 1680s a substantial part (sometimes amounting to practically the whole) of the Lordship rents, paid in butter and oil, were sold by the local landowning chamberlain to the merchants.[59] These were the largest single export items apart from fish, due to the large size of the Lordship estate in the seventeenth century. These transactions, although not regulated in the legal manner of the late sixteenth century, were nonetheless subject to strict bargaining procedure, with precise instructions as to how the merchants were to be dealt with in the negotiation of prices and letting of booths at most advantageous rates.[60] There is also record of small sums being paid by merchants to the landowners for permission to trade with the latter's tenants,[61] although it is not clear whether this had anything to do with the payments of rents for the use of beaches and booths. The closeness of commercial relationships is instanced by the fact that by this time some merchants had obtained liferent tacks* of beach areas,[62] and were hiring landowners' flitboats.[63*]

The landowners also engaged in other buying and selling transactions with the merchants, especially towards the end of the period, although it is likely that rents paid in kind by the tenants continued to form the basis of many transactions. For example, the chamberlain to the Lordship in 1682 was also negotiating on behalf of Sinclair of Burgh in Nesting for the disposal of Sinclair's butter, oil and fish.[64] In 1703, there are records of Westshore

buying brandy and tobacco from the German merchants;[65] more significantly in the context of the landowners' increasing interests in trade, when
the ship *Grace* was stranded at Uyeasound in 1680, Laurance Stewart of
Bigton and James Leslie bought a two-thirds share* of her and sold one-third
to a German merchant.[66]

The merchants generally dealt directly with the tenants,[67] even as late as
1701 when the landowners as a class were adopting a more commercial outlook, relative to earlier times. The process is well described by Brand:[68] 'And
these merchants seek nothing better in Exchange for their Commodities,
than to truck with the Countrey for their Fishes, which when the Fishers
engage to, the Merchants will give them either Money or Wares which they
please, and on the Fishers going to Sea, what they take, they bring once in
the Week or oftener as they have occasion, and layes them down at their
Booth Door, or in any other place where the Merchant appoints them to be
laid, and they being numbered, the Merchants account for them accordingly.' Such a list[69] of 'Fish put in to Otta Macke' and 'Ane nott of geir taikin
out from Otta Macke' both confirms and illustrates the operation of this
arrangement for the year 1653 ('Otta Macke' — i.e. Otte Meyer, a Hamburg
merchant). It is likely that the tenants would bave been at an increasing disadvantage as the century progressed due to the augmentation of weights
and measures and the parallel depreciation of currency, and the probable
increase in dealings with landowners in the latter part of the seventeenth
century discussed above may be related to such a change; in other words,
the landowners may have been acting as middlemen to some extent by the
end of the period.

The apparently increasing commercial interests — or at least awareness —
of the landowners with regard to the German trade may also be significant in
assessing the changing character of the import[70] and export trades. It has
indeed been contended that by the end of the period the balance of the
import and export trades was becoming increasingly unfavourable to the
Germans in that there were too many merchants for the scale of the import
trade,[71] the numbers being presumably more closely a reflection of the
requirements of the export trade.

The imports of Shetland from the German merchants during the period
fall into a simple pattern of five categories. First of all were those items
required for commercial production, restricted generally to fishing gear (the
merchants seem to have had no part in the Norway trade in boats and other
wood goods). The principal items were hooks and lines, hemp and tar, and
salt, some of which was Scots salt originally taken as back freight[72] by the
merchants on return journeys to north Germany. The second category consisted of essential foodstuffs, limited almost exclusively to rye meal to
supply the shortfall in local subsistence produce, but also some wheat flour
and bread, probably for the landowners. The third item was closely related
to the first, consisting of beer, spirits (mainly corn brandy) and tobacco
principally — and on occasion expressly[73] — for the use of the fishermen.

Table 1. Imports, 1669-1673.

These statistics are taken from the Customs Accounts. As various measures (units) have been used for the same quantities in the original records, no attempt has been made to change this in the table. In the case of goods which are sometimes given by weight and sometimes by value, for example, the price is often not given, so that it is not possible to quote equivalents.

Goods	Units	1669	1672	1673
salt	barrels	462	—	—
	lasts	14½	—	—
hooks and lines (sometimes	value: dollars	210	20	180
includes nails)	value: £ Scots	140	941	290
hemp	value: dollars	—	40	
	value: £ Scots	124½	—	—
	lb. wt.	30	250	—
tar	barrels	6	8	8
iron	lb. wt.	—	—	—
rye meal	barrels	173	190	131
wine	hogsheads	—	—	—
brandywine	pints	—	100	—
beer	barrels	—	9	3
	satts(?)	—	7	6
mum beer*	barrels	—	18	—
mead*	barrels	—	25½	—
	£ Scots duty	—	—	£2-8-0
corn brandy	ankers*	—	—	2
	pints	—	—	35
tobacco	cwts.	4	—	—
	lbs.	395	850	565
linen cloth (sometimes included	value: dollars	370	20	207
'creme ware', i.e. other textiles)	value: £ Scots	430	1589½	580
soap	kegs/firkins*	20	6	6
shoes	value: £ Scots	—	30	—

The fourth category comprised 'household' items, mainly in the form of linen cloth and small quantities of other textiles such as muslin, shoes, and soap. Finally was money: in 1700 seven ships were reckoned to bring in 3,600 dollars (i.e. rixdollars*) used in buying fish and other produce,[74] for example.

The table of goods imported for the years 1669-1673 (Table 1) constitutes the only detailed statistics available locally, and it is worth noting the fluctuations in the various classes of imports. The fact that salt is recorded for 1669 only, and spirits not at all in 1669 is probably due in part to administrative factors. That salt imports tended to fluctuate from year to year can be demonstrated from eighteenth-century records (Chapter 3). Such fluctuations were related to the degree of success of the fisheries, and in some years no imports were necessary. The appearance of wine, spirits and beer, and tobacco in quantity would suggest that smuggling was not practised as extensively as in later times, when these commodities seldom, if ever, appear in Customs records of imports. Beer and spirits often could not be 'had for money' until the merchants arrived,[75] although in the early part of the century at least, ale was brewed in Dunrossness.[76]

During the sixteenth and early seventeenth centuries, barter seems to have been more prevalent than subsequently, as evidenced by the frequent allusions to the wadmel measure* and its money equivalent prior to 1628.[77] The merchants generally dealt in dollars, particularly the rixdollar*, although other currencies and their respective coinages* were in common use, especially in the late sixteenth and early seventeenth centuries,[78] including Danish (shillings), Scots (pounds, marks, groats, bawbees), English (angels or angel nobles), and German (dollars and zopindales). As the Dutch fisheries expanded in the Shetland area, Dutch coinage no doubt also circulated in quantity. On the whole, however, it is likely that the merchants remained the chief importers of coinage, and their import trade, apart from maintaining certain sections of the commercial economy and supplementing the subsistence food supply in both essential and non-essential items, thus signified a constantly favourable balance of payments for the Shetland economy as a whole which was used to finance trade links with other areas, notably Orkney.

In the seventeenth century the products of the sea formed the basis, indeed the vast bulk, of export commodities. The staple throughout the period was the ling; cod, though significant, were much less important, followed by skate. Unfortunately there are no runs of statistics to illustrate the scale of exports, but there are some precise estimates for the period 1700-1710 based on the reckonings of Scots and English merchants hoping to engage in the trade. In 1700-1701, Robert Jolly (see below) estimated that the whole Shetland fish exports could be handled by five ships carrying 1,400 cwt. of ling and 240 cwt. of cod each, a total export of 8,200 cwt. per annum, which he alleged was being carried at that time by eight or nine north German ships. In addition he reckoned on a total of 600 cwt. of skate being exported every year.[79] In a subsequent contract dated 1709 by Captain Robert Jolly (almost certainly the same man), 800 lasts* (c. 1,600 tons) of fish, butter and oil were reckoned as having been carried away every year by the Germans in ten or twelve cargoes, the fish consisting of ling, cod, tusk, skate and herring. Taking the last as equivalent to two tons or six barrels,[80] and allowing for a substantial export of herring, it suggests a figure of well over 10,000 cwt. of dry ling and cod.

Fisheries were of course subject to various wide environmental fluctuations from year to year, though 1700 itself was reckoned as having been a good year.[81] On the whole an annual figure of around 10,000 cwt. (500 tons) of white fish (mainly ling) seems a reasonable estimate of exports per annum in the latter part of the seventeenth century at least, when the fisheries generally were poor. This scale of production was not greatly different from that of the mid-eighteenth century (Chapter 3). It has been estimated that Shetland contributed over 10 per cent by value of stockfish entering international trade in the sixteenth and seventeenth centuries. In addition, substantial quantities of herring were exported in the early seventeenth century, being some 270 tons annually to Hamburg between 1629 and 1633.[82]

The other principal commodities in the merchants' export trade were butter and oil, which were to a considerable extent the produce of rents paid in kind, although it is likely that from time to time substantial quantities of oil entered into purely commercial transactions. In the assessment of the trade by Jolly in 1700-1701, 80 barrels of butter and 50 of oil were reckoned as being exported in every cargo, giving a figure for five cargoes of 400 barrels of butter and 250 barrels of oil exported per annum. This figure is less certain than that for the fish exports insofar as the merchants had a virtual monopoly of the former at this time, whereas in the case of the latter the substantial butter and oil rents of the Lordship (100-130 barrels of butter and about 50 barrels of oil per annum in the second half of the seventeenth century) appear to have been increasingly exported to Scotland from the 1670s onwards.[83] That these exports could be subject to physical environmental influences of an annual kind over and above normal exigencies is illustrated by Brand's reference to fish having had little or no oil in their livers in the year 1699.[84]

Other exports carried by the merchants were comparatively unimportant, most significant being probably woollen goods, though the position regarding these is none too clear, especially in the closing decades of the sixteenth century. It certainly appears that rents were still paid partly in wadmel[85] rather than in money, but after 1628 this seems to have been permanently converted into a money payment.[86] Although the German merchants dealt in wadmel,[87] the part played by them is not known in detail. In the latter part of the seventeenth century the quality of Shetland woven cloth was reckoned to be poor,[88] and in any case the staple of this section of the economy — woollen stockings — was largely directed towards the trade with the Dutch fishermen from early in the seventeenth century. Hides, tallow, feathers and skins were also bought. Rabbit skins, in particular, were an item in the Earldom rental in the sixteenth century,[89] and rabbit warrens were sufficiently esteemed to receive special mention in seventeenth-century accounts, such as those of Unst in Captain John Smith's account of 1633,[90] and of Minn and Meil in the description of Burra in 1654.[91]

The Rise of Scotland and England

Competition with the Germans must be viewed in conjunction with the attitude to the fisheries in Scotland and England as the mercantile outlook gained momentum in the sixteenth and seventeenth centuries. Develop-

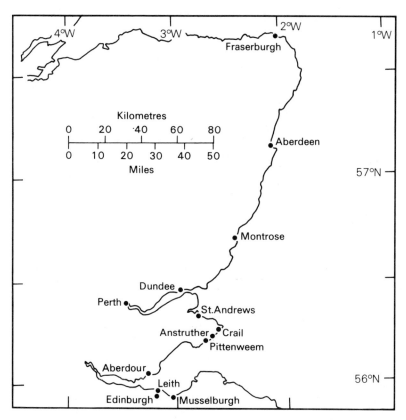

Figure 5. Scottish links

ment of the fisheries generally was a recurrent theme, especially in periods of relative peace in the 'home countries', and there appear to have been two phases of development which took place before and after the periods of the Civil War and the Commonwealth respectively, with important bursts of initiative around 1630 and again in the 1660s. As English and Scottish fishermen also operated in the Shetland area (Chapter 6), it is not invariably clear whether fishing and merchant activity were mutually exclusive. Indeed the same remarks apply to some extent to the German merchants themselves, at least in the seventeenth century, as they certainly carried fishing gear for subsistence fishing[92] at least.

In the first phase, until the 1630s, the opposition consisted of both English and Scottish merchants (Fig. 5), of whom the English tended to be the more important competitors. Thus Earl Patrick made an agreement for the use of Shetland as a fishing base by the English in 1594.[93] In 1603 there was an English merchant based at St. Ninian's Isle and probably one at Gluss in Northmavine,[94] and in the 1680s it is recorded that 'in olden time' English merchants occupied a booth at Aith Voe in Bressay[95] — no doubt the one built by Captain Thomas Knychtson for the two German merchants just after 1600.[96] The most notable incursion of the English, or at least the best documented, took place in the years round 1630 in a general wave of interest in trade which was sweeping England at that time. In 1629 Sir William Monson wrote[97] that fishing establishments should be set up in Orkney, Shetland and Lewis, and a principal town established in each group of islands for the purpose. In 1632 there was a Scottish Act of Parliament establishing a fourteen-mile fishing limit for foreign vessels. It was designed to protect and encourage Scottish and English fishing interests, including those around Shetland, at the expense of the Dutch.[98] In 1633 John Smith traded in Unst for twelve months as factor for the Earl of Pembroke, and freighted a cargo of fish to London.[99]

The earliest specific record of trade with Scotland is in 1573, although this was a case of piracy. A ship was stolen from Burntisland to Shetland, where the king's rents were loaded on board and taken to Aberdeen for sale.[100] The Dundee Shipping Lists[101] for the 1580s contain several references to arrivals from the 'north Ylles' — almost certainly Orkney and Shetland — with ladings of herring, dried salt fish and oil. James Lindsay, a burgess of Dundee, freighted a ship to Shetland in 1591, and in 1610 David Hill, burgess of Musselburgh with five or six others undertaking voyages from the Forth area to Orkney and Shetland for ladings of oil and fish, was forbidden to take victual over and above the ships' requirements.[102] In the period 1612-1618 there are several arrivals at Dundee from Shetland, including four in 1612, one in 1615 and one in 1618, all laden with dry salt fish, herring and oil.[103] The overall picture presented, therefore, is one of a small but significant amount of trade being carried on.

The distinction between fishermen and merchants is particularly blurred in the Scottish case. Thus Orkney and Caithness fishing boats had booths at Sumburgh at the beginning of the seventeenth century,[104] and Earl Patrick seems to have been involved in the fisheries in some way, as appears from an allegation against him in 1611: '. . . that the Erle has compellit the inhabitants to contract to his lordship the haill commodity of fischingis'.[105] Also, in 1624 Ninian Neven, a leading landowner, refers to his 'fisheing trade' although whether this was in any way associated with the Scottish merchants is not clear — certainly his business transactions were being carried out at Leith. The debts of the tenants[107] indicate Scots merchant activity, and almost certainly are related to the fish trade of Dundee and Crail merchants, though the latter port also sent fishermen to Shetland in the sixteenth and seventeenth centuries (Chapter 6). Also there were a significant number of dealings between Scottish merchants — who may not all have been itinerant — and the landowners (Fig. 5).

The events of the years after 1660 posed a much more serious threat to the German merchants' trade. Although Parliament[108] and the Privy Council[109] were forced to acknowledge the indispensability of the Germans in the Shetland economy in 1662, several acts had been passed[110] in the previous year authorising merchants in Edinburgh, Kilrennie, Crail, Anstruther Easter and Pittenweem to have preference over the German merchants in the fishing trade at Shetland. Some of them may have intended merely to fish on their own account, using Shetland as a base, but this was not the case regarding two Dundee merchants granted permission in the same year to trade in Shetland *provided* they imported the goods normally imported by the German merchants.[111] Merchants from Dundee remained in Shetland until the close of the century, and were based at Grutness, adjacent to the 'Dutch Pool' which had formerly been occupied by German merchants.[112] They were also based in Fair Isle in 1695, and had the use of Sinclair of Quendale's boat for travelling to and from the island.[113]

In the latter part of the century also, the materials of the Lordship rentals paid in kind were being transported more frequently to Scotland, rather than being sold to the German merchants. Thus in 1669 it was noted that in the previous Dutch War a large part was being transported to Leith when taken by a Dutch privateer.[114] When Andrew Dick, the tacksman, lost his ship off Fraserburgh in 1677, she was on her way to Scotland with the rents.[115] Finally, the importance of this trade is illustrated by the remark of Sibbald[116] about ". . . all . . . Necessaris . . . for which . . . they trade with their barks loaden with fish and Oyl to Scotland, and bring home such Commodities from thence as they want . . .'. By this time, of course, the German merchants' trade was virtually at an end, and that of the landowners had scarcely got under way.

The third and final phase of active and increasing competition occurred in the decade 1700-1710. In all, at least three enterprises were either mooted or established. These were designed to gain a foothold in the Shetland fish export trade, with a view to eventual creation of monopolies at the expense of the Germans. The first scheme[117] of note was that of Robert Jolly, factor in Hamburg to Alexander Pyper, a leading Edinburgh merchant. Jolly devised a scheme whereby the Shetland fish trade might be monopolised by five ships operated from Hamburg by a Scottish company, and his scheme is the most detailed British source of information on the operation of the itinerant merchant system for the period. Whether anything came of his scheme at the time is uncertain, although Brand, writing in 1701, mentions that 'Consideration of this great Gain that doth redound to the Trading Merchants hath of late animated some Gentlemen and others in Zetland, to enter into a Society or Company for Trading in Fishes . . .'.[118] The 'great Gain' referred to by Brand no doubt means the 40 per cent profit margin calculated by Jolly in his scheme — a high profit designed to offset the high risks involved in all sea trading operations of the period.[119]

A still more concrete cause of competition was the joint-stock company floated by the Earl of Morton[120] (who acquired the Lordship estate at the time) in London in 1706 with a capital of £2,000 sterling, of which one-sixth was to be used in whaling, and one-twentieth in fishing, the butter and oil of the Lordship rents to be delivered free of freight charges at Leith or London from time to time as required. It is almost certainly this scheme which was referred to by Thomas Gifford of Busta, one of the great fishing landowners of the eighteenth century. Writing over three decades later,[121] he stated that the company failed because only two ships were sent — an insufficient number to cater for the numerous fishing areas (Fig. 62), with the consequence that neither of the ships could obtain a full cargo. The capital, which had been partly raised locally, was soon exhausted, resulting in the failure of the enterprise. Gifford himself lost £150 sterling as a result. The interest in whaling can be seen in the context of the desire in Scotland and England to emulate the great seventeenth-century successes of the Dutch in whale fishing.[122]

The final scheme was a contract drawn up in 1709[123] by a Captain Robert Jolly, probably the same man who had formulated the 1701 scheme, and some London merchants with a few of the leading Shetland landowners, for the disposal of Shetland's exports. In this scheme the local landowners had to organise all the local elements of the trade, including provision and supervision of booths, and the company's vessels were responsible only for taking the fish away. Thus this enterprise in its geographical organisation was intermediate between the true itinerant merchant system with its external control and the system of the landowners who became established to the virtual exclusion of all others in the years after 1712.

Links with Orkney were of a different character to those with mainland Scotland and England, being based mainly on the import of meal into Shetland by Orkney merchants. There is no evidence to suggest that there was any substantial export of fish by these merchants. Although there were trade connections with Orkney in the first half of the seventeenth century, the majority of references date from the last few decades of the period. Significantly, the few early references are connected mainly with debts owing to skippers in Orkney,[124] and it may be that Orkney merchants were supplying Shetland with wood imports as they did to some extent as late as the middle of the eighteenth century. It is interesting in this connection that the extant customs returns indicate no imports of wood into Shetland, but considerable quantities into Orkney. From the discharge of the Lordship rents in 1664[125] it appears that there were small quantities of fish, butter and a few live cattle sent to Orkney, and from the 1680s onwards there are references to saddle horses being imported from Orkney.[126] The South Harbour of Fair Isle was reckoned in the 1680s to be 'very commodious' for Orkney boats which travelled to Shetland,[127] indicating that the trade was in the hands of itinerant Orkney merchants. Sibbald, quoting in part from Smith (1633, published 1662), indicates that the principal import from Orkney was corn,[128] as indeed it appears to have been as early as the 1610s.[129]

The trade seems to have reached a peak around 1700, possibly due to the declining influence of the German merchants, who had formerly imported large quantities of rye meal (Table 1): 'Beside their fish-trade with foreign merchants, they do likewise drive a great trade with Orkney, from which every year several boats do pass to Zetland Loaden with Corns, Meal, Malt, &c. upon the coming whereof they often wait for barley seed, tho' the last Year (1699) they had a Considerable Crop, so that the Barley Seed was sown before the boats came across. The Orkney men also bring sometimes Stockinis, Ale and the like, which they know to be vendible here. Hence every year considerable Sums of Money go from Zetland to Orkney, and some have told that most of the Money they have in Orkney is from Zetland. So great is the advantage that these Isles do Reap by their Neighbouring Commerce with one another, for Zetland could not well live without Orkney's corns, so neither could Orkney be so well without Zetland's money.'[130] Thus the Orkney trade was an important element in the trade pattern as a whole by the end of the period, although it declined shortly thereafter (Chapter 3).

The Dutch Fishermen

One of the principal sources of cash used in the Orkney trade derived from the commercial relationship between Shetland and the groups prosecuting the fisheries carried on by various European nations in the waters round the archipelago. During the latter half of the sixteenth and the whole of the seventeenth centuries, these external fisheries, mainly to the east of Shetland, played a significant role in the economy of the islands. Although by far the most important of these was the Dutch herring fishery, which bids fair to be ranked as the third major external commercial influence on the island economy after the German merchants and other merchants discussed above, there were also cod and ling fisheries carried on by the Dutch, English and Scots.

The importance of the Dutch herring fishery in the present context lies in the considerable amount of trade which it engendered between the fishermen and the local inhabitants in the course of the seventeenth century. This trade consisted of numerous small-scale transactions, but it is unique in relation to other external fisheries developments in the Shetland area (Chapter 6) because of its very large scale in terms of the number of vessels engaged, and its varying impact on the economy as a whole. It appears from the evidence below to have increased in direct proportion to the increasing numbers of vessels engaged following the expansion of the Dutch herring fishery in Shetland waters and to have varied according to its subsequent vicissitudes.

The distant water fisheries of the Dutch appear to have grown in the fifteenth century contemporaneously with the development of the buss*, and operations in the Shetland area date from around 1500.[131] The first local references relate to the 1530s when one Robert Fogo of Leith attacked Dutch busses,[132] including some fishing in the vicinity of Shetland, which he was ordered to restore around 1540.[133] The fishery was not as highly organised as it was to be subsequently, a major disadvantage being friction with the

States General Administration of Holland, which was however finally resolved by co-operation in the years after 1575.[134] This paved the way, with the gaining of independence by the Dutch in 1581, for the expansion of the herring fishery which began about that time.[135]

The majority of English contemporary sources referring to Dutch fishing consist of English political pamphleteers of the first half of the seventeenth century, who were intent on the replacement of Dutch commercial supremacy in the North Sea fisheries generally by that of England. Thus figures tend to be high, varying between 1,000 and 3,000 vessels, with around 2,000 being a favourite estimate.[136] However, Beaujon reckoned that 2,000 was the maximum possible limit of all fishing vessels belonging to the Dutch, not only the summer herring fishers.[137]

For the Shetland herring fishery, therefore, perhaps more reliable evidence is available from local sources which are less likely to be biased in favour of large and exaggerated numbers. In 1594, over 100 vessels were referred to by the Earl of Orkney as disturbing the peace in the Shetland area.[138] The first reference to regular trading in Bressay Sound between the Dutch and the local people dates from 1615,[139] and in the first written account of Shetland dating from the period 1615-1618, 200 or 300 busses are referred to as resorting annually to Bressay Sound.[140] Prohibitions on trade at Bressay Sound were issued in 1615 and 1625,[141] suggesting continuing expansion, and the development continued until mid-century.[142] It is perhaps significant that although Brand and Gifford both allude to 2,000 busses in the area,[143] Brand states that 500 to 700 came into Bressay Sound every year, while Gifford, who was born in 1682, states that he never saw more than 500 to 600 before the burning of the fleet in 1703,[144] which is probably a fair reflection of the period of prosperity which the fishery enjoyed in the 1680s.[145] This figure agrees well with modern Dutch informed opinion that the maximum number was in the region of 500.[146]

After the mid-century, the fleet was subject to periodic interference and partial destruction as a result of war. In the summer of 1652 about fifty busses were taken by the English near Fair Isle,[147] and thereafter the herring fleet was kept at home during the Anglo-Dutch Wars[148] (Fig. 8). During the war with France in the 1670s, the fleet's operations were virtually suspended at times,[149] and a few who ventured out in 1677 were caught and destroyed by the French in Bressay Sound.[150] A writer, describing Bressay in 1684, states that only 200 to 300 regularly came into Bressay Sound.[151] The fleet was kept at home during the hostilities of the 1690s[152] (Fig. 8), and the most severe blow was dealt in 1703 soon after the outbreak of the War of the Spanish Succession, when over 100 were burnt by the French in Bressay Sound.[153] It was a setback from which neither the fleet nor the trade with the fishermen recovered, and may have been reinforced by a similar attack in 1722.

The atmosphere between the locals and the fishermen appears to have been hostile to some extent at first, although it is worth noting that the chief complainers were the 'vested interests'. Thus, in the 1540s, James V refers to the Hollanders and Flemings appearing in greater numbers than previously, and with more menacing weapons.[154] In 1594, the Earl of Orkney mentioned that over 100 sail had been involved in depredations locally[155] while, as late as 1618, the Privy Council was instructing the collector of the assize on herring to mention the stealing and trouble caused by the fishermen at Fetlar and Unst if he was unable to obtain the assize money by straightforward means.[156]

As early as 1614, the Dutch were alleged to 'frolic it on land',[157] but as noted above, the first substantial reference to market activity as such in connection with the fishery occurs in 1615, when it was forbidden to trade at Bressay Sound and booths erected for the purpose of trade were to be demolished forthwith.[158] The first mention of the name 'Lerwick' in a trade connection is in the second, 1625 prohibition of trade, due to the lawlessness associated with it, in which drunkenness, theft, prostitution, assault and murder were all alleged. The sheriff principal, 'being informit of the great abominatioun and wickednes comittit yeirlie be the Hollendaris and countrie people godles and prophane persones repairing to thame at the houssis of Lerwick quhilk is a desert place . . . Ordaines the said houssis to be utterlie demolished and downe cassin to the ground be the haill awneris thairof . . .'[159] In the same year a complaint was made to the Privy Council that the Dutch were damaging the fisheries all along the east coast of Scotland by coming in much closer to the land than usual,[160] and this may have been a source of friction in Shetland then as in later times.

The cycle of activity in Shetland waters began about the middle of June (Fig. 1), when the fleet assembled in order to commence fishing after St. John's Day on the 24th of the month. It was probably at this time that the peak of marketing activity was reached, although there is little direct evidence before the eighteenth century. After the 24th, the busses fished practically continuously, sending their early catches back in fast carriers known as 'vent-jagers'* (first mentioned in 1604)[161] and moving gradually south about the end of July or the beginning of August to the grounds east of Fair Isle. Thence they followed the shoals southwards along the western margins of the North Sea outwith the Shetland area, returning home when they had full cargoes.[162]

Trade was organised in what amounted to a fair at three localities: Bressay Sound, Hollanders' Knowe above Gulberwick, and Levenwick (Fig. 4). All these locations were governed primarily by their proximity to the east-coast location of the fishery, and of these Bressay Sound was undoubtedly the most important. The Hollanders' Knowe seems to have been of importance, possibly after the temporary demise of the town of Lerwick in 1625, although there is little left apart from the name and local tradition to support this contention.[163] It was inaccessible from the sea, but was relatively central to people coming from far afield, as indeed they came to the third location of Levenwick.[164]

The commodity basis of the trade was fresh provisions and woollen stockings. In both the 1615 and 1625 references bere* is particularly mentioned, while in the later part of the century there are also references to fresh meat (mutton and lamb). Stockings and mittens are mentioned from the beginning of the seventeenth century, and later also garters and feathers. In exchange the locals received tobacco, brandy, shoes, boots, and — most important of all — money.[165] Although by the mid-1650s there were two 'Holland' merchants,[166] indicating that trade had assumed greater proportions than mere barter between locals and fishermen, it was not generally so highly organised, being based on bilateral transactions between the foreign fishermen and the local people. However, its significance was well-known, even to the English, who, referring to the 'fair' which the Dutch held in Shetland, were particularly anxious as to its effects on the security of the Commonwealth on the outbreak of war in 1652.[167]

In spite of loose organisation, the cumulative effect on the trading economy was considerable, and the periodic cessation during the Anglo-Dutch and other wars (Fig. 8) must have been noticeable. By the end of the century, Brand records that the presence of the Dutch caused the price of provisions in Shetland to be higher than in Orkney, and that the sale of stockings brought in considerable quantities of money to the poorer people.[168] Gifford states that the import of money in this trade was sufficient for the poor people to pay their rent and buy supplies.[169] It is thus hardly surprising that the burning of the Dutch fleet in 1703 was held at the time to be one of the most important contributory causes of the decline in the economy in the 1700s, and the cause of poverty among the lower classes.[170]

Shetland Interests and the Norway Trade

There were two kinds of local merchants: those who occupied a fixed location, and those who were itinerant. It is not possible to distinguish sharply between the two on the available evidence, which is limited almost entirely to the first half of the seventeenth century, at which time there seems to have been an influx from Scotland in the wake of the landowners' immigration.[171] There were also tradesmen who may have been in part itinerant.

By the late 1640s there were individual merchants in Scalloway, Hillswick, Baltasound, Uyeasound and Neshion (Delting),[172] locations which correspond to those commonly in use by the German merchants with the exception of Neshion, which is, however, near to Tofts Voe, an important trade centre in the eighteenth century (Fig. 11). There were also skippers and a number of tradesmen in Scalloway. The type of trade engaged in by these merchants indicates that they were operating on a comparatively small scale. For example, Michell Craig on his death in 1618 left in his booth (the testament is signed at Scalloway):[173] 5 lispunds (c. 90 lb.) of wool, a few ox and cow hides, 2 barrels of oil, some cloth, and one little otter skin, with £50 in ready money. His household goods and clothes were worth only £20, bringing the gross value of his estate to £137, plus debts owing to him of £106 by various tenants and payable mainly in wool. Possession of a booth and a substantial number of outstanding debts suggests that he was still in business at the time of his death.

The arrival of local itinerant merchants created a problem through forestalling, that is buying produce from the tenants before they had the opportunity to sell direct to the fish merchant. This, which bore heavily upon the tenants, was usually only possible by offering the tenants below-market prices and selling the goods later to the fish-merchants. Thus their activities were regulated by the parish bailies on more than one occasion in the 1610s[174] by forbidding them to trade until several days had elapsed after the arrival of a ship. The emphasis in their trade was on stock products, particularly hides, skins and wool — about the only commodities which do not appear to have been of much importance either in the landowners' or the German merchants' transactions.

The coming of Scottish landowners to Shetland formed a small part of a much wider movement into Europe generally associated with the general expansion of the Scottish nation.[175] Although the search for land was the most important motive in a Shetland context, other purposes of this expansion included trade, professional work, especially to do with the Church and the law (which often resulted in churchmen and lawyers becoming landowners also), and, in the sixteenth century, a certain amount of raiding activity.

Landowning was, of course, a family business organised on the basis of the family unit, and fortunately there exists a fairly detailed printed record of the vast majority of country family genealogies[176] from which it is possible to construct in rough fashion a chronology of establishment families. The construction can only be approximate since the dates of establishment are not always available. Without detailed research, beyond the scope of this study, it is impossible to ascertain the time at which these families acquired land.[177] This is particularly true of the later part of the seventeenth century, when landowners were often more directly involved in the legal or church professions. However, these drawbacks do not obscure the basic pattern of immigration. The first notable immigration was by Sinclair families from Orkney and Caithness,[178] who seem to have occupied some of the best land in the south and central Mainland, especially on the sandstone lowlands (Fig. 6), in the latter half of the fifteenth century and the first half of the sixteenth. The first major wave of immigration occupied the second half of the sixteenth century.

That the land, and the land alone, constituted the economic interests of the early immigrants, particularly the Sinclairs,[179] receives strong support from the high degree of correlation between the sandstone and limestone areas and the Sinclair holdings in particular, and a general distribution over the best central land areas in the case of the families arriving before about

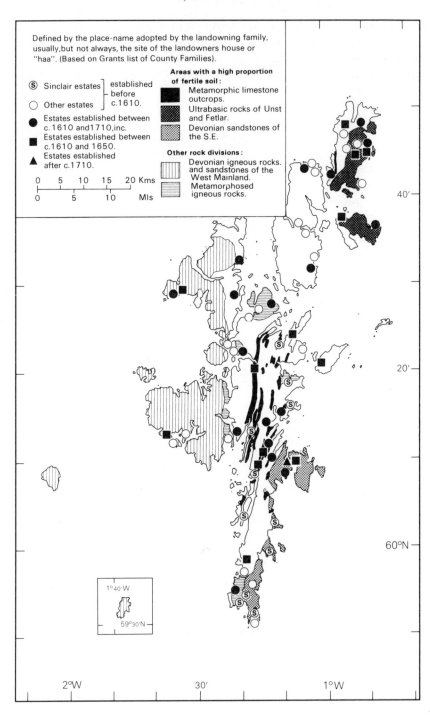

Figure 6. Estates

1600 (Fig. 6). In contrast to succeeding developments in the eighteenth century (Chapter 3), it was a situation where the land took precedence over the sea in determining the interests of the leading local inhabitants and locations of estates. However, although the central portions of the estates were generally situated at the locations shown on the map, estates as a whole bore little relation to the geographical units of production already outlined. This was due mainly to the extreme fragmentation following the subdividing of property among heirs which had taken place under the udal system of land tenure. Thus, the incoming landowners tended to acquire land in bits and pieces related to family and other social connections, and resulting estates consisted geographically of many fragments, both at the scale of the individual township and on the scales of the parish and even the archipelago as a whole. Despite the complex pattern, several individual estates were growing in size during the period, notably the estate of the Earldom, which came to occupy approximately one-fifth of the total arable land by the first half of the seventeenth century,[180] and which had considerable influence on trade.

It is, on the whole, uncertain to what degree the landowners took part in the day-to-day running of their estates. The few large landowners, ministers and lawyers probably delegated much of the work, either through tacks* or, in the case of the Earldom, through factors* known as chamberlains.[181] However, the bulk of the landowners probably ran their estates personally and had few possessions beyond their land. No doubt they took part in the seasonal production cycle through the general supervision of operations and collection of rents, examples being Ninian Neven of Windhouse and Christian Stewart of Bigton; the latter is recorded as personally taking up her rents in Papa Stour in the 1630s.[182]

Apart from the Norway trade described below, it is clear that a few at least had interests, direct or indirect, in trade, which probably expanded in parallel with the growth of individual estates. Several estate inventories, including that of Robert Bruce of Symbister in 1609,[183] indicate that the landowners owned boats and herring nets from the very beginning of the seventeenth century, although their interests apparently were not large, possibly because of the fact that the bulk of the fishing trade was in the hands of the German merchants. Ninian Neven in 1624 specifically refers to his 'fisheing trade' after Lammas being held up by legal proceedings being taken against him.[184] He also mentions £1,000-worth of salt and provisions he had bought at Leith, and his tolbooth charges outstanding (presumably at Leith also). This strongly suggests direct participation in the fishing industry. Apart from the above activities and the operation of the Norway trade, the landowners were also involved in the supervision of wrecks, which were sometimes of great economic importance for individual landowners in this, the age of mercantilism (Chapter 6).

The landowning links with Norway merit special consideration because of the close relationship with the development of the Norway trade. The tack system was used for the administration of outlying parts of the Norwegian-owned estates in Shetland, a legacy of the later Middle Ages. This type of contact was most important in the sixteenth century, and, as the seventeenth century progressed, the Norwegian landholding connection gradually dwindled, principally through the sale of lands to Shetland landowners, such as to John Neven of Lunning in Lunnasting, who acquired property in this way around the middle of the seventeenth century.[185]

Landowners resident in Shetland also owned land in Norway, the outstanding example being the Mowats in the late sixteenth century. Andrew Mowat of Ollaberry travelled regularly between Norway and Shetland in his own ship, sometimes staying in Norway for extended periods and conducting trade between the two areas; his near relative Axel Mowat is recorded as having possessed large estates in Norway and having been experienced in the timber trade.[186] It is from this type of connection that the Norway trade of some of the landowners expanded rapidly in the second half of the sixteenth century.

The entry of the landowners into the Norway trade must be seen as due to a combination of factors, namely, the landowning links, the need for the wood goods which could best be supplied from Norway, and the fact that, in the absence of any substantial local merchant class throughout the period, only the larger landowners had sufficient capital to pursue trade on any scale, generally in the prevailing itinerant merchant fashion of travelling to Norway and conducting business personally.[187]

The trade required ships and specie with which to pay for imports. Contemporary records indicate that the large landowners were plentifully supplied with both. Robert Sinclair, baron of Burgh in Nesting, had at the time of his death in 1616 a ship valued at £2,000 Scots and £5,000 Scots-worth of gold, besides £1,400 Scots-worth in French crowns and English angels.[188] Robert Bruce of Symbister had, among other goods, £1,400 Scots-worth of gold 'spoiled' from him by Patrick, Earl of Orkney in 1609;[189] Andrew Mowat of Ollaberry (above-mentioned) was robbed of 2,000 rixdollars-worth of gold, silver, money and other goods from his home in Ollaberry in 1586, and of 4,500 rixdollars-worth when his ship was captured by pirates en route from Norway to Shetland in 1590.[190]

The trade between Shetland and Norway extended back to the Norse settlement, although it underwent a period of depression between 1350 and 1500.[191] The second half of the sixteenth century was a period of expansion, although the incompleteness of the Norwegian records makes any detailed account impossible. The trade continued throughout the seventeenth century, probably altering in character by the end of the period as it became increasingly channelled through Bergen and Godøysund (Fig. 7).

In 1519, of 88 foreign ships visiting Bergen, one belonged to Shetland; in 1521, of 108, two.[192] By the middle of the century there was a well-established trade, though as regards the number of traders we have only the number of ships operating in the first half of the seventeenth century as a

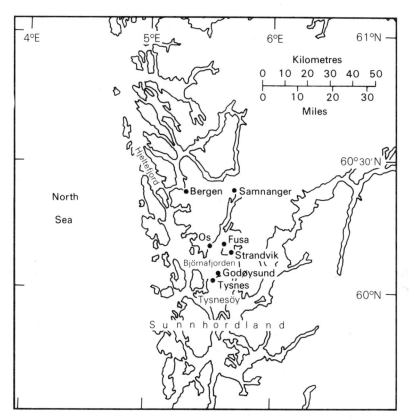

Figure 7. Links with Norway

Table 2. Vessels clearing from the ports of Sunnhordland (Fig. 7), 1597-1642.

The statistics are available for a few years only.

Date	Orkney and Shetland	Scotland	Total
1597	12	41	82
1610	18	57	114
1611	12	39	76
1612	12	44	76
1614	11	43	73
1620	6	39	67
1621	19	66	107
1624	19	47	86
1627	14	62	90
1634	17	63	88
1639	12	22	35
1641	11	48	62
1642	15	66	84

guide (Table 2). However, it is likely that these represent fairly closely the number of traders involved, as in general the ships engaged in this trade were small — 6 to 12 lasts were common, compared to 30-50 lasts for the German traders (Chapter 6). Variations in the numbers of vessels cleared for Orkney and Shetland from year to year are substantial, and probably due to the small scale of the trade, where variations in demand for such durable items as boats are likely to have been appreciable. Although there are no statistics for the trade in the latter part of the seventeenth century, it continued to be important. In 1651 one of the special requests from Shetland, when acceding to the establishment of the Commonwealth, was that the Norway trade be allowed to continue uninterrupted,[193] and Sibbald, writing in 1711, and probably quoting Smith (1633, published 1662), suggests that, in wartime, there tended to be an increase in the Norway trade,[194] presumably to obtain items which normally were brought from Scotland and even North Germany.

All the references for the period suggest that trading was limited mainly to Bergen and the Björnafjord area of Sunnhordland immediately to the south. Shipping was geared to the scattered organisation of timber production in seventeenth-century Norway, and ships generally received their cargoes direct from the production areas — 'the woods' — although they sometimes called at Bergen en route. In the first hundred years of the period under consideration cargoes were loaded at a variety of places in the Björnafjord area (Fig. 7),[195] but by the end of the seventeenth century there was a high degree of localisation, notably to the areas supplying boats, with Godøysund in Tysnes the leading port at which, along with Bergen, the trade was concentrated in the first decade of the eighteenth century.[196]

The Norway trade was a summer trade, geared to the production of timber in the woods of West Norway, and to the advantages of travel by sea in the better weather which usually could be expected in summer — a factor probably of greater significance in this trade than in the German trade due to the comparatively small size of the craft used. In 1627, for example,[197] the entries of cargoes loaded in Sunnhordland all fall into the period between the beginning of May and the end of August. The majority of vessels made just one trip per season, though a few made two trips, as in 1627 when three of the eight vessels involved did so.

In common with the British Isles as a whole, the Shetland trade was one in which the balance of trade was firmly in favour of Norway, in contrast to Orkney, which supplied exports of corn in exchange for wood goods.[198] It is in this context that the gold and silver of the landowners referred to above appears to have been mainly used, and it is likely that some of the English coinage circulating in Shetland may have reached the islands by this route because of the preponderance of English coinage in many areas of western Norway as a result of timber trade contacts with England.[199] An outward trip from Shetland in ballast, therefore, with a return trip with cargo was the most common mode of trading, a good example being the four vessels engaged in the trade in 1577-78.[200] These arrived at Bergen from various parts of Shetland in ballast, and returned with timber and boats.

The great bulk of the commodities imported from Norway were wood goods of various descriptions, usually semi-manufactured or manufactured. The principal categories of timber in the first class were deals, balks, small masts and spars and 'boats in boards' (see below), and small quantities of such items as tar and spirits, and wood for agricultural purposes, such as ploughs and harrows, referred to under this broad heading in 1651.[201] Many of the deals were used as house-timber, while spars were for boats. In 1620-21[202] there was an import of 300 deals, 234 balks, 1,500 'Hjeltespirer' ('Shetland-spars' — probably small spars for boats); three dozen cars; in 1627,[203] 180 balks, 247 deals, 3,900 poles, 4,450 hoop-poles (most likely for making wooden barrel hoops), 48 oars, and 2 fathoms of firewood. All these imports came from Sunnhordland.

The second category consisted almost entirely of boats, although it is probable that ships were also acquired from Norway at this time. Many of these boats were completed, unlike the 'boats in boards' which were in fact built and exported in what today would be termed 'knocked-down' form to be reassembled in Shetland. The numbers imported were variable, and consisted of six-oared 'sixerns' and four-oared 'fourerns'. In 1566-67, 17 boats were received from Bergen;[204] in 1610 Scots and Shetland ships loaded 46 boats in Os;[205] in 1620-21, 11 fourerns and 6 sixerns were imported into Shetland;[206] and in 1664, 44 fourerns and 8 sixerns were sent to Scots and Shetlanders.[207] By the end of the period, Tysnes was specialising in supplying boats to Shetland,[208] with the emphasis on 'boats in boards', a major advantage of this form of export being that more boats could be stowed per cargo than if exported in built form. It is worthy of note that the numbers of fourerns exceeded the numbers of sixerns, thus supporting the contention that the fishery in the seventeenth century was predominantly an inshore one.

Change and Decay

From the perspective of today, the events around 1700 appear almost cataclysmic — war, famine and the first great smallpox epidemic wracked the land. The world of divided initiatives which had lasted for three centuries appeared to have come to an abrupt end. While the interplay of factors involved is complex and not invariably clear, they may be regarded as a combination of external influences operating at a European scale on the one hand, and internal changes on the other, so that there was more continuity than would appear at first sight.

On the European stage Shetland trade was subject to gradual change, much less spectacular than the disruption caused by the almost endemic warfare among the major European powers in the seventeenth century. The pattern of imports from north Germany, Norway, Scotland and Orkney

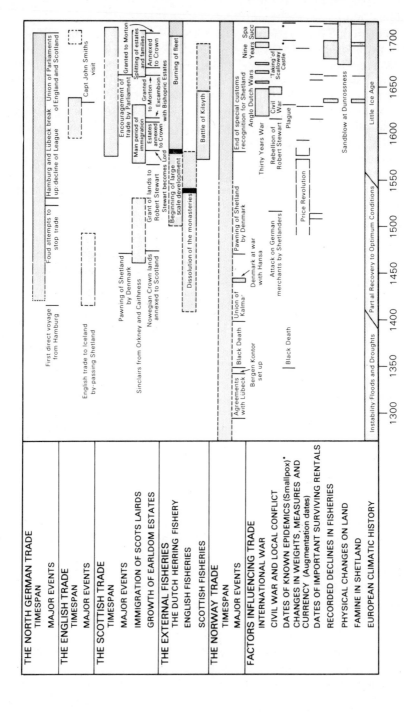

Figure 8. Medieval and early modern times

remained stable, while the major export products continued to be directed towards Germany, Scotland and England, although it seems likely that in the seventeenth century Hamburg and Bremen were increasingly becoming entrepot ports in the fish trade for southern European markets.[209] Prices, although subject to fluctuations, remained remarkably constant in the seventeenth century, notably in butter and fish, which changed little between 1630 and 1730.[210] The growth of the Dutch herring fisheries may have contributed to the decline of the northern continental dried fish markets in the long term. Evidence is insufficient to be certain about any such competition.

There was a decline in wadmel exports. Wadmel still constituted an item of rent payment in the 1570s, and in 1616 an edict was issued for its continued payment.[211] However, by 1628 it was apparently permanently converted into money equivalent in the rentals,[212] and in 1633 John Smith mentions its poor quality.[213] It seems reasonable to suppose that the great expansion in the woollen stocking market at this time was also a major factor in the decline of wadmel as an item of rent payment and for export, as it is not mentioned after the middle of the seventeenth century except for domestic use.

It is worthy of note that throughout the later Middle Ages there is no mention of oil as a rent payment, rents being returned chiefly in wadmel and malt (later butter).[214] By the 1570s butter, oil and wadmel were the principal commodities,[215] although some church revenues were paid in fish which the tacksmen of the church revenues insisted should henceforward be paid in butter and oil only.[216] The increasing demand for fish oil probably had the same roots as that which supported the rise of the Dutch whaling industry in the seventeenth century, and that of Britain in the eighteenth. In the days before the introduction of mineral oil on a large scale, it was of particular value for lighting and lubrication purposes.[217]

War contributed to price rises and the desire for gold to finance the wars. In a Shetland context, beginning with the short interlude in the Thirty Years' War in the 1620s in which Charles I became embroiled, the primary significance of war was to demonstrate Shetland's strategic position on the trade routes of Europe. Direct attack caused disruption of local trade, and being caught in the cross-fire between warring nations also had serious consequences, the prime example being the disruption of the Dutch fisheries. Direct attack occurred in 1627, when cattle and other goods were plundered,[218] in 1673, when the Dutch burned the fort and the few houses which by that time constituted the town of Lerwick,[219] and in the 1690s, when French privateers did some plundering.[220] The German merchants' trade seems to have been uninterrupted by the Thirty Years' War and the Dutch Wars,[221] although a ship carrying the King's rents to Scotland was intercepted by a Dutch privateer in the second Dutch War.[222] Trade in general was probably affected to some extent in the Civil War, being prohibited for a time in 1644.[223] It was certainly disrupted during the Nine Years' War and

D

the War of the Spanish Succession. French privateers cruised round the islands, bringing in prizes, including a few of the German merchants.[224] They intercepted vessels trading to Scotland, including those carrying the rent commodities, and extensively disrupted the trade with Orkney.[225] It was also near the outbreak of this final war that the Dutch fleet was partly destroyed by the French in 1703, with grave consequences for the trade with the Dutch fishermen. During wartime, local initiative was forced to turn more to the Norway link for all import requirements. On the whole it is difficult to avoid the conclusion that the pressures of war were of importance in the break-up of the itinerant merchant system discussed below, in spite of the fact that Thomas Gifford, writing in 1733, thought the French a more liberal enemy than the Dutch.[226] The system remained remarkably resilient in the face of difficulty. One reason was the rudimentary nature of foreign exchange procedure[227] which, until the beginning of the seventeenth century, was maintained by the transfer of specie as in the Norway trade, and the German merchants' trade. Under such conditions, coupled with the manifold dangers of sea trade, not least of which was piracy, it is scarcely surprising that the merchants carried out every stage of their trading operation personally.

In the latter half of the seventeenth century, the 'commercial revolution' of bills of exchange and the increasing sophistication of foreign exchange markets[228] made it increasingly possible to operate the financial arrangements of trade independently of locational considerations of the commodity trade itself. Although the fish trade still required money in the form of coinage because the merchants were dealing directly with the tenants, this change in financial practice, coupled with the rise of nationalistic mercantile philosophy epitomised in the Navigation Laws of 1651,[229] increased the possibility of trade without transfer of specie. Further, it generally favoured division of labour between production, transport and marketing in the trade system, thereby contributing to the success of political pressures in 1707 which were unsuccessful in 1662 when Scottish trading interests had attempted to engage in Shetland trade. This division of labour indeed could not have been successful on any account before 1651, when the English Navigation Laws were first enacted.

Nevertheless, the decline of direct external control of trade cannot be explained merely in terms of technical developments in international financial procedures. It was also associated with certain basic changes in mercantile outlook. The persistence of the fish merchants in particular is all the more remarkable when it is realised that the itinerant merchant had to be totally committed in a sense undreamed of in later times. Not only capital and contacts were at risk, but also his life as well — from the elements, pirates and privateers. And yet the merchant carried on with practically nothing between him and disaster but a calculated high profit margin, in lieu of insurance in the modern sense, which was small consolation if his ship was wrecked, as was a German merchant's in Sandwick Bay in 1602,[230] or taken by privateers, as happened to some of the German merchants in the 1690s.[231] The most convincing evidence of the outlook of the German merchants is that when they were finally prevented from trading, some of them were willing to stay on.[232] Meanwhile, the attitude to Shetland trade in Scotland and England, apart from the few merchants who engaged in it, was largely a contrived political matter, especially as regards the outbursts of interest in the 1630s and 1660s. These were sustained by much political pamphleteering and by parliamentary enactments, but not much else. Real commercial interest only becomes apparent in the 1690s and 1700s, and provided a strong element in the reasoning of the government of the day in prohibiting the trade of the German merchants.

Apart from these international developments in the theory and practice of trade, there was a third political factor which was decisive in prohibition of the German merchants' trade. Behind the act of government prohibiting this crucial component in the whole structure was a record of fiscal and political pressures of varying significance which extended throughout the period and even further back.

Local pressures were partly political and partly fiscal. As early as 1521 the Foud had tried to prevent trade, and there were various subsequent conflicts with the merchants, particularly in the sixteenth century. The first significant build-up of fiscal pressure, which it was alleged at the time would be likely to lead to the decline of the trade, occurred in the 1570s at the instigation of the Earldom estate. This pressure took the form of rents for shore facilities and harbour dues.[233] By the middle of the seventeenth century, this estate was receiving £800 Scots yearly in the form of dues from foreign merchants.[234] As previously noted, the individual landowners received payment for the use of their land, but this was probably not onerous. Occasionally extortion appears to have been resorted to, as by the collector to the tacksman of the customs in 1669. James Moodie of Melsetter in Orkney had, upon a pretext of deputation of Admiralty*, forced some Hamburg merchants to pay him money 'unwarrantably and illegally'.[235]

Although there seems to have been a phase in the early seventeenth century in which additional dues were imposed at national level by the tacksmen of the customs, subsequently ordered to be rescinded in 1613,[236] and there was some interference with the trading privileges of the merchants by the Scots in the mid-seventeenth century,[237] serious fiscal pressures exerted by the state at local level date from the latter half of the seventeenth century. Nevertheless, in the Act establishing general increases in customs duties in 1661, wood goods, fishing materials and salt used in fisheries exports were specifically exempted.[238] In 1662 a petition[239] that the German merchants be allowed to continue their trade was successful on the understanding that they would give it up when Scottish and English companies were organised to take it over[240] — evidence of the state's desire to establish a national monopoly over the fisheries. Although duties were subsequently raised on these goods and in contemporary opinion this was held to be more important than, for example, the decline in the fisheries in discouraging the trade,[241] it by no means stifled it, since by an Act of 1705 all materials imported for fishing purposes were to be entered free of duty.[242] Thus, in spite of the fact that the local lobby in favour of the German merchants considered that the high duties were the prime cause of the cessation of the trade, it is clear from the memorandum sent by Treasurer Godolphin to Queen Anne[243] in connection with the respective petitions of the merchants and the locals for the continuance of the trade that the real reason was rooted in the assertion of the navigation laws which forbade the import of salt in foreign bottoms, coupled with the ruling that foreign salt only was to be used in curing fish for export. The government opinion was backed up by merchants in Scotland[244] and England.[245] This time, by contrast with 1662, there were to be no special dispensations in favour of the German merchants. For the first time the power of the state with regard to trade in Shetland was equal to its long-held desire to change the patterns in favour of Britain.

In Shetland itself, there were also a number of influences promoting change. At the basic level of production, climatic disturbances of the long-term variety (Chapter 3) produced famines, and similar long-term changes in the marine environment produced decline in the fisheries. As noted in Chapter 1, the period from around 1550 until 1600 was one in which famine was frequently prevalent in Scotland, coincident with the onset of the 'Little Ice Age' climatic deterioration, but there is no record of such events in Shetland. The seventeenth century witnessed two major recorded periods of famine in the islands, both of which had serious repercussions. The first was in the 1630s,[246] particularly the years 1633-35, and this was perhaps the most serious in terms of starvation. A vivid picture of widespread death through starvation is painted in the petition for its relief, and a public subscription was put in train;[247] thus in 1635 it is recorded that in Stirling 500 merks were to be put at the disposal of the relief organisation, 'or to some uther gude and pious use . . .'[248] In 1663 there is a record of the crop having been blasted, and shortage of fish coupled with cattle disease,[249] but as the Lordship accounts show the usual quantities of rents paid in kind, this would seem to have been a much less serious outbreak.[250] The second major famine period ran in parallel to some extent with the 'seven lean years' in Scotland as a whole,[251] and probably permanently undermined the financial position of some of the landowners. The worst years appear to have been 1693-1696, though it is notable that the tacksmen of the Lordship between the years 1693 and 1700 had not paid up their tack duties in 1712.[252] The resort to a public appeal in the 1630s and an appeal to government in 1698[253] indicates that prolonged severe famine could not be counterbalanced by the normal adjustments of the trade system and were liable to cause permanent financial damage to individual landowners and tacksmen, as in the 1690s, and indirectly probably also resulted in depopulation through disease, as in the very serious smallpox epidemic which swept Shetland in 1700.[254]

The problems of famine were accentuated for a few estates by the commencement of persistent sand-blowing in the Dunrossness area which is first recorded in the 1670s, resulting in the gradual over-running of the rich agricultural land north of the Bay of Quendale by wind-blown sand. This resulted in the virtual wiping out of the estate of the Sinclairs of Brew by the middle of the eighteenth century,[255] and partial inundation of the neighbouring estate of Quendale; thus in 1718, the laird of Quendale considered that his estate had lost £200 Scots per annum in rent payments from sand-blow between 1676 and 1706, and £300 Scots from 1706 until 1718,[256] all of which contributed to the financial difficulties of this large and important estate at this period. Linked with the extensive sand-blowing was the progressive silting-up of the neighbouring 'Dutch Pool' — now known as the Pool of Virkie — which was almost useless as a harbour by the end of the century,[257] necessitating the use of the much more exposed and dangerous location of Grutness Voe nearby as the main trade point for Dunrossness.[258]

The close connection between land and sea in the production of the islands takes on a new significance when it is noted that failure of the fishings is mentioned in all three periods of famine (see also Chapters 3 and 4). However, the most important recognisable change which can be attributed to environmental causes paralleled the onset of the sand-blowing and resulted in a decline in the fisheries. It began in the early 1680s, and persisted until 1700 or later. This deterioration was considered by writers in the 1680s[259] and by Brand in 1700[260] to have contributed to the 'decay' in trade of the period, and appears from the comments of Brand to have been characterised by seaward migration of the fish. The fishermen had to go much further to sea in order to catch fish, which many of them were not disposed to do. This directly affected the operations of the German merchants, one of whom complained to Brand about the decline and the unwillingness of the fishermen to do anything about it.[261]

A second local influence promoting change was the economic and social changes associated with landowning, following upon the immigration of the Scottish landowners who acquired large estates, exemplified by the Lordship estate which was the direct descendant of the Earldom, though modified in one or two important respects. The Earldom estate was a powerful political force during the phase of its evolution in the period 1565-1610, when Robert Stewart and his son Patrick succeeded in expanding it from its very minor position in the landholding structure to a primary estate occupying at least one-fifth of the total Shetland rentalled land.[262] Thus a major sector of the agricultural economy came under the direct control of the estate.

During the subsequent phase in the evolution of the estate — now termed the Lordship — from 1611 until 1706, it was externally controlled by the Crown and its tacksmen or grantees. In the phase of heightened commercial awareness which seems to have pervaded Scotland after the Restoration,[263] a large part of it was feued out in 1664 to local landowners,[264] and an unusually commercial outlook was adopted when it was rouped* for the first time to local tacksmen from 1670 until 1680, when it again reverted to tacksmen from Scotland.[265] This post-1660 phase was one of the major influences in the development of trade links with Scotland, due in no small measure to the trading of the rent commodities to Scotland by these tacksmen, rather than sale of commodities to the German merchants.

Although Shetland appears to have shared in the general rise in prices which occurred in Europe in the sixteenth century, this seemingly did not affect the predominantly barter economy to any great extent until the 1570s, the changes of greatest import being those in weights and measures, including an augmentation of 33 per cent in the cloth measure, 25 per cent in the butter weight standard, followed by a further 25 per cent in the 1590s, and 35 per cent in the oil measure.[266] As rents were paid largely in these commodities, this resulted in a strong pressure for increased agricultural production, especially of butter. In practice, it probably resulted in increasing absorption of surplus agricultural production in the rental system until at least the 1620s, when for the first time it was recorded that the rents could not be increased further, and indeed could no longer be paid by the tenants without the support of the fisheries.[267]

The result was the secure establishment of the landowners as middlemen selling the rent commodities to the merchants as described above. Depreciation in the value of the rents continued on a reduced scale throughout the seventeenth century, although in 1614 the numerical value of the rents had probably been fixed.[268] In the first extant rental of 1628,[269] the wadmel measure* appears to have been permanently converted to a Scots money equivalent — the value of the £ Scots fell by about half between 1570 and 1600.[270] The butter measure which in the early 1570s had stood at 12 lb. per lispund stood at 18 lb. by the 1590s, and was probably about 20-22 lb. by the early 1680s. It was raised to 24 lb. by 1691,[271] thus tending to maintain pressure on agricultural production while lowering its value in the internal trade system.

It goes almost without saying that the Shetland trading economy, indeed the whole economy of the islands, could have faced total ruin after the Act of Union in 1707, particularly in view of the conspicuous lack of success of Scottish and English trading ventures to the islands in the decade 1700-1710. It was all very well in theory to wield the political 'big stick' against the Germans; it required no small change in local circumstances to put it into practice. The fact is that there were some shifts in the theory and practice of trade taking place in Shetland which paralleled European developments to some extent, but which at the same time took a distinctive local form.

The first important change to occur was a gradual, at times almost imperceptible, shift in the attitudes of the landowners to the trade of the archipelago as a whole in contradistinction to the Norway trade in particular. In the early part of the period, even up to the 1630s, there is convincing evidence which bears out the contention that the landowners, who were the only people with sufficient capital, were, with notable exceptions, basically uninterested in trade beyond the Norway link, which in any case had had landowning connections allied with it from the beginning.[272] In the period 1570-1600, far from the encouragement of trade, there was considerable effort among the most powerful landowners to disrupt it by piracy. The German merchants were attacked by some locals in 1566,[273] and two Shetlanders undertook a piratical expedition round the islands in 1573.[274] In 1576, no less a person than Robert Stewart himself was accused of piracy, including the plundering of a ship of Emden of 2,000 Spanish royals in 1574, and in the following year the protection of pirates in an operation involving the taking of 'nine great ships' with cargoes valued at £100,000.[275] English pirates robbed Andrew Mowat of Ollaberry on two occasions, in 1586 and 1590,[276] and as late as 1614 the Privy Council granted a commission for the arrestment of pirates infesting the waters between Peterhead and Shetland.[277]

Apart from this, it is an historical fact of some moment that, besides the Norway trade, local trading interests of any other kind are seldom mentioned in the records. In this situation it is highly unlikely that the generality of landowners possessed other extensive trading interests. On the contrary, in the period between 1600 and 1640, there were no fewer than five serious disputes among landowners involving land and related non-trading interests. Only one of these, the case involving Ninian Neven already discussed, specifically refers to trade as an interest. It is of some consequence, therefore, that John Smith should have remarked in 1633 that the people were interested 'neither in improving anything by land nor sea'.[278] This is in striking contrast to Sibbald's observations in 1711 that the landowners were well-educated and widely travelled and interested in trade generally.[279] It illustrates that shift of interest which was taking place in the second half of the seventeenth century.

At a more practical level, there is concrete evidence of changes in the landowners' business interests towards the end of the period, by which time of course a number of landowners had acquired considerable estates. However, there is a twofold distinction apparent between estates in financial trouble on the one hand, and those associated with early trading ventures on the other, significantly those which survived the economic vicissitudes of the late seventeenth and early eighteenth centuries.

The estates in the first group are distinguishable through two main sources — rent accounts,[280] and various eighteenth-century documentary references. From these sources it is evident that the most serious blow in the short term had been struck by the series of disastrous harvests, particularly between 1693 and 1696. The tacksman* of the Lordship* was seriously in debt due to the inability of the landowners, who were also in debt, to pay their superior duties*, and who were claiming large deductions for 'ley lands', as ley (i.e. unworked) lands — probably related to the smallpox epidemic of 1700 — were exempt from payment of scat*.[281] Such abatements first appear in the middle of the seventeenth century in the rent accounts,[282] but are absent from the rental of 1628. It was suggested in 1785 that these were introduced by the tacksmen who had only short-term interests in the revenue, probably to tide over some economic disaster,[283] which on the basis of the above evidence would appear to be the disastrous famine of the 1630s.

However, these deductions were small throughout the seventeenth century, and then reach major proportions suddenly in the early eighteenth century,[284] which strongly suggests an attempt to compensate for the non-receipt of rents. In the rental accounts of the 1710s[285] it is significant that those landowners who were seriously in debt with their superior duties were the same ones who claimed large deductions for ley lands in the accounts of ley land debts for 1712-1719,[286] and that these estates were situated mainly in Unst, Fetlar, Yell and Dunrossness — the first three areas being characterised by relatively small-scale landowners with small resources.

It is yet more significant that the financial weaknesses of these estates exposed by the 1690s famine and the 1700 smallpox epidemic were due to a variety of other basic causes. Thus the Quendale estate — the only big debtor in Dunrossness — was afflicted by sand-blowing, and injudicious financial management due to the proprietor being appointed Receiver General of the Land Tax in Edinburgh.[287] The small but significant Fracafield estate was in difficulties because of the inability of the proprietor to settle the vast debts incurred by his grandfather Sir William Dick of Braid in financing the Covenanters' cause in the 1630s, again hardly a local cause.[288] Finally, another major debtor, William Bruce of Turhoull in Unst, was ruined by the depredations of French privateers in 1695.[289] The seriousness of the whole position is highlighted by the legendary story of his maidservant, Madge Louttit, who pursued a marauding Frenchman and succeeded in strangling him using the neckband of the kishie* he was carrying[290] — a tale distinctly out of character with the relatively meek submission towards privateers normally referred to in the seventeenth and eighteenth centuries.[291] On the whole, the picture presented is one in which many estates were under severe pressure from the combined effects of famine, smallpox, war and external financial difficulties.

The second group of estates were quite distinct from the first, and continued to expand in the first decades of the eighteenth century while the others went bankrupt.[292] All of these proprietors engaged to a significant degree in trade. The four leading pioneers were Gifford of Busta, Mitchell of Girlsta, Henderson of Gardie (these three acquired sectors of the large Muness estate which had gone bankrupt due to a 'spendthrift' laird)[293] and Nicolson of Bullister and Lochend. It is worthy of note that these four estates secured joint tacks of the large Lordship estate during the early eighteenth century mainly in order to further their trading interests. By the end of the period, therefore, the landowners were finding it increasingly difficult to live off their estates and in the absence of alternative merchant capital were already turning to the development of trade when the Act of Union and subsequent prohibition of the German merchants' trade provided the decisive opportunity.

3

The Lairds, 1710-1790

By the early 1710s the German merchants had left, and Scottish and English mercantile ventures had met with little success. The new British Government had willed the means for changing the system, but the new 'Shetland' lairds were on their own as the chief source of initiative for any direction which the economy might take. Thus they took up the 'fishing trade' as they called it, the initiative coming from a handful of small-scale landowners with mercantile interests who nonetheless rapidly became the largest landowners. The main starting point in this subsistence-based society was the haaf fisheries. Successful development depended upon the nature of the local society and especially upon the economic and social relationships of landowners on the one hand and tenants on the other. It also depended upon the nature of the external trade organisation which was built up and which fostered a network of new European links. (Fig. 9). Most of all, the distinctiveness of the following period was defined by the enterprise of the much maligned lairds. There were economic and social parallels with Scotland as a whole in an advance with increasing momentum towards greater prosperity as the century progressed,[1] until eventually the lairds lost the initiative.

The Far Haaf

The haaf — the open boat line fishing — had its roots in the early medieval world of the Norse settlers. By the eighteenth century it was the cornerstone of Shetland's commercial surplus,[2] and its requirements for boats and gear were strongly reflected in imports. The nature of the haaf fishing was intimately related to the land and sea, with the greatest development occurring in the exposed peripheral coasts nearest the fishing grounds of the 'far haaf' on the one hand, and local fisheries in the more sheltered waters of the central parts of the archipelago on the other.

Before 1700 commercial activity seems to have been limited mainly to inshore fishing, perhaps not further than five or ten miles offshore, and it is likely that this pattern continued for some time in the eighteenth century. The boats used were of two types, the fourern* and sixern*, which had four

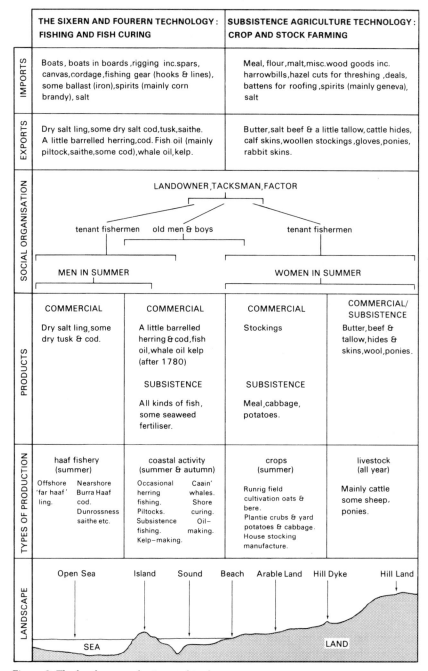

THE SIXERN AND FOURERN TECHNOLOGY: FISHING AND FISH CURING			SUBSISTENCE AGRICULTURE TECHNOLOGY: CROP AND STOCK FARMING	
IMPORTS Boats, boats in boards, rigging inc.spars, canvas,cordage,fishing gear (hooks & lines), some ballast (iron),spirits (mainly corn brandy), salt			Meal, flour,malt,misc.wood goods inc. harrowbills,hazel cuts for threshing ,deals, battens for roofing ,spirits (mainly geneva), salt	
EXPORTS Dry salt ling,some dry salt cod,tusk,saithe. A little barrelled herring,cod. Fish oil (mainly piltock,saithe,some cod),whale oil,kelp.			Butter,salt beef & a little tallow,cattle hides, calf skins,woollen stockings ,gloves,ponies, rabbit skins.	

SOCIAL ORGANISATION

LANDOWNER,TACKSMAN,FACTOR

tenant fishermen   old men & boys   tenant fishermen

MEN IN SUMMER   WOMEN IN SUMMER

PRODUCTS

COMMERCIAL	COMMERCIAL	COMMERCIAL	COMMERCIAL/ SUBSISTENCE
Dry salt ling,some dry tusk & cod.	A little barrelled herring & cod,fish oil,whale oil kelp (after 1780)	Stockings	Butter,beef & tallow,hides & skins,wool,ponies.
	SUBSISTENCE	SUBSISTENCE	
	All kinds of fish, some seaweed fertiliser.	Meal,cabbage, potatoes.	

TYPES OF PRODUCTION

haaf fishery (summer)	coastal activity (summer & autumn)	crops (summer)	livestock (all year)
Offshore Nearshore 'far haaf' Burra Haaf ling. cod. Dunrossness saithe etc.	Occasional Caain' herring whales. fishing. Shore Piltocks. curing. Subsistence Oil– fishing. making. Kelp–making.	Runrig field cultivation oats & bere. Plantie crubs & yard potatoes & cabbage. House stocking manufacture.	Mainly cattle some sheep, ponies.

LANDSCAPE

Open Sea   Island   Sound   Beach   Arable Land   Hill Dyke   Hill Land

SEA   LAND

Figure 9. The haaf era: production and trade

and six oars respectively, the smaller fourern being usually used in the near-shore fishing areas. (Fig. 10) both for subsistence and commercial fishing, while the larger sixern was used mainly in offshore fishing and in transport of cargo such as cured fish from outlying stations to main shipping points. The hull form of these boats in the eighteenth century was of the 'Shetland model' type, the basic design being Norwegian in origin with modifications to suit Shetland conditions,[3] and the import of these boats remained the staple of the Norway import trade. These modifications applied more or less uniformly throughout Shetland, with the exception of the Dunrossness area, where a much longer, narrower hull form known as the 'Ness yoal'*[4] was evolved to suit the requirements of fishing in strong tidal streams. The boats were constructed mainly of Norwegian fir planks ('boatbuilders' deals') in the eighteenth century. In later time larch was increasingly used.[5] Although it has been suggested that the boats depended entirely on oars in the eighteenth century,[6] there were considerable improvements in design effected during the period,[7] and there seems little reason to suppose that the sixerns at least did not have sails as well, especially in the second half of the century. The imports of large numbers of spars and small spars (Fig. 19) is strongly indicative of this.

The method of fishing was by means of a long line,[8] which consisted of a series of separate lines or 'baukts'*. On each baukt, which was 40-50 fathoms long, hooks were spaced at regular intervals of $3\frac{1}{2}$ to 5 fathoms, attached by means of snoods or 'toms' 3-4 ft. long. The baukts were tied together as the lines were laid, the number of baukts per boat varying from as low as 30-40 to a maximum of 120, depending on whether the boat was engaged in near-shore or offshore fishing.[9] Each long line, consisting of the requisite number of baukts, and ranging up to 6-7 miles in length, was held in position on the bottom by a number of stone sinkers attached to surface marker buoys by ropes. Hooks and lines were imported mainly from Hamburg, and to a lesser extent from Leith also.

The usual sequence of operations in the haaf fishing was for boats to go off in the morning after having obtained bait, and lay their lines in accordance with wind and sea conditions, with particular regard for the state of the tide insofar as it influenced the directions and strengths of current flows on the fishing grounds. Depending on the length of time taken to reach the grounds, primarily a function of distance, but influenced also by wind and sea conditions, the lines were laid or 'set' in afternoon or evening, and hauled after a few hours. In those areas where the fishing grounds were close to the shore this was a daily sequence of operations. On distant grounds the boats might stay at sea, setting* and hauling lines continuously for 36 hours or so, depending on the weather and the quantity of fish caught, and make only two trips per week. After the final hauling of lines, the boats proceeded to the shore station, where the fish were discharged for curing.

The fishing stations consisted invariably of stony beaches or ayres*, which were most suitable for drying fish as their hard, dry surfaces permitted free circulation of air round the fish. The beaches also possessed good drainage qualities for the carrying away of water from the wet fish during the initial stages of drying.[10] Such beaches were also often the only points of access on the exposed coastal areas closest to the fishing grounds, especially along the west coast of Northmavine and the east side of Fetlar where the largest stations were situated, and had the advantage that boats could be hauled up fairly readily. Near the beach on each station was a booth for the storage of salt and other fishing materials, and dried fish awaiting export. Those stations serving the most distant ('far haaf') offshore grounds also possessed a number of fishing lodges* in which the fishermen stayed between trips to the haaf.

When the fish were brought ashore, the curing operation began as soon as possible.[11] The stations were manned mainly by older men and boys, who first split and boned the fish, then washed them thoroughly to prevent the blood entering the flesh, after which they were placed in large wooden tubs called vats in alternate layers with salt. After four or five days, the fish were removed from the pickle, cleaned and washed, and placed in a long pile (or if rainy — in clumps) on the beach to drain. Drying was subsequently accomplished by alternately spreading the fish out on the beach first the flesh, then the skin side uppermost, and gathering them into clumps at night or if it rained. This protected the fish from moisture which tended to destroy their sweet flavour,[12] and also allowed air to circulate, which kept the fish cool.[13] In the final stages of drying the fish were built into very small clumps or staples* in order to ensure complete and uniform drying, a process known as pining*, which was necessary for the fish to maintain their quality during the long sea voyage to market.[14]

Salting was usually done twice a week,[15] depending on the quantity of fish caught. Upon the quantity and quality of salt used largely depended the quality of the finished product, so that the technological requirements of curing underlie many of the characteristics of the salt import trade. Different markets required different salting and drying techniques. For example, the greenish colour of fish required by the Spanish market was attained by laying the fish skin side uppermost during the later drying states, whereas the white appearance of fish for the German and home markets was obtained by constantly keeping the flesh side facing the sun.[16] Fish for the Irish market were split differently from those for other markets.[17]

Apart from the curing* of ling and cod, and occasionally small quantities of herring (in barrels), the production of fish oil for export was an important ancillary activity at some stations. Although a certain amount of oil was produced from cod and ling livers, by far the greatest proportion was derived from the young coalfish (piltocks and sillocks), the livers of which were boiled in salt water and the oil skimmed off[18] and barrelled at the rate of roughly one barrel per boat per season for the islands as a whole.[19]

Throughout the period, ling was the staple export, with cod coming a very poor second — a proper method for curing cod for the Mediterranean markets was not mastered in Shetland till the close of the century and beyond.[20] The ling was most abundant on the wide, even expanses of the

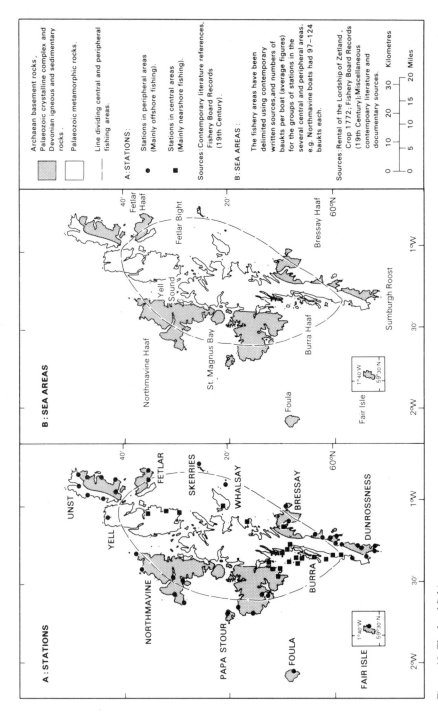

Figure 10. The haaf fishing

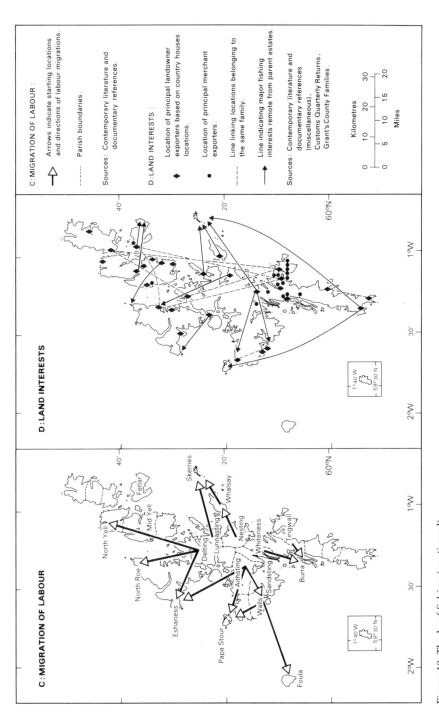

Figure 10. The haaf fishing (continued)

continental shelf (Figs. 2, 62) in the deeper water — in other words, generally furthest from land. Consequently, the most important haaf fishing areas tended to be situated round the periphery of the archipelago (Fig. 10a), particularly the 'far haaf' stations*.[21]

Stations from which the near-shore fishery was prosecuted can be distinguished to a large extent from those concerned with the offshore fishery by studying the average number of baukts carried by each boat at the several stations as recorded in documentary and literature sources (notably the Fishery Board statistics), the number of baukts being roughly proportional to the distance offshore simply because the room available for laying lines also increased in direct proportion with the distance from shore. Due to the great total length of lines belonging to any particular boat, it was nevertheless necessary to delimit strictly by crossbearings the areas of sea which could be fished from each particular station, especially in constricted areas such as the Burra Haaf,[22] and in areas where the length of line per boat was very great, such as west of Northmavine.[23]

In the peripheral zone, where the sea area was most extensive, the number of lines carried per boat was the greatest, Northmavine being the outstanding example. In outlying areas where there were shallows and strong tidal conditions, inshore fisheries tended to be dominant, with relatively small numbers of baukts per boat, the most important of these areas being Dunrossness, where the saithe fishery was of greatest consequence, Foula, which specialised in cod fishing to some extent,[24] and Fair Isle. Unst was to a small extent a saithe fishery centre,[25] and Skerries was in a favourable location for both inshore and offshore fishing.

The central near-shore waters consisted of five areas (Fig. 10b). Undoubtedly the most important of these was the Burra Haaf, in which cod fishing was probably marginally of greater importance than ling, and fishing was carried on commercially in winter as well as summer, the nearness of the grounds being a major advantage. The second most important area was the deep basin south of Fetlar, known today as the Fetlar Bight, utilised by boats from Whalsay, Skerries, and south and east Yell. Yell Sound was the leading piltock fishing area. St. Magnus Bay and the area north of Bressay were much less significant. Along the west coast of Mainland herring were sometimes caught in the voes in the harvest months, but this was an intermittent and unimportant fishery in the export trade as a whole (Fig. 63).

The growth of trade or shipping points was governed by the distribution of the main fishing districts and rent collecting points in the major settled areas, sites providing accessibility, good anchorage and shelter for sailing ships. The principal legally defined trade points,[26] although previously in existence as such (Fig. 4), tended to lie on or within a few miles of the zone of transition between the very important peripheral and less important central regions, with one for each major peripheral land-sea production region, such as Northmavine and Dunrossness. With the exception of Fetlar, which had no proper harbour (Fig. 11), all major islands such as Whalsay and

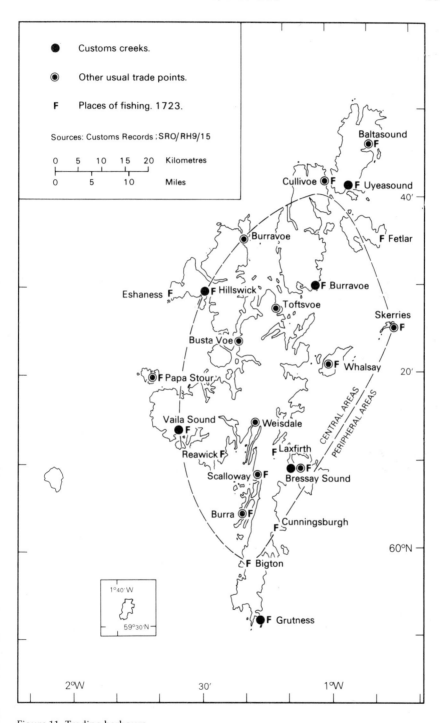

Figure 11. Trading harbours

Skerries also had recognised trade points, although these were not necessarily customs creeks.

During the period, the legally defined customs creeks tended to become the most important centres. Each of these major points (Fig. 11) was at the centre of a sea region (Chapter 6). Thus, for example, Burravoe drew business from Fetlar, eastern Northmavine and north Delting, Uyeasound was the focus for North Yell and Fetlar, while Scalloway was the centre for the great bay of islands south and west of it. The most important commodity handled was dried fish, carried along the coast from the individual stations to the trade points in sixern 'flitboats' (Chapter 6), while the small trade surpluses and rent commodities such as barrels of butter from the agricultural sector were transported by land and sea to the central places.

The summer seasonal migration of labour to the haaf fisheries (Fig. 10c) from the central area to the periphery was very marked, particularly in the latter half of the century, being often remarked in the Statistical Account. For example, the men of Sandsting went to Papa Stour and Northmavine stations.[27] The concentration of the major expansion into the latter half of the century is also often hinted at with references to the earlier greater importance of farming — especially stock-rearing — in many of the central parishes[28] and even specific references, such as the reference — again in the account of Sandsting — to the first 'far haaf' skipper to go from the district as still being alive in 1791.[29] This migration of labour was parallelled as the population increased by the growth of new arable enclosures known as outsets, which were most abundant in these peripheral areas and which were perhaps the most tangible evidence of that second indicator of expansion, the landowners' interest in expanding the fisheries.

This growth can also be traced through the landowners' landowning interests *per se* which generated an appreciable outward pressure from early on in the period, not at once reflected in increased production and exports. To begin with, there was a tendency for those more powerful landowners whose estates were centred in areas remote from the periphery, where most of the expansion was taking place, to acquire land interests in these outer areas (Fig. 10d).[30] As time progressed and the estates were handed down, these outlying sectors sometimes became separate estates, a good example being the Walls and Sandness portion of Mitchell of Girlsta's estate, which passed to John Scott, grandson of James Mitchell, and the first Scott of Melby, who became established on Vaila.[31]

On occasion competition for favourable locations was exceptionally fierce. For example, as early as 1726, in a conflict between Sinclair of Quendale and Mitchell of Girlsta over a booth at Skerries, Sinclair sent a party to take over the booth, one of whom was killed in the ensuing skirmish.[32] In 1771, when the landowner-merchant controversy was beginning, competition for these locations was renewed. Bruce of Symbister accused Henry Blair, a merchant in Sound, West Yell[33] of trying to destroy Symbister's booth at Skerries and otherwise take over the fishing at that locality.[34] The pressure of competition is further illustrated by the development of the principal absentee landlord's estate — that of the Lordship — which was often left with the poorest and worst-tenanted land in the most unfavourable locations for fishing.[35]

A parallel development of long-term significance was the increase in land values which occurred in those areas most suitable for fishing irrespective of the quality of the land for agriculture, such land selling at 50 to 70 and even 100 years' purchase of the rental value in the 1780s.[36] Land such as that of Scousburgh in Dunrossness, which was well-situated for both the winter and summer fishings, fetched highest prices.[37] By contrast, land in areas remote from offshore fishery development, such as Upper Weisdale, remained relatively stable in price after the Napoleonic Wars (Chapter 4).[38]

Lairds and Tenants

The collection of rent was the central business transaction in the running of an estate, and as rent continued to be paid largely in kind, the commodities of payment continued to play an important part in the export trade. Payment in kind was necessarily tied to the seasonal production cycle (Fig. 1); thus butter rents were generally payable on 1st August (Lammas) and money rents at Martinmas (11th November).[39] Often small cargoes of butter and oil were shipped out early in the year (Chapter 6). In bad years, when it was not possible to pay the rents in kind — if, for example, there had been a high stock mortality as in the winter of 1783-84, or a poor piltock fishery — rents might be paid in other commodities, particularly fish, although it is uncertain to what extent this was done in practice.[40] Such fish payment tends to confuse the distinction between the rent and trade transactions of the landowners with the tenants.

The difficulty of distinguishing the rent and trade sides of the landowners' businesses[41] is reflected in the geographical distribution of rent levels at the end of the eighteenth century. In most of the good fishery locations, rents were low, and compensated for by the profits accruing from the fisheries. In those parts of the central zone least well placed for the fisheries, notably Sandsting, Aithsting, Weisdale and Tingwall, rents were high and the landowners tended to force the tenants to sell them their fish at prices below the current market price. In a few areas the landowner relied upon rents only for his estate income and had nothing to do with the fish trade, which was carried on between his tenants and merchants. The first estate to implement this scheme successfully was that of Sumburgh in the 1770s;[42] the only other estate of note to attempt a similar scheme at this period was Lunna in 1799,[43] but this was unsuccessful owing to the lack of co-operation of the tenants, who like many landowners preferred the 'social security' of the old system to the winds of market change implied by the new.

Throughout the period there were two distinct kinds of business conducted between the landowner and the tenant. In the first kind, the landowner transacted with the tenant for his rents, usually paid in butter, fish oil and money when possible, as described above. In return, the landowner was generally obliged to keep up the estate, notably to supply the tenants with suitable houses to live in,[44] and even provide stock and seed corn on credit when these were in short supply, usually after bad winters and poor harvests respectively. The second type of business was purely a trading concern — contracting with the tenant for the supply of fish in return for supplying him with 'fishing necessaries'*, chief of which were boats completely fitted out, lines and other fishing gear, meal, tobacco and spirits (usually corn brandy)* for use while at sea. As noted above, these functions were very seldom distinct in practice.

The results of the rent and trade sides of the business in terms of production are illustrated for a typical large Shetland estate for the latter part of the eighteenth and the beginning of the nineteenth centuries in Fig. 12.[45] The most important points which the diagram illustrates are the great dependence of the average estate on the success of the fisheries, and the lesser, but significant, positions of butter, fish oil and (after 1780) kelp production. Hides, skins and woollen goods were very much incidental, although it is to be noted that in the famine of 1782-84, when there was a very heavy stock mortality, the sales of hides helped to offset the loss of revenue from other sources. The year-to-year variations do reflect variations in quantities to some extent, subject to the fact that the graph shows incomes, and the fluctuations therefore also reflect price changes (Fig. 36). Perhaps the most significant development overall is the decrease in the dependence on the fisheries and the corresponding increase in the worth of kelp, and to a lesser extent oil, in the gross proceeds of the estate.

In theory, there is no reason why the two functions of estate-owning and trading should not have been carried on independently, and in years of good harvests and fishings this may well have been so. Evidence to support this contention is present in the first half of the century. Thus, for example, there is virtually no mention of fish entering any transactions in the Daybook of Thomas Gifford's dealings with his tenants covering the 1720s.[46] Thomas Gifford himself, writing in 1733,[47] complained of the 'high price' which the landowners had to pay the tenants for their fish — this price was of the same order as that in the contract of Robert Jolly of 1700 discussed in Chapter 2, and indeed not greatly different from that prevailing in the days when the tenants sold their fish to the itinerant merchants a hundred years previously.[48] In the Old Statistical Account there are references to the relative prosperity of the tenants in the early part of the century; in Northmavine, the fish were considered to have been more profitable to the fishermen.[49] In areas remote from the main haaf fishing locations, such as Sandsting and Aithsting, the tenants were stated to have formerly had large flocks of sheep, considerable numbers of cattle and comparatively unimportant fishing interests.[50]

However, there were several factors in operation which made independence of landowning and trade at best precarious and, at worst, inseparable.

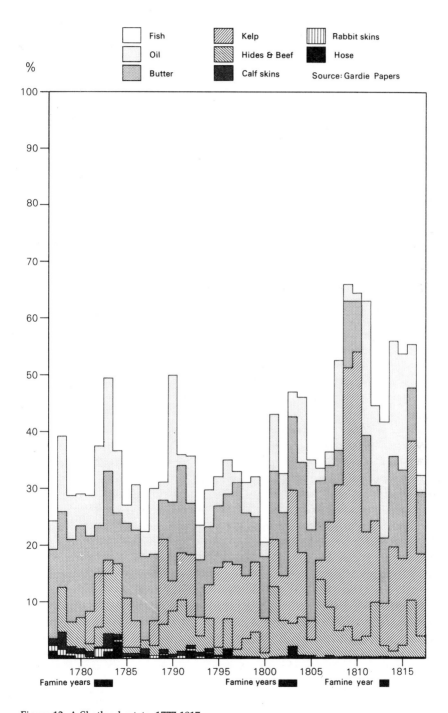

Figure 12. A Shetland estate: 1777-1817

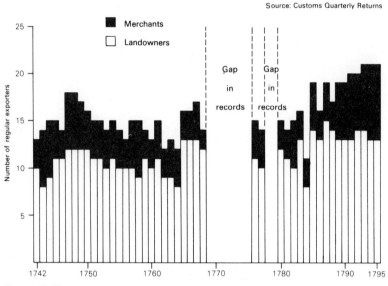

Figure 13. The exporters

Perhaps the most important of these was the seasonal nature of agricultural and fishery production, a direct consequence of the environmental relationships of the production system (Fig. 1) which caused a summer peak in business transactions. This, coupled with the basic shortfall in agricultural production due to increasingly inadequate land resources as population expanded, rendered necessary the advancement of credit to the tenant (usually in the form of meal) and the 'fishing necessaries'. As a direct extension of this was the sometimes extreme variability in both agricultural and fisheries production from one year to the next (Figs. 14, 21). Poor fishings and bad harvests were of frequent occurrence — sometimes simultaneous — and the long run of these between 1769 and 1784 was well-nigh disastrous for both landowners and tenants. The former suffered from over-extended credit (which necessitated considerable Government assistance in the form of meal supplies for the first time in the eighteenth century)[51] and the latter from being put in the position of bad debtors. However, little could be done about this situation apart from the time-honoured social adjustments of short leases* for the tentants and short tacks* for the tacksmen* which, through making it possible to evict the tenants, minimised risks to some extent. It did not get rid of the credit problem, which was only avoidable, at least from the landowners' point of view, by the appearance of independent parties to handle the fish trade. This was just beginning to come about on an appreciable scale by the 1770s and 1780s.

A second important drawback was the products used in rent payment, especially the butter and oil, which remained for a long time of poor quality and consequently at low market prices. In 1733 the landowners decreed that butter must be clean salted with British salt and free from hairs, and that oil must likewise be clean. No single stockings were to be presented for sale.[52] These exhortations, at least in the case of butter, appear to have had the desired effect, as from 1740 onwards the price of Shetland butter on the Hamburg market began to rise steeply, and remained relatively high for the remainder of the century,[53] probably mainly due to wartime demand. This caused further blurring of the distinction between rent and trade commodities. When the butter price was high, tenants and tacksmen alike tended to sell it direct rather than pay it in rent, while if prices were low the reverse was the case.[54] Further, the pressure on the tenants to pay in kind when high prices prevailed was great, and it has been suggested that this tended to cause overstocking of cattle.[55]

These problems of seasonality of credit and blurring of distinctions between rent and trade commodities might have been ameliorated had there been an adequate money supply to iron out the fluctuations in liquidity to which the tenants were subject. However, the supply of money was generally inadequate, although it is on record that the tenants had small money savings before the great famine of 1782-84.[56] The decline in the money supply was initially an important and much deplored consequence of the decline in the Dutch fisheries (Chapter 6) and remained a persistent problem, especially in the first part of the century when almost the only coinage current was German. In 1718 it was remarked that had the German coinage not been passable in Orkney, there could have been no British coinage at all in Shetland.[57] Apparently Orkney was the only area among Shetland's British trade contacts where German coinage was acceptable as a medium of exchange.[58] In 1727 and 1733[59] regulations were passed governing exchange rates, which were unfavourable to Shetland trade due to the fact that the German stivers* in particular were held to be virtually worthless outside their country of origin.

The cumulative effect of the above three factors was that by the 1770s and 1780s a significant proportion of rent was from time to time being paid in fish,[60] the chief trade commodity, thereby strengthening even further the socio-economic bonds of landowners and tenants, which had grown out of necessity in the first part of the century to be something of a burden for both by the close of the period. Any liquidity which the tenant might possess tended to appear as a credit balance in the landowner's ledger rather than money in the tenant's pocket, and by 1785 the usual procedure was a simple one of deducting the land rent from the tenant's share of the summer fishing along with his other debts.[61] In 1785 few tenants could have been solvent after that operation. However, the position was aggravated to some extent by certain other internal trade developments.

Although the landowner-tenant relationship formed the cornerstone of the internal trade structure, there were significant developments in other forms of trading during the period. Until the 1740s, there was some resemblance to the seventeenth-century system in the presence of itinerant merchants, who continued to buy up hides and skins in particular, even to the extent of depriving the landowners of sufficient beasts for slaughter, as in 1729.[62] Their activities smacked of, and were indeed alleged to constitute, forestalling, which led to artificially high prices. The trade was regulated by the landowners in 1733,[63] but chapmen* were still being complained of as late as 1745.[64] This provides supporting evidence for the contention that the tenants, particularly in the central area with its high stock population, were comparatively well-off in the first half of the century.

Meanwhile, the tenants continued to dispose of surpluses of provisions, meal and woollen stockings to foreign fishermen. This trade, although on a smaller scale than previously, was still important enough to warrant the holding of a fair in Lerwick in the month of June (Chapter 6). In areas of increasing peat shortages, peat was bartered with neighbouring districts; thus the people of south Unst, for example, imported peats from Yell.[65] Also, the corn surplus areas of Dunrossness and (sometimes) Walls and Sandness supplied adjoining areas.[66]

The beginning of the most important long-term development, that of the emergence of merchants occupying fixed locations, and engaging in retailing to a significant degree, can be dated to around 1760, and is connected mainly with the development of external trade. From the 1760s onwards they began to encroach on the island economy, first through the retailing of linen and other good-quality manufactured cloth and clothing, which made serious inroads on domestic subsistence manufacture of coarse woollen cloth for clothing.[67] This was followed by the introduction of the second main retail commodity of smuggled gin (and to a lesser extent tea). By 1791, Sandsting and Aithsting alone boasted thirty to forty 'gin and tea shops'.[68] Most of these were almost certainly casual places of sale, rather than approaching even a true general merchant's establishment in character, but there is no reason to suppose that this trade was any less important in other rural areas.

There tends to be a clear division into a pre-1760 phase, when itinerant merchants were still of importance, and thus internal trade was fluid in location, determined only by the settlement pattern and the long-standing trade points (Fig. 11) discussed above, and a post-1760 phase paralleling the rise of general merchants, in which local trade outside the staple exports became increasingly concentrated on Lerwick. Indeed, towards the end of the period Lerwick may also have been making substantial inroads into the export trade, as many of the merchant agents resided there (Fig. 10d). By the end of the century the people of Sandsting and Aithsting were bringing their black cattle, ponies and other products to the town for sale,[69] rather than disposing of these to itinerant merchants as had been done in the first half of the century. In the early part of the century also, the town had declined in parallel with the trade with the Dutch fishermen upon whom it largely depended,[70] but by 1764[71] it was 'rather increasing', though Low in 1774[72] thought the town had never been bigger in spite of the fact that his estimate of the number of families was only half that of Brand's in 1700[73] (Brand's estimate was certainly a gross exaggeration, as the town at this time had a population of about 700).[74] The key to the expansion of the town was undoubtedly the expanding merchant class. The number of retail shops alone increased from two to three around 1760 to twelve in 1785.[75] By the end of the period the town was just entering a phase of rapid expansion (Chapter 4), with the building of the private piers known as lodberries*, which still lend a distinctive appearance to its South End.

Lairds and Merchants

It is clear that the earliest attempts of the landowners to engage directly in trade were limited to contracting with external merchants to buy the product and carry it away, as in the contract of 1709 (Chapter 2). One or two subsequent early contracts involved partnership of one or more landowners with a single external trader, such as the 1716 contract between Robert Blellock, shipmaster in Leith on the one hand, and James Scott of Voesgarth (Unst), Andrew Bruce of Urie (Fetlar) and Thomas Mouat, merchant in Unst. Blellock was to buy or build a ship to the value of £200 or £250 sterling, and have her ready for sea at Unst by 1st July 1717.[76] Each of the four subscribers had a quarter share in the project.

However, as the landowner became more securely established in trade in the 1720s and 1730s, there were three basic variations in trading organisation. First was the 'company trade', which was probably the earliest, and of which the Blellock example is one with an external partner. In this method of operation, two or three landowners would enter into an agreement, for perhaps up to three years at a time, to pool their resources (ship(s) and cargo(es)) and employ local agents where necessary to deputise for them. In 1721 George Pitcairn of Muness (Unst) and Magnus Henderson of Gardie (Unst) undertook such a contract for three years to trade within the whole south parish of Unst and all of Fetlar.[77] William Bruce was to be agent in Unst, and John Scott of Clothan was to manage their affairs in Fetlar. The fish was to be divided equally, and each was to export his own share. Another variant on this was for a landowner not directly engaging in trade to agree to sell his produce to one who was. A good example of this arrangement is that of 1727 in which Hector Scott of Scottshall agreed.to deliver to Magnus Henderson of Gardie at Bressay all Scott's cod, ling, saithe (Scottshall was situated in the saithe fishery area of Dunrossness) and oil caught and made by Scott's tenants that year.[78]

The second basic variation in organisation was sometimes implemented by the largest landowners, who had sufficient capital and produce to carry on trade independently of others. The outstanding example was Thomas Gifford of Busta (Delting), who was the pioneer of the landowners' fishing trade, both in respect of his large scale of working and his opening up new markets. A good description by Bruce (1922, 1931),[79] giving some idea of the wide scope of the day-to-day operations in such a venture, has been provided using extracts from Gifford's letter books of the 1720s and 1730s. Such a landowner supervised all aspects of the trading operation, from the production side including fishing and shore curing and settling with the tenants, through owning and freighting his own ships (Chapter 6), to not infrequently going personally to market to dispose of the cargoes. Indeed it was the itinerant merchant's trade in reverse in the sense that the landowner was situated at the production end, while the itinerant merchant operated from the market end. Some of these early 'landmaster-traders', such as Magnus and William Henderson of Gardie, received a mercantile education at Hamburg[80] in the Scottish merchant tradition.[81] The largest operators, notably Busta and Gardie, were among the first pioneers of the fishing trade, being the principal Shetland partners in the Jolly scheme of 1709.

The third and final method of trading employed by the landowners was the tack system, which was used for the landowning side of the businesses as well. Its use took place under four circumstances. The first was for the running of estates with absentee landlords, of which the Lordship estate was by far the most important. Until 1734 the estate, which was very scattered, was let to three or four tacksmen who were empowered to run it and dispose of its produce, including the delivery of the rents — butter and oil — by ship, usually to Leith.[82] Significantly, the tacksmen involved were the most notable large-scale pioneers of the fishing trade — principally Gardie and Busta, with Lochend and Girlsta at various times. That the development of trade was their main reason for holding the tack is evident from a letter[83] of Thomas Gifford of Busta to Magnus Henderson of Gardie and Arthur Nicolson of Bullister (and later Lochend) in 1722. Gifford did not expect much profit from the tack — 'yet it could not but produce a greater stock in the Cuntrie and thereby contribute something for carrying on our Company trade . . .' He pointed out the virtue of the usual three-year tack as virtual insurance against 'unforeseen accidents'. From 1735 the estate was let to ten or twelve tacksmen — usually local landowners in the respective parishes — probably largely due to the arrears of tack duty built up by the previous tacksmen. 'Unforeseen' setbacks such as failures in markets were at least partly responsible, along with the practice of claiming retentions for ley lands and famine which by 1733 had wasted away about one-tenth of the revenue of the estate.[84] However, as the pressure to develop the haaf fisheries increased, some of the best areas of the estate — an estimated one-twelfth — were surreptitiously taken over by these tacksmen leaving the poorest areas, so that by the 1780s, after the series of poor harvests, arrears of £5,000 Scots (£600 stg.)[85] had accumulated. This demonstrates the increasing disadvantages of the tack system in the new economic climate.

The second case was the administration of outlying parts of estates, often by landowners who did not engage directly in trade, of which Westshore was the principal example in the second half of the century. Again, the various parts were usually let — or 'set'* in the terminology of the times — to the principal landowners in adjacent parts, Gifford of Busta, for example, obtaining tacks of the Westshore lands in Northmavine.[86]

The third case, of landowners who wished to expand their fishing interests, was in some respects a small-scale version of the first. It involved these landowners obtaining tacks of land in favourable fishing localities. Busta obtained tacks in Papa Stour[87] from the Westshore and Lordship* estates in the 1750s in this way, and Andrew Scott of Greenwall, a small Unst landowner in the 1740s, was likewise able to engage in trade through his holding of many lands in tack.[88] The tacks of the church revenues were a special case in that although the landowner could use the commodities gained in trade, he was obliged first of all to support the minister on the proceeds. The best example of this arrangement was Sinclair of Quendale's possession of the church revenues of Dunrossness, worth about £5,500 Scots (£300 stg.) per annum, which the minister, the Rev. John Mill, had much difficulty in extracting from him.[89]

Although the amount of land held in tack was considerable — the Lordship and Westshore estates together amounted to roughly one quarter of the total rentalled land in the second half of the century — the tack system tended to work only in the important respect of making more convenient the running of very fragmented estates, often with the aim of developing trade also. Despite the fact that Low mentions the propensities of tacksmen to oppress the fishermen,[90] the great majority of the landowners engaging in trade before about 1790 were resident on their estates,[91] and as the tacksmen were generally the same group of landowners, there was no real tendency to promulgate a race of tacksmen *per se* as happened, for example, in the western Highlands of Scotland.[92] The rise of the merchants was further insurance against such a development in trade.

From the available evidence, it appears that the true 'merchant-laird' system described above persisted throughout the 1710s, 1720s and 1730s as the only method of trading. However, that a number of merchants, who were not themselves landlords, were entering the import-export trade by the 1740s is borne out by the evidence in the Customs returns (Fig. 13), and the comment of Thomas Gifford about 1740 that 'Landowners cure and export the fish of their tenants themselves, or set their tenants who are fishermen to merchants, who do the same'.[93] Gifford himself set his fishings in 1753.[94] In this fourth use of the tack system, some of these early traders styling themselves merchants were in fact close relatives of the landowners who handled the export-import side of the business, such as Patrick Gifford, brother of Thomas of Busta, who often handled the merchant business at Hillswick.[95] Others were small landowners in their own right such as William Bruce of Burravoe, who belonged to the Symbister (Whalsay)[96] family. There is some evidence to suggest that a few of these early merchants were gaining a small footing in the export trade through the export of butter (the price of which rose steeply after 1740) and woollen stockings, and in the import trade through the import of salt. James Craigie, merchant in Lerwick and Collector of Customs for a time, often imported salt on behalf of the landowners.[97]

The first major development, involving merchants who had no land-owning interests of consequence, arose through the development of agencies handling at local level the import and export trade of the land-owners, who tended to establish semi-permanent trade relations with one or more merchant agents, depending on the scale of the individual land-owners' business. From around 1760 onwards, when the Spanish market was opened up, merchants acting as agents became more firmly established. They often owned their vessels and took an increasing share of the import trade as well as acting as shipping agents on behalf of the merchant houses in London and elsewhere (see below, and Chapter 6). Some of these agents were involved in developing new markets. Andrew Bruce of Hogan (Bressay) and Thomas Bolt of Cruister (Bressay) stand out as leading developers of the Spanish market in the late 1750s and early 1760s.[98] James Henderson of Gardie contracted with Bruce to handle the Gardie fish trade throughout the 1750s,[99] and Henderson subsequently made a similar arrangement with Arthur Nicolson of Lochend, a landowner who, in the early 1760s, engaged in agency work.[100] This was the same Arthur Nicolson whose Day Book for 1762[101] illustrates that these merchants engaged with the local people in many small transactions of a general nature as well as with the landowners, although at this time there were only two or three shops in Lerwick.

By the mid-1770s the merchants were recognised as a separate class inter-posed between the landowners and the tenants, handling part of the land-owners' shipping business. They were just beginning to handle the production side of the fishing trade as well. Some of them, notably a few members of the merchant houses (see below) who had settled in Shetland after 1760, were accused of taking the best fish from the tenants in contra-vention of the latter's agreements with the landowners.[102] They were also acting as wholesalers and retailers for landowners and tenants alike by virtue of their increasing share of the import trade, including smuggling. By 1785 there were twelve shops in Lerwick selling 'every fashionable and expensive article of dress . . .', and one shopkeeper alone in 1782 had sold £1,000 sterling-worth of drapery among the ordinary people.[103] However, the merchants, despite their increasing numbers (Fig. 13), had not ousted the landowners from their commanding position in the trading economy. That only occurred after 1790.

When the Shetland landowners entered trade on their own account for the first time, the factor system was more or less universal in international trade in Europe outside the big trading companies,[104] and operated both in the Shetland import and export trades. It consisted simply of a mode of dealing by means of an agent at the market port, who handled all the business of any individual landowner or group of landowners for a fixed commission, usually a percentage of the market value of the cargo. In the 1709 contract of Robert Jolly (Chapter 2), for example, Charles Mitchell of Uresland (Tingwall), who was a merchant in Edinburgh, was appointed to act as agent there for the enterprise, to handle advice to and from London. More commonly the factor, who was generally a Scot resident in the port of trade (Hamburg and Bergen were the main foreign ports), arranged the docking, cargo-handling and customs formalities of his clients' ships both on entering and leaving port. He organised the warehousing and disposal of the cargo to local merchants and obtained cargoes; he also attended to all financial transactions pertaining to these functions. The contacts built up were usually of many years' standing and were sometimes held to restrict trade developments as a consequence. Thus Henry Blair, shipmaster and merchant in Sound, West Yell, had dealt with James Stephen, factor in Hamburg, for forty years by 1776. James Stephen also did business with other Shetland traders, and Henry Blair had at that time been his agent in Shetland for twenty years.[105]

The factor system persisted for most of the period in the Hamburg and Bergen trades. However, the Spanish trade saw the introduction of a new system of marketing which, in contrast to the essentially bilateral type of trade relationship of the factor system, was multilateral and therefore more flexible in operation. Merchant houses — the Greenock and London merchants referred to as having begun to buy Shetland fish in 1759 and about 1763 respectively[106] — were large-scale import-export agents centred mainly in London, Liverpool, Leith and Glasgow. They were also shipowners, shipping agents and even finance houses at this time.[107] These houses, which made prior contracts with the producers for fish, usually had branches scattered in various ports in the market area (in Shetland's case mainly Spain), which handled the business at the market end in much the same way as a factor. This type of organisation at the market probably largely explains the variety of ports to which Shetland fish were consigned in the latter part of the century compared to the former (Fig. 11), since if one market port was unsuitable, a ship could be sent to another with little delay.[108] One such firm which developed Shetland contacts in the 1780s was Sellar and Henderson of Liverpool, the Henderson partner being a Shetlander. Their ships carried Shetland fish to Spain, and brought back cargoes of Spanish salt on return voyages.[109] As a result of this type of organisation a small proportion of fish was exported coastwise for re-export from these merchant house centres, and sometimes was warehoused till demand or other circumstances were more favourable.

The European Dimension

The eighteenth century is the first period in Shetland history for which detailed statistical coverage of production and import-export figures exists in any degree of precision. There are two basic problems in dealing with the information. First, prior to 1742, statistics of production must be derived from shreds of evidence, and the best that can be attempted is an estimate for the export level of fish (Chapter 2). After 1742, more or less continuous coverage of foreign and import statistics exists until 1796 in the Quarterly Customs Returns,[110] although there are a few gaps, notably in the export statistics from 1769 until 1775 inclusive. Other imperfections have made it necessary to restrict the material plotted to the years 1744-1795 inclusive.

The second point, which at first would appear to be a major drawback — namely, the absence of detailed statistics of the 'coastwise' trade with Britain (Chapter 6) — is in fact not of great consequence in the export sector, as frequent historical references indicate that most of the staple commodity, fish, was exported to foreign ports, and hence is recorded in the Quarterly Returns. A few precise figures do exist, notably in the 1776 export figures (Table 3),[111] which indicate the relative scales of foreign and coastwise trade, tending to corroborate the other evidence regarding the low level of dried cod and ling exports to Britain. The gap in coastwise import statistics is more to be regretted, as this trade included the all-important grain and meal imports, the most reliable possible indicator of the shortfalls in agricultural production and hence the general state of the subsistence agricultural economy. The final major statistical gap, relating to both foreign and coastwise trade, is that for smuggled goods, principally spirits, tobacco and tea, which are very difficult to estimate, except possibly to state that these figures almost certainly rose in parallel with two other trends, the increase in population and the steep rises in duty, especially toward the end of the century (Chapter 4).

Because of the primary importance of fish exports in the trading economy as a whole, and the relative abundance of statistics relating to these, special mention is required of fish export statistics. There are three separate sets of these, all incomplete in one way or another, but which together give some idea of the pattern (Fig. 14a). The most complete set is of the totals of the entries outwards which each exporter had to submit to the Customs and which appear in the Customs Quarterly Returns. The second series is of the weights on which debentures* were granted, the fish being weighed before shipment by the Customs officers to assess these weights.[112] The resulting figures were entered in the Customs books as a record of debentures paid, and thus do not reflect accurately the annual production statistics in the way the first series does. For example, in the winter of 1744-45, when exports were delayed by bad weather, many of the debentures for 1744 were not granted until 1745. The debenture figures tend to be consistently lower than the merchants' entries totals, which may mean that some of the fish exported did not qualify for the bounty,* or that some of the fish was exported coastwise first. The internal consistency of the figures and their relation to independent evidence of the state of the fisheries, particularly with regard to bad years, rule out large-scale fraud. The only such fraud on record was detected in 1723, and the Customs staff were replaced as a result.[113]

The third set of statistics is from the Treasury returns, 1751-1782.[114] These appear to have been derived from the debenture figures and may therefore tend to exaggerate the decline in exports in the period 1769-1775. This is supported by the figure of 7193 cwt. given by Low for fish exports in the foreign trade in 1774 — almost twice as much as that shown in Fig. 14a. The explanation of this discrepancy possibly lies in the fact that in 1774, and for several years thereafter, fish 'not completely dry' seems to have been refused the bounty, and hence would not have been entered in the Customs Records.[115]

There were two basic factors underlying the demand for fish in eighteenth-century Europe. First, there was the importance of fish as a supplementary item of diet in what was, by and large, a subsistence agricultural economy, so that it tended to occupy a more important place relative to other foodstuffs than in later times. The second factor was institutional, namely, the insistence of the Roman Catholic Church on diets of fish during Lent and on one day per week (Friday) throughout the year. This second factor was of more significance for the Shetland fishing trade in the long term, as it led to a gradually increasing emphasis on southern European markets for the dry white fish which formed the staple of Shetland production. In the case of the northern European markets, herring caught by the Dutch and other nations in Shetland waters tended to be predominant,[116] and throughout the period this market was consequently of much less direct significance in the island trade as a whole. A third factor which began to assert itself in the second half of the century, especially in the Spanish market, was the growing size of the market itself, caused by population increase, notably around Barcelona.[117]

The basic requirement of all the fish markets in Europe, both white fish and herring, was for salt fish. In the case of white fish, sometimes dry fish with practically no salt was favoured. Salting (or drying) was the only way of preserving fish on a large scale. In the case of white fish, there were distinct requirements regarding the degrees of salting and drying in northern and southern European markets respectively. The German market required heavily salted fish, white and almost salt-burned in appearance and not too dry, in contrast to the relatively light-salted, hard-dried product preferred by the Spanish market.[118] Although the hard-dried variety had been cured in Shetland as early as the 1730s,[119] it was not until the 1760s that the different curing techniques required for the Spanish market were widely mastered and applied in Shetland,[120] a necessity for successful penetration of this market. Even so, there were occasional complaints from the merchant houses in Barcelona to the effect that they were receiving too heavily salted fish from Shetland.[121] The expansion of the Shetland fishing industry after 1760 helped to make possible the curing of large batches to a uniform standard which also encouraged development of this market.[122]

The variations in supply, i.e. the exports, are summarised in Fig. 14a. Estimates for the late 1710s and early 1720s are difficult to come by, although the amount paid out in fish debentures[123] (complicated by the fraud referred

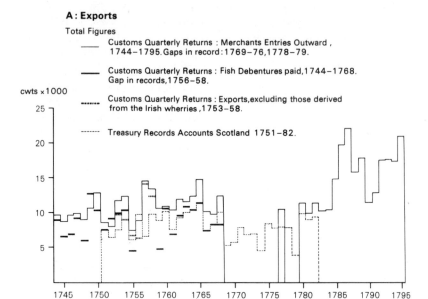

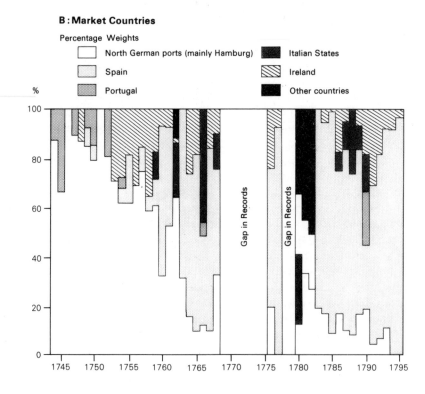

Figure 14. Dry salt fish

to) suggests levels of production considerably lower than in both the late seventeenth century (Chapter 2) and the early 1740s. Apart from the period 1760-1784, there was a basic upward trend which can be attributed to the increase in catching power brought about by an increase in the number of boats, and the use of more large boats (sixerns) and longer lines. It is recorded that these changes brought about increases in catches in the important Northmavine area, for example.[124]

The year-to-year fluctuations and the prolonged slump of 1769-1784 are mainly due to the influence of natural causes, which affected the fish trade in two ways, short and longer term. First, there were the short-term fluctuations relating mainly to weather and sea conditions, which ranged from the sudden storm which interrupted the fishing and not infrequently led to loss of life, to the onsets of several days or weeks of unsettled weather which greatly impeded the prosecution of the summer fishing, and on occasion even led to its premature abandonment, as in 1774.[125] Although the sudden storm was to have its greatest effect in the nineteenth century (Chapters 4, 5), between 1745 and 1791, for example, thirty boats belonging to the leading offshore fishing area of Northmavine (Fig. 10b) were lost.[126] It is not clear if this includes the eight or nine lost in 'the north of Shetland' in 1791.[127] Such losses, quite apart from the human tragedy involved, signified considerable losses in production and expense in replacement of boats and gear for landowner and tenant alike.

The second effect on supply was the seasonal and longer-term variations related to climatic and oceanographic changes, of which the most notable example was the large number of poor years between 1769 and 1784 (Fig. 14a), the years before 1779 in particular being remarkable for the large quantities of small fish caught.[128] This probably contributed to the tenants' poor economic position at the end of the eighteenth century, and may well have aided the merchants in their competition with the landowners over the buying of fish, as the former often acquired the larger, better fish at the expense of the latter.[129]

Concerning variations in demand little is known apart from the long-term upward trend associated with the expansion of population in the principal market area of north-eastern Spain. In the short term the factor of competition is the only one which appears to have significantly affected demand. In the eighteenth century there were four major sources of supply for the European dry salt fish market, namely, the Newfoundland area, the western and northern coasts of Norway, the waters round Iceland, and the waters round the northern half of the British Isles. Although Shetland was by far the most important supplier in Scotland (Fig. 15), the island production occupied a relatively small share of the total market, being only about 7 per cent in Barcelona in 1790, for example.[130] While competition among the four major supplying areas sometimes led to short-term slumps in demand, the Shetland share of the market was so small that it remained reasonably assured in the long term. The position of Shetland fish in the market was

F

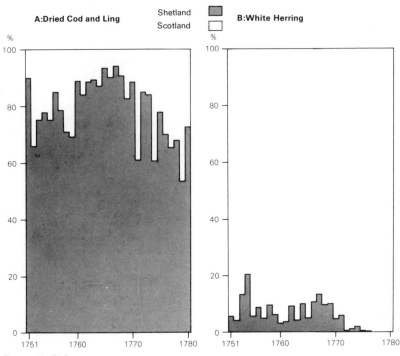

Figure 15. Fish exports

further secured by the higher-priced ling[131] in which the islands specialised. Ling was generally in short supply in a market dominated by cod.

Competition from Norway was offset by the fact that this area concentrated on the production of wind-dried stockfish, which on the German market at least seems to have been complementary to salt fish, rather than in competition with it.[132] On the whole, probably the most serious competition came from Newfoundland. This was felt for the first time in the 1720s on the German market as the Newfoundland fisheries expanded after the War of the Spanish Succession,[133] and was mentioned again in 1744, when Thomas Gifford declared that the superiority of Shetland ling over Newfoundland 'poor jack' in the Lisbon market made the ling the first choice of the poor people,[134] although it was probably rather more expensive. Indeed, fish prices as a whole were considered low until the mid-1730s,[135] and it was the attraction of higher prices which was one of the main spurs to the development of the Lisbon market by Gifford at this time. Finally, in the late 1780s and early 1790s large supplies of Newfoundland fish were dumped on the Mediterranean markets, thus bringing down prices sharply[136] (Fig. 36). During the latter part of the period, from, 1760 onwards, the price of fish doubled relative to the first half of the century,[137] and Shetland trade was undoubtedly aided in its expansion by competition between the German and Spanish fish markets.[138] However, the competition between the supplying areas was also sometimes severe, prices in any given season being liable to rapid fluctuation, which was the main reason for the exporters' anxiety to 'catch' the markets as early in the season as possible.

There were basically two phases in the development of market links, falling before and after 1760 respectively (Figs. 14b and 16). During the first phase of development the links of the preceding century to Hamburg remained dominant (Fig. 16a). Although as early as 1719 there is a reference to trade contact with Bilbao,[139] before about 1750 the small surplus remaining was usually sent to Portugal. The different requirements and higher profitability of the Portuguese market were recognised, but the development at this time was hampered by war and the generally higher risks of transporting fish to this distant market (Chapter 6 and below). Contact with the Irish market was established more or less permanently in 1751 through the arrival of the Irish wherries* (Chapter 6), which were responsible for most of the exports before 1760, and the market remained a significant outlet for Shetland fish after the wherries were prohibited from operation in 1763 (Fig. 16b, below).

During the second phase of the development, which was associated with the taking over of the trade at the market end by the merchant houses, and improved curing techniques at the production end, trade links became more diversified, with a relatively sudden shift to the Iberian market, particularly Barcelona, a shift also parallelled by the Newfoundland trade.[140] There were lesser, but significant, contacts with other Iberian ports and ports in the Italian peninsula, notably Ancona, Naples and Leghorn (Fig. 16b, c). Barcelona was well placed as the chief port of Cataluña, the most economically progressive part of Spain in the latter part of the eighteenth century, and the seat of the Spanish equivalent of the English Industrial Revolution, spearheaded by a developing textile industry.[141] Between 1760 and 1800 the volume of trade handled by the port trebled, its profits increased ten times,[142] and it appears to have acted increasingly as an entrepôt port for the whole fish trade in the Western Mediterranean. The port received cargoes of cod, the chief import, from all the production regions mentioned above; in 1790 there were 33 cargoes amounting to 4,300 tons, of which Shetland provided 300 tons[143] (1790 was a poor year for the Shetland fisheries compared to the late 1780s and early 1790s generally — Fig. 14a). However, Shetland ling, 'les langues d'Ecosse',[144] were as highly valued in the Barcelona market as they had been in the Lisbon market in the first half of the century, and fetched higher prices than the ubiquitous cod.[145] This probably helps to account for the continued emphasis on ling in the haaf fisheries, rather than cod, which were not caught in as great quantities as in the nineteenth century,[146] and the curing technique for which was not properly mastered in the islands in the eighteenth century.[147]

Throughout the period war, apart from having significant effects by virtue of Shetland's strategic position in the north-west approaches to Europe (Chapter 6), also hampered the fish trade through the closure of markets.

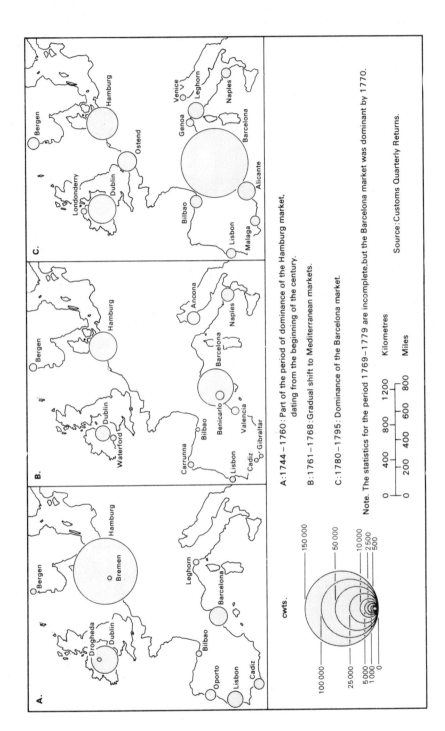

Figure 16. Development phases in the dried salt fish trade

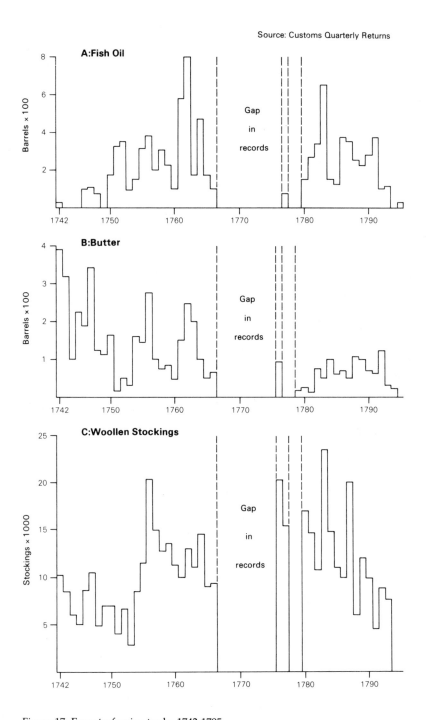

Figure 17. Exports: foreign trade, 1742-1795

Thus the lucrative Lisbon market was cut off by the War of the Austrian Succession,[148] and it may be significant that the change from Germany to Spain as the main fish market occurred during the Seven Years' War,[149] as imports from Hamburg were also cut off at this time. Most of the subsequent wars with France did not disrupt the trade links to any great degree until complete closure of the Mediterranean markets in 1798 (Chapter 4), but the Dutch War cut off the Spanish market completely, and large consignments had to be sent to Ostend, Bergen, and some even to Riga[150] (Figs. 16c, 21).

Although fish was the staple export product, there were appreciable quantities of other products, which can be classified as surpluses from the subsistence sector of the production economy (Figs. 1, 9), most important being fish oil, butter and woollen stockings. Exports of fish oil show wide fluctuations, probably mainly due to local production factors, principally the occurrence of piltocks (Fig. 12) and the scale of the fishing effort, which tended to intensify in years of poor haaf fishings and harvests, as in the period 1782-84 (especially in 1784 — Fig. 17a). By the end of the century, production was said to vary between 200 and 800 barrels per annum,[151] which agrees well with the export statistics (Fig. 17a) and indeed suggests that most of the oil was exported abroad. However, these statistics only partly reveal the true level of production, and do not, for example, show the exceptionally high production of 2,000 barrels in 1791, which was due to the great abundance of piltocks,[152] thus drawing attention to the fact that much of the oil production went coastwise (Tables 3, 4 below). Oil sent abroad invariably went to Hamburg.[153]

As in the case of oil, much of the exported butter went coastwise, and the steady decrease apparent in the quantity exported (Fig. 17b), especially in the latter part of the century, is probably mainly due to the increasing dominance of the coastwise trade. Before the mid-1730s, the quality of Shetland butter for export was very poor, consignments being frequently contaminated by hair[154] and of uneven quality due to collection in small lots.[155] In 1735 it was losing ground on the Leith market to superior English butter for these reasons,[156] and was also in competition with Orkney butter.[157] Pressure by the landowners in 1733 caused gradual improvements to be made,[158] and about 1740 the price on the Hamburg market rose steeply,[159] and although subject to downward fluctuations, as in 1765 with the dumping of excessive quantities of Irish butter on the Hamburg market,[160] tended to remain high for the remainder of the century[161] and beyond. In the 1770s it was increasingly diverted to the home market, and was particularly valuable in wartime, as although some was used by bakers,[162] most of it — again the quality seems to have declined — was used as grease butter, first mentioned in the Customs Returns for 1776-77. The Royal Navy was an important customer in this respect.[163]

The export of woollen stockings (which went almost entirely to Hamburg) was considerable, and tended to increase as time went on (Fig. 17c). This export was in addition to the large but unknown quantities sold to foreign fishermen (below, and Chapter 6), and those sent coastwise. The steady decline in the 1780s and 1790s was probably the result of the outbreak of sheep scab (Chapter 4) and the increasing importance of the Leith market, where the low quality of the stockings was such that by 1790 the Highland

Table 3. Foreign and coastwise exports, 1776.

This table is compiled from Thomas Mouat's Vade Mecum in the Gardie papers, and all figures have been rounded off to the nearest whole number. CQR figures in brackets where known.

Products	Foreign		Coastwise	
	Quantity	Value £ stg.	Quantity	Value £ stg.
dried fish to Barcelona & Dublin	7065 cwt @ 17/6	6005		
—coastwise for export	478 cwt. @ 13/–	407		
(Hamburg)	(712) +(13,700 by tail)			
(Dublin)	(840)			
(Barcelona)	(1990)			
dried fish @ 3/– bounty to Hamburg	(This is probably the 13,700 above)	462		
bounty @ 5/– p.120		934		
dried ling, cod, tusk			2703 cwt. @ 15/–	2027
dried saithe			16105 cwt. @ 25/–	100/201
barrels butter	86 @ 60/– (82. ½ x 5.37 ankers)	257	332 @ 55/–	913
barrels oil	185 @ 40/– (353. ½ x 8.16 ankers)	371	462 @ 44/–	1017
hides in salt			481 @ 9/6	228
barrels herrings			208 @ 18/–	197
barrels beef			148 @ 30/–	222
ankers tallow			19 @ 40/–	38
calf skins (no.)			6156 @ 11d.	282
coarse stockings (pairs)	18020 @ 6d. (20220)	450	2618 @ 6d.	65
barrels wet cod			233 @ 20/–	233
ankers fish sounds			21 @ 8/–	8
rabbit skins (no.)			2506 @ 3d.	31
tallow			2 cwt. @ 30/–	5
		8887		5471

stockings sold to foreigners at Lerwick, provisions to ships & goods exported not cleared at the Cu. Ho. is thought to be about   3000

TOTAL VALUE: £17,357

Society were pointing out that the market price had fallen below the value of the wool contained in the stockings.[164]

The basic import pattern of the seventeenth century with its five categories of items (Chapter 2) remained remarkably unchanged during the eighteenth century, particularly during the first half. The only major difference appears to have been a decline in the money supply in terms of coinage, due to the decline of the Dutch fisheries and the disappearance of the German merchants, and also probably to the increasing financial dealings with Britain, which consisted largely of paper transactions. Meanwhile, the import of meal and household goods tended to come more and more from Scotland rather than Hamburg, and spirits imports were drawn with increasing frequency direct from Holland rather than Hamburg as the taste for gin became established alongside that for corn brandy.

In an economy which was based on primary food production both for subsistence and commerce, salt was the only preservative and thus occupied a central place in the trading economy, being used in the curing of white fish and herring and in the preparation of butter, beef and hides. Of these uses, the curing of ling, tusk, cod and saithe was most important, the quality of the finished product depending to a large extent on the quantity and quality of salt used. Fish required approximately one third of their dry weight in salt,[165] depending on the quality used. The technical requirements of curing were thus basic in determining the character of the salt trade, particularly the dominance of foreign salt, which was of superior quality to home salt and essential in the proper curing of fish for export markets.[166]

Most of the salt imported in the first half of the century came via the entrepôts of Hamburg and Bergen (see below). For example, in 1743 Anthony Simpson, Thomas Gifford's factor in Hamburg, was negotiating the import of a cargo of salt from Lisbon for re-export in part to Shetland.[167] It was variously referred to as foreign, white, Spanish, or Portuguese salt,[168] and so is impossible to trace exactly to its origin. However, a few cargoes were brought direct to Shetland, notably from Faro, Oporto and Lisbon in Portugal, Cadiz in Spain, and even one from Cagliari in Sardinia.[169] The best salt[170] came from 'St. Lucar' in Spain (Sanlucar de Barreda at the south of the Guadalquivir and probably the source of cargoes from Cadiz), 'Fugerie' or 'Figura' in Portugal (Figueira da Foz on the coast near Coimbra and most likely the source of the Lisbon cargoes), 'Ivica' (most probably Ibiza in the Balearic Islands), and the 'Isle of Rhi' in France (Île de Ré on the coast off La Rochelle). Scots salt from the salt pans in the Forth was unsuitable for fish curing for foreign markets,[171] as it was not as 'strong' as foreign salt and did not preserve the fish so well,[172] the only time it was used extensively being temporarily during the Dutch War in 1780-81.[173] However, it was used for curing saithe and other fish for the home market and in the preparation of butter, beef and hides.[174] English rock salt began to be imported after 1760 and took the place of foreign salt to an increasing extent, especially in the 1780s and 1790s,[175] as the activities of Sellar and Henderson of Liverpool

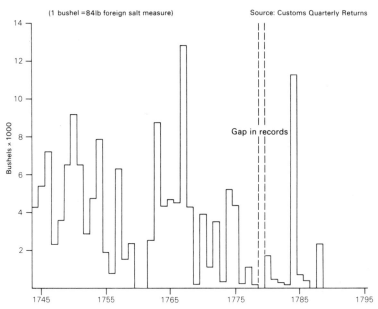

(1 bushel =84lb foreign salt measure)   Source: Customs Quarterly Returns

Gap in records

Figure 18. Imports of foreign salt, foreign trade

gained momentum in the island trade. During wartime (Fig. 21), from the Seven Years' War onwards, supplies of foreign salt were often interrupted, which also encouraged the use of English salt and was probably a major contributory factor in the overall decline in foreign salt imports (Fig. 18, Chapter 4). The wide year-to-year fluctuations are largely explicable by the varying relation between bulk supply on the one hand and demand governed by wide fluctuations in the quantity of fish landed on the other.

Because of the key role of salt in the economy and the large quantities required, it was most frequently the object of Government regulation of trade and revenue-raising generally. It was the prohibition of the import of salt in foreign bottoms which was technically responsible for the demise of the German merchants' trade, as is specifically stated in the contract of 1709. This part of the navigation laws remained in force throughout the period. Subsequent rules and regulations governing the salt trade were many and complex, and beyond the scope of this study. The potential disadvantage of having to pay duty on foreign salt essential for the Shetland fishing industry was avoided in practice, from 1718 onwards, by the regulation that duty paid on imported foreign salt was offset by the payment of a bounty, out of the duty itself, while British salt could be imported duty-free provided it was used only in fish destined for export.[176] If the fish subsequently entered the home market, duty had to be paid, which was an important factor in the use of inferior Scots salt for the curing of fish for the home market. The circumstances of the salt trade highlight the principal influence of Government during the period as a whole, which by allowing the fishery salt used in exports to be entered effectively duty free, acted in a rather negative way to promote conditions of 'free trade'.[177]

There were four main import links, viz. from Hamburg, Bergen, Holland and Britain — the last named being a rather special case (below). Of these links, the Hamburg link, based on the factor system, led in importance in the first half of the century. It remained significant, although not of first importance, in the second half (Chapter 6), chiefly in the supply of 'fishing necessaries' and household items.[178] Although the statistics are not consistent or full enough to plot in graphic form, it is clear that the bulk of fishing gear came from Hamburg, including hooks and lines, as well as a whole range of shipchandlery such as bales of hemp, mats used in the stowing of fish cargoes (Chapter 6), tar, and unwrought iron used by blacksmiths. Intermediate between fishing materials and household items was the large import of corn brandy, used mainly by the fishermen when at the fishing, tobacco, some meal, and pots and kettles. The household items contained a whole range of goods, too numerous to mention. These consisted of everyday requirements including cheap textiles, soap, and luxury goods such as expensive wines, brandies, and fine-quality textiles.

A further important group of items from Hamburg were those necessary in the commodity export trades, including salt (see above), barrel hoops and staves (Fig. 19a, b), and occasionally numbers of empty barrels. These barrel items came mainly from Hamburg, and were used in the export of oil, butter and occasionally locally caught herring, as well as providing storage for every conceivable type of goods from salt beef and potatoes to lines. The erratic variations in quantities of hoops and staves cannot be readily explained, although the relatively continuous import of hoops probably signifies the difficulty of obtaining supplies from alternative sources (hoops were generally of wood at this time). A large quantity of barrel staves may also have come via the coastwise trade. The boom in imports in the early 1780s correlates well with the increase in fish oil production during the famine years (Fig. 17a).

The Norway trade seems to have continued little changed into the eighteenth century, at least up to the 1740s, particularly the purchasing of cargoes 'at the woods'. Godøysund was the main centre for the export of boats, mainly in boards, in the first half of the century.[179] As time went on, Bergen became virtually the sole centre and, although like Hamburg it was to some extent an entrepôt port for the Shetland import trades, the staple commodities were wood goods, which can be grouped into three main categories, wood for boatbuilding, for housebuilding, and for miscellaneous agricultural purposes. Again, due to the quality of the statistics, only those for deals and spars can be properly summarised in graphic form.

Deals* and deal ends* (short versions of deals) were used both in boatbuilding and housebuilding, and in the eighteenth-century Customs returns there is seldom any distinction between the two. In 1755-57, it is recorded that 75 boats were exported from Bergen to Shetland, Orkney and

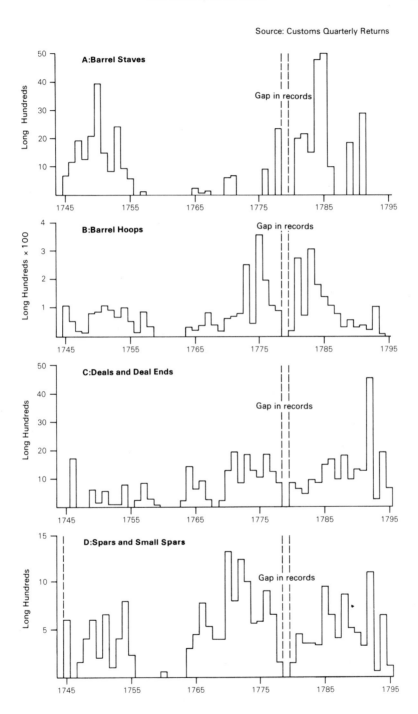

Figure 19. Import of wood goods, foreign trade

Scotland,[180] but the first mention of boats as such in the Shetland Customs records is in 1792, when 22 were imported. The long-term increase in deal imports from the 1770s onwards (Fig. 19c) strongly suggests expansion of the haaf fisheries as well as the first stage of housebuilding in Lerwick (which was, however, probably more accurately reflected in the beginnings of timber imports from southern Norway — see Chapter 4). The contemporaneous expansion in the import of spars* (boat's masts) and small spars (boat's yards*) (Fig. 19d) is perhaps more clearly evidence for the expansion of the 'far haaf' component in the fisheries. Besides these items were a number of others, such as oak knees*, tafts* (seats) and tilfers* (bottom boards) — all for boats, 'parcels' of birch and occasionally oak bark* for tanning* lines, and scoops* for bailing*.[181] Building timber, such as battens* and lathwood*, appears increasingly in the closing decades of the period as evidence of building expansion. Wood for agricultural purposes included hazel cuts* used as flails in threshing, harrowbills* and plough timber*, and spokes for cart-wheels.

Links with Holland, in which Amsterdam and Rotterdam only are mentioned in the records, are difficult to trace, probably because the principal commodities were smuggled and, in any case, often reached Shetland indirectly through the entrepôts of Hamburg and Bergen. In the 1730s, Thomas Gifford regularly obtained supplies of tobacco via Hamburg from Charles Roosen, his factor in Amsterdam, to whom he remarked in a letter in 1731 that 'It is my misfortoun that I finde non of our Country product can answer in Holland otherways you should be trubled with more of my business.'[182] In 1742 there is a mention of a cargo from Amsterdam,[183] and in 1775 one of the Shetland merchants is recorded as having dealings with Rotterdam,[184] about which time it is likely that direct contacts were increasing as smuggling activities expanded. However, some at least of that great Dutch export, gin, also came via Bergen.

The definition of 'to smuggle' runs: 'to import or export illegally or without paying duty'.[185] The smuggling trade in eighteenth-century Shetland consisted overwhelmingly of importing without paying duty, although, to begin with, there were some instances of exporting illegally as well. This may be linked to a few lingering German merchants after the cessation of the German merchants' trade. It is worth noting that in 1708 the Collector of Customs complained that 'the justices had set him in the stocks, and declared that wool might be exported from thence'.[186]

In the import trade, there were two distinct phases of development in smuggling. In the first phase, smuggling went on almost entirely as part and parcel of the ordinary trades described above, and consisted in evading as far as possible the duty on goods required for everyday use that were liable to high duties, principally tobacco, tea and spirits (mainly corn brandy). Comparisons of cargo invoices with entries in the Customs returns reveal the working of this system very well: for example, when the *Sibella* imported a cargo from Hamburg in 1752, the only goods listed in the Customs returns were those paying little or no duty — salt, lines, iron, and tar; in addition there were corn brandy, French claret, cognac brandy and a variety of wines including Rhenish, which made up about half the total value of the cargo, which was worth just over £6,000 Scots (£500 sterling).[187] Occasionally salt was smuggled in, as in 1742, when two cargoes were intercepted while being run ashore in Yell by two local landowners,[188] but comparison of the statistics of salt imports (Fig. 18) with those for dried fish exports (Fig. 14a), on the basis of the quantity of salt required for curing (above), suggests that this was unimportant on the whole.

This type of smuggling continued throughout the century, if anything becoming more intensive as the duties rose steeply in the 1770s and 1780s,[189] but from the 1760s onwards it was supplemented by a 'true' smuggling trade, based on the import of Dutch gin, one of the first references to the carrying of gin by local merchants occurring in 1765.[190] In the records this development is presaged by an attempt by the Customs in 1764-65 to get all ships unloaded at Lerwick,[191] probably to forestall these developments; the landowners retorted quite reasonably that this was impossible (Chapter 6). The first serious clash with the Customs came in 1768-69, when the Lerwick Customs house was found to be implicated,[192] although in a petition of 1769 the landowners established the plea (which was to be maintained thereafter) that spirits and other fishing materials ought to be imported duty-free, which, they contended, would soon put a stop to smuggling.[193]

In the 1770s smuggling intensified as external merchants began to be involved. The possibilities for smuggling in busy shipping lanes were of course almost limitless, and a considerable amount of trade was done with passing ships, the Dutch busses perhaps being the most obvious example (Chapter 6). However, in 1770 there is the first record of a full-time smuggler being captured,[194] and another was seized in 1776.[195] The following year a smuggler came from Gothenburg with tea, but the Customs were afraid to touch him, as there had been violence in earlier seizure attempts in 1774 and 1775.[196] One of the sources of gin was ships bound from Holland to the Faroe Islands, which put in for shelter on the way, such as the *Young Jacob* of Rotterdam, which lay in Grutness Voe with a cargo of gin for a time in July 1780, and was guarded continuously by the Customs.[197] In 1786 John Logie, merchant in Scalloway, was jailed when he could not meet debts on goods which he had bought from a Faroese firm and smuggled into Shetland.[198] By this time there was a distinction between the 'Rotterdam gentry', mainly merchants, who carried on the true gin-smuggling trade, and the 'Hamburg gentry', mainly landowners, who carried on the time-honoured smuggling of 'necessaries',[199] especially spirits and tea. The competition between merchants and landowners in this field ceased around 1791, when the landowners renounced any open connection with the gin trade,[200] and it became the preserve of Shetland merchants (Chapter 4).

The principal import links with Britain were Orkney and the Forth area respectively. The seventeenth-century links with Orkney persisted probably until the early 1730s. However, by the early 1740s Thomas Gifford was lamenting that '. . . Orkney . . . has annually supplied the Zetland fishers with as much meal, stuff and linen as carryed of most of the cash they made by the fishing besides wool and horses, and since (*sic*) the Orkney trade with Zetland has very much failed of late . . .'[201] This decline may have been due to the effects of war (Fig. 21), and was superseded by a phase of what was apparently more intermittent activity. Open boats from Sanday brought cargoes of wood goods from Bergen to Shetland on several occasions in 1749,[202] and Orkney vessels continued to take a small part in the Shetland import trade thereafter (Chapter 6). The principal trade points seem to have been at Lerwick[203] and Weisdale,[204] where meal and linen were bartered for wool and ponies, and contact was still being maintained in the early 1790s when the minister at Delting recorded that '. . . thy often sell their wool to the Orkney people at a very low price, and next year but their stuffs made of the same wool at a very high price'.[205]

Contact with the Forth area, especially in the early part of the century, was based on the need for meal, which increasingly came from points along the east coast between Peterhead and the Forth. It was a trade which was a direct consequence of certain characteristics of the agricultural system, namely, that even in the best of times the agricultural production was insufficient for the needs of the islands, and not infrequently the situation was adversely affected by poor harvests as a result of unfavourable weather.

Agricultural production was basically organised on two distinct planes: first, growing crops for subsistence consumption, and second, producing livestock for subsistence and commercial purposes (Fig. 9). The growing of fodder in connection with the second function was affected by those climatic factors of most significance for the first function. These two functions tended to be affected by different aspects of the seasonal weather pattern in the sense that whereas the crops (and fodder) were most vulnerable to summer and autumn climatic anomalies, stock were most affected by severe winter and spring conditions. The most common causes of crop failures were wet summers and/or early snowfalls.[206] The first produced crops which might never ripen or at best produce a very late harvest which was liable to be over-taken by these snowfalls between the end of September and the beginning of November. Wet summers in particular cut fodder production, and the ensuing shortage was generally felt during the following late winter and early spring, when many animals died for want of fodder, as happened in 1781-82.[207] The second great danger was a severe frost, sometimes coupled with snow in winter and spring, which was liable to cause heavy losses of livestock, especially sheep and ponies which were left out all winter. Many cattle also died. It was the death of cattle which caused the effects of the 1782-84 famine to be so severe in the winter of 1783-84.[208]

Because agriculture was largely subsistence, the most immediate effects on trade were steep rises in meal imports from Scotland. If there was a heavy loss of cattle, the export trade in hides was stimulated (Fig. 12), and the effects might be further offset by increases in oil production if piltocks were reasonably abundant (Fig. 17), both of which occurred in the 1782-84 shortages. However, that the general effects were deleterious in the extreme, undermining the credit of both landowners and tenants, is revealed by a contemporary landowner's remark after the 1782-84 economic disaster that '. . . it has been observed, with much Justice, that the success in the Fisheries is found very inadequate to the making good the misfortunes of a Bad Crop and Loss of Cattle . . .'[209]

It was undoubtedly because the landowners' credit was at an end that Government assistance in the form of meal cargoes from England was sought in 1784[210] — the first time since 1698. It had not been required in the severe shortages of 1740-1, 1760-1 and 1766.[211] By and large, landowners were not in a position to withstand losses on the agricultural operation of their estates beyond a year or two. The only quantitative estimate of Shetland's meal requirements in the eighteenth century comes from an approximate calculation in 1784 of the quantity required to maintain the islands for a year given a population of 20,000 — which was probably in excess of the true population at that time.[212] It was reckoned that 22,500 bolls were required, of which the poor 1784 crop would only supply 5,000 bolls, or less than three months' supply. Since six to eight months' supply could be produced locally in good years, and the population was much increased by the 1780s, one can assume imports were substantially lower on average, perhaps in the region of 5-10,000 bolls per annum, an estimate which agrees well with the figure of 6,000 bolls imported in 1778, an average year for local agriculture.[213]

Other imports from Britain included salt from the Forth salt pans and the whole range of household and fishing goods also obtained from Hamburg and to a lesser extent Bergen, particularly after the advent of the merchant houses from the 1760s onwards, when the landowners can sometimes be found comparing the prices at Leith with those abroad.[214] The first recorded imports of coal into Shetland came from this area in 1781 for the use of the garrison in Fort Charlotte,[215] and thereafter small quantities were imported from time to time for the use of the 'gentry', although the cost was prohibitively expensive, as there was a duty on the coastwise trade in Scots coal carried past the Red Head of Angus.[216]

Export links with Britain were predominantly with the Forth area also — at least until the activities of merchant houses became established. Although fish, butter, oil and stockings tended to form the staple items, as in the foreign export trade, fish was comparatively less important, and the trade as a whole rose from a very minor position in the early part of the century to a significant, but still secondary, position in the latter half (Table 3). As in the preceding century, the staple of the fish trade was saithe, exported to Leith and Dundee,[217] where it was considered the 'food of the poor' and fetched low prices;[218] by the end of the century exports averaged about 50 tons of dry saithe per year.[219] In addition, some cod, ling and tusk, especially those caught in spring at the inshore fisheries, were exported, notably after the advent of the merchant houses. Cod at this time were caught in relatively small quantities, and the technique of curing these to withstand long voyages appears not to have been known in Shetland; tusk could not withstand long voyages[220] and were sent entirely to Britain. By the end of the period, about 65 tons of these 'winter fish' were being sent coastwise every year,[221] and a few hundred barrels of herrings were also exported from time to time.

Overall there was a gradual shift in emphasis towards the development of trade with Britain, especially after the Seven Years' War, which was of deeper significance than that implied by commodity trade developments alone. The most important aspects were the development of financial links, relating to imports and exports and pioneered from the 1760s onwards by the merchant houses of London, Liverpool, Leith and Glasgow, and strengthened further by the increasing dealings of the landowners with the emergent Scottish banks, notably Sir William Forbes, James Hunter and Company of Edinburgh.[222] The merchant houses were generally also ship-owners, which led to the growth of shipping links for the import and export trades and the pioneering of mail services. Finally, the expansion of the whaling industry was linked to the increasing use of Shetland men for crews and led to the growth of agencies.

The Spirit of Improvement

Throughout the eighteenth century, the outlook of the landowner with regard to trade and economic change was at once that of the pioneer and continuing developer, well-educated and informed on contemporary affairs in general, and trade concerns in particular. As the only possessor of adequate capital resources for the undertaking of trading ventures, his attitude was of paramount importance in the development of Shetland trade, particularly during the early part of the period. Thomas Gifford, whose numerous writings[223] reveal the many problems encountered in carrying on trade, including the high prices he had to pay his tenants for their fish, the uncertainties of markets and the disruptions of war, was undoubtedly the leading figure in early development. His political affiliations to the Whigs and the Hanoverian Succession contrasted with the Jacobite sympathies of the majority of contemporary Shetland landowners, and undoubtedly was instrumental in his acquisition of tacks of the Lordship estate, with concomitant trade opportunities. Another notable example of individual initiative was displayed by John Bruce Stewart of Symbister — by his own admission the 'second' in Shetland to improve the fisheries, Thomas Gifford presumably being the first in his estimation — who was responsible to a large degree for the pioneering of the improved curing techniques so necessary for the development of links with the Spanish market.[224] The landowners, both as individuals and as a group, by their initiative led in many of the subsequent developments. They acted as guardians of the local interest generally and of trade in particular, from the exposure of the fraud of the Irish wherries (Chapter 6) and the drawing up of a scheme to supply labour to the Greenland fleet, to warning the government of the day on the manifold dangers of the Dutch War of 1780-81.[225] Above all, their interest lay in expanding the labour force so necessary for fishing improvement and trade expansion: in the words of Arthur Edmonston, '. . . to increase the number of fishers was their greatest object'.[226]

However, the landowners remained strongly bound to their land, which eventually proved a brake on their trading activities. Failure of the crops put them in a serious financial position, and they were not disposed to take too many risks, such as investing in the herring fishery. As one of them wrote: 'very few have ever been able to advance their circumstances much, and when individuals do it costs them so dear that they are extremely careful not to risque, but in the Business they have succeeded in, or in the purchase of lands — while the greater part are still struggling on the old line, and have enough to do to preserve themselves from falling back . . .'[227] Nonetheless, in the course of the century there were some notable attempts, mainly by the landowners, to introduce new ideas of various kinds, which merit closer examination.

Innovation in the haaf production system was conspicuously lacking, apart from the use of bigger boats and longer lines, until after mid-century, and consisted of ideas and attempts directed towards improving the efficiency of the open boat fishery and of agriculture. Apart from the Earl of Morton's unfulfilled intention to set up a waulkmill (a fulling mill) in the 1730s,[228] no attention was being given to the improvement of woollen manufacture till 1790.[229] As early as 1740, it was averred that no improvement in the haaf fishery could take place because of the necessary preoccupation of the fishermen with subsistence agriculture,[230] while by the 1780s it was reckoned that the fishery generally could only be improved by the abandoning of open boats in favour of decked vessels.[231]

The only two significant innovations which got off the ground for a time were, first, that of attaching floats to the tom-lines which, by holding the hooks clear of the bottom, greatly improved the catching power of the long-lines. This project failed due to the conservatism of the fishermen.[232] The second was the use of 'mother sloops' to attend the sixerns at sea, thereby facilitating fishing operations by cutting out return journeys to the stations. This scheme was first suggested in 1769[233] but abandoned towards the end of the period due to the loss of boats by smashing together while under tow among various fishing grounds, or when transferring fish to the sloops while at sea. It was also impracticable to keep in touch with scattered boats in adverse weather conditions, thus offsetting the advantages of increased catching power.[234]

In agriculture, there were few improvements apart from the dubious one of breaking in new outsets* in association with fishery development and population increase. Interest in better methods was manifested by the sending of an agricultural apprentice to one of the great Scottish improvers as early as 1756.[235] Around 1770 the first recorded building of a proper large-scale mill for grinding corn on Bruce of Symbister's estate near Bigton[236] was a forerunner of things to come (Chapter 4).

The most notable examples of unsuccessful externally inspired new systems of production were flax-growing, lead-mining and herring fishing. Around 1740 the Earl of Morton was enquiring as to whether hemp might be grown in Shetland,[237] while an attempt to grow flax in Unst around 1770 proved unsuccessful.[238] Interest in lead-mining was first stimulated soon after the Earl of Morton acquired the Lordship Estate. The Earl endeavoured unsuccessfully between 1709 and 1714 to interest the Governor and Company for smelting lead in Scotland to prospect for lead in the islands,[239] and in 1740 Robert Dick of Fracafield contracted with John Leslie of Ustaness in Whiteness for 'the inspection of a suspected lead mine',[240] but it appears that mining never reached the practical stage until after 1790 (Chapter 4).

Although it was going on all round them, the Shetlanders showed little interest in developing the herring fishing on their own account, apart from a scheme drawn up by Thomas Gifford as early as 1718,[241] and even the small-scale West Side fishery was often thwarted for the want of barrels and salt.[242] The usual reasons advanced were the conservatism of the fishermen, the lack of sufficient capital, and the uncertainty of the herring markets. Nevertheless, this was the most 'successful' of the unsuccessful ideas, as there were at least three herring fishing ventures in the latter part of the century.[243]

Apart from production innovations, there was a fairly strong and consistent pressure in the first half of the century to develop new market outlets, the most notable result being the pioneering of improved curing techniques in conjunction with the development of Iberian markets, which foreshadowed the main pattern in the second half of the century. The Lisbon market was the main aim, although William John Neven of Windhouse (Yell) tried the Irish market as early as 1744, but because his ship arrived when the Lent season was over, he obtained a very low price.[244] There is no further reference to this market till the 1750s (above, Chapter 6). The other point of interest was the improvement of the merchanting organisation, which was also foreshadowed in the first part of the century. As early as 1718 one Captain Drummond was enquiring about setting up a fish-buying enterprise in Shetland,[245] and in 1740 Thomas Gifford considered that the method of exporting fish could be much improved to the benefit of the exporters.[246] Although he does not elaborate, he probably envisaged the merchant house organisation operating in Shetland twenty years before it became a reality.

There were three innovations which bid fair to be termed new types of production, although they did not, with a single exception, become permanent at the time. They lasted long enough and augured, in one way or another, developments which were to become of great significance in the subsequent period of trade development. The first innovation, cod fishing from sloops, was really an extensions of the haaf production system, whereas the other two, linen and kelp manufacture, were new departures. All were notable in that the enterprise was in all cases of local origin, although the developments, at least in the case of linen and kelp manufacture, parallelled developments taking place elsewhere at the same time.

The first of these, cod fishing from sloops, was pioneered in 1742 or 1743 by a vessel fitted out by Arthur Nicolson of Lochend, suitably encouraged by a bounty from the Board of Improvement.[247] Unfortunately, she was intercepted and plundered by a French privateer (Fig. 21), which put an end to her operations, and when in 1744 William Mouat of Garth approached the Board with a view to a similar venture in 1745, they were of the opinion that, in view of the dangers, it was 'not fit to treat with him this year'.[248] Nothing more is heard of cod fishing until after the Seven Years' War, when bounties were doled out to various landowners and merchants prosecuting the fishery between 1765 and 1773.[249] The advantage of this fishery was that it required no great capital investment, as the participants could use their own cargo ships (Chapter 6).

Cod were of course caught in the open boat fishery, and as early as 1742 Robert Dick of Fracafield contracted with a London merchant for the supply of cod,[250] although his name is not associated with the developments outlined above. These 'open boat' cod were caught mainly in spring, and the method of curing was not well understood,[251] although a little was exported wet-salted in barrels after the Dutch manner.[252] Those dealing in this trade are recorded as having almost always lost money.[253]

The other two production systems, linen and kelp manufacture, parallelled developments which were taking place simultaneously in Scotland,[254] the former largely under the auspices of the Board of Trustees for Fisheries and Manufactures in Scotland and the landowners, and the latter mainly under the aegis of the landowners. The linen manufacture in Shetland followed this pattern, and was established for six years between 1770 and 1776. From as early as 1765, Lady Mitchell of Westshore was awarded premiums to encourage the spinning of flax,[255] and James Hay, who was later to become one of Shetland's leading merchants (Chapter 4), was apprenticed under the auspices of the Board to the linen trade in Scotland, before being put in charge of the bleachfield at Catfirth in Nesting.[256] The company, established 'for carrying on the linen manufacture to its ultimate height', was backed mainly by landowners and merchants with indirect interests in the haaf fisheries,[257] and in practice existed not so much to manufacture and sell linen as to serve people in Shetland who furnished materials and paid for the weaving of these. After its failure an unsuccessful attempt was made to resuscitate the enterprise under Orkney management,[258] the linen trade at this time being much more highly developed in Orkney.[259]

The third new production system of kelp manufacture, although not on the large scale of similar developments in Orkney and along the western seaboard of Scotland, was the most enduring, and it is worthy of note that kelp production was well-suited to the landowning management of trade, as it involved no great re-organisation of outlook or management. Several landowners employed someone from Orkney who was knowledgeable in the trade to survey their shores as early as 1760,[260] but production did not really get under way until around 1780 (Fig. 12), from which time two to three hundred tons were exported per annum.[261] The industry continued to expand in the early years of the nineteenth century (Chapter 4).

If the landowners tended to be conservative in their approach, the tenants were no less so, and the common outlook is perhaps well expressed by the note of Thomas Mouat of Garth taken from *The Wealth of Nations:* 'Tho' the success of a particular day's fishing may be very uncertain, yet in the course of a year or of several years together it is certain enough'.[262] It was something of a fatalistic approach instilled by the hard school of unpredictable failures in fishing and agriculture. In spite of complaints against the landowners, such as that to Low in 1774 on the low price the lairds gave them for their fish,[263] tenants were reluctant to forego the comparative security of the land-owner-tenant relationship. Bruce of Sumburgh met considerable opposition from his tenants when he disposed of his fishings in the 1770s,[264] and Hunter of Lunna had to give up a similar first attempt in 1799.[265]

This philosophy of 'better the ill kent as the gude unkent' ('better the known evil than the unknown good') may have been rooted in the tenants' view that going to sea was their best opportunity of economic self-improvement. Around 1740, Thomas Gifford thought that not more than a hundred would ever undertake to fish from ships, either for cod or herring 'for any encouragement may (*sic*) be offered them'.[266] After 1750, however, many went to the Greenland whaling, which had several advantages, including the fact that it was seasonal (from March to August), well-paid, and the Shetland men were both picked up and landed at home. The same could be said of the Royal Navy, which resorted to impressment in order to obtain men, and the competition between the two forms of employment in times of war is largely responsible for the contraction of the fishery in wartime and its expansion in peacetime (Fig. 20).

Although the Greenland whale fishery is first mentioned in Shetland sources in 1733, when it was suggested that Lerwick might be used as a base,[267] the practice of going to Greenland did not begin until sometime around mid-century; it is first mentioned as an established practice in 1755.[268] The importance of the fishery to the Shetland economy, apart from the introduction of the agency business, is reflected in the fluctuations in the numbers of vessels engaged in the Scottish and English fisheries as a whole (Fig. 20), many of these vessels calling at Shetland *en route* for the fishing grounds to pick up part of their crews. The agencies were set up by local Shetland merchants in Lerwick to supply stores on credit to the Shetland

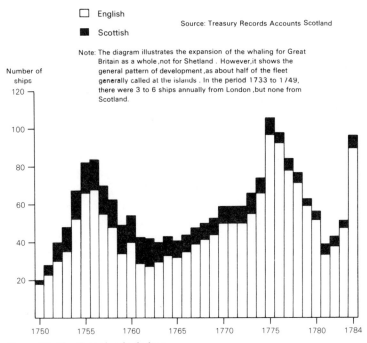

Figure 20. The Greenland whaling

members of the whaling crews and to handle the men's wages on behalf of the whaling companies through the masters of the whale ships. As a result these agencies became an important influence permitting expansion of merchants' businesses. The trade had expanded considerably by the 1780s when a scheme was drawn up for the supply of about 1,000 men to the Greenland fleet under the supervision of the landowners, who resented somewhat the 'usurpations' of the merchants in the developing economy.[269] From the 1770s, an additional trade item was ponies, sometimes exported to England by the returning Greenland ships.[270]

The second major source of new employment, in the form of the Royal Navy, also became important around mid-century. The first mention of impressment is in 1755,[271] and sometimes the threat of impressment induced more men to go into the whaling, as in 1777.[272] In 1774, it was stated that for twenty years previously, an average of 100 men had gone every year into the Navy and the merchant service;[273] in 1763, 900 were paid off from the Navy on the cessation of the Seven Years' War,[274] and in the wars of 1776-1783, 2,000 were estimated as being in the Navy and the merchant service.[275]

By 1755, although the landowners were complaining that there was a shortage of labour due to the demands of these two main new branches of employment,[276] it is likely that these alternative occupations contributed to the stability apparent in the development of the fish trade, and explain, to some extent, the virtual absence of emigration. This diversification of

employment was, however, only made possible by the increasing population. It appears that the population of the islands remained relatively static
until around mid-century; around 1740, there were an estimated 2,000
fishermen,[277] but by the 1780s this figure had risen to around 3,000.[278] The
fundamental reason for the increase in population was undoubtedly the
control of smallpox epidemics,[279] which tended to strike once every twenty
years, on average, and probably had a generally depressing effect on the
economy. The first recorded epidemic of 1700[280] was extremely severe, and
undoubtedly had some effect on the decrease of cultivation (Chapter 2) at
that time. It was followed by another in 1720, later termed the 'mortal pox' in
Foula, where it practically wiped out the population.[281] The third and fourth
major epidemics occurred in 1740 and 1760-61 respectively, the latter
causing a reduction in the population of Unst which it took until 1766[282] to
make up. From around 1770 onwards, inoculation* was practised on a wide
scale, and further outbreaks were much less serious.[283]

The only other factor which might have radically affected the level of
population and the pattern of employment was emigration, which at that
time was taking place on a wide scale in the Highlands of Scotland.[284]
Despite the hard times, however, particularly in the 1770s and 1780s, few
emigrated, and it seems likely that the whaling and the Navy played a part in
this. Although Low considered that, given the chance, many would have
emigrated,[285] in fact 1774 was the only year when appreciable emigration
may have taken place,[286] probably because the poor fishing coincided with
the provision of an emigrant ship.[287] This opinion was still held by some of
the landowners in the 1780s.[288] The real situation was well summed up by
the minister of Unst, writing in 1791: 'Their resisting all temptations to join in
the emigrations to America induced me to think they are contented with
their situation, if not absolutely, at least comparatively'.[289] His observation is
supported by the fact that if the fishing was good, as in 1781, the tentants
could not even be prevailed upon to go to Greenland, unless wages were
very high;[290] nor would they go if there was danger of impressment, as
happened in 1785, when during the previous season many had been pressed
on their return through an arrangement between the landowners and the
pressgang officers made in the tenants' absence.[291] A few had the necessary
spirit for emigration, especially among the young: 'the youth being generally of spirits and seeing the sunshine days of the seamen' went to sea in
passing merchant ships and were often never heard of again,[292] as also
happened to many of those who entered the Navy. However, the majority
again preferred the 'known evil'. This decision not to emigrate was crucial to
the further development of the trading economy.

It is likely that the political controversy over the alleged oppression of the
tenants by the landowners which erupted in the 1780s[293] was inspired by the
keen competition between the merchants and the landowners in the trading
economy, and was probably sparked off by one or more of the merchants.[294]
The great advantage which the merchants possessed was that, not being tied

to the land, they were in a relatively flexible position in the pursuit of trade. Although they necessarily suffered in hard times, they could recover fairly quickly in such activities as shipowning, whaling agencies, and smuggling, which were not entirely bound up with local trading conditions. However, with one or two exceptions, the merchants did not immediately assume the initiative in trade development at this period.

In view of the relative freedom from bad debts apparently enjoyed by the tenants in the first half of the century, the subsequent expansion of the fisheries even in the poor times of the 1770s and early 1780s, and the diversification of employment represented by the whaling and the Navy, it may well be asked why the tenants were so heavily in debt and the landowners' credit so severely strained by the shortages of the period. It would appear that the forces promoting continued development were stronger than the very considerable ones tending towards the collapse of the economy. This is nowhere more evident than in the depression of the 1770s, when the expansion of deal and spar imports — the key to investment in new fishing boats — proceeded apace (Fig. 19c, d). The evidence for the answer, if not the answer itself, would appear to lie in the expansion of retailing and merchant activity generally, the import of textiles, and the rise in gin-smuggling, while the conflict of interests between the merchants and the landowners suggests that the economy as a whole was strained to the limit. There were those who believed strongly in the mid-1780s that the haaf fishing was incapable of further development in its then form,[295] and their opinion is borne out by the pressure of new ideas regarding development at this time, and the increasing engagement in other branches of trade after 1790.

The picture which emerges from the history of innovation is that of two phases of development, namely, the first half of the century, when concentration was on maximising the potentialities of the then existing system, with only a small minority of landowners — usually the most important — possessing advanced ideas on production and marketing. In the second half of the century, innovation and new production systems designed to develop trade spread rapidly with varying degrees of success. Most of the potentially significant of these, such as linen manufacture and kelp production, although parallelled in Scotland, proceeded under the direction of local enterprise, while practically all the externally inspired innovations were failures. In spite of the fact that the landowners were the chief innovators at all times, it is noteworthy that the only really successful innovation in terms of permanence, kelp production, could be successfully added to the existing economic and trading structure which they dominated without a high degree of commercial risk. This investment pattern was also parallelled in Scotland, where landowners tended to lay out money in relatively 'secure' undertakings such as agricultural improvements, kelp-making and rural textile industries rather than large-scale manufacturing industry, where higher risks were involved.[296]

Contemplation of further expansion and improvement, such as the scheme for supplying men to the Greenland fleet, and agricultural improvement, required further division of effort — in short the rise of the merchant class, first alongside, then supplanting the landowners in trade. The position has been perhaps most succinctly put by Rostow,[297] discussing the ideas of their great contemporary, Adam Smith: 'At the core of the *Wealth of Nations* . . . is Adam Smith's perception that surplus income derived from the ownership of land must, somehow, be transferred out of the hands of those who would sterilise it in prodigal living, into the hands of the productive men who will invest it in the modern sector, and then regularly plough back their profits as output and productivity rise.' By 1790, accompanied by a considerable friction between landowners and merchants, this was just beginning to happen in Shetland trade.

4

The Shetland Traders, 1790-1870

The changes which took place around 1790 were much less clear-cut than those which had occurred in 1707, in the sense that there were no sudden changes, but rather subtle shifts of emphasis taking place over a period of years rather than months. On the surface this was manifested in a variety of ways, beginning with the controversy between the landowners and the merchants in the mid-1780s. Soon afterwards small but significant changes in trade patterns began to occur, such as the more frequent appearance of Christiansand in the record of import trade links,[1] signifying the increasing import of timber for construction of buildings rather than boat building, and borne out by references to the wave of building of lodberries and merchants' houses in Lerwick in the 1790s and early 1800s.[2] In the export trade it became the practice to send a shipload to Barcelona early in the season, which consisted of many small consignments from a relatively large number of merchants, to catch the early dried salt fish market.[3] Unlike the eighteenth century as a whole, when references to smuggling coincide almost entirely with the years of peace, after 1790 smuggling was being carried on in wartime also, and the number of trading vessels registered at Lerwick increased sharply in the decade from 1790 until 1800. In the key export trade sector of the economy, practically all the agency work was in the hands of the merchants by 1806,[4] if not earlier (unfortunately this is not certain due to a gap in the customs records from 1796 to 1806). Meanwhile, the Spanish market was cut off in 1795,[5] to remain more or less closed until 1814 as the battle against Napoleon intensified.

Merchants and Smugglers

While the chief sector of the merchants' business was that of agency work handling imports and exports, by 1790 it was extending gradually into the buying of fish directly from the tenants as well. The merchants were also acquiring shipowning interests and were in the process of developing retail trade which, along with buying fish, helped to erode the landowner-tenant relationship, itself hardly of a retailing nature, although fulfilling a similar

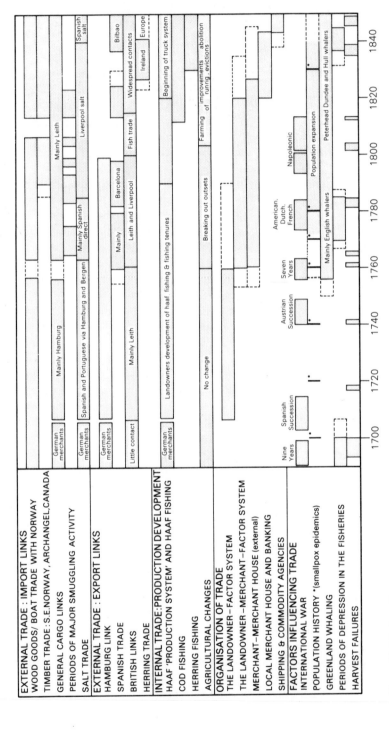

Figure 21. Modern times

function in the economy. Between 1790 and 1820, the increase of merchant power to a position of dominance in the trade system was accomplished simply by the continuing extension of these functions, the driving force behind the expansion of trade being the individual merchant working very largely on his own. They co-operated in the chartering of ships for fish cargoes and in other such trade matters, but true business partnerships seldom extended beyond the family variety of father being followed by son. The crucial element, and often the largest part of their businesses, was agency work of various kinds, the most important being the fish export and general import trades.

The role of the agent in the export trade continued on the same basis as in the latter half of the eighteenth century, the landowners having trading relationships with one or more agents which were semi-permanent in nature, while the external links were operated by the merchants in conjunction with British merchant houses. A good example of this arrangement is to be found in the correspondence of Irvine of Midbrake, a small estate in North Yell. James Linklater, a Lerwick merchant, wrote to James Irvine in November 1795[6] to inform him that he wanted '. . . the buying of your Fish next year for exportation at the Currency to be shipt at Uyasound as usual . . .

'I beg also you will converse with Mr. John Spence and your other friends in your quarter, and if they will sell to me I will take their fish, and come under the necessary engagements.

'If you have any goods for the Leith market of good quality you may ship them for me and advise . . .'

These were largely speculative ventures on the part of the merchants, as appears from a similar letter of Linklater's in 1797,[7] in which he promised to take all of Midbrake's 1798 fish on condition that all of Irvine's produce for the Leith market was included as well. In this same year, the Spanish market was finally cut off (Chapter 3 and below), and thereafter most of the fish went coastwise to Britain until the second decade of the nineteenth century, although an appreciable amount was eventually exported by devious routes. Thus the number of agents in the direct export trade to foreign ports declined sharply in the early 1800s to as few as four or five merchants,[8] and it is likely that the remainder of the agents (see Fig. 13 for the approximate number in the 1790s) were exporting to the British market and thus do not appear in the records. The continuing connection with the merchant houses after the Napoleonic Wars is illustrated by a letter of William Henderson of Bardister to James Irvine in May 1813;[9] Henderson had received from 'Commercial Houses of high respectability in London, orders to purchase 500 tons of Shetland ling and cod' for the Spanish market.

The principal components of the import trade remained similar to those described in the previous chapter. The trade in wood goods expanded to include increasing quantities of timber for house-building while the salt trade, which became centred more or less entirely on England after the blockade of Spain, was in the hands of the merchants at the Shetland end.[10]

The final important category of items, goods paying high duty, were also imported by the merchants, the principal items being gin, tea and tobacco. However, the attractions of this trade encouraged its development to assume characteristics beyond that of the mere import trade, and smuggling merits separate treatment.

It was through the import trade that the merchants were enabled to establish their retailing businesses more readily, and thereby gain a foothold in the internal trade system through buying fish and other goods direct from the tenants on a cash or barter basis. The growth of retailing can be inferred only from references to shops (Chapter 3), the increasing number of small merchants, and the expansion of mercantile activity generally. As early as 1794, the small shopkeepers and tradesmen of Lerwick founded the Lerwick United Trades Society,[11] a friendly society aimed at the 'relief of their widows and of infirm and unfortunate citizens'. The first of its kind (it appears to have been resuscitated in 1809),[12] it was an indication of the growing importance of the merchant class. The merchants sold a wide variety of imported goods, including the basic necessities of meal and textiles for clothing, and most of them dealt in tobacco, tea and spirits, which was especially convenient as some of them engaged directly in smuggling. Sometimes buying between merchants and tenants became in part a fishing-tenure type of relationship, as some of the merchants were small-scale landowners, while others obtained tacks or bought themselves into the landowning fraternity (Chapter 3). For example, James Hay in Lerwick bought Braewick in Northmavine in 1814[13] because of its favourable location in relation to the fishing, it having the privilege of a booth and beach at Hamnavoe a mile away. Later, in 1820, his son William obtained tacks of Oxna and elsewhere[14] and proceeded to build fishing stations for the prosecution of the developing cod fishery. By this means a number of the merchants were becoming substantial landowners by 1820, the Hays of Laxfirth being indeed the outstanding example.

The agency function for the Greenland whaling was in large part a retailing one, and was of great importance to the Lerwick merchants in particular. It must necessarily have been subject to considerable variations in importance, as the Greenland whaling tended to decline in time of war — almost continuous decline is evidenced between 1793 and 1815 (Fig. 20, Chapter 3). The merchants acted for the whale-ship owners, supplying the crews shipped at Shetland on credit with all necessaries for the outward voyage and setting this against their wages paid out on the return from Greenland. In 1821 it is recorded that in order to pay for the outfitting and wages of sailors going to Greenland, the shopkeepers were under the necessity of importing £10,000 sterling in money every year.[15] The whaling was in a prosperous state about 1790,[16] and underwent considerable expansion again in the 1810s and 1820s, as the Scottish whaling industry grew up alongside that of England.[17]

It is difficult to ascertain precisely the relationship of shipowning (Chapter

6) to the other branches of mercantile business at this period, but it is likely that it helped greatly in their expansion, especially in the import trade in general and smuggling in particular. Ever since the 1770s, most of the import trade had been carried in Shetland vessels, but the number of ships remained small and relatively constant. In 1789, for example, there were only 6, totalling 258 tons.[18] Very soon thereafter, the shipping industry expanded: in 1794 there were 8 ships totalling 389 tons,[19] and by 1800 this had increased to 17 of 552 tons[20] (Chapter 6). Undoubtedly the most important single factor in this increase was the obtaining of naval prizes in the war of 1793-1801. However, although often mentioned in the Customs records, there is no exact tally of the number of vessels obtained in this way. The ships were cheap, and thus conditions for entry into the shipping business were favourable in this respect, notwithstanding the dangers of having ships retaken by the enemy. The most profitable part of the shipping business, which engaged the merchants for most of the time before 1801, was the smuggling of timber and gin — the former from Norway, and the latter from Norway and Holland. The imposition of high duties to help finance the ongoing wars was the chief reason behind this profitability.

When war broke out again in 1805, this same pattern continued, though trade was more intermittent: there tended to be outbursts of smuggling followed by periods of quiescence. From 1807 until 1814 the British blockade of Norway put a virtual stop to the Norway timber trade. There is some evidence to indicate that the number of ships declined, but that their average size increased and that they were engaged increasingly in freighting all over Europe. In 1809, for example, there were ten ships totalling 768 tons,[21] and Edmondston stated that these figures were 'greater than . . . at any former period'. As an example of this freighting trade, it is recorded that the brig *Don* of Lerwick was at Pillau, which had no trade connections with Shetland, where she sustained damage from a bomb in her ballast.[22] By this time, peace was imminent, and merchant interest was beginning to expand even further into the development of the cod fishing, which could be combined with shipowning to some extent. Smuggling became increasingly dangerous as a campaign for its suppression was waged by the Government, and soon passed into the hands of others.

The pattern of smuggling continued during the 1790s and early 1800s to be similar to that in the few preceding decades (Chapter 3), although there was a great increase in the smuggling of timber and wood goods after the duty was raised on wood imports. The principal ports from which cargoes were smuggled were, apart from Rotterdam (the centre of the gin trade), Hamburg, Bergen and Christiansand (Fig. 22).[23] The goods involved were mainly timber, tea, tobacco and spirits. In 1792, Walter Scott of Scottshall, who was the sheriff-substitute and charged with the responsibility of apprehending smugglers, wrote that[24] 'Altho' Hamburgh cargoes are not smuggling ones, yet if the vessels carry trifles, it might give trouble to fall in the way of King's ships . . . — As to your Rotterdam gentry, they deserve punishment, for their trade will ruin this country compleatly'. The beginning of smuggling *per se* as a fully independent branch of trade was marked by the withdrawal of the landowners from direct participation in the gin-smuggling trade at about this time (Chapter 3), although they continued smuggling on other trade routes.

This pattern was disrupted by the blockage of continental ports by the British Navy which commenced in 1807, cutting off these routes. In 1808 the Customs recorded[25] that there had been no smuggling the previous year, and that the commodities formerly smuggled were now obtained from Leith and Aberdeen, although they warned that an increase in smuggling could be expected when these foreign ports re-opened. Writing in 1809, Edmondston referred[26] rather optimistically to 'the abolition' of smuggling as having recently taken place, but the fears of the Customs were justified in the long run, as smuggling recommenced with renewed vigour in 1814, the year in which the blockade ended.

The decade which followed, between 1814 and 1823, was a veritable 'golden age' for smugglers. Although casual smuggling, particularly of timber, continued as before, there arose a situation in which the local merchants began to withdraw from direct engagement in smuggling using their own ships, and concentrated more on acting as agents for international smuggling rings based in London, Holland and Western Norway. This important phase was brought to an end by the pressure of Government acting through the Navy. Although isolated reports continued to filter through, by 1825 the Customs in Lerwick[27] considered that 'regular smuggling is at an end in this country'. As the 1820s progressed, the losses sustained by smugglers through capture were reinforced by the great reduction in duties on home-brewed spirits. The Dutch herring fisheries became the only source of gin in appreciable quantities — a return to the pre-1760s situation — while the import of whisky seems to have increased. After the mid-1820s the only smuggling carried on was in the course of normal trade, and by 1841 the Minister of Unst (one of the principal smuggling localities — Fig. 24) noted that the quantity of spirits consumed in the parish had fallen to half of what it had formerly been.[28]

During the period there were three basic types of smuggling trade. The first, direct participation by local merchants, was most significant for Shetland in the long run, and for the rise of the merchants, as it was combined with shipowning and was a potential source of capital which could be invested elsewhere. Although the landowners gave up participation in the gin trade around 1791,[29] they continued to engage in the Norway trade, smuggling in as much timber as possible, and usually entering a little presumably to allay suspicion.[30] Such cargoes included a little gin, and judging by the frequent references to it in the Lerwick Customs' letter books, it seems to have reached a peak during the short interlude of peace after 1800. In 1800 one prominent Yell landowner sued a number of merchants for 'debauching fishermen with spirits and making them give their fish in recompense'.[31] No doubt, also, it was such an adventure that was referred to by the mining engineer at Sandlodge in a letter to his superior in December 1802:[32] 'What think you,' he wrote, 'of gin £5–10 to £6 per anker* — there is great preparations making for large supplies soon'. In 1804 and 1805 there was a renewed outburst which ended in seizure of the vessels and much of the cargoes involved,[33] and thereafter activity was less prominent.

Writing in 1871, Robert Cowie summarised[34] the pattern of activity of the Shetland merchants engaged in smuggling: 'The ordinary practice was for a vessel (probably not larger than a sloop), after clearing the Custom-house at Lerwick, for Norway, to proceed directly to Holland, where she loaded gin and tobacco, which were quietly landed at Unst, or some remote part of Shetland. The smuggler then made all haste for his acknowledged destination, loaded timber, and returning to Lerwick, reported himself as having been at Norway all the time'. However, judging by contemporary evidence, it is likely that the pattern was more complex than this, due mainly to the integration of smuggling into shipowning as a whole. It was a more efficient utilisation of cargo space to have cargo on every leg of the journey if at all possible. This was certainly the pattern after the resumption of foreign trade, including smuggling, in 1814, the classic example being the well-documented[35] smuggling voyages of James Hay of Laxfirth, Shetland's leading merchant and smuggler in the early 1810s.

On more than one occasion during these voyages the vessels used the newly established cod fishing as a cover for their smuggling operations. Clearing out on the cod fishing, they proceeded to Norway and loaded timber and gin, or perhaps obtained a cargo in Norway and proceeded to London before picking up a cargo of gin in Holland and returning to Shetland. It was on what proved to be the last recorded voyage of this kind that James Hay was caught in 1814. The voyage of the sloop *Catharine* (Fig. 22) commenced in May 1814 when she cleared out on the cod fishing and proceeded to Sanday in Orkney where she loaded a cargo of meal. Although the export of meal was illegal, she proceeded to Bergen, discharged, and loaded a cargo of hides, skins and tallow for London. After unloading on the Thames, she took on 22 coils of rope and cleared coastwise, but on reaching the Thames Estuary sailed 'to the other side', as James Hay put it, and loaded a cargo of 600 ankers of gin in Rotterdam. This cargo was run at a number of points in Shetland before she set course again for Orkney, and unloaded the rope taken aboard at London. The intention was to take on another load of meal, this time for Gothenburg, but unfortunately they had been reported from Shetland, and were seized *en route* for Sanday, and ship and cargo were impounded at Kirkwall. However, the case was never satisfactorily brought, and in the words of the Lerwick Customs[36] 'the party was exchequered and the case compromised on payment of a penalty of £1,000, also expenses and forfeiture of vessel and cargo'. Luckily, as a precaution, James Hay had disponed* his estate to his son William just previously,[37] and the 'large fortune', which the Customs alleged[38] had been gained by him in smuggling, was preserved intact for the very considerable investment in the economy which the Hay family undertook in the 1820s.

Apart from the early phase of smuggling by outsiders into Shetland in the 1760s and 1770s, and a brief interlude in the late 1790s, the local merchants seem to have maintained a virtual monopoly on spirits imports in the 1780s, 1790s and early 1800s. Other smugglers are seldom mentioned. This may be partly due to the eclipse of Holland in the wars of the late 1770s and early 1780s, followed by the Napoleonic wars. Once peace was declared, outsiders began to participate once more, and their activities soon surpassed the efforts of the local merchants.

The most important of the agency smuggling ventures in which local merchants acted as agents for outside merchants, including smuggling rings, was carried on by two local merchants, John Ross of Sound, Weisdale and Balfour Spence in Lerwick (who was also agent for Lloyds), in conjunction with the London 'smuggling house' of Ewarth and Sons.[39] The basis of the trade, which commenced in 1814, was the running of part-cargoes of spirits by ships on voyages from London or Holland to various ports along the coasts of western and northern Norway (Fig. 22). The ships were often specially constructed with false bottoms and secret compartments, and were registered in the name of a Norwegian firm, C. J. George of Nyholm, although on occasion flying Danish colours. The spirits consisted generally of rum and brandy, with appreciable quantities of wine and other goods subject to Customs duties, and the scale of the operation was considerable. For example, in 1817 the *St. Johannes* (built in Christiansand by English carpenters on the model of a Yarmouth shallop)[40] smuggled 10 puncheons of brandy (800-1,000 gallons) at Whalsay and Skerries *en route* for Antwerp with a cargo of stockfish. The following year the *Forsoget* was seized in Lerwick harbour.[41] Purporting to belong to the same port, she had cleared out from Antwerp bound for Bodo, but had in fact gone to Shetland. As an indication of the scale and variety of commodities carried, she had on board 84 barrels of gin, each of 30 gallons capacity; 1 puncheon of brandy containing 100 gallons; 23 boxes of tea weighing 90-100 lb. each; 2 barrels of snuff weighing 7 cwt; a 3-cwt. bale of pepper) and 5½ tons of biscuit. The determined character of the smuggling ring is revealed in that when she was released in June 1818 she proceeded to Bodo and was seized attempting to smuggle her cargo there.[42] When the crew were released they seized the ship, broke open the Customs warehouse and took the cargo, setting sail for 'Faroe, Iceland or Britain'. However, the law was closing in, and Mr. Ewarth himself was in another of the company's ships, the *Commerce*, seized at Aberdeen in the same year. By April 1819 Ewarth & Sons were, in the words of the Customs in Lerwick, 'done up'.[43] Tradition has it that the Ross family of Sound were bankrupted over smuggling ventures.[44] However, it could not have been this one, as their names appear throughout the 1820s as pioneers of the cod fishing.

The smuggling of wood goods by local merchants seems to have been

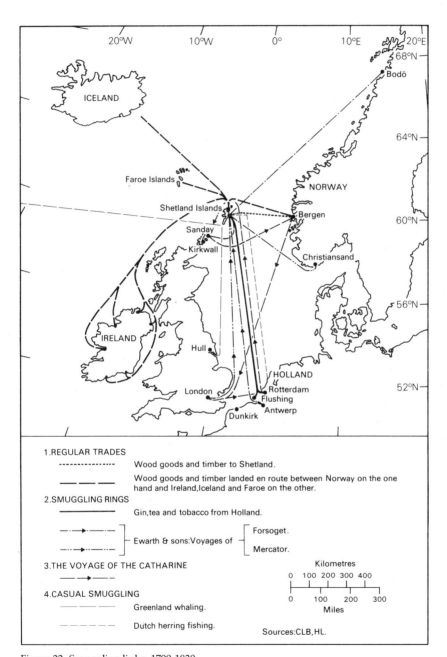

Figure 22. Smuggling links, 1790-1830

H

much less important after 1814 than it was before 1807, although there is reference to the local merchants around 1820 bidding up the prices of boats in Norway and entering these below their true value, thus evading a proportion of the *ad valorem* duty*.[45] From around 1822 till 1827, most wood smuggling seems to have taken place from ships bound from Norway to Ireland, Faroe or Iceland[46] (Fig. 22), and after the suppression of the smuggling rings this route seems to have specialised to some extent in the smuggling of spirits and tobacco as well, to judge from the several references in the letters of the Customs. The Customs considered that this trade could have been considerably reduced by a reduction in the high duty on wood, at that time in the region of a 50 per cent *ad valorem* duty. The chief places of landing used in the illegal timber trade were the North Isles and West Side, and it is likely that direct buying took the place of agencies.

There were two periods in the Shetland smuggling trades dominated by trade in gin to the virtual exclusion of all else, carried on by Dutch vessels. The first phase was comparatively short-lived during the late 1790s, and some of these vessels were bound for Faroe and discharged only part cargoes.[47] However, in 1798 it was recorded that so much gin had been paid for in money by the merchants during the two previous years that there was a shortage of money in the islands.[48]

The second, and by far the most important phase, followed on the cessation of direct participation in the gin trade by the Shetland merchants after the seizure of James Hay's sloop the *Catharine,* and lasted from around 1816 until about 1823. It marked both the peak and the end of the smuggling era in terms of its existence as a separate trade. During this period an estimated 10,000-12,000 gallons of gin were landed every year,[49] usually at the remote peripheral localities of Skerries, Foula and Fair Isle from which Quendale Bay, Scalloway, Burra, Papa Stour and Bressay Sound could be supplied (Fig. 23).[50] These smugglers, sometimes English, but more often Dutch cutters* or luggers* fitted out at Flushing,[51] were fast, heavily armed sailers and generally arrived in the spring and fall of the year, both before and after the fishing season. They carried a certain amount of tea and tobacco as well as gin, all of which was considered by the Customs to be of the very worst quality. It is undoubtedly this period to which the minister of Unst was referring when he said that the import of gin equalled half the rent of the island. The dealers in spirits and tobacco complained along with the Customs that smuggling had reached such proportions that it was proving detrimental to the economy of Shetland as a whole.[52] The smugglers were alleged to have 'already drained the poor of this country, who we believe have been almost the only buyers, of every shilling they could spare or raise'.[53] In 1821, the smugglers traded at sea with the forty or so cod sloops.[54]

A decisive decrease in the trade occurred in 1822, when no cargo was landed.[55] One of the smugglers, the *Earl Spencer,* was wrecked on St. Ninian's Isle; another lugger was captured off Fair Isle; and luggers were chased from the West Side and Baltasound. The determination with which

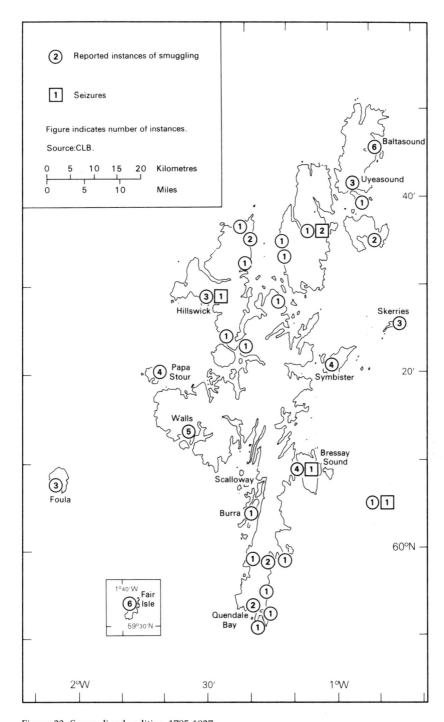

Figure 23. Smuggling localities, 1795-1827

these smugglers ran their trade was demonstrated forcibly by an incident in this latter chase, in which a man was killed when an attempt was made to board the smuggler from the revenue cutter.[56] The year 1823 is the last in which large-scale gin-smuggling is recorded, '. . . a vast quantity of spirits' being landed by the fishermen from smugglers at sea.[57]

The passing of the great smuggling era was due to a variety of reasons. Although the suppression by the Navy was undoubtedly the most immediate, it was reinforced by the poor economic state of the tenants, the Customs remarking[58] in the early 1820s that there was 'Absolutely no means wherewith to buy contraband'; and the relative poverty of the population referred to by the Customs in 1831[59] helped to ensure the long-term stability of the new situation, as did the relative cheapness of imported spirits from Scotland following a reduction in the excise duty. The increasing scale of whisky imports is shown, for example, in 1825, by William Hay, Shetland's leading merchant, arranging for the import of almost 1,700 gallons of whisky (though he subsequently lost 600 gallons of it by shipwreck).[60] A final factor was that by the mid-1820s the interests of the merchants were firmly engaged elsewhere.

The Capitalists

All the mercantile interests described above, especially import-export functions, shipowning and smuggling, permitted the accumulation of capital in the form of ships or money. After 1820, much of this capital was diverted by the merchants into the expansion of production, and the size of some businesses began to increase in parallel. The leading sectors in capital investment were the cod and herring fisheries, discussed more fully below. Investment in the cod fishing got fully under way around 1815 and reached a peak about 1830, while the herring fishing was somewhat later, beginning about 1825 and expanding until about 1835. The most striking feature of the development of the cod fishing was the large number of participants in the initial phases of the industry in the 1820s (Fig. 24). Most of the men involved owned or part-owned one vessel only and were often masters of their vessels as well. This, in fact, is the earliest recorded significant investment by the fishermen themselves clear of the landowners.

The close link between the growth of the cod fishing and business firms respectively stemmed from the business organisation of the cod fishing. Unlike the haaf fishing, the cod fishing, on which many businesses were primarily based, was more in the nature of a partnership between owners and crew.[61] Many sloops* were owned by more than one person on a share basis, and the remainder of the crew were paid wages with some share of the fish and oil, of which the owner had preference as a buyer. The crew were responsible for the supply of fishing materials and provisions while the owner provided the vessel. It was this provision — that the owner had the buying of the fish — which provided a basis for the expansion of the

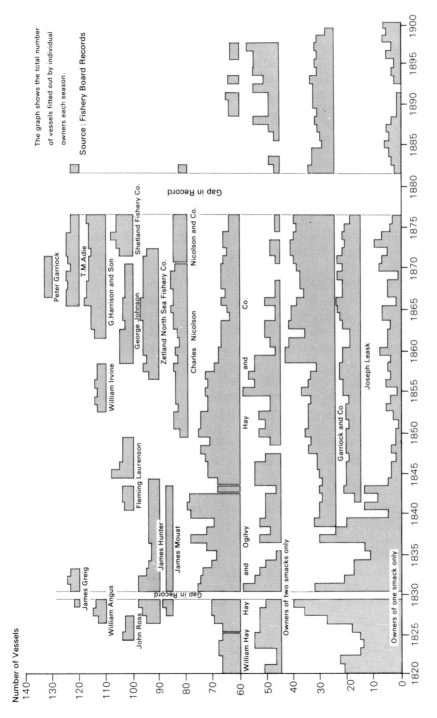

Figure 24. Investment in cod fishing vessels

business-firm type of organisation in the industry, and for the gradual growth of business firms at the expense of small operators, as the cod fishing was thereby strongly bound to the export agent function. The firm, with its larger financial resources, could withstand depression, such as occurred in the 1830s, better than the small operator.

The result of these developments was the eventual predominance of large family business firms together with one or two joint-stock companies, including Hay and Ogilvys (Hay and Ogilvy after 1832).[62] In 1837 Arthur Anderson established the Shetland Fishery Company[63] along the same lines, getting English smacks to fish for him, although he allowed freedom to the haaf fishermen to sell to whom they pleased once capital advanced for boats had been repaid. In 1839, several of the leading sloop owners combined to form Garriock and Company (Fig. 24). After the collapse of Hay and Ogilvy in 1842 (see below), a new pattern of business firms emerged, in which the great majority of sloops and smacks* were owned by six to ten leading firms, most of whom had their roots in one-man businesses set up in the 1820s and 1830s.

These firms, although almost always family concerns, were the direct extension of the individual merchants as regards function, investment in the cod fishing being generally the 'leading sector' in their activities. They were in addition usually import-export agents, shopkeepers, entrepreneurs in the herring fishing and haaf fishing, and shipowners. The situation was well summed up by a respondent to the Poor Law Enquiry Commission in 1843:[64] 'Shetland business consists of everything a man can make profit by. The merchants here do not confine themselves to any particular branch of business'. The only extensive operation of the business-firm principle independently of the production sector of the economy was in shipowning, where a series of firms were set up to provide mainly links with Scotland[65] (Chapter 6) and in banking (see below).

As regards the detailed organisation and operation of these firms, the affairs of Hay and Ogilvy and the Shetland Bank (a separate banking business set up by the same partners) merit special consideration, as these firms brought together locally for the first and only time the various functions relating to Shetland trade which had been developing since the middle of the eighteenth century — notably the merchants house and banking functions which had hitherto been a part of external organisation. The Shetland Bank was established in 1821 and Hay and Ogilvys in the following year,[66] both by William Hay, son of James Hay of Laxfirth, Charles Ogilvy of Stove and his two sons John and Charles, Junior.

Hay and Ogilvy entered business as import-export ('commission') agents and speculators, which included activity in the fish trade and early development of the cattle trade, and moved into fishcuring, retailing and shipbuilding afterwards, the business expanding greatly when the separate trading interests of William Hay were merged with it in 1825. Thus in 1826 the firm entered the cod fishing, and also began to engage in the herring fishing using half-decked boats*, fulfilling a similar role in Shetland to that of the curers in the Scottish herring industry, which was developing at the same time.[67] By the late 1830s, the firm owned about 100 half-decked boats, and were supplying an additional 120 or so.[68] They also acquired substantial interests in the haaf fishing, mainly by acting as tacksmen*, and in the herring curing industry (Fig. 25). Perhaps most important of all from the point of view of trade, they were a merchant house in the full sense of the word (Chapter 3) and, as well as dealing as import-export agents on behalf of other houses, dealt directly with market areas in Spain and elsewhere, generally using their own considerable fleet of merchant ships (Chapter 6). By the late 1830s the firm had a virtual monopoly of the foreign and much of the coastwise trade.[69] In addition to these internal and external trade functions, William Hay was responsible for establishing a shipbuilding, ship-repair industry and dock complex at Freefield,[70] just to the north of the then town of Lerwick in the area now known as Hay's Dock.[71]

Although there appears to have been an agent of the Commercial Bank in Shetland in the 1810s,[72] it is likely that most of the banking business in the islands, apart from the necessary functions of the merchants in this capacity, was externally situated. As late as 1817, for example, Sir William Forbes, James Hunter and Company of Edinburgh (Chapter 3) were responsible for bringing the supply of new coins to Shetland.[73] The history of local banking, *per se*, began in the late 1810s. In 1818, a small savings bank was set up in Lerwick,[74] and in 1819 the Shetland Society proposed to establish a Shetland County Bank.[75] The culmination of this local interest in banking was the establishment of the Shetland Bank in 1821. Although the same business partners were involved as in Hay and Ogilvys, the Shetland Bank was nominally a separate business with separate books,[76] and was in fact run as such (but see below). Issuing its own notes until 1828,[77] it was a local joint-stock bank after the Scottish fashion of the late eighteenth and early nineteenth centuries,[78] and operated apparently without any local competition until the 1830s when a branch of the National Bank was set up but subsequently withdrawn in 1838.[79]

The rise of Hay and Ogilvys can be seen in perspective as the culmination of the development of trade under local initiative since 1707, and the epitome of local trading and general economic development in the islands both with regard to initiative and organisation. The financial collapse of both Hay and Ogilvy and the Shetland Bank in 1842, therefore, apart from marking the end of an era in mercantile development and reverberating throughout the total Shetland economy, was a fact of the greatest possible historical significance. Although detailed financial study is beyond the scope of this work, it is clear that the basic underlying reasons for the collapse were the remarkable series of failures in the harvests and fishings in the late 1830s.[80] Not only were there three disastrous harvests between 1835 and 1839, necessitating the usual advance of credit (Chapter 3), so that by 1838 Hay and Ogilvy were at their lowest ebb at any time (even including the

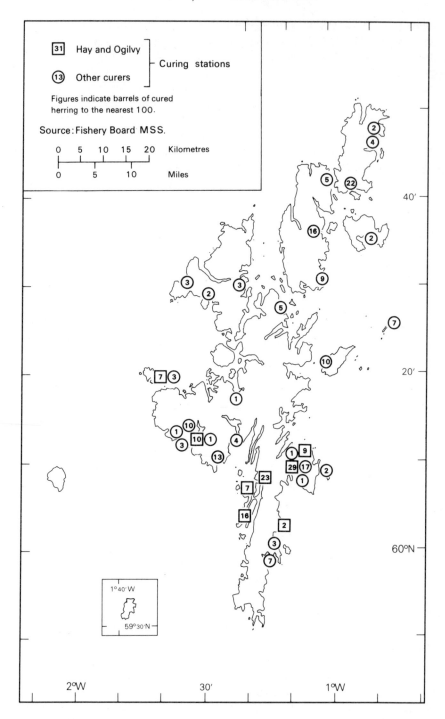

Figure 25. The herring fishing, 1839

time of collapse)[81] and bill protests for thousands of pounds were circulating among the leading landowners, merchants and Scottish banks,[82] but also there were steep declines in the cod and haaf fisheries simultaneously. In 1840 the herring fishery also failed,[83] while in the same year a disastrous gale caused great loss among the herring boats, from which the fishery never recovered.[84] These heavy losses were sustained for a while with the aid of the Royal Bank of Scotland, and the eventual collapse was precipitated by the refusal of this bank to make any more advances.[85] On 26th June, 1842 Hay and Ogilvy and the Shetland Bank were declared bankrupt for a sum of almost £60,000[86] — a vast amount of money in those days. In the investigation of the firms' financial affairs it was discovered that the Shetland Bank had made successive huge advances to Hay and Ogilvy amounting to not less than £40,000,[87] and that the outstanding debts to the Royal Bank amounted to some £26,000.[88] Although this policy had borne fruit in the building up of large cod and herring fisheries and creating much employment, it was, to put it mildly, if not euphemistically, imprudent banking.

The consequences of the bankruptcy were considerable. Foreign trade was completely paralysed for about two years, as the firm had a virtual monopoly[89] outside the relatively small-scale activities of the Shetland Fishery Company. Although the country districts were not so severely affected, hundreds were thrown out of work in Lerwick and Scalloway, contributing greatly to the poverty witnessed in these districts by the Poor Law Enquiry Commission[90] in the following year. A large part of the historical significance of the collapse lies in the continuing power of physical environmental factors over the trade economy. It also reflected the fact that this was the only attainment of almost complete monopoly over most of the import and export trades, with the implication that the island's economy was very much 'going it alone'. The structure of business after 1842 was more securely based in terms of organisation in that although trade continued to be dominated by a few large firms of which Hay and Company, the successor of Hay and Ogilvy, was the largest, there were no monopolies (Fig. 24).

The effects of the merchants on the expansion and diversification of the economy after 1820 were nonetheless stable and a solid contribution to the life of the islands. The most important enterprise was the cod fishery. The first cod fishing venture seems to have taken place in 1811, according to Edmondston, writing in 1820.[91] In 1822 Hibbert stated[92] that the first attempts had been undertaken 10-12 years previously, that is, in the period 1810-1812; so they agree. Earlier, in 1809, Edmondston had noted[93] that there had been no previous attempt to fish for cod separately for commercial purposes — he being apparently unaware of the eighteenth century attempts (Chapter 3). It is a curious historical fact that the first cod fisher met a similar fate to that other first one in 1742. She was taken by a Danish privateer, and soon afterwards retaken by a British warship and returned to her owner John Ross of Sound.[94] By 1813, there were complaints that the cod fisheries were destroying the mussel scaap* in Bressay Sound,[95] while in

1814 the cod fishing was being used as a cover for smuggling operations. However, the fishing was limited to inshore grounds and does not seem to have been outstandingly successful to begin with. In 1817 activity moved out to the large fishing bank south-west of Foula (called by Hibbert the Regent Bank), rediscovered in that year after having been first noted by a Shetland merchant-ship skipper in 1788.[96]

The reasons behind the establishment of the cod fishery are not entirely clear. Bearing in mind that it was carried on for the first few years mainly by Shetland's leading smugglers, James Hay of Laxfirth and John Ross of Sound, coupled with the evidence that it was used as a cover for smuggling activities, it would seem that smuggling was an important factor. In 1809 Edmondston remarked[97] that the quantity of cod around Shetland had increased greatly since the Dutch had ceased fishing for them, and the prolific nature of the West Side fishing grounds undoubtedly spurred new effort. It is likely also that the introduction of the tonnage bounty[98] had a beneficial effect, especially for the numerous small operators owning one sloop only, many of whom were fishermen. The result of these factors was a rapid expansion in the scale of activity around 1820, which continued on to a peak around 1830 (Fig. 26).

In the early 1830s, as the herring fishing expanded, the cod fishing failed, and between 1833 or 1834[99] until at least 1836 a few of Hay and Ogilvy's smacks went to Faroe.[100] This failure signalled ruin for some of the small operators (note the steep decline in owners of one sloop only, Fig. 24), and some of the men would not engage in the cod fishing unless they had the chance of the herring fishing also.[101] Some improvement in the later 1830s coincided with the abandonment of Faroe, except by one or two English smacks landing at Shetland,[102] and the industry suffered from the collapse of Hay and Ogilvy and the effects of declining fish stocks in the 1840s (Fig. 26).

It became increasingly apparent throughout the 1840s and 1850s that if the industry was to expand it must range much further afield than the 'home' cod grounds, as the home cod fishery continued to languish. Accordingly, between 1846 and 1850 Hay and Co. sent a number of their largest schooners* across the Atlantic to the Davis Straits to fish for cod.[103] This venture was followed in the 1850s by the growth of the fishery at Faroe, and to a lesser extent Rockall, based on large smack-rigged vessels rather than the smaller sloops which had been the basis of the first great phase of expansion in the 1820s. The decade between 1855 and 1865 was characterised by the great expansion of the Faroe fishing and the growth of large family businesses based on this industry (Figs. 24, 26). In addition to local smacks, these firms bought large quantities of fish from English smacks fishing at Faroe. By this time three voyages were being made per season, the first two to Faroe or Rockall, depending on the abundance of fish, while the final one was usually to Iceland.[104] The Shetland smacksmen, who bought bait from the Faroese, were alleged to sell their curers' salt to buy brandy,[105] and certainly by this time an appreciable quantity of smuggling of corn

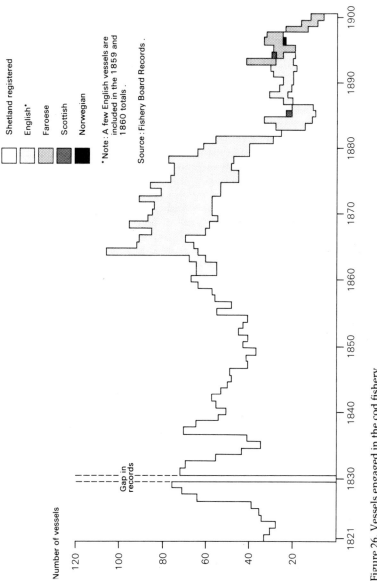

Figure 26. Vessels engaged in the cod fishery

brandy and Cavendish* tobacco into Shetland was taking place. In the peak year of 1866, the Customs estimated[106] that more smuggling was being done in this way than from the time-honoured Dutch herring busses. Meanwhile the home cod fishery remained on a small scale, and became the preserve of the largest firm in the cod fishing trade, Garriock & Co.[107] (Fig. 24).

Through their fish-curing activities the cod firms soon became involved in the haaf fishing as well, if not directly, then through landowning. Despite the great expansion in the cod fishery, however, the open-boat fishery remained consistently more important in terms of scale of production, although detailed statistics prior to 1850 are not available to confirm this (Fig. 27). At the beginning of the century there were over 450 boats engaged in the haaf fishing,[108] and the number probably increased somewhat in the 1820s, judging by the large import of new boats (Fig. 35). In the 1830s and early 1840s there was a decline which in part at least parallelled that of the home cod fishing, not surprising, perhaps, in view of the fact that both fishings were working to some extent over the same grounds. The number of boats on the West Side declined considerably, due, as the minister of North-mavine put it,[109] 'to the scarcity of fish, the lowness of the price, and the great expense with which the fishery is attended'. Although the great fishing disaster of 1832 struck heavily in certain areas, especially on the east side, it did not have a long-term effect.[110] By the 1860s, encouraged mainly by the high prices for fish,[111] the catch of the open-boat fisheries was expanding, albeit less spectacularly than that of the cod smacks (Fig. 31).

Although there are not many data relating to the details of the open-boat fisheries, it is apparent that there were improvements throughout the period. In particular, there was a significant increase in the size of the larger class of boats used in the far haaf fishings, where boats of eighteen feet of keel and over became increasingly common (see Fig. 35 for the level of import of these in the 1811-1829 period). Also, there were signs of increasing specialisation. In Dunrossness, attention became exclusively centred on the saithe fishery,[112] and although there is little record of a continuous piltock and sillock fishery as in the eighteenth century, in some years such as the winter of 1865-66 large numbers were caught and sold to the curers for oil.[113] In the Scalloway and Burra areas fishing all year round for local markets was well established in the first half of the century, and the beginnings of haddock fishing for local markets seem to date from the 1840s. By the 1860s Hay & Co. were even exporting a few barrels of wet-salted haddocks from Scalloway every year.[114]

For the first three decades after 1790 the pattern of casual herring fishing established in the eighteenth century continued. One of the three attempts at 'buss fishing' mentioned previously took place in 1793, but the vessel was subsequently lost on passage to Leith with her cargo of 225 barrels of herring.[115] There is no further evidence of this type of open sea fishing until 1809, when an attempt was made by a local shipowner, followed by another attempt in autumn 1813, when James Hay had the dogger* *George Rose* fitted out. He seems to have bought this vessel with a view to engaging in the herring fishing after the establishment of the bounty scheme in 1808.[116] The venture was not particularly successful, although Hay fully intended to repeat it in 1814, this time in June. Edmondston considered[117] that the stipulations regarding the size of vessel and number of nets were too high for Shetland conditions, and that provision to use boats the size of the cod sloops with fewer nets would have effectively promoted the industry in Shetland because of the lower level of capital investment required.

The initial impetus in the establishment of the herring fishing (Fig. 25) proper came from a small influential group of landowners,[118] and drew its inspiration from the open boat fishery which was by that time rapidly expanding all along the east coast of Scotland. In 1820 two half-deck herring boats of the kind used in the Firth of Forth were purchased by subscription, but the experiment was unsuccessful because of bad planning.[119] However, a few boats continued to be acquired, especially after 1825 under the aegis of Hay and Ogilvys. By 1827 three or four boats of the kind used on the Caithness coast had been bought,[120] and many of the subsequent half-deckers came from the Wick area, such as those purchased by James Garriock of Reawick.[121] The example of Hay and Ogilvys was closely followed by that of the major east-side landowners, notably in Dunrossness, Sandwick, Cunningsburgh, Bressay, Fetlar, Unst and Whalsay. The engagement of the landowners in the business was significant, as the herring fishing could be organised along the lines of the fishing tenure system, whereas this would not have been possible using busses. It demonstrates that landowning enterprise in promoting trade was still potentially active so long as it did not interfere with landowning interests *per se*. By the late 1830s — after the peak of fishing — Hay and Ogilvy had about 100 half-deck boats, out of a total of well over 200 of these engaged in the fishing (and in the region of 500 altogether, counting sixerns).[122] It was thus a fishing in which both the landowners and the merchants participated, although there were a few outside curers: the Garth estate in particular entered into a five-year partnership with a Belfast curer in 1834,[123] for example.

Herring production remained at a high level throughout the 1830s (Fig. 32), reaching a peak in the region of 50,000 barrels, or approximately one-tenth of Scottish production, in 1834. However, the Shetland industry was different from the Scottish industry in one vital respect. While the Scots herring curers were dependent more or less entirely upon the herring industry, the Shetland curers were landowners and merchants who had substantial interests elsewhere. This may partly explain the decline which set in during the 1830s, and why the great loss and damage sustained by the fleet in a great gale in October 1840 virtually put an end to the industry based on half-deckers.[124] At the same time the herring catches were declining (see below), and Hay and Ogilvy, who owned almost half the fleet and supplied a great many more, were tottering financially. There were marketing difficulties too, including the entry of speculators in place of merchant houses in the West Indian trade.[125] Much of the herring was spent* and made a poor cure*, suitable only for Irish and West Indian markets. This was because the industry was secondary to the cod and ling fisheries, the season beginning only in August, by which time the herring had spawned and were in poor condition.[126]

The industry after 1840 was a pale reflection of the one that had collapsed. Nevertheless, it is significant that it remained a recognisable occupation and did not sink into its pre-1820 oblivion. This was due in large part to the continuing interest of the large cod merchants. The fishing was carried on using sixerns, and expanded greatly in parallel with the Faroe fishing* in the 1850s. Production reached a peak of over 17,000 barrels in 1857 (Fig. 32), and a large number of boats were engaged (Fig. 27), although fewer than thirty were exclusively herring boats.[127] However, the fishing declined more or less completely soon afterwards, most likely because of the greatly increased prosperity of the ling fishing noted above.

The spirit and enterprise directed towards the increase and diversification of production on land, if less spectacular than that at sea, was no less apparent, and contributed substantially towards the variety of export commodities in two main sectors, agricultural products and minerals. Throughout the period, the landowners' enterprise was predominant, although some of the most important advances were made by landowners who were also merchants, such as the Hays and Garriocks, whose estates were in the central area. That the landowners specialised in improvement of agriculture and exploitation of minerals is a reflection of the fact that these were the two major areas worth developing without risking 'landowning capital', as the former provided reasonably sure returns on investment, albeit in the long term, while the latter could be developed using mining capital where necessary or desirable.

The spirit of improvement in agriculture went right back to the 1790s, and is evinced in the desire to substitute proper agricultural holdings of the croft* variety in place of the system of runrig.[128] In the period until about 1830, however, there was little advance, although there was much animated discussion of the possibilities. In fact the export of livestock in the form of cattle and ponies predated significant agricultural improvement by a long way even though it was on a comparatively small scale. The main phase of improvement occurred between 1830 and 1870 and was directed towards the general abolition of runrig in most areas,[129] with the laying out of large arable farms in those areas with the best agricultural land. However, one or two sheep farms were established, the first being near Lerwick in 1820,[130] followed by Weisdale in the 1840s (see below) and Sandsting by the 1860s.[131] The large merchants were among the first in the field in the central area in which their estates lay, especially in the limestone valleys which are associated with the most fertile farmland. William Hay was largely responsible for the establishment of the farms of Laxfirth and Veensgarth in Tingwall at this time,[132] for example, while Andrew Umphray of Reawick

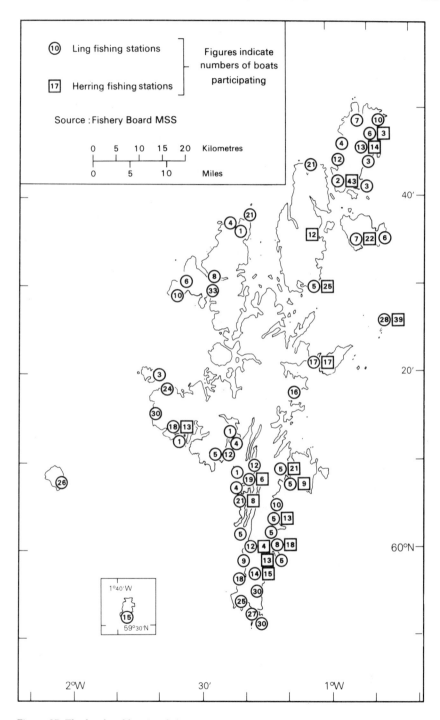

Figure 27. The haaf and herring fisheries, 1857

carried out extensive improvements in the Reawick area.[133] Other notable improvers included D. D. Black of Kergord, who cleared the Upper Weisdale area and established a large sheep farm in the 1840s and 1850s.[134] Various farms were also laid out in the peripheral areas possessing good land in Unst and Dunrossness (Fig. 28).

The chief reason for these improvements was the rising export of live cattle (Table 4, p. 147), further encouraged after the coming of steam communication in the late 1830s (Chapter 6). These improvements in cattle production were in sharp contrast to sheep production, which in any case had never been for commercial ends beyond obtaining wool. The principal reason for the decline was the appearance of sheep scab in 1786 in the South Mainland, ironically during an experiment in sheep-breeding.[135] By 1809, scab and bad seasons had reduced the number so much that it was remarked that 'There is not one left in fifty of the number that was a few years ago'.[136] Combating this state of affairs was virtually impossible until the number of livestock on the scattalds was properly regulated, something to which attention was just being turned by the end of the period. The seriousness of the situation was well summed up in 1841 by that great improver, the Rev. John Turnbull. Speaking of Tingwall, Whiteness and Weisdale, he stated that[137] in 1797 there were about 10,000 sheep in the parish, and that this number had now been reduced to 1,000: 'The want of them is very much felt'. Little attention was paid to the population of Shetland ponies either until after mid-century, when a market grew for ponies for use in the mines (Chapter 5).

The possibilities for mineral exploitation were a theme not unfamiliar even in the eighteenth century (Chapter 3), but this only assumed concrete form from around 1790 onwards. Perhaps more obviously than any other island product, it was related to market demand, and prospectors of one kind or another sometimes visited Shetland in the search for minerals, although the enterprise of the landowners was of decisive importance in promoting exploitation. There were basically two groups of minerals involved, iron and copper, and iron chromate, the former mainly in the Sandlodge area of Sandwick, and the latter mainly in Unst. Exploitation naturally lay particularly with the landowners on whose grounds the minerals were located, although the interest of the landowners generally is demonstrated from time to time in various small trial excavations and the great interest in mining exhibited from time to time by most of them. For example, in an express letter[138] to John Bruce of Sumburgh during the first phase of mining at Sandlodge, Robert Bruce of Symbister remarked on 'the generality of mining lodes' in Whalsay, and sought expert inspection. After the first phase of mining ended in 1808, the continuing interest of the Sumburgh estate was shown in 1826[139] in correspondence between Bruce and the Scottish National Mining Company, an interest which did not receive practical expression again until the re-establishment of mining operations in the 1870s (Chapter 5).

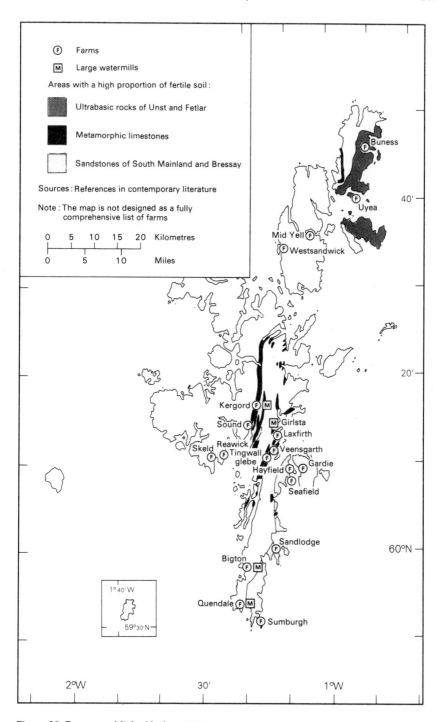

Figure 28. Farms established before 1870

J

The purpose of the initial opening up of the Sandlodge Mine was the extraction of copper ore.[140] Although some samples were taken in 1789 by a party of Welsh miners,[141] mining proper was confined to the period 1799-1808, beginning with the Angelsey Mining Company, which took away samples but did not work the mine.[142] Afterwards, several English mining companies took an interest,[143] and at least two successive Shetland mining companies were formed in which the Sumburgh estate had a substantial share.[144] However, managerial inexperience, labour troubles including the departure of local labourers for Greenland,[145] the involvement in smuggling of the mining engineer, and high costs due to difficult rock structure and transport to and from the distant locality of Shetland, combined to hasten the closing down of the enterprise. Only several hundred tons of copper ore were shipped to Swansea.[146]

Of more long-term import was the discovery and exploitation of iron chromate in Unst and elsewhere. First discovered by Professor Jameson in 1789,[147] it was rediscovered in large quantities by Hibbert in 1818,[148] and quarrying under the direction of the Unst landowners commenced in the mid-1820s[149] (Table 6, p. 150). 'Chromate', as it was termed, was used as the source of yellow pigment used in the paint and dyestuffs industries.[150] At the time of its initial exploitation it was the only major source in Europe and fetched high prices. Quarries were worked at various times in Fetlar,[151] Haaf Gruney[152] and Sand (Sandsting).[153] As competition from other suppliers began to intensify, prices fell,[154] but operations continued throughout the period (Chapter 5).

As to internal trade, increasing use was made of lime and local building stone, which was transported over long distances. For example, the big house in Uyea was built using lime transported by sea from Girlsta in the mid-1810s.[155] Other important lime-kilns situated at Fladdabister were in use throughout the period. The house of Symbister in Whalsay was built from Nesting granite quarried from neighbouring Stava Ness.[156] Cargoes of Bressay flags were transported everywhere for building and roofing, and Hay and Ogilvy even shipped a few cargoes to Faroe around 1840.[157]

Manufacturing was the final important category in the diversification of production, and can be considered under two main headings, the traditional and the new. The two most important traditional manufactures, kelp and whale oil from caain' whales*, were in reality processed goods obtained from raw materials, in much the same way as dried fish. Woollen stockings declined considerably after 1790, in part because of poor markets, as well as through inability to obtain wool as the sheep scab epidemic spread. The most important new introductions were straw-plaiting, boat and ship-building, and Shetland hosiery.

The history of kelp production (Table 4, p. 147) was one of increasing quantity and increasing prices until the end of the Napoleonic Wars, while during the 1820s the bottom dropped out of the market with the reintroduction of barilla from Spain,[158] used in soap-making and glass-manufacture. Kelp manufacture continued on and off on a small scale for the remainder of the period in some districts. The importance of whale oil varied a lot and probably declined on the whole, although it averaged out at several hundred barrels per year. Between 1800 and 1833 some 12,000 caain' whales were stranded,[159] which on average yielded about a barrel of oil each.[160]

Straw-plaiting was introduced by a London company in 1802 and at its height employed about 200 girls in factories in Lerwick and Dunrossness.[161] The straw was brought in from Dunstable ready for plaiting, and finished articles were exported to London (Tables 4, 5, pp. 174, 176). This industry ended sometime around 1820.[162] Shipbuilding and boatbuilding were begun in a big way around 1820 at first under William Hay[163] and later under Hay and Ogilvys. Although boatbuilding continued in Shetland for the remainder of the period and beyond, shipbuilding as such did not survive beyond the demise of Hay and Ogilvy, who built cod sloops and trading schooners, and brigantines* and barques* of 2-300 tons.

The industry of most long-term significance was Shetland hosiery. Although the Highland Society had reported on this subject in 1790 (Chapter 3), nothing was really done to develop the industry until the late 1830s, by which time demand had fallen to little more than the few stockings and other goods bartered with the Dutch fishermen for smuggled tobacco and gin. By the mid-1840s there was a considerable demand, mainly from the London market, for shawls, and by the early 1850s for veils also. The industry, based on female labour, continued to expand thereafter.

Merchants and Tenants

In the local economy there was a shift in emphasis from the peripheral area to the central core region, following the development of the cod fishery, and associated with certain other features of landholding and agricultural improvement. There was also a secondary influence brought about by the rise of the herring fishery which tended to cut across this central-peripheral pattern. In the peripheral areas the haaf fishing remained of great importance, although there were certain shifts in emphasis of various kinds.

The growth of the cod fishing was closely governed by two factors, the location of the fishing grounds in relation to certain physical features of the central region particularly suited to this type of fishing,[164] and the contrasting patterns of landholding interests between the central and peripheral areas. The cod-fishing grounds were situated almost entirely to the west and south-west of the archipelago to begin with, and these central areas were reasonably accessible to the grounds. When the fishery expanded to Faroe and other areas, the northern part of the central zone also became of importance. However, accessibility was only part of the reason, as the western peripheral areas were equally or more accessible in terms of distance.

The decisive factor was that the central core area was more suitable because of its physical characteristics,[165] which are in sharp contrast to those of the peripheral zone. Here, the characteristic alternating ridge and valley topography intersects the coast to produce the long, narrow and comparatively sheltered voe* with small offshore islands as the typical coastal form (Fig. 1). Coastlines are generally rocky, and drift deposits covered by green sward come down practically to water level. Often there are shingle spits and bars, and the floors of the voes generally consist of sand and mud which is often, but not necessarily always, good anchorage ground. Practically all the coastlines of the parishes of Delting, Nesting (Mainland), Yell, Tingwall, Sandsting and Lerwick fall into this category. It is this combination of room, anchorage ground and shelter which was the important factor in the determination of location of shore stations, some of which became trade points (Fig. 30).

A final factor in the location of the shore stations of the cod fishery was the pattern of landholding. By this time, of course, the peripheral areas tended to consist of relatively few large estates dominated by the haaf-fishing landowners, and the central area consisted of a greater number of smaller landowners, some of whom had entered business as merchants and were foremost in the investment in the cod fishing. These included the Hays of Laxfirth, Ross of Sound, Umphray of Sand, Garriock of Reawick, and Greig of Sandsound (Fig. 29). These men were also among the foremost in agricultural improvements, the central area containing much of the best agricultural land and growing in importance as far as agricultural production was concerned.

The result was the growth of a number of additional trade points to the main ones on the boundary zone between the peripheral and central part of the islands (Fig. 30). In the first expansion of the home cod fishery, places around the West Side in the vicinity of Scalloway tended to predominate, such as Weisdale, Whiteness, Sand, Sandsound and Skeld, and Hamnavoe in Burra, while Scalloway itself increased greatly in importance. During the second phase of expansion of the cod fishery, western and northern districts also came into prominence, trade points such as Voe, Brae, Collafirth in Northmavine, and Tofts Voe being most important in these districts.[167]

In the case of the herring fishing, the most important factors in the location of the herring fishing stations were nearness to the fishing grounds, as a round trip had to be made daily, and adequate harbour facilities. As the major herring fishing grounds were located along the east side, the distribution of stations bore only a limited relationship to the central-peripheral subdivision so prominent in the pattern of the open boat and cod fisheries, and cut to some extent across this division. The availability of harbours tended to favour, in the central area, places such as Lerwick, which increased in importance as a trade centre, and Burravoe in Yell, which gained new importance.[168] In the peripheral zone, important new trade points appeared on the east side in areas as near as possible to the grounds, the suitability of the harbour being secondary, notably at Skerries, at Cullivoe in Yell, and

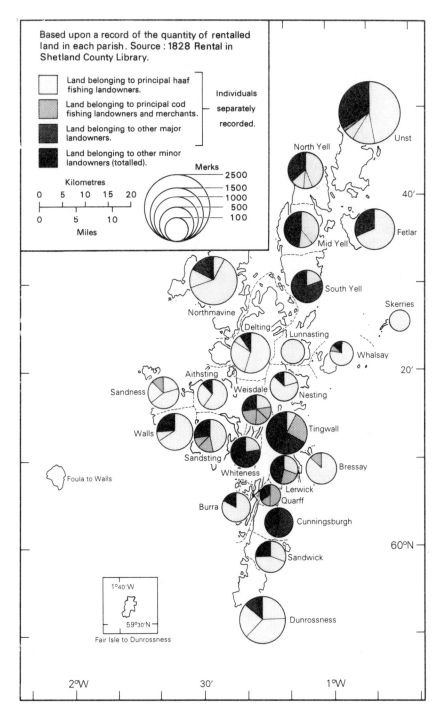

Based upon a record of the quantity of rentalled land in each parish. Source : 1828 Rental in Shetland County Library.

☐ Land belonging to principal haaf fishing landowners.

▨ Land belonging to principal cod fishing landowners and merchants.

◩ Land belonging to other major landowners.

■ Land belonging to other minor landowners (totalled).

Individuals separately recorded.

Merks
2500
1500
1000
500
100

Kilometres
0   5   10   15   20

0   5   10
Miles

North Yell

Unst

40′

Fetlar

Mid Yell

South Yell

Skerries

Northmavine

Delting

Lunnasting

Whalsay

20′

Aithsting

Sandness

Weisdale

Nesting

Walls

Tingwall

Sandsting

Bressay

Whiteness

Lerwick
Quarff

Burra

Cunningsburgh

Sandwick

60°N

1°40′W

59°30′N

Fair Isle to Dunrossness

Foula to Walls

Dunrossness

2°W   30′   1°W

Figure 29. Landowning and fishing interests in the 1820s

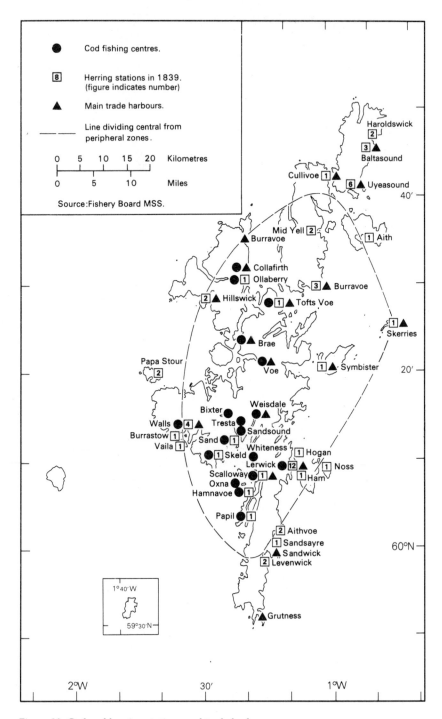

Figure 30. Cod and herring stations and trade harbours

Sandwick and Hoswick in Dunrossness;[169] while Uyeasound and Baltasound gained new significance (Fig. 30). The integration of the herring fishing with the cod and haaf fisheries previously in operation, combined with the collapse of the herring fishing in 1840 and the short seasonal nature of the industry throughout the whole of the period, ensured that these herring stations did not develop further as trade points. The only exceptions were those areas in which other activities were in progress, notably in Lerwick, where trade, rather than production, factors were at work.

The rise of the large merchants and also of the shopkeepers implied the growth of shops as well as stores and fishing stations. This element of retailing strengthened many of the 'production' trade points and created small spheres of influence around many of these. However, by far the most significant growth took place in Lerwick and Scalloway, the expansion of which was also aided by the herring and cod fisheries respectively.

The first phase of the nineteenth-century expansion of Lerwick can be detected in the course of the 1790s, and was closely allied to the expansion of activity by the merchants at that time. By 1814 there were 21 lodberries* built out into the sea as extensions of the merchants' shore premises.[170] The local trade of the town consisted partly in acting as a centre for distribution on the east side of the islands, and partly in drawing in produce from rural areas within a radius of ten miles or so.[171] Commodities included livestock and woollen stockings, which were sold both in the town and to shipping. However, the town had no regular market, and it was suggested in 1817 by the Shetland Society[172] that one ought to be established for the purpose of encouraging the cattle trade in particular. This wish was reiterated the following year, when the town was erected into a burgh of barony, principally to obtain a police force and a magistracy, reference being made in the petition for burghal status[173] to the population increase of the town, and the great use of the port as a fishing base and by the Greenland whalers. This event marked the end of the first phase of development at Lerwick.

The second phase in the expansion of trade in Lerwick commenced with the building of the first proper dock facilities in Shetland by William Hay at Freefield and John Mouat at Garthspool around 1822,[174] for the purpose of laying up the newly acquired cod sloops and, in the case of William Hay, for the establishment of shipbuilding and ship repair facilities as well. However, an application[175] to include these docks as part of the port of Lerwick was not finally accepted until ten years later, in 1832,[176] when the herring fishing was well under way and presumably put pressure on the authorities. The Lerwick merchants were afraid of the potential competition for trade as the town itself, with its lodberries, was little better than an open roadstead in comparison to the sheltered docks (Chapter 6). The Customs, ever mindful of smuggling activity, pointed out[177] that this was a favourite smuggling location, and that '. . . the foreign trade of the Port is so very insignificant that to talk of an increase of accommodation being wanted and that at a distance from the town (½-mile!) is truly preposterous'.

Despite this strong local opposition, the docks and ship repair yard proved to be a positive attraction to trade and a great asset to Lerwick. As the Rev. James Catton observed[178] in 1838: 'It is a place of great extent and business for Shetland. Here is the principal fishing station in the Islands, and the great numbers of coopers are employed in making herring barrels. Boat and Ship-Building is going on; sawyers, smiths, masons, all are busy; vessels and boats loading and unloading; indeed, the business done here, in a good fishing season, is astonishing'. As early as 1832, an extant list[179] of sloops and boats hauled up or lying in the dock indicates its importance (Chapter 6), and for the remainder of the period the majority of the Faroe smacks were laid up in these docks in winter, notwithstanding the fact that the cod fishery was centred on the West Side.[180] The dock area was also a key site for the establishment of herring-curing stations when the herring fishery got under way in the late 1820s and early 1830s.

In contrast, the contemporaneous growth of Scalloway, which commenced in the 1820s, was due to the growth of the cod fishing. The trade of the village received an additional boost when Hay and Ogilvys built the quay and curing station at Blacksness around 1830.[181] By 1843 the population of the village was estimated to be in the region of 500, and there were 'many incomers',[182] although there is some evidence of subsequent decline to 350 by 1863.[183] Trade expanded further in parallel with the cod fishery in the 1850s, and in 1857 a petition[184] for a Customs Officer to be stationed in Scalloway was granted by the Customs because of the increase in foreign trade. It was common for the Spanish schooners, which arrived to take away the fish cargoes (Chapter 6), to smuggle wine and brandy in substantial quantities on their arrival.[185] Timber was also imported direct from Norway.[186] Scalloway acted as a centre for the various curing stations in the surrounding area at which the majority of the cod fishers landed their catches: Hamnavoe, Papil, Trondra, Oxna, Papa and Nesbister stations all belonged to Hay and Company, for example (Fig. 30).

As regards outwith Lerwick and Scalloway, it is worth noting that as late as 1838, Lerwick still had no regular market,[187] although cattle were brought there in considerable numbers, sometimes for shipment to Scotland. Nonetheless the practice of stock sales twice or three times yearly had taken root in the country districts, and there are mentions of these being held in Northmavine[188] and Sandsting by 1841,[189] for example. After the building of roads in the late 1840s, this livestock traffic increased, and by 1862 many of the roads required repairs as a result.[190] Although country shops were to be found in all centres of population and trade, people did not necessarily patronise their nearest shop. Under the Truck System (Chapter 5) the tie to the fishcurers' shops was much stronger than that to others, and as many fishermen did not fish in their home area for their local curer, it was not uncommon for a man to walk up to twelve miles to deal with the fishcurer to whom he was 'tied'.[191]

The business of the landowners changed little during the 1790-1820 period, in the sense that fishing tenures were still prevalent. They were nevertheless becoming increasingly aware of, as Hibbert put it, '. . . the advantages to be derived from letting land at a definite price, independent of the obligation of fishing, and of paying tenants a regular price for their fish, that may correspond with the fluctuations of the market'. Desire to change the system appears in the experiments of Bruce of Sumburgh and Hunter of Lunna described in Chapter 3, and in that of Scott of Melby,[192] who raised both the land rent and the price of fish to his tenants, so that they could benefit from high market prices. Usually there was no opposition by the tenants to these schemes. According to Edmondston,[193] the landowners rather than the tenants had the best part of the bargain, as they had the potential benefits of increased profits from increased sale of, or high price of, fish at the market, while the tenants had the benefit of profit from the low rent only. This reluctance to change may be partly explicable by the fact that the tenants could do reasonably well through the sale of surplus butter, oil, and sometimes fish to the rising class of merchants, who supplied them with smuggled tea, spirits and tobacco. There were, however, two other important forces at work between 1790 and 1820 which contributed to the weakening of the fishing tenure system. One was the changing economics of landowning, and the other the changing attitudes and interests of the land-owners with respect to trade.

The gradual undermining of the landowner-tenant relationship by the advent of the merchants (Chapter 3) was reinforced by certain further changes in the economic position of landowning after 1790, which affected the engagement of the landowners in trade to the point of their losing the initiative in trade development to a great extent in the 1790s and early 1800s. First, the increased wealth brought about by war conditions and the activities of the merchants made the landowner-tenant relationship less worthwhile, as the profits from the fishing were inadequate to balance the frequent necessity of advancing credit to the tenants in poor seasons, and there was no profit to be made in other directions such as the supply of fishing necessaries.[194] Second, beginning about 1790, the value of all land — not just that in the fishing districts — began to rise. This started with the demand by landowners for land adjacent to their estates when the very large Westshore estate (Chapter 3) came on the market in 1791, and led to a gradual increase in the rents which soon became general.[195] Demand for land in the fishing localities continued, and after the wars the value of good agricultural land not situated in the fishing districts (such as Upper Weisdale)[196] rose with the increasing attraction of land for agricultural improvements. Finally, the rent system had become very much out of date. Not only was the levying of rent inequitable in relation to the true value of land, but payment in kind was considered a 'heavy exaction' upon the tenants.[197] The problem of inequity loomed largest on the Lordship estate, now the only large estate with an absentee landlord. In the words of John Bruce in 1785:[198] '. . . it is absolutely necessary that some rental or other, more accurate and just, and of more authenticity than the vile contradictory scraps hitherto existing should be made ever hereafter the Constant rule of exaction . . .' The bulk of the Lordship duties were eventually sold in 1812,[199] and between then and around 1840 the payment in kind of rents and teinds was finally converted into money payment.[200]

Partly as a direct result of these economic changes, and of independent changes in outlook, such as the desire for agricultural improvements, the attitudes of the landowners to trade were changing, as was their direct participation in it. Whereas in 1786 they were 'Labouring to reduce the profits of Fishing to an Ideal shadow',[201] by 1809 they were much less keen on promoting the haaf fisheries, at least on the fishing tenure basis. Thus they were encouraging early marriage much less frequently[202] and were often, it seems, glad to be relieved of the responsibility of conducting even internal trade, implied by the fishing tenure system, which had of course by the 1810s passed to a great extent into the hands of the merchants. Nevertheless they were keenly aware of the necessity of retaining the population despite the weakened landowner-tenant relationship, and recognised that depopulation was the 'worst calamity'[203] which could befall the islands. So there arose a somewhat paradoxical situation in which the increase of eviction notices to an apparent peak in the 1800s and 1810s (which can be detected from the admittedly imperfect series in the sheriff court records)[204] contrasts with the words and even deeds of the landowners. Favouring the unity of agriculture and fishing in terms of division of labour, they generally recognised the deleterious effects upon the economy and the resultant traffic for the 'emigrant-ship owners'[205] which would be the logical outcome of a widespread eviction policy or the complete separation of agriculture and fishing as occupations, advocated by some, such as Shirreff.[206]

These attitudes would seem to explain to a large extent their continuing interest in the promotion of trade and of economic development generally, first with special reference to agricultural improvement in the late 1810s, including the beginnings of the cattle trade, demonstrated so clearly in their participation in societies directed to this end. Second, their interest was apparent in their engagement in the herring industry in the 1820s and 1830s. The herring trade, like the kelp trade which preceded it, could be run on the basis of the fishing tenure relationship. By the 1830s, therefore, despite the fact that few apart from those engaged in the herring fishing were directly involved in trade, the landowners as a group were generally Whigs, and favoured the expansion of Free Trade.[207] Thenceforth, they were beginning to turn their interests increasingly towards the running of their estates and agricultural improvements generally, as these became fully separated from and independent of the fishings. They were also interested throughout in developing alternative forms of production and increase. Sumburgh promoted copper and iron mining in the 1790s, and again in the 1870s (Chapter 5). The Unst landowners turned to the exploitation of chromate in the 1820s, while others became absentee landlords, such as Grierson of

Quendale, who spent most of his life in the East Indies.[208]

By 1840, therefore, the landowner-tenant relationship in the form of fishing tenures, built up in the course of the eighteenth century, had virtually passed away, although fishing tenures continued in many places until the early 1870s. The results of these changes were expressed in two main ways. First, no sooner had the problems of rents been sorted out than a new financial problem loomed on the horizon — that of assessments on the land for the provision of services, which had of course to be paid out of the rent revenue. These 'public burdens' included teinds, land tax, rogue and prison money, building and repairing parish churches and parish schools, schoolmasters' salaries, assessments for the poor, and building and repairing tenants' houses, the cost of which was particularly high because of using imported wood. By 1851, all this amounted to 10/8½ in the £1, or £7,500 out of £14,000, which was the estimated value of the Shetland rental.[209] Clearly, landowning by mid-century was becoming an uneconomic proposition, and such conditions strongly favoured both evictions and agricultural improvement.

Second, there was the question of evictions. Unlike parts of Highland Scotland, Shetland did not suffer seriously from evictions, principally because of the continuing 'symbiotic' relationship of land and sea in the island economy. Despite the fact that eviction notices were often issued for debt and other reasons, and in fact were never put into practice (many of those in the 1800s and 1810s fall into this category), real evictions did begin in the 1840s in a small way, especially in those areas where new farms were being laid out. In certain areas, such as Tingwall, this involved merely shifting the tenants to another part of the estate.[210] In other, rarer, cases the people were thrown off the land by force with nowhere to go, the most notable example being Upper Weisdale[211] (Fig. 28).

Meanwhile, in the majority of cases the landowner had by this time become merely the tenant's 'confidential agent' as far as trade was concerned, standing between him and the merchant,[212], and there often existed a tacit or open agreement that tenants were to fish for certain merchants exclusively when fishing tenures were done away with.[213] The agricultural improvements promoted by the diseconomies of landowning thus proceeded with very little eviction. This was made possible in economic terms by the fact that the mainstay of the islands' income came from the sea, and in social terms by the fact that the great merchants had become by the end of the period landowners also, while other 'non-merchant' landowners granted leases of fishings to these and other merchants. By 1870, the landowners as a class, if not in every individual case, no longer participated in trade. When they did so, it was as merchants or businessmen first, and landowning was a distinct occupation not necessarily connected directly to trade as it had been previously.

The position of the tenants and fishermen throughout the period thus scarcely altered in effect, and landowners were replaced by merchants. This was strikingly demonstrated right at the beginning of the period by a court case[214] in 1794 in which Charles Ogilvy (later of Hay and Ogilvys) charged tenants on the Sumburgh estate with selling fish illegally to another merchant (the Sumburgh estate was the first to grant the tenants freedom to sell their fish to whom they chose). This case demonstrates that the outlook of the merchants tended to be the same as that of the landowners as a whole earlier in the eighteenth century, in that they favoured some sort of monopolisation of the tenants' produce. It is perhaps significant, therefore, that from the 1780s into the early years of the nineteenth century, there are a considerable number of cases brought for the breach of fishing 'contracts' between landowners or merchants on the one hand and fishermen on the other.[215]

The weakening relationship with the landowners was not lost on the tenants, and their position was well expressed by Edmondston:[216] 'The young men witness this change, and observe the effects of it; and they become sensible, that the only means left of diminishing their calamities, is to guard against engaging in that line which leads to them (i.e. of becoming bound to go to the haaf fishing). They generally, therefore, leave the country, or if they remain in it, do not evince a disposition to marry, until they have previously obtained what they think will enable them to support a family'. This statement is particularly significant in the context of the expansion of the cod fisheries and Greenland whaling in the 1810s, followed by the herring fishing in the 1820s, and contrasts sharply with the eighteenth-century picture (Chapter 3). The successful establishment of these fisheries, which were new in the island context, would appear to have been aided by a favourable psychological 'climate' on the part of the tenant fishermen.

When the shopkeepers took over a sizeable proportion of internal trade from the 1820s onwards, there was further weakening of the link, but credit was still necessary, as Thomas Leisk of Uyea complained. The material condition of the tenants probably did not improve greatly until the expansion of the cod fishing in the 1850s, which parallelled the growth of the hosiery trade, and the increasing sale of other produce such as eggs. However, the principle of truck* inherent in the fishing tenure system continued in force and almost certainly became stronger. In part this was because it was an established way of doing things against a background in which subsistence was being gradually undermined, implying that less and less was being produced on the crofts, and hence that more and more had to be bought and paid for at the merchant's shop. It was also in part because the seasonal fishing industry still constituted the mainstay of the economy, necessitating advance of seasonal credit.

The period from around 1790 until 1820 was the era of the rise of the individual merchant engaging in as many branches of trade as possible. The remarks made in the previous chapter about the outlook of the merchants apply also in large measure to this period, when they were still in the process of building up their businesses. With the advent of the business firm after 1820, their interests turned more towards the development of production, especially investment in the cod and herring fisheries. After 1820 also, as the economy expanded in response to the development of these fisheries, opportunities for mercantile enterprise increased accordingly, and a class of small merchants or shopkeepers came into being both in Lerwick and in the country districts. These shopkeepers were 'general dealers' trading in more or less every item possible, including spirits, tea, foodstuffs and household necessaries. In 1838, Catton remarked that[217] 'The street [of Lerwick] consists principally of shops, which are termed by the people "merchants", but what in England would be called shopkeepers. They are a kind of general dealers, and most of them sell bottled ale, porter and whiskey'. The scale of the 'tea trade' is evident from Laurence Edmondston's assertion in 1841[218] that in the late 1830s the population was consuming in the region of 40,000 lb. of tea per annum, which, it was reckoned, might well exceed the gross annual value of the rental. The shopkeeper class also had to advance credit to the tenants in the country districts especially, and often did so beyond the capability of their small resources, which resulted in their living, as Thomas Leisk of Uyea put it,[219] '. . . on the purse of their creditors' (i.e. the large merchants). In the hard times of the 1830s, many of these small shopkeepers went out of business, and there appears to have been some return to the fishing tenure system. Indeed Laurence Edmondston further emphasised the position by stating that the seriousness of the want in the 1830s, although due directly to famine and poor fishings, was due no less to the breakdown of the landowner-tenant relationship with no alternative security for the tenants.[220] He saw the maintenance of fishing tenures as the only substitute for evictions.

As economic conditions improved after mid-century, the number of shopkeepers expanded, so that by the early 1860s there were over 200 small shops in the country districts alone,[221] excluding the large number in Lerwick, which by the end of the period possessed specialist shops dealing in various branches of the retail trade[222] as well as general merchants. Meanwhile, the original class of merchants became the great fishcurers and import-export agents, and shipowners of the period after 1840. The major undertakings expanded into family businesses and had shops as well. It was here that the commercial power with respect to internal and external trade lay, and it was remarked in the evidence of the Truck Commission in 1872[223] that it was very difficult to run a country shop without being a fishcurer as well, as the fishcurers were generally the tenant-fishermen's only source of credit.

In retrospect it is obvious that it was practically impossible to replace the fishing tenure system until there arose a class of merchant *with sufficient capital* to fulfil the role of the landowner in supplying credit to the tenant-fisherman: something which began to happen after 1820. After 1840, the merchant-fishcurer had virtually replaced the landowner, and his advancement of credit, especially from this time onwards — by which time all rents had been converted into money payments — led to the establishment of a truck system to replace the fishing tenure system, although the latter arrangement continued to exist in several areas, mainly on small estates in the peripheral haaf-fishing region. The merchant-fishcurer had replaced the landowner from whom he had obtained tacks or leases of ground for his fishcuring establishment, while the largest merchant-fishcurers had become by the end of the period large landowners as well. In the great haaf-fishing area of Northmavine and on the west side of Delting, for example, a complete monopoly of the fish trade was possessed in 1872[224] not by the landholders or their tacksmen, but by three merchants, Adie of Voe (Fig. 24), Inkster in Brae, and Anderson in Hillswick, all of whom leased curing premises from the trustees on the Busta estate. For all practical purposes, therefore, the landowner had been replaced by the merchant as the 'kingpin' in the internal trade structure.

Markets

The nineteenth century, at least until about 1870, was characterised by the diversification of commodity production, and the diversification of markets followed from this fact. It was an era of commodity trades — in dried salt fish, in herring, in cattle, in minerals — but these still emanated from a few closely integrated systems of production. The haaf production system (Chapter 3) was not dead, and subsistence agricultural production, although being slowly eroded, was still the basis of the economy on land, despite the advent of the cod and herring fisheries, stock farming, and retailing. Above all, trade was still in the hands of the large merchants, a relatively small number of whose activities spanned all the commodity trades. This may explain why there appears to have been a lack of inclination or ability to exploit market potential to the full in such areas as the Spanish fish trade.

    The development of the salt fish trade during the period was fairly complex compared to that of the eighteenth century. Three major phases in development can be distinguished: 1798-1814; 1814-1837; and 1838-1875. The eighteenth-century pattern of fisheries exports continued well into the 1790s, long after the outbreak of the first war against Napoleon. By 1796, when the Customs records' continuous coverage ceased (Chapter 3), the Spanish market was still open, despite the fact that Spain had changed sides from Britain to France in 1795.[225] The disruption of the trade did not come until 1798, when the Spanish market was cut off by the hostilities, including the decree of the French Convention[226] that all neutral ships of whatever description were to be taken if they were found with British goods on board. This act introduced the pattern of activity which was to continue throughout the Napoleonic Wars, of overwhelming reliance on the home market, which previously had hardly provided an outlet at all for Shetland dry salt fish, except for 'winter' cod and ling, and saithe (Chapter 3). During 1799 and 1800, trade in Barcelona came to a complete standstill,[227] and there is no evidence of any resumption of direct trade from Shetland during the short interlude of peace which commenced in 1802. By February 1803 the war clouds were gathering again. Fourteen English merchantmen in Barcelona could not get a freight as the local merchants and the shipowners were apprehensive of war soon commencing.[228] Until the blockade of Norway and Denmark began in 1807, a certain amount was exported to Norway, especially to Bergen,[229] being bought by Danish merchants and passed off as Norwegian fish in the Spanish market, where it in fact fetched higher prices than the Norwegian fish.[230] This blockade, combined with that of the Mediterranean and other Spanish ports, cut off Barcelona and the other Spanish ports completely.

Although precise export statistics are sparse (Tables 4, 5, 6, pp. 147-150), the level of exports was similar to that of the 1790s, namely, from 800 to 1,200 tons[231] per annum, with an average of 1,000-1,100 tons.[232] The only exact figures are for the year 1st May 1808 until 1st May 1809,[233] when 19,107 cwt. were exported coastwise, and 3,159 cwt. abroad. In general, it appears that the home market consumption was about six times that of the foreign markets.[234] During this period the Irish market became 'quite over-stocked',[235] and after the union with Great Britain and Ireland in 1801 the encouragement to trade was further lessened by the fact that this ceased to be a foreign market eligible for the 3/– bounty per cwt. dry fish.[236] The capacity of the home market under such circumstances was of course more limited and 'precarious', and in 1809 it was suggested that a weekly fish dinner for the Navy should be inaugurated to support the market.[237] Nevertheless the economic conditions of war helped to maintain the price (Fig. 36), although of course most of the export bounty* was lost.

The period which succeeded the peace from 1815 until 1837 was an uncertain one for the dry salt fish markets to which Shetland was exporting, and was characterised by a predominant home market while the Spanish and Irish markets, although of importance, were less than half their size in the 1780s and 1790s (Fig. 31b, c). Statistics for home consumption again do not exist, although it can be inferred from the production statistics (Fig. 31a) that production for direct export was increasing, the open-boat catches remaining relatively constant while the cod sloops provided the extra cod destined for the Spanish market, which would therefore appear to have been an attraction in the development of the sloop fishery. Home consumption fell sharply after 1815 following the liberation of the French prisoners of war,[238] but this was partly offset by attempts to re-establish contact with the Spanish market by way of Minorca as early as 1812,[239] although market conditions were unstable due to the uncertain political conditions of Spain itself.[240] In 1820, Edmondston considered[241] that the fisheries could not be expanded without an increase in the demand for cod, as there was keen competition in the markets, especially from Newfoundland. When the fourth of the five vessels sent from Shetland to Spain in that year arrived at Bilbao, for example, there were eleven vessels from Norway and Newfound-

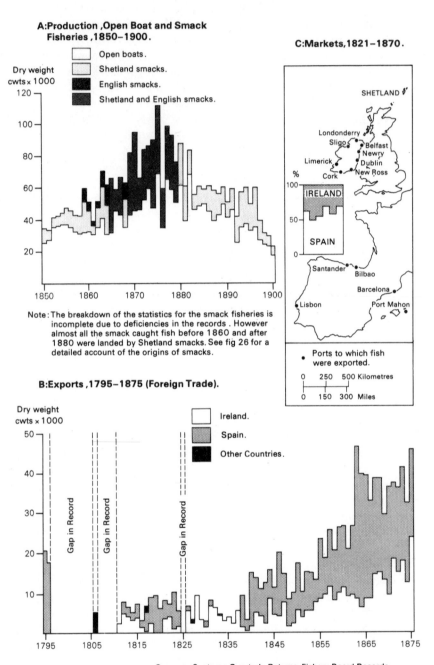

A:Production ,Open Boat and Smack Fisheries ,1850–1900.

Open boats.
Shetland smacks.
English smacks.
Shetland and English smacks.

Dry weight cwts × 1000

Note: The breakdown of the statistics for the smack fisheries is incomplete due to deficiencies in the records . However almost all the smack caught fish before 1860 and after 1880 were landed by Shetland smacks. See fig 26 for a detailed account of the origins of smacks.

C:Markets,1821–1870.

SHETLAND

Londonderry
Sligo
Belfast
Newry
Limerick
Dublin
Cork
New Ross

IRELAND

SPAIN

Santander
Bilbao
Barcelona
Lisbon
Port Mahon

Ports to which fish were exported.

0   250   500 Kilometres

0   150   300 Miles

B:Exports ,1795–1875 (Foreign Trade).

Dry weight cwts × 1000

Ireland.
Spain.
Other Countries.

Gap in Record
Gap in Record
Gap in Record

Sources: Customs Quarterly Returns, Fishery Board Records.

Figure 31. Dried fish

land discharging, and the Shetland fish had to be stored to await better market conditions. The dependence upon the British market for so long seems to have led to a decline in the quality of cure, and the fish were generally not sufficiently pined* to withstand the long voyage to Spain[242] (Chapter 3).

During this period an uncertain quantity of the fish shipped coastwise was probably eventually exported by the Scottish and English merchant houses — Hibbert records[243] that some were sent by these merchants to Barcelona, Lisbon, Ancona and Hamburg. Unfortunately there is no supporting evidence for this, except that home demand was falling. By this time the beneficial effect on trade which the bounties were designed to promote was debatable as far as the merchants and curers were concerned,[244] and these were abolished in 1830.[245] Apart from apparently poor curing standards, the trade with Spain was further discouraged by the high import duty on fish, which in 1837 was equal to the cost price.[246] From 1831 to 1837 inclusive, no fish was exported direct to the Spanish market (Fig. 31b).

The third phase in market development commenced in 1838, with the reopening of direct contact with the Spanish market by the Shetland Fishery Company under the direction of Arthur Anderson. That the quality of cure had declined to the point at which it was adversely affecting demand is apparent from contemporary remarks of one writer[247] who attributed this to the want of the 'beneficial superintendence of the lairds' and its replacement by the 'pseudo-free system' of the merchants and shopkeepers. It was also evident from battles which Anderson had with the Fishery Board over the marketing of Shetland fish for the Spanish market.[248] Contrary to the opinion expressed by Ployen on his visit in 1839,[249] and by the Fishery Board itself,[250] that their mark constituted a guarantee of quality in the Spanish markets, Anderson, by using a mark of his own, coupled with the introduction of drying using wooden flakes* instead of beaches, demonstrated conclusively that this was not the case by increasing the demand for Shetland fish apparently beyond the productive capacity of the fisheries.[251] The Government mark was subsequently abolished.[252] The Shetland Fishery Company operated in conjunction with Spanish merchants,[253] apparently situated mainly in Bilbao, which became the chief port of export, followed by Santander[254] (Fig. 31c).

For the first ten years or so after 1838, progress in the markets was a bit uncertain. In the case of the Spanish market, this seems to have been mainly due to the activities of the Shetland Fishery Company. After supervising operations for a year or two, Anderson delegated responsibility for the running of the company for two seasons, and when he returned in 1844 discovered that demand had again fallen off because of inferior cure. He redressed the situation by substitution of his own mark for that of the Fishery Board[255] before winding up the company in 1847, allegedly for personal reasons.[256] In the Irish market there were wide fluctuations in demand occasioned mainly by the potato famine, which brought the market

K

very low.[257] This also happened to some extent in Scotland.[258] In 1850 a memorandum[259] was sent to the British Government asking them to apply to the Spanish Government for the relief of the heavy import duty on salt fish. The duty remained, being almost half the price of the fish in 1864,[260] for example, but thenceforward the market expanded in step with the great expansion of the Faroe fishing, an expansion paralleled in the Irish market (Fig. 31b, c). In this third phase of expansion, the Spanish demand was limited mainly to cod, while most of the ling went to Ireland and the home market.[261] Also, from the 1850s onwards, practically all the dry salt fish was absorbed by the Irish and Spanish markets (Fig. 31b), and only the poorest quality fish found its way to the home market.[262] At the same time there was some pioneering of new markets, of which the most notable was Australia in 1854,[263] and the beginnings of import of fish for drying and re-exporting. Such fish first came from Norway in 1850,[264] Faroe in the late 1850s and of course English smacks from the late 1850s also (Fig. 26).[265]

It is difficult to date the end of this period of expansion and renewed interest in the market with any degree of precision. In 1863 Spain adopted a free trade policy,[266] which greatly encouraged Spanish trade, but by 1869 large quantities of Shetland cod were lying unsold[267] due to the constant arrival of cargoes from abroad, and the dull state of the home market. This, probably as much as anything else, was the turning point. Although there was little visible difference in the level of exports in the short term (Fig. 31b), a free-trade policy in the long term encouraged more efficient producers, and Shetland after the 1870s was being slowly but surely overtaken by other areas, such as Faroe, in this respect (Chapter 5).

The herring trade was probably the first conscious large-scale, locally inspired effort to encourage the development of an entirely new system of production specifically aimed at developing certain new markets. In contrast to the ling and cod fisheries, which were in many ways part of the naturally evolving order of things, the ling fisheries and markets in particular having been established from time immemorial, the herring fishing was brand-new in almost every sense of the word. Owing to the policy of not disrupting the fishing for cod and ling by undertaking herring fishing in the haaf season, a policy seemingly favoured by both merchants and fishermen alike, the season was too late to take advantage of prime quality fish. This resulted in a large proportion (probably nearly all in most years) of the exports consisting of spent* fish, which were saleable only at low prices in the Irish and West Indian markets. In the latter they were fed only to the slaves.[268]

The development of the herring markets is separable into three very distinct phases. The first, pre-1825 phase is hardly worth noticing because of the small scale of operations (Table 4, p. 147), which were of the casual eighteenth-century variety, amounting to a few hundred barrels per year exported generally to Leith. The great phase in the herring trade lasted from 1825 until 1840. Practically all the fish directly exported (Fig. 32b) went to Ireland, with negligible quantities to the northern European ports (Fig. 32c),

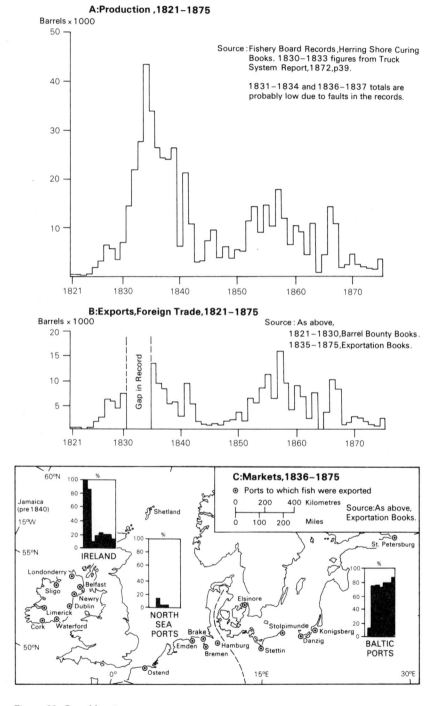

Figure 32. Cured herring

and the remaining larger proportion went coastwise (Fig. 32a). An unknown quantity — but probably the greater part — of this coastwise export was re-exported to the West Indies, one or two direct cargoes being sent from Shetland to Jamaica also. Apart from the decline in production due to local causes, both these markets were in decline in the late 1830s. The West Indian market disappeared very quickly with the emancipation of the slaves,[269] and seems to have been adversely affected also by the operation of speculators instead of the more usual London merchant houses.[270] Shetland herring seem to have been falling into disrepute in the Irish market because of their poor quality.[271]

The third phase in market development falls between the years 1842 and 1875. The emphasis continued to be on spent herring for the same reasons as before, but the roles of the Irish market on the one hand, and the southern North Sea and Baltic markets on the other were reversed (Fig. 32c). This time, practically the whole production was exported direct, and it is a striking fact that this level of direct export was for most of the time of the same order as that prior to 1842 (Fig. 32b, c). Most of the cure* went to the Prussian ports of Stettin and Danzig[272] (Fig. 32c), but the price of spent herring was so low that in the later 1860s and early 1870s it was hardly worth catching the herring,[273] and the trade withered away to practically nothing by 1875.

Despite the different courses of development of the fish and herring markets, there was a certain striking similarity in the fluctuations of fish catches upon which the fish trades were based. In the case of the cod and ling fisheries, there appear to have been two great peaks of effort, namely, the 1820s and early 1830s, and the late 1850s until the early 1870s, with a slump during the later 1830s and 1840s. This was parallelled in the late 1830s, and the overall pattern of white fisheries was repeated in the whale fisheries, where there was a virtual collapse of the industry in the 1830s. Finally, the events at sea were parallelled in the late 1830s by successive failures of the grain harvests and in the late 1840s by similar failures in the potato harvests. The common link between all these was the physical environment — a variety of climatic and hydrographic influences acting apparently on a North Atlantic scale, with profound repercussions for the Shetland trade economy.

These long-term downward fluctuations in fish catches, combined with poor harvests, which were the greatest single influence on the level of pro-duction, can unfortunately be outlined only uncertainly owing to lack of detailed research. Only a tentative explanation can therefore be given. The starting point for discussion would appear to be that changes in water mass characteristics tend to follow changes in air mass characteristics. Thus there is an annual seasonal fluctuation in the Shetland area in which Atlantic water predominates over North Sea water in winter, while the reverse is the case in summer. This probably follows from the increased vigour of east-west movement of air masses in winter compared to summer caused by the passage of successive cyclonic disturbances.[274] Also, the ascendancy of polar continental or polar maritime air masses, represented by prolonged easterly or northerly winds respectively, tends to favour the ingress of cool surface water masses from the Norwegian Sea over the warm Atlantic surface waters of the North Atlantic Drift from time to time.[275]

The most important consequence of these fluctuations in the present context was their influence on the abundance of fish stocks and hence the success of the fisheries and trade generally. In particular the distribution of herring shoals on the west and east sides of Shetland caught variously in early and late summer and autumn in different historical periods is closely related through the distribution of the plankton on which they feed to the first, 'east-west' set of variables outlined above, while demersal* fish species distribution (the cod in particular) is probably more affected by the ingress of cool waters from the north. That this was in fact the case in the 1830s seems highly likely in view of the fact that this northerly influence accompanied by persistent northerly and easterly winds, sometimes with snow, was often responsible for harvest failure,[276] and was parallelled by the severity of conditions in the sub-Arctic oceanic regions which was in large measure the cause of the disruption of the whale fisheries.[277] The cool easterly wind component in this system persisting for several seasons in succession, as it appears to have done, correlates with the parallel decline in the herring fisheries in the 1830s. Again it must be emphasised that research is inadequate for determining the degree of significance which can be attached to this correlation. The effects of these climatic and hydrographic fluctuations have already been outlined (Chapter 3, and above), and their far-reaching nature is strikingly illustrated in the fact that between 1780 and 1850, practically one year in four was a famine year, with particularly bad series of seasons in 1782-84, 1802-04, 1835-38 and 1846-49.[278]

With mercantile enterprise concentrated on the potentialities of production from the sea, it is not surprising that trade based on production from the land appeared to lag behind. In fact this is more appearance than reality, as there were vast problems to overcome. The first great necessity was to divide the arable land lying in runrig into separate workable holdings, and the desire to do this began to be translated into action in the 1790s.[279] However, progress was extremely slow until after 1840, and most of this task accompanied the laying out of the farms between 1840 and 1870. The Shetland Society reckoned[280] that the two first essentials in the improvement of agriculture were the valuation of teinds* and the division of commonties*. The first was accomplished by 1840, the second scarcely begun until after 1870. The position was well foreseen by Edmondston in 1809.[281] He pointed out that concentration on sheep farming would not only cause depopulation, but 'would operate powerfully in checking the breeding of cattle', which in Shetland possessed 'a decided superiority over sheep as an article of general sale'. His philosophy was generally adhered to until close to the end of the period, by which time sheep, including southern breeds, were being raised in large numbers,[282] and the pace of evictions was beginning to

rise (Chapter 5). The major object and result of the improvements was therefore directed towards the expansion of the export trade in Shetland cattle.
Little attention was being paid to the breeding of livestock until the end of
the period (Chapter 5), although there was some crossing of Shetland ponies
with Norwegian horses in Unst in the early 1800s.[283] Nevertheless, by the
1860s agricultural produce, consisting of cattle, some sheep, ponies and
eggs, was a major item in the export trade of the archipelago.

As regards livestock, the earliest exports were undoubtedly Shetland
ponies, which were shipped regularly to England on the Greenland whale
ships from the 1770s onwards until at least the 1820s in appreciable
numbers.[284] Although a few Faroese horses were being imported for re-
export as early as the 1830s,[285] this trade did not become regular until the
late 1850s, when the returning cod smacks were utilised.[286] The beginning of
the large-scale pony trade came around 1850, when demand for use in coal
mines accelerated after the statutory prohibition of the employment of
women and children in the pits.[287] By the end of the period, the price of these
animals had increased from four to five times, and the export of ponies was
becoming established as a regular trade (Chapter 5).

The debut of the live cattle trade seems to have taken place as a result of
large numbers being exported to the east coast of Scotland in return for
imports of meal during the famine of 1802-1804 (Fig 33). In the early 1800s,
the number of live cattle regularly exported was in the order of a hundred or
so every year,[288] and by 1816 it was recorded that 'Livestock even under the
present very imperfect system of management [has] become an important
article of export'[289] (Table 4, p. 147). Several hundred animals were exported
annually in the 1820s and 1830s,[290] and in 1841, three years after the introduction of steam communication, the price of live cattle had consequently
risen 50 per cent.[291] By the end of the period the trade had expanded as a
result of the spread of farms, crofters' cattle being seldom exported (Chapter
5). Cattle were the most important element in the livestock exports, and the
creation of farms at this time was largely aimed at production of cattle for
export and subsequent fattening along the eastern lowlands of Scotland.

The sheep population of the islands was decimated in the first half of the
century, and only began to expand significantly thereafter. Consequently
trade in sheep was very limited till the 1860s (Chapter 5). The progress of the
hosiery trade followed that of the sheep population for much of the period.
In 1809 the export of woollen stockings had fallen to about £5,000-worth
from about £17,000-worth in 1795,[292] although the absence of the Dutch
during the Napoleonic Wars accounted partly for this. Nonetheless a great
decline in demand in the home market had also occurred, which was
attributed to the huge expansion in sheep numbers in Scotland and
England.[293] The trade was encouraged a little by the activities of Arthur
Anderson in the late 1830s,[294] but it did not really get under way until a
London merchant, Edward Standen, took an interest in it in the mid-
1840s.[295] He opened up the English market — after the disappearance of the

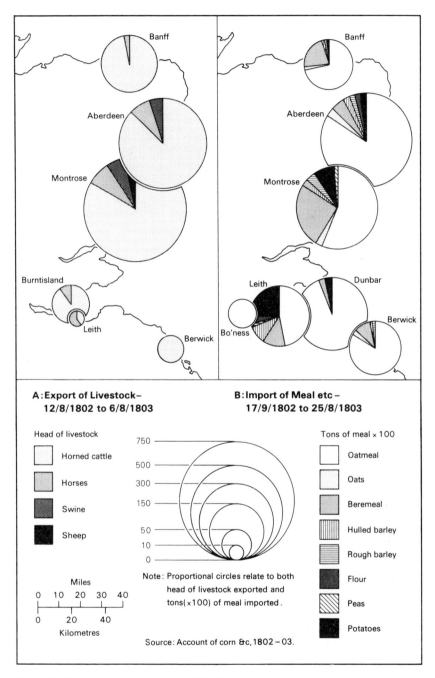

Figure 33. Trade links with Scotland, 1802-03 famine

Dutch, production had tended to go mainly to Scotland — and soon fine-quality shawls were being sold widely, followed by veils in the early 1850s.[296] By the early 1870s the hosiery exports were worth around £12,000 a year,[297] and included woven rugs as well as a wide variety of fancy goods. In 1874 'Fair Isle' knitted goods* were even being sold to the Spaniards in London[298] (Chapter 5).

As for miscellaneous exports, the first half of the period, until about 1830, was characterised by the passing away of the old subsistence surplus trades (Chapter 3), along with the kelp trade, and their gradual replacement by livestock, hosiery and a number of other items. By the late 1820s, fish oil, butter and woollen stockings were of little real importance in the overall export pattern, although still exported. Meanwhile, to Faroe went cargoes of Bressay slates and flags, while from 1841 peat was sometimes sent to Leith for use in the distilleries,[299] latterly because of high coal prices.[300] The coastwise trade in cattle and peat was reinforced by the export of salt beef and bone dust (cattle and whale bones) (Table 4, p. 147), and in the 1850s eggs and periwinkles became regular items — in one year in the 1860s, £9,000-worth of eggs were shipped on 'the steamer'.[301]

The increasing export of goods coastwise was matched by the establishment of the coastwise* trade as the dominant link for practically all imports — imports which were becoming more and more diversified than in the eighteenth century as the mercantile system developed. Only the import of fishing stock (salt and barrels) and timber diverged from this pattern.

During the Napoleonic Wars, particularly between 1798 and 1814, virtually all trade, whether destined for export or import, was coastwise, and after 1815 the coastwise trade continued to expand, in parallel with changes in trade links, in which transport gradually emerged as a separate business organisation (Chapter 6). Meanwhile, imports gradually became the most valuable component in this coastwise trade as the dried fish and herring markets abroad expanded. There is little need to itemise the various categories of commodities. These were basically the same as in the previous century (Chapter 3), together with an ever-widening variety of groceries and household goods of many kinds, encouraged no doubt by an increase in the number of shopkeepers. The trade was carried on mainly by the merchants and larger shopkeepers and was partly bilateral. For example, William Hay bartered stockings for rum and apples in Leith, oil and butter for pitch and tar, and often small quantities of wet-salted tusk with merchants in the north of England.[302]

In times of scarcity, large imports of meal were brought in coastwise, notably in 1802-1804, when this import was valued at some £30,000, a sum greatly exceeding the value of all the fish exports, and very nearly all the exports.[303] Although the major point of contact was still Leith, there were a large number of contacts with other places. Fig. 34 illustrates the wealth of William Hay's contacts from 1819 until 1825,[304] when he merged his business with that of Hay and Ogilvys. At this time he was Shetland's largest

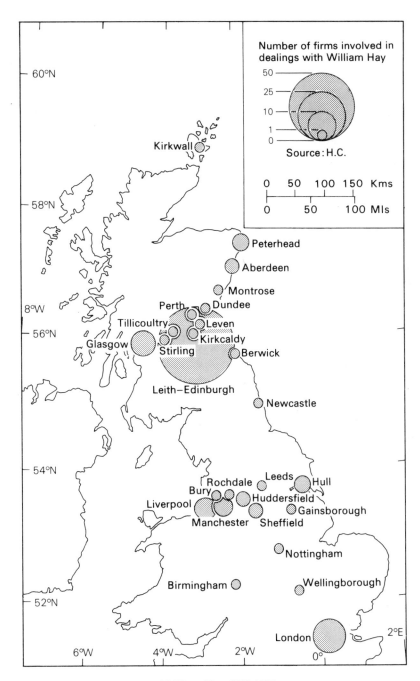

Figure 34. Business contacts of William Hay, 1819-1825

merchant, and the distribution reflects the relative importance of the various centres. London and Liverpool were the main destinations of fish exports, and the source of 'colonial' produce such as tea, coffee and spices, with tobacco coming from Glasgow. Ironwork and shipchandlery came from Glasgow, Newcastle and Leith. Textiles came from Manchester and the West Riding towns, steel from Sheffield, and lace from Nottingham. Kelp was exported to Hull and Gainsborough. Finally, there was a consistent small import of coal, often only a few tens of tons per year, at this time. The overall patterns were a microcosm of the commodity trading relationships of the Britain of the Industrial Revolution.[305] The coastwise trade was of course much reinforced, and possibly more concentrated on Aberdeen and Leith, by the establishment of regular packet services in the 1820s and 1830s, followed by the steamer service in 1838 (Chapters 5, 6).

The import of fishing stock* was a special case. Although almost all hoops and staves for barrels appear to have been imported coastwise until after the 1810s (many probably came originally from America), the salt trade was primarily dependent on Liverpool, although Sellar and Henderson (Chapter 3) also brought cargoes from Spain before 1820 or thereby.[306] In the herring trade, herring destined for the West Indies had to be re-packed in Spanish salt, although Liverpool salt was sufficient for other markets.[307] Although the benefits of Spanish salt in the dried fish trade were recognised (Chapter 3), Liverpool salt seems to have been dominant, judging from the extant arrivals and sailings records (Chapter 6). Certainly after 1840 some Spanish cargoes were imported, although the obvious source of the Spanish fish schooners (Chapter 6) was by no means always used, these vessels often arriving light.

There were some interesting developments in the timber and boat trades in the course of the nineteenth century. The first of these was the increase of timber imports for housebuilding, which parallelled the increase of merchant activity in the period 1790-1820, and led to important changes in the pattern of imports. Foremost among these changes was the entry of other Norwegian ports into the import trade, in addition to Bergen. The most important new port was Christiansand[308] (Chapter 6). These developments were further strengthened by the import of timber direct from America — mainly the Maritime Provinces — from the 1810s until the 1830s, and by the activities of Hay and Ogilvy, who in 1839 began to land part-cargoes of timber, pitch and tar from Archangel en route for British ports,[309] a practice carried on by Hay and Company until the 1860s. Unfortunately, detailed runs of statistics do not exist beyond 1829 (Fig. 35).

The imports of boats from Norway continued until the early 1860s — the latest Norwegian source is for the period 1856-1860,[310] and the latest Shetland reference appears to be 1861.[311] The source of the trade remained Bergen, with boats built at Tysnes (Chapter 2), and this trade was interrupted only between 1807 and 1814 during the blockade, when it has been suggested that Shetland boatbuilding began through necessity.[312] The level

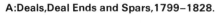

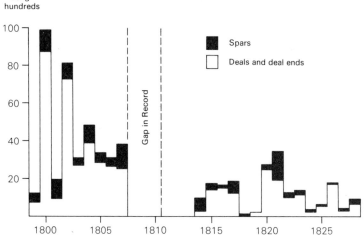

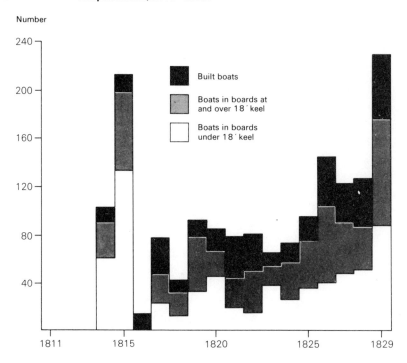

Figure 35. Wood goods imports

of imports of the different kinds of boats until 1829 is illustrated in Fig. 35, and it is notable that there was a gradual upward trend throughout this period, which even allowing for smuggling probably signifies some expansion in the open boat fisheries. In the period 1842-1844 inclusive, 78 boats were imported[313] — an average of 26 per annum, which compares with about 30 per annum in the period 1856-1860.[314] This provides evidence for a decline in the trade after 1830. Afer 1860 the demand of fourerns* and sixerns* declined for reasons to do with the changing patterns of the fisheries and the growth of local boatbuilding (Chapter 5). The import of cod sloops, smacks and other large vessels is dealt with in Chapter 6.

There were two phases of development in the timber trade as a whole which cut across these commodity boundaries. The first was the era of high duties which began in the 1790s and ended in the 1840s, and the post-1840s period of decreasing duties. Until the blockade of Norway between 1807 and 1819, large quantities of timber were smuggled, and constant complaints were made throughout the 1820s and 1830s about the high duty of 50 per cent *ad valorem** on most wood goods, culminating in a petition in 1844 for the abolition of timber duties.[315] From the 1840s onwards these duties were progressively reduced, and a new pattern of trade with Norway had emerged by the 1860s, in which large amounts of fishing stock (especially staves) were brought over from various southern Norwegian ports, and Norwegian vessels came over with cargoes of timber on purely speculative ventures.[316]

The overall pattern of development of the trading economy of Shetland from 1790 until 1870 was characterised by three main features, namely the impact of economic factors and local trade relationships, followed by the phases of development of external marketing, and the changing economic character of island trade revealed in the balance of trade and diversification of the economy. These economic factors helped to maintain the general social and economic equilibrium of the island community, although the increasing prosperity which eventually derived from these towards the end of the period may have been instrumental in promoting the emigration which began in the 1860s.

At the local scale, apart from the fluctuations due to climatic and oceanographical factors reacting upon agriculture and fisheries, attention focuses upon the impact of economic factors on the social structure. The character of the first phase of trade development from 1790 until 1820 was well summed up by Edmondston.[317] 'War,' he wrote, 'appears to be more beneficial to Zetland than peace.' This period was largely one of war, and the great rise in the price of Shetland export commodities was occasioned principally by this fact (Fig. 36). Large sums of money were also remitted to the islands from Shetland sailors in the Navy, and because of the shortage of men, wages paid to those who went to Greenland were high. The advantages of high export prices and full employment by war were further accentuated by the fact that prices of local produce varied little. Thus,

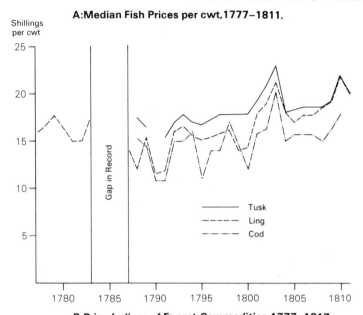

Source : Book of Zetland Product , GP.   Extracts by J.Wills

A:Median Fish Prices per cwt,1777–1811.

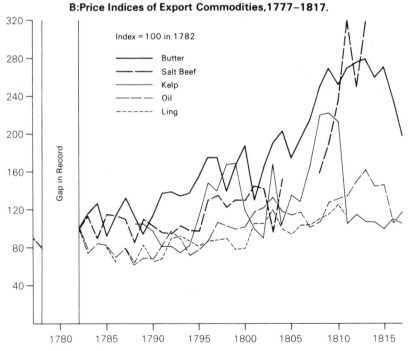

B:Price Indices of Export Commodities,1777–1817.

Figure 36. Export commodity prices, 1777-1817

although the war caused much disruption of markets in particular, and much general suffering, conditions were favourable for the accumulation of capital, and the following two decades until about 1835 saw the investment of this capital in the development of the cod and herring fisheries. Nevertheless, it was a sytem in which the rich got richer and the poor, if they did not actually get poorer, were at best only a little better off. In 1837, for example, it was circulated in *The Shetland Journal*[318] that on £40,000-worth of herring there was a profit of £20,000 of which the fishermen received only £4,500, or £1–16–0 each for a season's herring fishing. This situation was aggravated by the great drawbacks to expansion of the local economy in the form of the successive failures in the harvests and simultaneous downturns in cod, ling, herring and whale fisheries, which brought financial disaster to great and small alike. In contrast, after 1850, conditions improved, so that by 1858 the Customs noted[319] that 'From various causes a rapid and apparently permanent improvement has been observable during the last few years in the material and social conditions of the inhabitants . . . hence an increased demand for many of the necessaries and even luxuries of life which they have hitherto been accustomed to, creating as a consequence an increase in the coasting imports'. By 1872, the general opinion was that this continuing prosperity had improved the condition of the fishermen, and decreased their debt.[320] It may also have encouraged them to emigrate by providing for the first time the wherewithal to do so. Poverty appears to have been an element discouraging emigration, at least until the 1840s,[321] as the wealth derived from trade was concentrated in the hands of the few large merchant capitalists.

At the market end of the chain there was evidence of two phases of development separated by the late 1830s and early 1840s which parallelled the two periods of expansion in production. The first phase of trade expansion showed little awareness of the importance of assessing market conditions. The standard of curing to take full account of market preferences declined in comparison to that developed in the eighteenth century, notably in the use of English instead of Spanish salt. The standard of herring curing was never very good — it could not be when spent* herring were used — and only the poorest Irish and West Indian markets could be exploited. In the second phase of development, with the establishment of individual commodity trades under separate business management, there was improvement in curing standards and market awareness pioneered mainly by Arthur Anderson, and maintained by the new generation of business firms which arose from around 1840 onwards (Fig. 24). By the end of the period, production levels and exports had reached an all-time record. Also, there were evident beginnings of new techniques, the introduction of well-smacks* and steam drying* of fish[322] — the first to pioneer the fresh fish market, and the latter to make possible drying all the year round. The herring fishing, although reduced to a shadow of its former self, and in spite of being a miniature reflection of the great industry then developing in

Scotland after 1840, nevertheless parallelled the Scottish fishery in its reliance on the northern European markets.[323]

In reviewing the development of the import and export trades, two general characteristics become apparent. In the first place, from the economic point of view, there was probably a consistent balance of trade deficit, as the value of imports tended to exceed the value of exports, though unfortunately detailed statistics exist only for 1809 (Table 4), with some useful estimates for the period 1814-1824 (Table 5). However, when the place of trade in the economy is reviewed, the position of the islands was much more favourable. This is one important reason why it is necessary to consider population and employment issues as a background to trade, as external sources of income eventually balanced the overall economy.

The second important point is the great increase in the variety of export and import commodities (Table 6), which is the best indication there is of such things as the gradual undermining of the subsistence economy, and the slow growth of a market-orientated economy which asserted itself after 1870. It is also worth noting that the value of exports and imports must have risen in like manner. As to imports, the only shred of evidence we have is the increase in the coasting trade already referred to. In the export sector, the value of all fish cured for market in 1859 was £63,000.[324] It was probably much higher by 1870, due to increased production, although prices were low in 1869.[325] To this must be added about £10,000-12,000 in hosiery exports, and several tens of thousands of pounds in livestock, and eggs. In 1862 alone, some £9,000-worth of eggs were exported.[326] All this added up to an all-round prosperity which had been hitherto unsurpassed.

Table 4. Shetland's Balance of Trade and Payments in the Early 19th Century
Source: Edmondston, 1809, *op. cit.*, Vol. 2, 20-23.

Exports		£
1,075 tons ling, tusk, cod @ £18–10–0		19,887–10/–
45 tons saithe @ £10		450
300 barrels herring @ £1–7–0		405
900 barrels fish oil @ £2–10–0		2,250
500 tons kelp @ £8	*Sea Products £26,992–10/–*	4,000
200 barrels beef @ £2–10–0		500
3 tons tallow @ £60		180
400 hides @ 10/–		200
20 tons of butter @ 50/–	*Livestock Products £1,880*	1,000
Stockings, gloves, etc.	*Knitwear £5,000*	5,000
100 doz. calf skins @ 12/–		60
150 doz. rabbit skins @ 7/–		52–10/–
12 doz. otter skins @ £4–16–0		57–12/–
Seal skins		12
Feathers	*Skins £232–2/–*	50

Table 4 *(continued)*

150 horses @ £3		450
100 cattle @ £3		300
50 sheep @ 10/–	*Livestock £775*	25
		£34,879–12/–

Imports

One regular trading sloop, Lerwick-Leith, 7 trips p.a. & imports each time, exclusive of provisions, goods to value of £2,000	£14,600
Freights on above	350
Another regular trader, 7 trips, £1,500 per trip	10,500
Freights on above	245
Goods imported by vessels not in Leith trade	4,000
Flour, barley, rice, bread, grain, meal	8,000
500 tons of salt, duty free	625
Freight on above	600
200 tons coal for inhabitants	200
Wood, boats, & boards from Norway inc. freight & duty	1,800
	£43,920

Balance of payments

Annual exports:	£34,879–12/–
Money left in Shetland by Greenland whale fishing	7,000
Money remitted by regular monthly allotments, by sailors in Royal Navy & money remitted from the Navy by independent bills	3,500
External employment £10,500	
Money brought in by straw manufactory	2,340
Money brought into Shetland by establishment of volunteers and sea fencibles	3,600
Profits derived from freights of vessels belonging to Shetland	1,000
Sale of beer to Royal Navy and other vessels	1,000
	53,319–12/–
Imports:	43,920
	£9,399–12/–

Table 5. Shetland Trade Figures, 1814-1824

1. *1814: Shirreff, 1814, 74:*		£
Exports, 'of late years' average		c. 30,000
+navy, Greenland whaling, freights of vessels, profits of straw-plaiting, pay of volunteers, &c.		c. 50,000
	Balance	c. 10,000 p.a.

2. *Thomas Leisk's computations on the Shetland economy:*

Suppose 1,200 tons of fish exported, & taking periods of peace & war together, say £24 per ton	30,000
Agents' commission for buying = 2½%	1,500
Money sent out of Shetland for fishing stock say £4 per ton	4,500
	up: 26,700

£4 perhaps too little: leaves summer oil to make

Cattle: suppose 20,000 inhabitants breeding cattle for sale — 3,333 families selling on average ½ a beast p.a. =1,666½ beasts. Price during peace and war, £3 per head	5,000
Total from fish and cattle	31,700
Estimates subsistence fishing at	9,000 p.a.

Shown that if fishermen became full-time farmers raising another ½ or 1 whole beast p.a., extra income would be only £10,000, still wanting £21,700, thus refuting Shirreff's arguments in favour of specialisation in livestock farming.

3. *NSA, 68* (published 1841)

Exports:	1823	1824	1825
fish, tons	1,866	1,284	1,575
oil, barrels	740	950	1,234
beef, barrels	140	—	435
oxen	—	367	1,250
sheep	—	69	76
kelp, tons	260	—	442
ponies	—	92	140
butter, barrels	—	106	119
chromate of iron, tons	—	—	180

Imports (precise year unknown, but annual import at same period):

oatmeal, bolls*	2,152½
tobacco, lbs.	4,788
spirits, gals.	14,830
coffee, lbs.	1,419
snuff, lbs.	1,073
tea ? (probably lbs.)	17,983

L

Table 6. List of Exports, 1861
Source: Duncan, 1861, 65

Livestock and hosiery		*Fisheries products*
cattle	geese	salt ling
ponies	ducks	,, cod
sheep	hens, &c.	,, tusk
pigs		,, saithe
		,, hake
Livestock products		,, sounds*
salt beef		,, herring
salt pork		smoked haddocks
beef and pork hams		oysters
salt tongues		periwinkles
smoked tongues		whale oil
tallow		seal oil
eggs, various		cod liver oil
hides and horns		other liver oil
calf skins		seal skins
rabbit and hare skins		otter skins
butter		
wool		*Minerals and metals*
bones		old iron
		old copper and brass
Woollen goods		chromate of iron
yarn*		[after 1872, copper and iron ore were
stockings		added to this category as were peats for
gloves		distillery use]
mittens		
mitts		
socks		
nightcaps		
comforters*		
Severra frocks*		
drawers		
shawls		
plaids*		
scarfs (i.e. scarves)		
veils		
haps*		

The Old Rock

The period between 1790 and 1870 was remarkable for its flood of new ideas on ways and means of promoting economic development. Indeed, as far as trade was concerned, it can be regarded as a period of continuous innovation directed at the improvement and diversification of production and trade, which to the merchants was almost their *raison d'être*. Great new fisheries were established, agricultural improvements were undertaken, manufacturing industries were set up. Although not every venture met with success, the flow of ideas from individuals, and the organisation directed towards improvement, played a recognisable role in the development of trade.

The ideas were many. In the realms of the sea-based economy, the suggestion that the Royal Navy should be provided with a weekly fish dinner to increase fish exports came as early as 1787[327] and was re-echoed in 1809. There were suggestions for a ropeworks, persistent discussions on ways and means of improving the haaf fisheries, notably through the use of sloops and boats, tried in the previous century (Chapter 3), and still favoured by the landowners,[328] only to be translated briefly and unsuccessfully into practice by Hay and Ogilvy after the great fishing disaster of 1832.[329] Laurence Edmondston wondered[330] as early as 1841 why steam had never been applied to the fishing. When it was, it was as steam drying in the 1850s, not steam propulsion. More unrealistic was the idea that dogfish skins might be used in the manufacture of sandpaper.[331] *The Shetland Journal* in 1837 advocated the production of finnan haddocks*,[332] although the first record of wet salted haddocks in barrels dates from the late 1850s, while smoked cod dates from about the same time.[333] It also gave detailed instructions for the construction of an icehouse, though ice was not applied to the preservation of fish in the Shetland industry until the 1870s. By the 1860s, the *Shetland Advertiser* was discussing[334] in great detail the advantages and disadvantages of fish-farming, while in 1853 a prospectus[335] was even issued for the setting up of a whale-fishing company in Shetland, with the comment that 'The advantages to the people of Zetland, of having vessels in the Whale and Seal Fishing Trades, is so obvious, that it is somewhat astonishing it has been deferred till now'.

Although land-related thinking and ideas were less numerous among individuals, being more common in the societies active in encouraging agricultural improvement, the planting of trees was tried at Kergord and in various landowners' gardens. The usual improvements in drainage, crop rotation, and the introduction of turnips were part and parcel of the Shetland improving movement, and as early as 1825 suggestions were circulating on the feasibility of shipping cattle by steamship,[336] seven years before the first steamship appeared in Shetland waters, and thirteen before the first steamer service was inaugurated.

The heyday of organisations dedicated to the promotion of new ideas was the early part of the period, during the expansion of the economy up to 1820. The first improvement society, the Iberian Patriotic Society, named 'to Commemorate the glorious exertions of the Spaniards in the cause of liberty and patriotism, against the unprincipled usurpations of France', was set up in 1808.[337] Beyond revealing the identification with Spain in the minds of its founders, probably traceable from the fish trade connection so rudely broken by the depredations of the French, it never really did much. The Shetland Society, on the other hand, established in 1815,[338] did much useful work in encouraging the improvement of agriculture, kelp production and improvement generally, including the supervision of the establishment of a wheelwright and blacksmith in the islands for the manufacture of agricultural implements. After 1820, in the heat of the great new developments in cod and herring fishing, there was a lull in improving zeal, but much of the philosophy was translated into practice after 1840, culminating in the setting up of the Shetland Agricultural Society, which held its first show in 1864,[339] in many ways the beginning of a new era in Shetland agriculture (Chapter 5).

The population of the islands continued to grow throughout the period, and had levelled off by the 1860s. By contrast with the previous century, there were virtually no limitations caused by famine or smallpox, although neither was by any means eliminated. The only way such a population increase could be maintained was by a parallel expansion in employment opportunities, over and above the requirements for local production. The principal attractions for the majority of ordinary men lay in the Royal and merchant navies, and in the Greenland whaling.

The Royal Navy re-asserted its claim on local labour on the outbreak of war in 1793;[340] by 1798 there were some 2,000 men in the Navy.[341] The activities of the press gang reached a new peak, especially until around 1810 or so.[342] By the end of the Wars it was estimated that the total number of men in the Navy was around 3,000, and their remittances home amounted to several thousand pounds annually[343] (Table 4).

During this time the activities of the Greenland whalers were curtailed somewhat, but immediately after the cessation of hostilities in 1816 many men went to the whaling,[344] which at the time was expanding rapidly, especially in Hull, Dundee and Peterhead (Tables 4, 5). Throughout the 1820s, over 1,000 went to the whaling every year. In 1825, for example, there were 1,400, and the income derived from this season was estimated at £50,000.[345] In 1821 the Greenland agents required about £10,000 a year in money to pay for wages and stores for the men,[346] and the whaling was an important means of entering business. It was all the worse, therefore, when a series of disastrous seasons in the 1830s, caused by lack of whales and extremely bad weather conditions, had by 1838, in the words of *The Orkney and Shetland Journal*, 'almost annihilated' the north-west fisheries.[347] During the 1840s the whaling began to pick up again, with the emphasis this time on Peterhead and Dundee whalers, rather than those from Hull,[348] and in the late 1840s and early 1850s from 500 to 600 men were employed annually.[349] In the 1850s there was another expansion to the 1820s employment level of around 1,000, which continued until the mid-1860s, after which a decline[350] which proved to be the beginning of the end set in (Chapter 5). An increasing number went into the merchant service, especially from the poor times of the 1830s and 1840s onwards, so that the comment[351] of the Customs in 1853 that '. . . the number of Shetland seamen abroad in the world is great . . .' was an apt one. In 1861 it was estimated that the census figure of 31,000 was about 2,000 short of the true population total owing to the absence of men at Greenland, the Faroe fishing and in the merchant service when the count was taken in April.[352]

Underneath the welter of events taking place in the nineteenth-century commercial development of Shetland, and notwithstanding the high proportion of the population which looked beyond the islands for employment opportunities, it is possible to detect from time to time the forging of a certain unity of outlook among all classes in the islands. Among the landowners, and to a certain extent the large merchants, this was evidenced in the long drawn-out battle from the 1790s until the 1820s to achieve separate Parliamentary representation for the islands.[353] At the practical trade level, it was demonstrated in the acceptance of the truck system by the majority of both merchants and fishermen. Among landowners and merchants it emerges in their joint interest in fostering economic development through the various improving societies. From the 1830s onwards it was increasingly evidenced in the new interest of the Commissioners of Supply in economic affairs. They petitioned the Government in the 1830s and 1840s during the famines, on the economic conditions of the islands in 1851, and on the remission of duties on Spanish imports of Shetland salt fish. Soon roads were also added to the list, culminating in the formation of the Shetland Road Trustees in 1868 (Chapter 6).

The resilience of the local community in the face of economic peril was demonstrated best of all perhaps by the lack of a desire to emigrate, notwithstanding the possibility that poverty prevented them doing so. In 1820, an observer commented,[354] after the setting up of Shetland's first sheep farm, that 'Whether, like the Highlanders, they will have to cross the Atlantic, or whether they will form fishing villages, and manufacturing establishments at home, are questions which cannot yet be answered, but which no one can reflect upon without anxiety'. In the event, no one need have worried. The 'spirit of emigration', as it was sometimes so aptly called, although alleged to be afoot during the shortages of the 1830s, for example,[355] was alleviated by the employment structure, which balanced work at home with work at sea.

If the community as a whole personified the spirit of 'The Old Rock' in the face of economic pressure and challenge, this spirit was exemplified along with the variety and spirit of the age in the activities of one of its leading — though not locally resident — native entrepreneurs, Arthur Anderson.[356] Between 1835 and 1865, he provided a bridge between the flow of ideas and their realisation. He set up the Shetland Fishery Company and revivified the Spanish market for Shetland fish, encouraged the hosiery industry (although without much success), was instrumental in obtaining steam communication for carrying the mails, petitioned vociferously against the Corn Laws and in favour of Free Trade and, in the all-important battle for minds, set up a newspaper, a school, and the Widows' Homes, and became a Member of Parliament for the islands.

What of the outside view of Shetland? Although the impressions of the 'south' merchants are unfortunately not on record (and in any case amounted only to a practical interest in existing situations), there perhaps tended to grow up a conception of Shetland as a 'Celtic twilight'[357] zone — a backward group of islands inhabited by oppressive landowners. This impression was fostered from a number of sources, including the Shetlanders themselves, as in the landowner-merchant controversy of the 1780s from which much of this sprang. It was fostered also by the writings of Sir Walter Scott, the first of a long line of nineteenth-century tourists.[358] The truth that Shetland was evolving a complex and increasingly prosperous life by the standards of the day completely escaped most of them. By the end of the period, 'The Old Rock' image of the islands and their socio-economic structure personified in the reluctance to emigrate, and in the deeds of Arthur Anderson, was on the point of fading over the horizon of time as emigration began to get under way.

5

Fishermen and Crofters, 1870-1914

As in the previous transition from merchant to landowner control of the trade economy around 1790, the changes which took place around 1870 were gradual, and were evidenced by a number of small outward signs rather than sudden, far-reaching events. The essence of the emerging new order lay in a shift away from local mercantile dominance of production and trade towards a trade structure increasingly based on the impersonal, abstract principles of 'market forces'. A glance at current developments reveals several apparent paradoxes. Production levels in the haaf and cod fisheries reached record levels in the early 1870s, and yet the Zetland North Sea Fishery Company, the only joint-stock company participating in the cod fishery which was not based on a family business, was wound up in 1871, while still paying a substantial dividend. The following year it was replaced by the Shetland Fishery Company, dedicated to the pursuit of the cod fishing 'free' of truck.[1] Meanwhile, prosperity among the mass of the population was also greater than it had ever been, and yet this period witnessed the beginnings of the first large-scale emigration from the islands. In common with the previous late eighteenth-century change from landowner to merchant domination of trade, there was some resurgence of the political controversy over the charge of oppression of the tenants, this time by both merchants and landowners. Evictions there were, certainly, and in the late 1860s sheep began to appear as an important export for the first time.

Among all these signs of impending basic change in the structure of the economy was one in particular which stood out, although its impact took some time to become fully apparent. This was the decline of truck, after the enquiries of the Truck Commission in 1872, which heralded the beginning of the end of the truck system, although the basic necessity for credit ensured that it was a long time in going. The Truck Commission's principal function was to investigate the compulsion for tenants and fishermen to trade with specified merchants, with a view to making such socially binding relationships in trade illegal. In internal trade it thus corresponded to the breaking down of the old external trade-link system in the wake of the Free Trade movement earlier in the century.

The Supremacy of the Market

Just how close-knit the social and economic framework of island society had become was brilliantly summed up by John Bruce Younger of Sumburgh in his evidence[2] before the Truck Commission in 1872: 'There are no doubt many things in the Shetland system of trade which might be improved, but the system has been of long growth, and is so engrained in the minds of the people, that any change must be very gradual: a sudden and sweeping change to complete free-trade principles and ready money payments would not suit the people, but would produce endless confusion, hardship, and increased pauperism. . . .

'Abolish the present system suddenly, and I am afraid our poor-rates would become unbearable, and nothing would save the country but depopulation.' It is arguable to what extent depopulation 'saved' the economy, but emigration is evidence of the changing outlook of the population towards material betterment; it was the most direct and possibly the simplest means of opting out of the Shetland system of trade.

The principal change was the gradual appearance of fixed agreements of one kind or another between the crofters and fishermen on the one hand, and the merchants on the other. The most important of these agreements included those following from the truck system legislation and those between curers and fishermen in the herring industry.

The decline of the truck system which followed the Truck Commission's findings[3] was by far the most important change in this sphere. As described in the previous chapter, the truck system was a key feature of the internal trade system by 1870, especially in its function of binding the fishermen to sell their fish to the merchants in return for the supply of shop goods. The Truck Commission, appointed to investigate the system,[4] did not consider that cash payments for fish were either impracticable or inexpedient, and the persistence of the system was attributed partly to the attitudes of both fishermen and merchants, who seemed in general to accept it, although not infrequently complaining about it. This was demonstrated by the rather meek submissions of the crofter-fishermen in particular, which contrast with the relatively forthright expression of views tendered by them to the Napier Commission investigating the land tenure problem little over a decade later.[5]

The immediate reactions to the new system were mixed. The most notable ones came in two of the major industries. In cod fishing, a number of businessmen, including one of the leading instigators of the truck system enquiry, John Walker, set up the Shetland Fishery Company, based in Glasgow to 'avoid' truck. Unfortunately the undertaking was established in a declining industry, although it invested in the most up-to-date techniques in the fishing. The second reaction was in the hosiery trade, which in its reliance upon female labour and its cottage industry characteristics, including the preponderance of a large number of small household transactions with the merchants, had evolved upon the basis of barter. In practice, the sanctions against trade were practically ignored here, although there was a certain amount of uncertainty with the advent of the Truck Amendment Act of 1887,[6] and in the 1900s, when the Government decided to enforce the provisions of the Act in the knitwear trade, and merchants temporarily suspended dealings in knitwear in case they were caught breaking the law.[7]

Apart from truck, agreements of one kind or another were still in force in most branches of production. In the livestock trade, for example, the auction system came into being in the early 1870s.[8] In the herring industry also, prior arrangements were made between the curers and fishermen for the supply of herrings by the latter at fixed prices. The fixed-price agreements came under heavy pressure in the mid-1880s due to gluts in the herring markets, but only began to be replaced from 1894 onwards by the auction system,[9] the practice of agreements continuing for some time afterwards alongside the new system. Auctions, by creating a more flexible relationship between supply and demand, could only increase the economic independence of fishermen from curers. Both, however, remained vulnerable to the exigencies of the fishing itself, while the fishermen as well as the curers were liable to become more exposed to the increasing uncertainties of the market, not least the political upheavals in Eastern Europe and the activities of speculators at the market end of the trade system.

The decline of the truck system could not of course remove all of the basic reasons for its existence, especially the seasonality of the fishing and the dangers of poor fishings and harvests (Chapters 3, 4). Thus it was still necessary to maintain a credit system of some sort, and there was little real alteration in practice immediately. Nevertheless, by the time the Napier Commission was conducting its enquiries into the crofting system in 1883, the problem of truck had largely gone, and, in their own words, it was '. . . not . . . in any great degree prominently urged on [their] attention . . .'[10] The continued prosperity of the knitwear trade and the rising herring industry ensured an increase in the general level of wealth associated with an increase in cash transactions rather than credit where feasible.

In retrospect, it seems likely that the breaking of the old bonds of truck helped to create opportunity for the ordinary people, opportunity made more realistic in that the implementation of the truck system proposals accompanied the most prosperous period up to that time in the Shetland economy as a whole. The possibilities for mobility of labour also increased with the growing availability of opportunities for employment outwith, as well as within, the islands. After 1870, there was a greater realisation of these opportunities among the crofter-fishermen, and a distinct increase in these other forms of employment, as well as in emigration. For the first time in over a century, the population of Shetland began to exhibit patterns of continuous decline, this time arising from emigration and the absence of a larger proportion of the younger sector of the population in the merchant navy and

Greenland whaling while, in the case of the girls, service employment on the mainland of Scotland was favoured, with a few going to work on the herring stations there also. It became increasingly difficult to obtain labour, especially in the cod fishing industry, and this was given as a major reason for the winding up of the Zetland North Sea Fishery Company.

The Greenland whaling was, in 1870, still probably the largest single employer of island labour outwith the islands: 5-700 men were going to Greenland every year in the 1860s.[11] In 1872 the Greenland agents withdrew from the agency business due to the alleged lack of profit in it,[12] the whalers often building up substantial debts in bad seasons. They no doubt continued to supply the whaling crews, their decision being influenced by the effects of the Truck Act, which applied in this, as well as other, sectors of the economy.

Meanwhile, technological advances were improving the economic possibilities. In 1858 one of the first steam whalers appeared in Shetland waters,[13] and from then onwards the fleet was rapidly converted to steam — larger ships but smaller numbers. This of course greatly improved voyage times and improved regularity of voyages. It became the practice to make two voyages per season instead of one, the first being a sealing voyage to the edge of the Arctic pack ice. This hunt for seals was becoming more attractive because of the growing scarcity of whales. After approximately six weeks the ships returned to Shetland for coal before setting off on the main whaling voyage to the Davis Straits. The seal fishing was most profitable for the seamen engaged, despite its short duration in comparison to the six months or so of the whaling trip.[14]

In the 1880s sudden decline set in, owing to overfishing of whales. The first year of failure was 1881,[15] and thereafter the situation steadily deteriorated. By this time the whalers came only from Peterhead and Dundee, and the last whaler to sail from Peterhead did so in 1893.[16] The remaining Dundee firms pioneered the Antarctic whaling the 1892, but their advertisement in *The Shetland Times* for crew met with only three offers.[17] One of the last recorded instances of whale ships coming to Shetland to pick up crew was in 1911, when two Dundee whalers set off from Lerwick to the Davis Straits.[18] The decline of the Arctic whaling was a clear case of the appearance of a fundamental imbalance between the resource base and catching power, the latter greatly outstripping the former. However, the Antarctic whaling was growing, and a new pattern of locally-based whaling by the Norwegians had appeared.

The decline of the whaling industry was offset by the rise of the merchant navy as an external employer in the 1870s and 1880s, which acted as a stabilising factor. After the rise of the herring fishing in the 1880s, there was a certain amount of transference of labour between one and the other, depending on the state of the herring fishing. Thus in 1888 and 1889, for example, when the herring fishing hit hard times, some men left it for the merchant service,[19] while the rising tide of prosperity in the herring industry in the late 1890s caused the reverse to happen.[20] From the 1890s until 1914 there were probably between 2,000 and 3,000 men in the merchant marine more or less permanently. The local newspapers carried weekly reports, culled from Lloyds, of arrivals and sailings of hundreds of ships with Shetlanders in their crews. Stars identified every ship with a Shetland master, signifying the large number of islanders who attained the top of their profession.

The final and most extreme form of mobility of labour was emigration. The prosperity of the 1860s undoubtedly aided matters, when emigration began in a small way, and for a variety of reasons. The islands as a whole were in a comparatively prosperous state in relation to the 1830s and 1840s, when people were too poor to emigrate (Chapter 4), and it is instructive to note that *The Shetland Times* was uncertain at the time about the reasons for emigration, which began on a big scale just after 1870.[21] No doubt failure of crops and fishings was partly responsible. For example, in 1863, one hundred people left Fair Isle due to destitution after harvest failure,[22] and widespread harvest failure and loss of stock in 1869[23] may have encouraged emigration. However, another decisive factor was the availability of assisted passages to such places as New Zealand, energetically canvassed by emigration agents in 1874 and 1875, although *The Shetland Times* warned that the 'land of milk and honey' image fostered by the agents contrasted with a much harder reality.[24] A final important factor promoting emigration was undoubtedly increased knowledge, based in part upon postal communication. As early as 1854 it had been remarked[25] that a great volume of mail was arriving from the colonies and America, from people who had left the islands, and as late as 1911 there is mention of fifteen emigrating to California to '. . . a Shetlander doing well there . . .'[26]

The movement towards more flexible external trade links was brought about less by the application of free trade principles as such than by a series of partly unrelated events which culminated in a more flexible structure of trading relationships. The first of these developments took place in the dried fish trade, and was symbolised by the establishment of the Shetland Fishery Company by Arthur Anderson in 1837 (Chapter 4). Direct links with the Spanish market were fostered, and the dried fish trade expanded greatly afterwards. The following year, Spanish vessels virtually monopolised the dried fish trade (Chapter 6), a situation that was to persist until the 1870s. Meanwhile, the hosiery trade with the London market became established largely through the efforts of Edward Standen in the 1840s, and was similarly organised on the basis of a separate trade structure, with gradually increasing specialisation in this trade by a group of Lerwick merchants in particular.[27] Overshadowing these events to some extent was the collapse of Hay and Ogilvy in 1842, contributed to by the failure of the 1830s herring fishery. This signified the end of a powerful locally based monopoly which extended its operations to external trade also. Hay and Ogilvy were succeeded by a group of large, independently organised family businesses, none of which attained a monopolistic position in the external trade of Shetland.

The end result was a great expansion in island trade based on the existing types of production, notably the cod and haaf fisheries, but with the beginnings of new trade links based upon specialisation in certain commodities. Under these more flexible trading conditions, it appears slightly paradoxical that the commodity trades should remain similar in kind to what they had previously been. The herring trade, for example, collapsed with remarkable suddenness, and was not revived. It seems odd that the great gale of 1832 could have so little long-term effect on the scale of the haaf fisheries, while a similar gale in 1840, without the great loss of life which had characterised the earlier disaster, was held to have had a marked effect in reducing the herring fishing.[28] The answer would appear to lie, as indeed averred by the Customs at the time, in the fact that the Shetland herring industry could not compete with that of mainland Scotland.[29] This was hardly surprising. It might have been possible to sell spent herring to the slaves of the West Indies; it was certainly not possible to do so in the more discriminating and competitive markets of Europe.[30] And so the persistence and expansion of the traditional commodity trades, together with the truck system, which maintained local mercantile power, tended to obscure the changes in the structure of trade and the greater opportunities for the development of external trade, such as those created by the developing knitwear market, and livestock production based upon improvements in agriculture.

The increasing importance of knitwear and livestock in Shetland export trades focuses attention on the role of communications. The influence of improved communications lay partly in their contribution to greater speed and regularity, and partly in their effects on outlook, both tending to break down or diminish the degree of isolation of the island environment. Summertime steamship services date from 1836, all-year-round services not being introduced till 1866 (Chapter 6). This was associated with the mail service, which received a boost with the beginnings of emigration in the mid-eighteenth century,[31] and which encouraged the expansion of the hosiery industry, especially with the introduction of the parcel post in 1883. The first telegraph link with the mainland of Scotland was completed in 1870. Finally the newspapers, although appearing irregularly in the mid-1820s, late 1830s and early 1860s, became permanent with the publication of *The Shetland Times* in 1872, followed by a variety of other newspapers of which the most important was *The Shetland News*, first published in 1885. These newspapers were valuable not only for the dissemination of local information, but also carried much news derived from national newspapers.

It would be an over-simplification to suppose that the introduction of steam communication in the late 1830s and the improved mail service were in themselves responsible for the growth which took place in trade from the late 1840s and early 1850s onwards. The petitioning for better services suggests rather that the forces promoting agricultural and fisheries improvements were the same as those fostering improved means of communication. There was rather a long way to go before the basic structure of the production and trading economy was changed, and it seems likely that this was the reason why the geographical patterns did not change for some thirty years.

Improved communications highlighted the relative economic advantages of different locations. For example, from 1866 onwards all-year-round communication by steamship made possible the introduction of the fresh fish trade. Nevertheless this opportunity was not taken advantage of for some ten years, despite constant advocacy in the columns of *The Shetland Times* and elsewhere, possibly because the dried fish market was by then showing signs of decline, with falling prices due no doubt in part to similar locational advantages brought about by improved communications. It was probably at this point that communication of ideas and information via the mail service and newspapers drew attention to the potential of the improved physical communications. Nevertheless, local enterprise was not correspondingly adventurous in pioneering new possibilities, and although the speculative element given rein by this increased regularity of communication did find outlets, it was still in proven fields such as cod fishing and iron-mining, rather than the fresh fish and herring trades.

The case of the telegraph exhibited similar delays between introduction and full utilisation. Its very rapidity was suited to circumstances in which no time could be wasted — speculative situations such as the fresh fish trade, where rapid deterioration of fish put time at a premium; or in industries in which supply-demand balances fluctuated rapidly and hugely, such as the herring trade. But the telegraph was also expensive to maintain and use, and it is thus scarcely surprising that it did not come into its own until the expansion of the herring industry and the fresh fish trade in the 1880s, when it was extended to rural areas as well as Lerwick.[32] By 1906, its importance was clearly indicated in the statement that 'To the fishcurer and herring merchant the telegraph is almost more than meat and drink — it is the sinew of war. Without it they would be groping in the dark'.[33] By passing messages from curing stations to herring curers' headquarters, it made possible better control of supply in relation to demand; rapid fluctuations in the catch could thus be coped with by bringing in barrels and salt at short notice from distant stations by steamship, thereby avoiding loss by deterioration of large quantities of herrings which could otherwise not have been salted.

Herring and Haddocks

It is a commonly held view that somehow the decline of population and the beginning of the disintegration of 'traditional' Shetland society was associated with parallel decline in the traditional fisheries, and in particular that the haaf fishing and cod fishing declined as the herring fishing rose in importance. To a certain extent this appears true at first sight, but it comes as

1,000 cwts

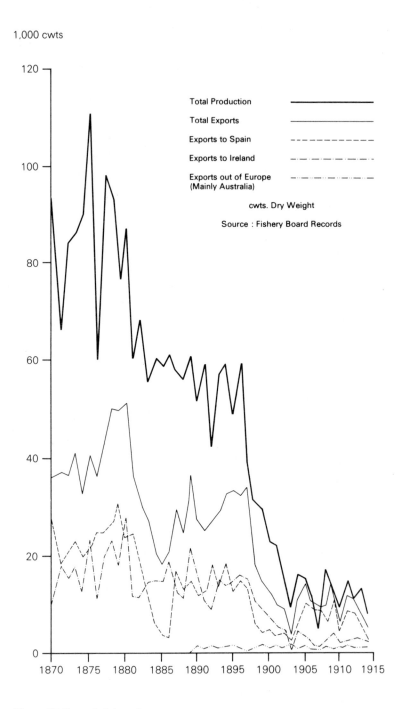

Figure 37. Dry salt fish trade

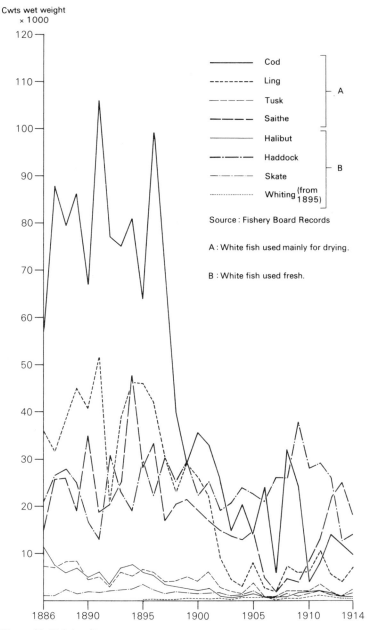

Figure 38. Fish landings

something of a surprise to discover that the cod fishing measured by number of boats engaged began to decline a decade before the herring fishing really got under way (Figs. 37, 38), and that the production of dried fish, apart from the very high levels of the 1870s, remained at pre-1870 levels until the late

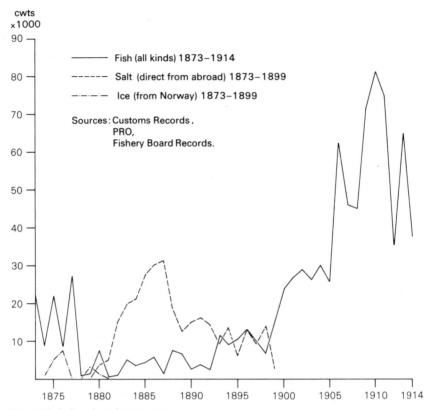

Figure 39. Fish, salt and ice imports

1890s when sudden collapse occurred in the levels of both production and direct exports (Figs. 37, 38). In order to account for this pattern it is necessary to consider certain elements both with regard to production and markets.

Production for the dried fish trade came almost entirely from the traditional cod smack fishery and haaf fishery, both of which had by the early 1870s reached their peak of development in terms of number of vessels employed, level of production, and general technological sophistication. Of the two fisheries, the haaf fishing was the more important in terms of its high level of production, although the cod fishing was not far behind in landings, as it was aided by substantial contributions from English smacks. The total quantity of dried fish was supplemented in the 1860s and 1870s by import of wet salt cod from Norway in considerable quantities (Fig. 39) by the large cod merchants, the drying process being completed in Shetland before the fish were re-exported. The firm of Garriock & Co., which was a leader in developing the cod fishery, also had business interests in stations in Orkney and Lewis at which some smacks, notably English ones, landed their catches.[34]

The developments leading to the decline in the cod fishing did not manifest themselves immediately. The first major straw in the wind was the winding up of the Zetland North Sea Fishery Company in 1871, allegedly due to the condition of their vessels, which needed replacement, and the difficulty of manning them, no doubt partly ascribable, as suggested by Halcrow,[35] to the relatively greater attractions of the 'great iron clippers' and steady wages of the merchant navy compared to toiling for uncertain rewards on the Faroe smacks. In 1871 the Faroe fishing was a failure, and many smacks were laid up, while a few went to Iceland.[36] In 1872 came the desire to participate in the growing fresh fish trade being developed by the English well-smacks* which ran to Granton and the Humber with live cod. Before their liquidation, the Zetland North Sea Fishery Company advertised for an augmentation of capital to take part in this trade;[37] this came to nothing possibly because the main shareholders were the other large smack owners, who were already contemplating reducing their commitments to the Faroe fishing. Meanwhile a new company, the Shetland Fishery Company, registered in Glasgow and led by speculative entrepreneur John Walker, commenced operations with six large new well-smacks designed to prosecute the Faroe fishing in winter as well as summer, and run to the fresh fish markets in the former season at least.[38] Winter voyages were undertaken on an irregular basis by other smack owners also at this time, especially before the advent of the herring fishing and spring line fishing (see below). However, the cod fishing continued to decline slowly but steadily in terms of numbers of vessels engaged (Fig. 26), although production levels remained high (Figs. 31a, 37). It declined rapidly when the herring fishing got under way around 1880.

The decline of the haaf fishing was related to several factors, of which the decline in subsistence agriculture, upon which the 'haaf production system' had been based (Chapter 3), may have been one of the most important. It remained relatively stable till the early 1880s, at which point it became subjected to the influences prevailing in the cod fishing, such as the comparatively greater attraction of the herring fishing using larger decked boats, and employment in the merchant marine. There was also the problem of declining dried fish markets encountered in the cod fishery. In addition, there were two factors peculiar to haaf fishing which contributed to its demise. The first was the great loss of life in the Delting disaster of 1881, in which 58 men were drowned.[39] By contrast with the 1832 disaster, after which the numbers of boats increased, there was little or no replacement of boats, and decline continued during and after the 1880s,[40] further reinforced by another disaster in 1900 involving the loss of four boats.[41] The second factor related to the introduction of trawlers. As in the case of the spring line fishing, the haaf fishing grounds were fished extensively by trawlers from the 1890s onwards, and the dangers of overfishing small areas, together with that of destruction of lines, was a discouraging factor. On the other hand, being a summer fishery geared to dried fish production, it was not in competition with trawl-caught fish at the markets, as occurred with the spring line fishing.

M

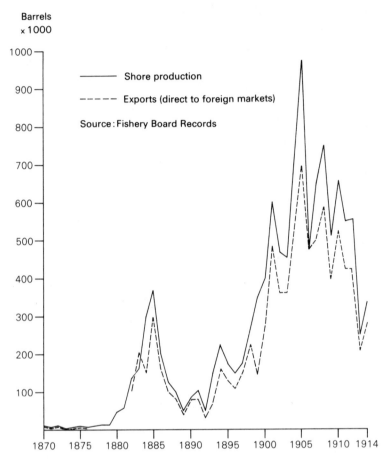

Figure 40. Cured herring

The premise that the comparatively greater attractions of the herring fishing caused the decline of the cod fishing after 1880 is strongly supported by the fact that there was a resurgence in the cod fishing in the late 1880s and early 1890s during the great depression in the herring fishing and herring markets (Figs. 26, 40). However, the fishing collapsed finally in the late 1890s due to successive failures in the Faroe fishing, and unfavourable market conditions. This accounts for the slump in production of fish for drying around 1900 (Fig. 38). In 1900 there were six smacks (Fig. 26); in 1906 the last Shetland-owned smack to take part in the fishing sailed for Faroe with a Faroese crew. As in the 1870s, the cod merchants made some attempt to redress the situation of falling production by importing wet salt cod, this time mainly from Faroe, in the 1880s, 1890s, and early 1900s (Fig. 39). After 1900 most of the fish imports consisted of herring. Refrigeration of bait was even put on trial[42] to replace the well, which was used for carrying fresh bait necessary to improve the chances of making good catches. Generally, however, the pursuit of the cod fishing was passing to Faroe. Beginning in the 1880s and continuing throughout the 1890s and 1900s a large number of the Shetland smacks were sold to Faroe,[43] where the cod fishing industry was being rapidly and effectively developed to challenge the Shetland dried fish trade, with the aid of Shetland skippers and crews.[44] By the end of the period, the Faroese industry was sufficiently developed to bypass Shetland altogether for the fresh fish markets on the British mainland and the more important dried fish markets of Spain.

The basic market influences acting on both the haaf and cod fishery production were thus similar. Shetland's position in the dried fish trade was undermined by the comparative attractions of the fresh fish trade, which derived in part from the better location of the islands in relation to the fresh fish markets in comparison with Faroe, while the Faroese obtained directly from the Shetlanders the skills required both in the cod fishing itself and in preparation of fish for the market. Competition was intensifed by the introduction of a system of differential duties into Spanish import trades,[45] extended in 1882 to the dried fish trade.[46] On the conclusion of commercial treaties between Norway and Denmark (to which Faroe and Iceland belonged) on the one hand, and Spain on the other, Norwegian and Danish dried fish were admitted to the Spanish market at about £2 less duty per ton (£7–9/– compared to £9–7/–) than British dried fish, a large proportion of which came from Shetland.

The potentially adverse effects of this unfair competition were offset to some extent by the development of new markets, the most important of which was the home market.[47] A large proportion of exports went to Britain from the 1870s onwards, probably approximating to the difference between total dried fish production and total recorded exports (Fig. 37). From 1881 onwards, some fish were also shipped coastwise for the Australian market,[48] and in the 1890s the West African market was added to this colonial trade.[49] Around 1890, direct exports to foreign markets virtually ceased, and most dried fish were consigned to Leith or Liverpool (Chapter 6). By this time, the supply of fresh cod and ling to the home market was more remunerative than the dried product, but the fisheries primarily responsible for the production of these were rapidly approaching extinction, and by 1905 Faroese cod had finally gained supremacy over the Scottish product in the Spanish market through the leading port of Bilbao.[50]

As in the case of the dried fish trade, the trades in the various kinds of fresh fish derived from two fisheries which developed with the prime purpose of supplying the fresh fish markets in Britain. These were the haddock and spring line fishings respectively, both being in essence 'winter' fishings, in contrast to the predominantly summer haaf and cod fishings. Indeed the cod fishing interest in the fresh fish market was always largely confined to the final autumn voyage to Iceland and the attempts at winter fishing.

The haddock fishing was a straightforward response to the development of the fresh fish markets in the late 1870s, and was principally an open boat fishery on inshore grounds using so-called 'small lines'*, which consisted of lighter lines with smaller haddock hooks, in contrast to the 'great' or long lines of the haaf fishing. The most important haddock fishing areas tended therefore to be the core area grounds (Chapter 3), with the Burra Haaf and Fetlar Bight predominant. Although 1879 was the first year in which appreciable activity was recorded, a 'few' boats participating,[51] it is likely that the fishing received considerable encouragement to expand with the improvement of steamer services upon the introduction of the West Side steamer service in 1881 (Chapter 6). In 1882 it was recorded[52] that '. . . a larger number of boats . . . were engaged . . . than in former years . . . and there are indications that this industry will in future be more extensively prosecuted . . . than has hitherto been the case'. Unlike the fishings prosecuted by large decked vessels requiring large merchant capital investment, the haddock fishery using open boats was begun by the capital investment of the fishermen themselves, and right from the beginning agreements were made between the fishermen and merchants about the beginning of November on the price to be paid to the fishermen, the merchants being in the main the same firms as those engaged in cod fishing and herring curing, with a few exclusively herring curers as well.

By the mid-1880s, haddock production (Fig. 38) had reached levels of between 20,000 and 30,000 hundredweights of wet fish per annum, at which level it tended to remain throughout the period, punctuated by fairly sharp fluctuations from season to season caused mainly by the exigencies of the fishing itself, the haddock fishing being noted for the variations in abundance of the species on the grounds, and the dangers of constant interruptions by bad weather as a result of fishing with open boats in winter conditions. In 1887 there occurred the most serious disaster in connection with this fishery, when 17 men were lost on the West Side in a sudden gale accompanied by snow early in December.[53]

Apart from the effects of the weather on landings, there is frequent contemporary reference to the depredations of trawlers. The first trawlers appeared on the rich grounds of the Burra Haaf in 1892,[54] heralding a long period of numerous disputes between the haddock fishermen and the trawlermen.[55] Although the fishermen alleged that the trawlers were overfishing the grounds, the general high level of haddock landings tends to negate this contention, at least as it applies to the long term. The most immediate danger was rather the destruction of lines by trawls being dragged over them. Nevertheless, the intricate relationships between the distribution of fish and ground conditions undoubtedly led to severe small-scale disruption of the haddock fishing on some grounds through overfishing. By 1909 there were some 600 men at the haddock fishing.[56] In the previous year the first decked motor fishing boat was introduced,[57] and by 1910 there were seven motor boats,[58] which apart from being much safer than the open boats, had greatly increased catching power. The principal centres of this innovation were Scalloway and Burra.

A fact of greater long-term significance for the haddock fishing than weather conditions and overfishing was that it was not in direct competition with the trawling industry at the market. In this it differed from the spring line fishing, which caught the same species as the trawlers, mainly in the form of cod, ling and halibut. Unlike the haddock fishing, the spring line fishing was not a direct consequence of the attractions of the fresh fish trade as such, but owed its initiation indirectly to the establishment of the herring industry. This was brought about by the fact that the large decked luggers used for the herring fishing, and introduced from 1876 onwards, were used during the spring season for great line fishing. In a sense this was an extension of the traditional haaf fishing into the winter season, insofar as the purpose was to catch the same types of fish — cod and ling — and the fishing was located predominantly on the same grounds around the northern half of the archipelago, based on such ports as Baltasound and Ronas Voe and North Roe in north Northmavine. The fishing was also joined by a few of the cod smacks, and in its business organisation resembled the cod fishing rather than the haaf or herring fishings, in that the boats fished for merchants. For example, in 1886 Hay and Co. had 9 boats fishing for them, Richmond & Co. (one of the leading Scottish herring firms) had 18, John Robertson Jr. 5, Garriock & Co. 6, and William Thomson of Scarpness 5, including 3 based at Lerwick and 2 at Sandwick.[59]

In the mid-1880s the merchants engaged in the spring line fishing began buying from Swedish line boats as well, based on such centres as Baltasound, Westsandwick and North Roe.[60] A few boats from the east coast of Britain as far south as South Shields (usually steam liners: Richmond & Co. introduced the first steam liner in 1885)[61] also landed their catches in Shetland. The spring line fishing had the great advantage that the main products, cod and ling, could be used for the dried fish trade, but this proved insufficient to offset the major disadvantage of competition with trawlers, due to the insecure position of the dried fish market itself. The most profitable item from the fishery was the highly valued halibut, sold iced to English markets in London, Leeds and Birmingham, and sent across to France also in the early 1880s.[62] The decline in halibut landings (Fig. 38) reflects fairly accurately the decline in the spring line fishing itself, which by 1904 had shrunk to 'vanishing point'.[63]

Although, as in the case of the haddock fishing, there was competition on the grounds from trawlers, the decline in the spring line fishing, especially after 1895, was almost certainly influenced much more by the competition of trawl-caught fish in the markets, as these could be brought directly and hence more economically (and fresher) to the market than the line-caught fish. Consequently the prices fell,[64] and even the Swedes* found it more profitable after the mid-1890s to carry their catches home rather than land them in Shetland. It seems possible that the trawlers caused some damage to the cod fishing grounds, although it is noteworthy that this did not kill the Faroese industry when trawling on a big scale commenced round Faroe after 1900. A northward movement in the distribution of cod due to physical environmental factors may also have played a part.[65]

The principal market for fresh fish was Aberdeen, the usual port of consignment, both for haddocks and for cod, ling and halibut. From there the fish were consigned by rail to various southern markets. In the case of the high-value halibut this market was mainly, as noted, in the large cities of the Midlands and South of England, with small quantities being exported to France. As these markets declined, the main market, and the most resilient, proved to be haddock. A large proportion of the haddocks were sold for smoking purposes on arrival at Aberdeen, while a considerable fresh fish market became established in Glasgow.[66] There were often difficulties of supply and demand, imbalances which could be particularly severe at times and which lay behind the formation of a co-operative marketing organisation by the Burra fishermen in the years immediately preceding the outbreak of war in 1914. These problems were not satisfactorily resolved until agents for the Glasgow market were established in Shetland in the inter-war period.[67]

By the early 1870s the herring fishing in Shetland had shrunk to near-vanishing point (Chapter 4), and in 1875 *The Shetland Times* was advocating another trial of the fishery.[68] The interests of merchants and fishermen began to turn to the industry in the second half of the decade, prompted — significantly — by the fishermen as much as by the merchants. The first two fully decked luggers were brought from Scotland in 1876, including one for a Burra crew,[69] and the success of this venture encouraged a steady investment in these boats from that time forward (Fig. 42a). The boats were generally owned on a share basis and usually bought initially by the merchants. By the adoption of the half-catch* system whereby the merchant bought the boat and maintained it, receiving half the value of the catch while the other half was shared among the crew, fishermen were enabled in successful seasons to accumulate sufficient capital to buy the boats, although as often as not a certain proportion of shares would remain in the hands of the merchant, who became known as a 'sleeping partner'. If the curer bought the boat, the fishermen were obliged to fish for him till the boat was paid off. Otherwise they could fish to whichever curer they pleased, an agreement being made between curer and crew at the beginning of the season stipulating prices. A settling* was made between the parties after the end of the season in October or November.

The merchants involved were the same large family firms as in the cod industry (Chapter 4), although as the industry expanded, many smaller merchants and shopkeepers invested in herring boats. Thus the financial structure of the herring fishing was securely based in the economic structure of the islands as a whole. However, generally only the largest firms, such as Hay and Co. and Garriock & Co., entered into the curing sector of the industry.[70] By 1880, the first year of major Scottish participation, about 50 luggers* had been acquired and most of the major Shetland curing firms were in business. The reasons for the expansion of the Scottish east-coast herring fishery into the Shetland area are more fully discussed below. The consequence for the industry in Shetland was its incorporation as a fully integrated part of the Scottish east-coast herring fishery region, based on the overwhelming preponderance of Scottish curing firms,[71] which formed the basis of the industry, both through capital investment and trade expansion. During the period of rapid growth between 1880 and 1886 the Shetland industry kept pace with Scottish developments in investment in boats (Fig. 42a, b).

This period of growth was followed by a slump which lasted from 1887 until 1894. On the Scottish scale this depression was initiated by the problem of over-supply of markets in 1884, a state of affairs which it took the industry several years to recover from. Many speculative curers supported by the banks failed,[72] taking fishermen along with them. In a Shetland context these problems were aggravated to some extent the following year by record fishings. At Baltasound and Cullivoe, for example, thousands of crans of herring had to be dumped or sold for manure because of lack of barrels and salt.[73] However, the depression was prolonged in Shetland by a succession of poor fishings which lowered production levels to those of the 1830s (Figs. 32a, 40). In 1887, after the gluts of 1885 and 1886, the curers delayed making agreements with the fishermen,[74] and continued instability eventually culminated in introduction of the auction system in 1894,[75] which had greater potential for balancing supply and demand, thereby safeguarding the liquidity of the curers. This system did not, however, gain wide acceptance immediately, the old system of agreements persisting alongside it for a number of years until the advent of the steam drifter after 1900.[76]

The 'golden age' of the herring fishing lasted from about 1895 until 1914, a period of some two decades, the first characterised by unprecedented expansion of production (Fig. 40), while the second period was notable for a great drop in production, which nevertheless remained at a relatively high level, accompanied by a technological revolution from sail to steam power for the fishing boats. From around 1895 the Shetland portion of the industry followed the general trend, there being renewed investment in boats (Fig. 42a) and a great expansion in the numbers of herring stations (Fig. 47). The type of boat acquired was a larger class of sailboat than the lugger, although some were lug-rigged and again came from the North-East of Scotland, sometimes new but more often second-hand. The boats were equipped with steam capstans to replace the 'iron-man' formerly used for hauling the nets, while the bush rope* replaced the balk ropes* in the late 1890s in parallel with the adoption of the steam capstan.[77]

The year 1905 was the peak year of the Shetland herring fishing. Over 1,700 boats, of which 400 or so belonged to the islands (Figs. 40, 48), landed the equivalent of approximately one million barrels of cured herring worth nearly a million pounds sterling.[78] In the following year the quantity of herring landed was somewhat less (Fig. 40) and was shared equally between steam and sail boats (Fig. 48b). In the eight years that followed, the steam drifter* swept the board in herring landings, and the numbers of sailboats belonging to Shetland fell sharply (Fig. 48). Local investment in steam drifters began in 1906, but the technological revolution implied by the steam drifter, the capital investment for which was to a considerable degree beyond island resources — at least on a large scale — practically passed the islands by as it was overtaken by that of the much more economical conversion of sailboats* to motor power which got under way after World War I.[79] The advent of the steam drifter with its fast and reliable communication with shore stations, and the preference of the drifter men for places offering the 'day's price' under the auction system,[80] had a powerful centralising influence on the herring industry locally, especially coinciding with the failure of the West Side herring fishing in the years from 1905 onwards. By 1914, therefore, the Shetland industry *per se*, taken as represented by the number of Shetland-owned boats, was in steep decline and on the verge of technological revolution from sail to motor power.

The European market for Scots herring[81] in the period 1880-1914 was dominated by the great, if uncertain, division between the German Empire and the Russian Empire (Fig. 41), with relatively minor outlets to the northern regions of the Austro-Hungarian Empire, notably the cities of Prague and Vienna. With the exception of Hamburg, all of the seven leading ports of entry to which herrings were exported were situated along the southern and eastern coasts of the Baltic. From these ports access could be gained to the principal interior market areas by river, and as time progressed, increasingly by rail also. The importance of river communication was greatest within the confines of the German Empire, where the Elbe connected Hamburg to the leading inland market area of Upper Saxony, the Oder to the market of Silesia via Stettin, and the Vistula to the markets of Eastern Pomerania and East Prussia via Danzig. The Russian market opened up as rail links were extended eastwards from the eastern Baltic ports. Despite its position in East Prussia, Königsberg was one of the leading ports for the Russian market, herring finding its way by rail to White Russia and the Ukraine as far as Kiev and Odessa. The major ports of Libau, Riga and St. Petersburg developed as herring outlets in the second phase of market expansion beginning in the later 1890s. Their importance was based partly on their connections with their immediate hinterlands and increasingly on their rail connections with Russia itself. By the end of the period, quantities of herring from these ports were penetrating the great heartland of the Russian Empire beyond the Urals, into Siberia, the desert areas of the south, and even to the far-eastern coasts — to towns such as Tomsk, Charkow, Tashkent and Vladivostok.[82] Finally, from the 1890s onwards, a growing market became established in America, encouraged by the migration of large numbers of German-speaking people in particular to the United States.[83]

The structure of trade links consisted of three parts.[84] At the production

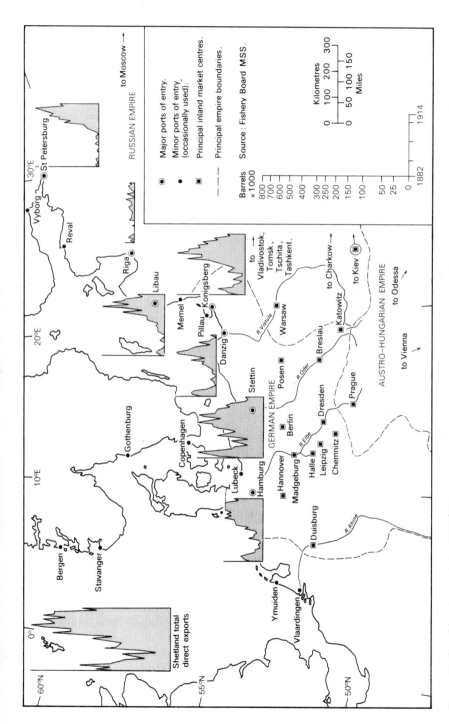

Figure 41. Cured herring markets, 1882-1914

end were the curers, who were responsible for the processing and export of the herring through shipping agents to the import agents at the market end of the trade systems. These import agents constituted the second link, and were responsible for conducting the sale of herring to the buyers, who came from the consuming centres.

The curers, as we saw, were largely responsible for the finance of the fishing industry itself as well as the curing. They were backed by the banks, and although there were a number of large firms, the basis of the industry was a large number of small family firms. The larger firms, especially among the Scottish curers, usually had several stations placed to take advantage of the East Coast, West Coast and Shetland fishings. Some curers, including those belonging to Shetland, had stations placed to take advantage of both early and late fishings. Although the majority of curers were based on the east coast of Scotland, there were also a number from East Anglia and even one or two from Germany and Holland.[85]

The herring were transported to the market ports mainly by steamship, although there was a substantial number of sailing craft involved also, especially in the 1880s (Chapter 6). At market, the herring were placed in the hands of the import agents, who stored them in special warehouses near their points of landing. The number of import agents[86] in the seven major ports of entry varied from five or six in less important ports such as Riga to as many as eighteen to twenty in the leading port of Libau during its heyday in the 1900s and early 1910s. The agents were often Jewish, particularly in the ports of the Russian Empire, and were enterprising men. Those in Libau, for example, were responsible for blocking the import of herring via Archangel, where it had been allowed in free of duty in 1905 and 1906, and their enterprise seems to have been largely responsible for Libau's pre-eminence as a herring centre.[87]

Although the importers had direct connections with the curers, a substantial part of their business was of a speculative nature. Their action as speculators was chiefly responsible for the disastrous consequences for importers and buyers at the market in 1907, when good demand the previous season pushed up prices quoted by the Scottish c.i.f.* agents beyond the capacity of the demand to support these prices when confronted by a very heavy fishing in the 1907 season.[88]

The buyers came mainly from inland centres of consumption (Fig. 41), some being also import agents operating in the coastal towns, while the majority dealt through import agents without taking part in the import business themselves. The buying of herring generally constituted only a small part of their business, and there were often a surprisingly large number of them, ranging up to fifteen in Breslau, for example, which was the distribution centre for Posen, Upper Silesia and West Russia. Many of the buyers were undoubtedly retailers also, and if they were not, the herring was resold to retailers for sale to the town-dwellers and peasants.[89]

The detailed operations of the market system were complex, but were affected by four main sets of factors — physical, quality, economic, and speculative — all to some extent interdependent, and of varying relative importance in the several market areas at different times.[90]

Physical factors consisted of location and climate. The location of the main German market areas in relation to the rivers Elbe and Oder in particular favoured the early development of these areas due to the facility and cheapness of transport by large barges carrying up to 2,000 barrels of herring each. During the early phase of development, prior to the mid-1890s, the cost of rail charges and absence of a well-developed rail network tended to discourage the development of the Russian markets, which depended to a much larger extent on rail connections in the absence of suitable river links from the ports of entry. In Germany rail transport was favoured for good-quality herring from the early fishing which, because of keen demand and higher prices, could better withstand higher transport costs.[91] The major disadvantage of the rivers occurred in seasons where early freezing impeded transport, necessitating greater use of rail, which could be financially ruinous in transporting the lower-value end of season products. The other climatic influence, of perhaps greater importance, was summer heat, which caused rapid deterioration of even the more carefully cured herrings, remedied to some extent by construction of special insulated warehouses in some of the ports, such as St. Petersburg.[92]

Broadly speaking, determination of quality was governed by the kind of herring — whether it was early*, large*, full* or spent*, which depended on the fishery from which it was derived, the quality and degree of salting, and the quality of packing. To ensure adequate marketing standards, the Fishery Board for Scotland had introduced early in the nineteenth century a system of branding herring barrels* to act as a guarantee of the quality, related to the kind of herring and the degree of salting. The best-quality herring received the Crown Brand*, upon which the reputation of the Scottish herring industry as the foremost in Europe rested, in spite of the fact that only a small proportion of the total exports were inspected by the Board officer. This was supplemented by a variety of other brands (Large Fulls*, Spents*, etc.), and individual curers had in addition their own marks. In the towns of Saxony, for example, market preference was for Shetland herrings. A watch was kept on the quality of the brand by the Chief Inspector of Fisheries, who after 1900 made periodic visits to the market towns to inspect the Scottish herrings.[93]

The problem of poor-quality cure was to varying degrees prevalent, especially in the 1880s and 1890s, encouraged by the speculative nature of the trade and the keen demand. Nonetheless the all-round quality of Scottish herrings secured for them a leading place in the herring markets as a whole, and there were frequent attempts at imitation, ranging from official visits of the Norwegian Inspectorate of Fisheries in order to ascertain the factors contributing to Scottish success,[94] to the extensive use of imitation Crown Brands on barrels of herring from other countries on sale in the same markets.[95] As in the case of the dried fish market in the eighteenth century, there were different requirements for salting in different markets. The German markets again preferred a well-salted product, whereas the Russian demand was for a lightly salted cure, which led to endless problems of deterioration through the inability of such herring to withstand the heat of summer, despite the provision of elaborate ice-houses in which to store the herring barrels in places such as St. Petersburg. During the initial process of gutting and packing, absorption of the brine by the herring, and settling of herring in the barrels, made it necessary for the barrels to be reopened and repacked after a certain time had elapsed. They were then ready for export. In the Russian market, however, the practice arose of repacking or 'bracking' the barrels yet again on arrival in the port of entry in order, it was alleged, to check on, and maintain, quality. This compounded the difficulties and delays caused by inadequate quay space and storage facilities.[96]

The market system was subject, thirdly, to influences deriving from economic conditions in the peasant communities upon which the eastern European economy was based, and the role of products competing with herring in the market. Above all, the market depended on the quality of the harvest. In the German markets of Saxony and Silesia demand was governed to a large extent by the success of the potato harvest, as herring and potatoes were a favourite dish, and potatoes were also used to pay for herring consumed. In the Russian market the grain harvest was probably of greater importance. Thus, for example, the famine in the Volga lands in 1906 adversely affected the market.[97] In Russian markets also, the production of timber, flax and other products could affect the market through their influence on general economic prosperity. These, together with harvest products, were influenced greatly by climate. The products in competition with herring were mainly salt beef, pork and vegetables, and in years in which production of these commodities was high, the market tended to ease.

Herring market conditions were influenced, finally, by individual speculative actions based upon judgement of these economic factors. The effects of speculation contributed towards supply-demand imbalances in most major crises in the industry prior to 1914. This is not to say speculation was unnecessary as a component of the trade system. On the contrary it was essential, especially for the import agents, to have considerable stocks readily available to supply buyers from the interior at short notice, an operation which not infrequently put them at risk, especially if other unsettling factors such as war and revolution were acting on the market. Good examples of this were the Russo-Japanese War of 1904-1905, which caused considerable uncertainty in herring markets,[98] and the Peasant Revolution in Russia in 1906, during which the import agents in the Baltic ports were reluctant to sell herring to the buyers, who tended for obvious reasons to be dilatory in their payments.[99] Speculation of another order was at work in the crises of 1884-86 and 1907, however, which was largely precipitated, in the first case, by the curers starting the fishing too early and flooding the market with immature and poor-quality fish, which seriously undermined confidence.[100] In the 1907 case the crises arose through import agents buying up large quantities of herring at too high a price early in the season, and finding them unsaleable when supply reached high levels in the late part of the season, with disastrous consequences for themselves and the buyers, especially in eastern Baltic ports such as Danzig.[101]

The overall development of the herring trade between 1880 and 1914 is summarised in Figs. 40 and 41. The two great phases in production expansion took place in the period 1880-1885 and 1895-1905, and the level of exports during these two periods was a direct consequence of the increased investment in the fishing and curing, supported by continuous expansion of demand. Although the great slump between 1886 and 1894 was sparked off by the effects of speculation on the Scottish industry as a whole, the dominant factor proved to be physical environmental influences causing decline in herring stocks. The relative greatness of the second phase of expansion compared to the first was the result of greater catching power provided by a greater number of boats, both in the Shetland-owned section of the industry and in the total number of outside vessels engaging in the fishery. This was aided by technological innovation which in the Shetland case took the form of adoption of larger sailboats and the introduction of the steam capstan, while the overall pattern was strongly influenced by the introduction of the steam drifter on a large scale in the years after 1900. The final decline was the result of several factors, including the decline in the number of vessels as a whole, a steep decline in participation by Shetland vessels as the economic advantages of the steam drifter became fully apparent (Fig. 42a, b), and the failure of the West Side herring fishing. It thus emerges that variations in production superimposed on a pattern of continuously increasing demand were the most important influences in determining the overall volume of herring exports.

In the case of market developments, there was a striking difference between the two major markets of the German and Russian Empires respectively. The pattern in the German market reflected the overall production pattern described above. However, the second phase of expansion in the market was tempered by the rise of competition through the establishment of a native German herring fishing industry on a large scale beginning in the 1890s. In contrast, the relatively less important Russian market of the 1880s and 1890s continued to expand enormously in the 1900s and eventually by 1912 had become the leading market (Fig. 41) despite an increase in duty of about 400 per cent between the early 1880s and 1914, by which time the duty on a barrel of herring was equal to the market value.[102] This was no doubt due in part to the efforts of the Jewish import agents, notably in Libau. It was due no less to the opening up of Russia by railway construction in the 1890s and 1900s, which made direct transit from the eastern Baltic ports to more and more new markets possible, rather than access via Germany. This is

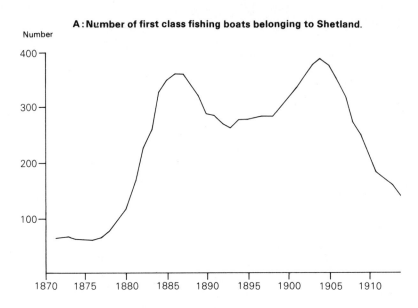

Source: Fishery Board Records.

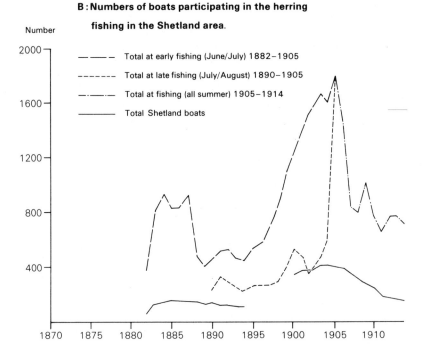

Figure 42. Fishing boats

strikingly shown by the fact that the Prussian port of Königsberg followed the Russian rather than the German pattern in the development of herring imports because its connections were mainly by rail to Russian markets.

After 1900 competition with Norwegian, Swedish, German and Dutch herring became keener in both empires, although the Scottish cure generally succeeded in holding its own.[103] The market in Austria-Hungary remained comparatively small, and it was often urged that contacts should be improved as it was capable of considerable development. For example, in 1896 the Fishery Board intimated the willingness of the Anglo-Austrian Bank of Vienna and London to act as agents for Scottish curers in this market.[104] The American market first became of importance in the 1890s, although Shetland herring were sent there intermittently to begin with, usually via Glasgow, but from 1907 via Liverpool also.[105] The total capacity of this market exceeded 100,000 barrels for the first time in the early 1910s.

The decline of the haaf fishery led to the extinction of the import trade in open boats from Norway in the early 1860s (Chapter 4), while the decline of the cod fishery was associated with the decline in the import of cod smacks, discussed in Chapter 6. The most notable development in boat imports accompanied the rise of the herring industry, the boats for which came almost entirely from the east coast of Scotland, especially the Moray Firth area. There were in fact two distinct phases in this trade, which was generally conducted between the Shetland fishermen on the one hand and the fishermen and boatbuilders of the Moray Firth area on the other. The first occupied the period 1875-1885 and was that of the import of fully decked lug-rigged* boats generally from 30 to 40 feet of keel. This phase corresponds roughly to the first phase of expansion in the herring industry and investment in herring boats (Fig. 42a, b), and was followed by a second phase lasting from around 1895 until about 1905. During this period concentration was on larger boats of 40 to 60 feet of keel, generally the 'fifie'* and 'zulu'* models, again acquired both new and second-hand mainly from the ports of North-East Scotland. Most of these second-generation sailboats were fitted with steam capstans, and those which did not go out of use with the advent of the steam drifter were gradually converted to motor power between the wars.[106]

During the period a substantial number of the smaller class of decked boat were built in Shetland, mainly by Hay & Co., who began building them in 1878, and by 1886 had built 34.[107] Building of the larger class of boat was not frequently undertaken, although some were constructed in Lerwick and Sandwick. After 1905, the innovations in the haddock fishing led from 1909 onwards to the building of the new class of decked haddock boats, which were built mainly in Burra and at Scalloway to a design based on the Shetland model*, fully decked and in the 30 to 40 feet of keel range. These boats were motor-powered and designed for the herring and haddock fishing, also being used for other purposes, such as line fishing for halibut.[108] Besides the building of large decked fishing boats, the development of the haddock fishing in particular stimulated the building of small, open 'haddock' boats*. The most important boat-building centres generally were in the haddock fishing areas of Scalloway, Burra and Lerwick, with other boatbuilders in rural areas such as Unst, Whalsay and Sandwick. This sector of the industry, which, in common with the other sectors, required the import of high-quality timber via Scotland, declined in part probably because of the underlying decline of open boat fishing as first the herring fishing and then the motor haddock boats were developed. By 1894, however, Shetland was one of the leading districts in Scotland for the building of open boats.[109]

The second major sector of the import trade consisted of timber, including staves. The timber was of course used for many purposes including house-building and boat-building, but a large proportion was used for the building of herring stations. The first phase of expansion in timber imports in the 1880s coincides with the development of herring stations all round the coasts, while the second in the early 1900s reflects the great expansion in the number of stations during this phase of growth in the herring industry. The final peak in the late 1900s and early 1910s reflects the wave of building of herring stations in Lerwick and Bressay as the herring industry became centralised in this area (Fig. 43a, b).

The trend of timber imports was reflected by that for staves until about 1910, after which the import of staves fell in reaction to the decline in herring landings. The history of timber imports is perhaps paradoxically reflected more precisely in the graph for the construction of barrels and half-barrels (Fig. 43b). This apparent paradox is an important indication of the differing character of the two phases of the herring boom. In the first, there was much greater emphasis on the carriage of salt and barrels from the curers' other stations on the east coast of Scotland, whereas in the second phase two barrel factories were established in Lerwick, the first in 1900 and the second in 1910, so that by the end of the period local barrel construction practically satisfied the demand for barrels for the herring exports (Fig. 43a, b).

Most of the timber imported was sawn timber, and both timber and staves came mainly from Norway and Sweden*, with a few cargoes from Russian ports such as Memel and Archangel.[110] Unfortunately detailed research into the ports of origin is extremely difficult, as records of this nature relate to arrivals and sailings of ships rather than cargo content.

There remain for consideration two important imports, salt and ice, the former used in dried fish and cured herring production, and the latter in the export of fresh fish. Unfortunately statistics are defective in coverage, both in time and quality. However, it is true to say in the case of salt imports that the patterns tended to reflect the two distinct phases in the development of the herring industry rather than those in the dried fish trade. During the first phase until the early 1890s, salt for both types of production was imported from Liverpool and directly from abroad (Fig. 39). After the mid-1890s,

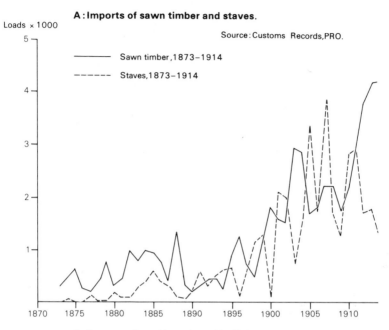

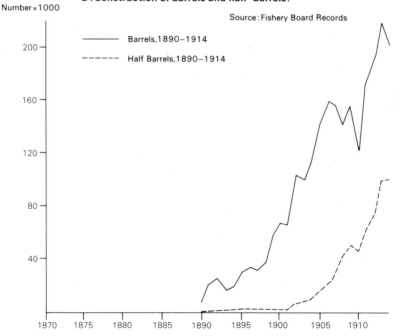

Figure 43. Timber and barrels

N

although most of the increased requirements of salt continued to be met from Liverpool, the declining dried fish trade was more than compensated for by the increase in the cured herring trade, and cargoes were also from time to time imported direct from Spain, Portugal and Italy.

The imports of ice from Norway began in the 1870s on a small scale, attaining much larger proportions in the 1880s with the development of the spring line fishery, and falling off in parallel with the decline of this fishery in the 1890s. Although records do not extend beyond 1899 (Fig. 39), ice imports continued beyond that date. Before 1900 most of the ice required came from ports in south-eastern Norway, such as Drobak, Drammen, Porsgrund, Kragero, Langesund and Mandal, and was often carried by Shetland smacks.[111] In sufficiently cold winters it was on occasion produced locally from frozen lochs, but after 1900 an increasing proportion was brought coastwise from ports with ice-plants such as Peterhead.[112]

Livestock and Hosiery

As discussed in the previous chapter, by 1870 a substantial amount of agricultural improvement had taken place, principally through the abolition of runrig and its substitution by separate small croft holdings, and in the laying out of large farms in those areas which were physically suited best to farming.

After 1870, the decline of subsistence agriculture can unfortunately by its very nature not be directly studied from statistics. Nevertheless there are some important indicators. One of these is the pattern of decline of the population, which was parallelled by the declining acreages of the principal subsistence crops of barley (bere)*, oats and potatoes (Fig. 44). Although detail fluctuations may be due to unreliable statistics, the overall trend is undeniable. That the subsistence type of economy was in decline is also suggested by a great increase in the use of bakers' bread in the 1870s,[113] although this was no doubt partly also due to the growth of Lerwick. Meanwhile, the relatively greater rate of decline in bere acreages infers a greater dependence on the potato crop, borne out by the statement made in 1898 that the potato crop was much more important than meal for subsistence.[114] The decline in the numbers of pigs and milking cattle (Fig. 46) is further evidence of the waning of subsistence agriculture.

In view of the lack of precision of the agricultural statistics,[115] perhaps the most important indicator of all is the decreasing significance of poor harvests. Although a prolonged series of bad years, such as occurred in the 1830s and 1840s, did not recur, poor harvests were by no means infrequent. The most serious failure seems to have been in 1869, when the corn was destroyed by hail and gales and the potatoes did not grow well.[116] Again in 1872 much of the potato crop was destroyed by blight, and this, coupled with the failure of the small-scale herring fishing (Chapter 4), presaged 'great hardship' for many small crofters.[117] In 1885 crop failure was wide-

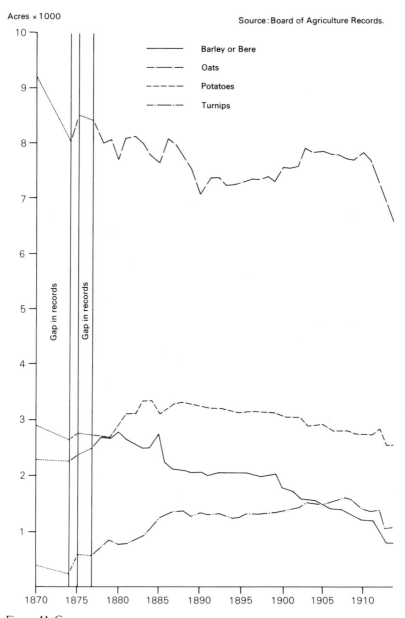

Figure 44. Crop acreages

spread, and a special request for assistance came from Foula, which was particularly hard-hit,[118] although there does not seem to have been large-scale emigration as there was under similar circumstances in Fair Isle in 1863.[119] Finally, in 1902, the poorest harvest for 'a generation' was experienced, and *The Shetland Times* remarked how such a poor harvest was no longer disastrous.[120] While the prosperity of the herring fishing was un-doubtedly the main reason for this state of affairs, the declining population pressure on land resources, greater commercialisation of livestock produc-tion, and in certain areas development of fisheries additional to the herring fishing, all contributed.

Livestock production fell into two main categories, that relying mainly on the arable land of the newly developed crofts and farms, and that from the unimproved hill land. There was a tendency towards the production of cattle on the better-quality and formerly arable land, indicated by an increase in acreages devoted to production of turnips, which were used in cattle rearing (Fig. 44), while the hill land was devoted mainly to raising sheep and ponies. In certain areas, notably on the Garth and Annsbrae estates, better-quality land was also used in sheep production through the laying out of large sheep farms.[121]

The cattle trade had of course become well-established by 1870 (Chapter 4), but it is unfortunately impossible in the absence of reliable statistics to be precise about its rate of expansion. Generally any number from a few hundred to 2,000 might be exported to Aberdeen every year (Fig. 45), depending on the overall quality of the season, which was of course strongly influenced by the weather. Nonetheless there were significant improve-ments. Whereas in 1874 it was noted that there were too many cattle on the land,[122] by 1883 it was observed that Shetland cattle* were being crossed with shorthorns to improve the breed.[123] By the mid-1880s there were small exports from spring cattle sales, as well as the main sales at the end of the summer.[124] In 1912, following the example of the more commercially minded pony-breeding fraternity, the Shetland Cattle Herd Book was estab-lished in order to preserve and improve the breed of Shetland cattle, and this had the effect of increasing cattle prices.[125]

The basis of the Shetland pony* trade from the 1850s onwards was their use in the coal mines (Chapter 4). After 1870 this was supplemented by the export of ponies for pleasure-riding. In order to maintain and develop those aspects of the breed suitable for the coal industry, a stud farm was estab-lished on Bressay and Noss in 1870 by the Marquess of Londonderry, one of the great coal owners. It remained in existence until 1899, during which time it produced hundreds of animals for the mines.[126] In the 1870s demand was so keen that agents travelled the countryside buying every pony 'that could be got', while inferior animals were imported from Faroe and Iceland[127] in the smacks and on the voyages of the *Queen* from Iceland to Granton (Chapter 6). These ponies were fed in Shetland before being re-exported to the south. Indeed in the early 1870s it was remarked that ponies were rather safer than sheep for the farmer.[128] After 1900 the use of machinery was in-creasingly supplanting ponies in the mines, and the market consequently declined, although a few were still being exported for this purpose in 1913.[129] This decline in the market was more than compensated for by the increase in market potential of ponies kept as pets. A shipment — probably the first —

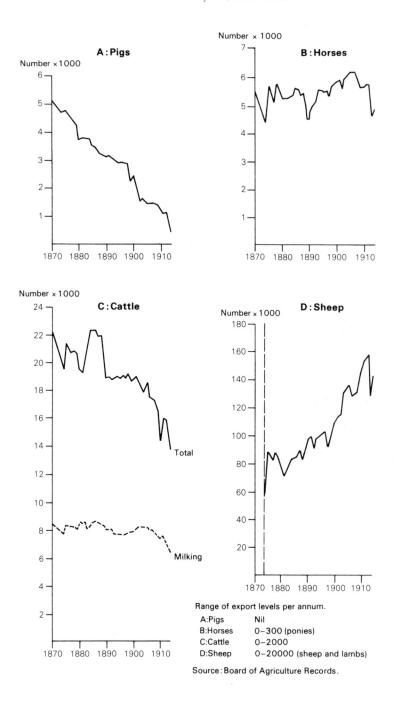

Figure 45. Livestock

was made from Unst to America in 1873,[130] and the American market continued to expand from that time onwards, interest becoming much stronger after 1890, when the Shetland Pony Stud Book was established to maintain the qualities of the breed and safeguard it against the export of the best blood to America.

The export of Shetland sheep* from Shetland was greatly hampered by inattention to the proper care of the animals and the decimation caused by scab (Chapter 4), and notable exports began to occur only in the late 1860s.[131] As in the case of cattle and ponies, imperfect statistics allow only approximate estimates; the numbers varied from a few thousand to figures approaching 20,000 (Fig. 45), depending, among other things, on the weather. The most serious disruption of this kind was in 1912, when tens of thousands of sheep were lost in a severe winter of snow.[132]

The initial development of sheep exports was associated with the introduction during the late 1860s and early 1870s of the first really extensive sheep farming on the Hay estate at Veensgarth and on the Garth estates, which possessed, apart from the farm on Bressay and Noss, five sheep farms laid out under the direction of entrepreneur John Walker, who was factor on the estate.[133] In practice only sheep produced from the sheep farms were exported, and the crofters' sheep and lambs were sold at the local sales.[134] The introduction of sheep farming on a large scale coincided with a period of very low prices from 1867 until 1871, but there were great improvements in 1872 when it was recorded that prices were double what they had been a few years previously due to the introduction of sale by auction.[135]

Although sheep numbers more than doubled in the period, there were obstacles to improvement, the most immediate of which was the regulation of the numbers of stock on the scattalds*. At the beginning of the period these were generally overstocked and run on traditional lines, each township being allocated a share of the scattald expressed as a certain number of livestock. However, the number of animals which each individual crofter could keep was not regulated, with the result that there was no proper control, and many scattalds were overstocked. Serious practical attention was first paid to the division of the commonties among the various proprietors in the early 1860s, and from then on slow and erratic progress was made.[136] However, a large proportion of the commonties remained undivided even in 1914, despite provisions for this in the Crofters' Act. By the end of the period renewed attention was being focused on the possibilities of completing the regulation of the scattalds in view of the importance of the sheep trade and the hosiery industry,[137] which derived much of its wool supply from local sources.

The trade in knitted goods, like the livestock trades, was already well-established by 1870, and exports were valued at £10-12,000 per annum. During the ensuing period, until 1914, the value of the exports rose by approximately three to four times, largely as a result of the continued development of the industry, which, throughout the period, remained a part-time cottage industry employing only female labour, except for the small amount of weaving of Shetland tweed which employed male labour, and which began about 1870 using natural instead of dyed yarn.[138]

The knitwear and weaving trades were operated locally on a basis of barter involving truck, and continued to be so virtually until the end of the period, when the Government enforced the provisions of the Truck Act. Both the traditional merchant class and the shopkeepers were involved in the buying of knitwear, and in Lerwick there was specialisation in the form of draper shops, of which seven or eight held most of the trade.[139] The nature of the cottage industry was such that it was based on processing the wool by carding* and spinning* it into yarn*, and carrying on to the manufacture of completed articles. In short, there was no division of labour, except insofar as Lerwick knitters generally had to buy their own wool in the absence of a sheep stock of their own. It is a measure of the commercialisation of the industry, therefore, that this pattern was beginning to change. The knitwear merchants were, for example, importing Scottish and Yorkshire machine-spun wool by 1870, especially for the use of these Lerwick knitters.[140] However, they would buy only pure Shetland wool goods from the country districts, which relied much more on native wool supplies, and the traditional methods of carding and spinning the yarn at home. Although by 1914 T. M. Adie, one of the leading merchants, had introduced a steam-operated carding machine,[141] by the late 1890s Shetland wool was beginning to be sent for spinning in the Scottish woollen mills.[142]

The principal markets for Shetland goods were in Scotland and England, and exports sent to London merchant houses dealing in the trade.[143] From the beginning of the extensive development of the trade, the principal problem was one of ensuring quality and maintaining the place of the articles in the market against fierce and not infrequently underhand competition. During the 1880s and 1890s in particular, there was a sustained slump in demand due in part to such factors, including underselling.[144] The introduction of the parcel post in 1883 aided development considerably,[145] as it permitted the growth of the private orders sector of the trade between individual knitters and customers independently of the merchant-merchant house organisation. In the words of the report on Highland Home Industries in 1914:[146] 'It would be difficult to find an industry of a similar comparatively small magnitude upon which so many and sustained attacks have been made — some of them insidious, some clumsy, but all tending to diminish the reputation of, and the demand for, the original hosiery'. A second problem, related to imitation, was the maintenance of the intrinsic quality of the products. At this time practically every conceivable item of indoor wear, including underwear, was made, and the merchant houses in London were complaining in 1896 of ill-shaped garments, while discriminating buyers were refusing to buy goods made with machine-spun wool.[147] There thus arose the need to ensure the genuineness of the hand-knitted article, especially in view of the problem of trade misdescription of articles as being

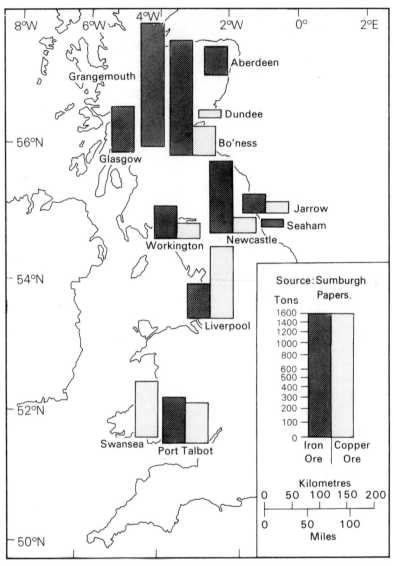

Figure 46. Exports from Sandlodge Mine, 1873-1880

of Shetland manufacture when these were in fact made elsewhere. The
report of 1914 recommended the setting up of a body to supervise the
industry, and look into the advisability of establishing a trade mark. However, in 1914 these problems, though real, were unsolved, and the industry
had done no more than develop, at times rather haphazardly, into an
important but secondary source of income in an economy still dominated by
the fishing industry in general, and the herring trade in particular.

Apart from the development of trade in agricultural and knitwear products, there were a number of short-lived ventures, prompted either by speculatively inspired moves to engage in business, or the need to fulfil short-term requirements for particular commodities. The majority of the commodities involved had initially appeared in the export trade prior to 1870, the most noteworthy being mineral exports, kelp and peats.

The Sandlodge mine was re-opened in 1872, under the auspices of the Sumburgh Estate and John Walker. Between the years 1873 and 1880, the mining operations of the Sumburgh Mining Company resulted in the export of some 10,000 tons of copper and iron ore,[148] principally to the iron and steel and other metal industries situated on the various coalfields of Britain (Fig. 46). The iron ore in particular was of high grade and, containing manganese, was suitable for use in the new Bessemer process for the manufacture of steel.[149] However, even the good market prospects were not sufficient to overcome bad management, particularly insufficient capital investment and delay in the installation of machinery, coupled, as in previous mining ventures, with difficulties in extracting the ore, and labour troubles caused by employing fishermen rather than miners. In 1879, John Walker sold his lease to the Sumburgh Mining Company, and in 1881 the company went into liquidation, 'starved of capital', according to one leading creditor,[150] although it is perhaps significant that a Government investigation in 1914 of mining possibilities suggested that a small mine was possible, which would not be able to carry much capital.[151]

The other mineral ventures were in quarrying, and more ephemeral than the iron-mining venture. In contrast to the resurgence in iron mining, chromate quarrying declined in the 1870s and quarrying operations ceased around 1877,[152] with only the odd cargo sent out thereafter, for example in 1883 and 1888.[153] Quarrying was resumed in 1910, and a cargo was dispatched in 1913. Soapstone or talc was also quarried and exported.[154]

A completely new venture in mineral exploitation began in the mid-1880s, when Hildasay granite was chosen for the new offices of the North of Scotland Bank in Wick.[155] From 1890 until 1894 the quarry was leased to MacDonalds of Aberdeen, a granite firm whose main purpose in starting operations in Shetland was to cope with the very high demand for granite at the time.[156] The first polished monumental stone was completed in 1890,[157] and it is recorded that the lessee of the quarry could hardly get the granite out fast enough to supply his orders. Some of this granite was shipped as ballast on returning wool clippers and found its way as far as Melbourne and Sydney in Australia where it was used as building stone.[158]

As in the case of mineral exploitation, kelp production was rather spasmodic. Around 1870 there was a sizeable export of kelp, and it is recorded in 1872 that in Whalsay 128 tons worth £768 were produced in that year.[159] Thereafter production was not continuous, although encouraged by a price increase in 1905.[160] In contrast to the early nineteenth-century use of kelp in glass manufacture, its chief value from the middle of the nineteenth century onwards was in the manufacture of iodine, where it came into keen competition with Chilean nitrate.[161] Another occasional export, especially in the year round 1900, was peat to Lossiemouth and Inverness,[162] where it was used by the distilleries, as it had been during the 1840s (Chapter 4).

The Communities of Land and·Sea

In 1870 the crofting-fishing system still remained basically intact in both central and peripheral areas. The abolition of the truck system was a starting point for change which of course had an influence on locational patterns as well as relations between merchants and fishermen. It was no longer necessary for the haaf fishermen in particular to remain burdened with debt to his landowner, and in the new economic conditions prevailing the opportunity to take up other forms of employment probably had the greatest effect. In the market economy the part-subsistence and part-commercial haaf production system, unchanged in principle from that of the eighteenth century, was in the weakest position economically, except in the conversion from fishing tenures to truck which in some cases, such as Burra and Whalsay, were little removed from fishing tenures in practice.[163] It was becoming much more efficient to conduct one's material existence by concentrating entirely on commercial production and buying the necessities of life in return.

In the central area, where cod fishing was more important, the position is much less clear, as the cod fishing, although governed by truck also, was not tied locationally to the land, but to the merchants alone. The labour might come from anywhere, although in practice the largest proportion appears to have come from the central zone. It is in this area, however, that the first clear evidence of the operation of locational advantages in production can be detected. The roots of this evolution have already been referred to (Chapter 3) and lie in the development of near-shore fishing and in the cod fishing. Briefly, those areas nearest the rich inshore grounds of the Burra Haaf and Fetlar Bight (which could be fished commercially all year round), and yet sufficiently far away to be free of having their labour drawn into the far haaf fisheries, tended throughout the nineteenth century to specialise more and more in fishing. This was especially so in Burra and Scalloway, and the other small islands in this district.

Even as far back as 1809 the Burra people were reputed to have been rich on the proceeds of fishing, and this West Side* area generally became the leading centre of the cod fishing (Fig. 30) for reasons already enumerated, among which the advantage of being near the principal fishing grounds ranked high on the list (Chapter 4). By the 1870s, therefore, the Scalloway-Burra district, and to a lesser extent Whalsay, developed as fishing communities, specialising in fishing to the increasing exclusion of agricultural activity. They were centres of innovation, leading in the development of the herring fishing by virtue of their traditions, and in the haddock fishing also by their advantageous location close to the rich inshore haddock fishing grounds in the Burra Haaf and Fetlar Bight areas respectively.

The first phase of expansion of the herring fishery, from 1876 until 1885, was characterised by a remarkably widespread acquisition of boats. However, there were certain areas which tended to specialise in the herring fishery, again mainly in the central zone where fisheries tended to be more important overall than agriculture, and again particularly in those areas adjacent to the Burra Haaf and Fetlar Bight, and south of Lerwick, which were also closest to the haddock fishing grounds. There were concentrations of boat ownership in Burra, Scalloway, Whiteness, Sandwick, Lerwick and Whalsay. In the development of the herring fishing the Burra men led the way, acquiring one of the first luggers in 1876, and the proportion of shore owners of boats in Burra tended to be much lower than elsewhere.[164] It was also in Burra that the only true fishing village in Shetland grew up in the 1880s and 1890s. Compared to the 'south end' of the island where the bulk of the population resided, Hamnavoe was more accessible to the fishing grounds. This favourable location, which had previously led to the establishment of a cod fishing station in the pre-1870 era and the setting up of three herring stations in the 1880s, caused a gradual migration of the fishermen from the south end to settle in Hamnavoe as the herring and haddock fishings expanded.

The great depression in the herring fishing in the late 1880s and early 1890s tended to hit the outlying areas hardest, and the centres of innovation — notably Burra, Scalloway and Sandwick — tended to strengthen their position as centres of investment by the fishermen and merchants in new, larger fifies and zulus in the late 1890s.[165] Meanwhile, herring boats gradually disappeared from many of the other areas, notably in outlying districts of the periphery and northern central zones. The position of areas possessing decked boats was further strengthened by their participation in the spring line fishing, in spite of the fact that these boats operated mainly from stations in the northern half of the islands far removed from the home base of the fishermen. Areas such as Burra and Scalloway, where a greater proportion of the tonnage was owned by the fishermen rather than the merchants, found themselves in a stronger position when the spring line fishing began to fail in the 1890s, because of their specialisation in the haddock fishing.

The haddock fishing was fairly widely distributed, especially in the central core areas near the haddock fishing grounds of the Fetlar Bight, Yellsound, east of the south Mainland and the Burra Haaf. In the case of the fresh fish market, however, the availability of steamer connections was of the utmost importance in order to get the fish quickly to market. In the winter months the principal connections were limited to Scalloway on the West Side, and Lerwick on the East Side — the internal steamer connection from Lerwick northwards being apparently often inconvenient for easy access to the 'south' steamer. Consequently, in those areas least well situated for steamer connections the fishing went into decline quite early, a good example being Yell and the northern parts of Mainland.[166] Prices paid in these areas were generally only 50 to 60 per cent of those paid at the main centres of Lerwick and Scalloway.[167] Those areas which were blessed by proximity to the grounds and strong fishing traditions were again favoured, and by the early 1900s the haddock fishing had become concentrated mainly in the Lerwick and Whalsay districts, Scalloway and Burra. The Burra Haaf was by far the richest fishing area.[168] Small open boats were still retained (the 'haddock boats,*'), and the herring boats* were laid up in winter.

By the end of the period, therefore, Burra had emerged as the leading fishing district in Shetland, with Scalloway, Whalsay and Lerwick of lesser but significant importance. In addition, Sandwick and Whiteness were important herring localities, but tended to decline with the decline of the sailboats in the period 1905-1914. It was from Burra that boats first ventured to the English herring fishing (as early as 1884),[169] and West Coast herring fishing, and there the first fully decked motor haddock boats began to be acquired from 1909 onwards.[170] The influence of proximity and strong community traditions arising out of early nineteenth-century economic conditions had combined in the evolution of the major fishing areas. However, rather strikingly and for the first time, the fishing areas had become separated from the trade points, a characteristic feature of the modern internal trade pattern. The contributory factors lay partly in the development of the herring fishing industry and partly in the evolution of 'central place'* forces independently of these.

At first the influence of the herring fishing was exerted through the need for herring stations to be sited as near to the fishing grounds as possible (Fig. 47), as the method of herring fishing with sailboats consisted of fishing at night and bringing the herring ashore early in the morning while still fresh, so that gutting and the initial process of curing could get under way without delay. The importance of proximity is well illustrated by the case of Mid Yell, which was virtually abandoned during the depression of 1887-1894 in favour of nearer stations such as Cullivoe and Uyeasound.[171] Any delay in landing the herring resulted in deterioration and ultimately in inferior quality of cure. The herring fishing grounds around the islands were generally offshore, ranging in distance up to forty miles, and thus the pattern of station location was peripheral. However, herring stations seldom occupied the same sites as haaf stations due to the fact that the fully decked sailboats required proper harbour facilities. Thus fishing stations were established in a series of small harbours in the peripheral areas, including new centres such as Baltasound in Unst, Cullivoe in Yell, West Burrafirth, Hildasay and Cumlewick (where the pier at Broonie's Taing was built) (Fig. 47).

All the curing operations were carried out on the herring station, including gutting and packing and making barrels. Stations were complete with living accommodation for the shore-workers (gutters and coopers), and cargoes of cured herring were taken direct from the curing stations to market

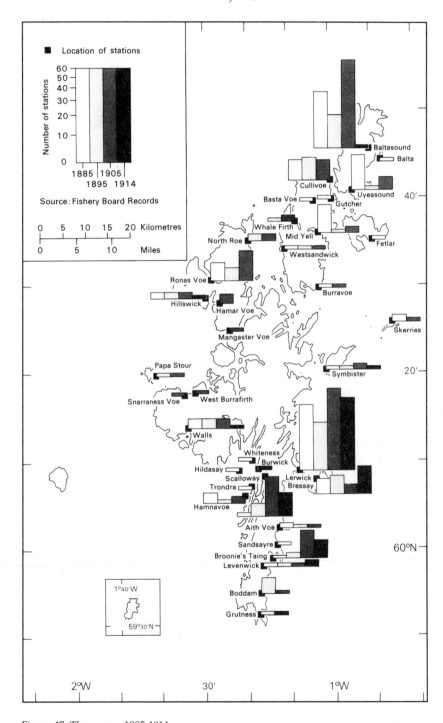

Figure 47. The curers, 1885-1914

in the vessels which brought in fish stock (salt, staves, barrels) direct to the station. However, although there were herring stations in the older trade centres such as Hillswick, Uyeasound, Burravoe and Lerwick, the herring stations did not attract new trade. It was only in centres otherwise favoured that the herring industry encouraged further development of services, establishment of manure and barrel factories being for example confined to Lerwick and Bressay. Most of the other stations, notably Baltasound, with its early summer fishing population of 10,000 in the early 1900s,[172] were too peripheral, and were hives of activity in the summer-time only, being vacated at the end of the fishing season.

Upon this pattern was superimposed the division of the herring fishing into early and late seasons. The early season, which lasted from May until the beginning of July, concentrated on fishing the Atlanto-Scandian herring stock off the west and north-west coasts from stations on the West Side, including Scalloway and Burra. Hillswick, Hamar Voe and Ronas Voe were the most important Northmavine stations, while centres in the North Isles included Mid Yell, Cullivoe, Uyeasound and, most important of 'all, Baltasound.[173] It was this fishing which attracted the great numbers of Scottish and English fishing vessels to the islands, and which provided the impetus for the Scots curers to catch the early continental herring markets with prime quality early Shetland herring — the Large Fulls so esteemed in the towns of Saxony and Silesia. Most of these 'stranger boats'* left at the end of this fishing. The late herring fishing began about the middle of July and lasted until the end of August or beginning of September. Many of the herring stations on the West Side were vacated and the fishing concentrated on the East Side grounds (Fig. 47), Lerwick and Broonie's Taing being perhaps the most important centres, although as the fishing moved south to the grounds east of Fitful and Fair Isle, it could be equally convenient to land catches in Scalloway.

In 1905, the peak year of herring landings, the West Side fishing un-accountably failed. At present we do not know the reasons for this, although contemporary opinion blamed the pollution caused by the whaling stations established in 1903. However, it is equally likely that hydrographical reasons were reponsible. Many West Side centres had disappeared by 1914, notably Ronas Voe and Baltasound, and with them the distinction between early* and late* herring fishings, a distinction further blurred by the advent of the steam drifter* capable of steaming long distances from West Side grounds to Lerwick in the course of a single night's fishing.[174]

The first year in which the steam drifter was much in evidence in the Shetland fishing was 1900,[175] and the numbers increased rapidly until by 1914 by far the greater proportion of the herring catch was being landed from drifters (Fig. 48b), although there was little local investment in steam drifters at this time. Drifter catches fetched higher prices than sailboat catches, as these could be landed more regularly and more quickly, thus being in a fresher state. The drifters had sufficient speed and independence of weather

A : Number of steam fishing vessels other than trawlers in the Scottish fishing fleet, 1892–1912.

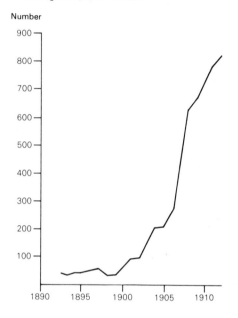

B:Division by steam and sail of herring taken by net, 1906 –1914.

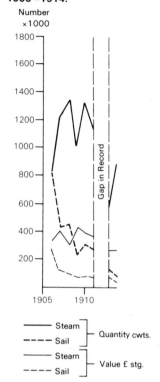

C:Number of boats built in Shetland, 1893–1914.

——— 1st Class (over 30ft keel).

··········· 2nd Class (over 18ft keel).

– – – 3rd Class (under 18ft keel).

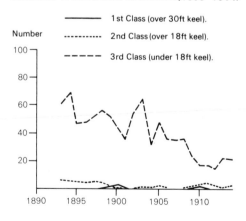

D:Number of first class boats in the Scottish fisheries, 1902–1912.

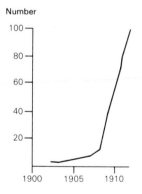

Source:Fishery Board Records.

Figure 48. Changes in the fishing fleet

conditions not to be tied to the nearest herring stations, as the sailboats were. They tended therefore to prefer stations offering the 'day's price' under the new auction system established at Lerwick and Baltasound in 1894, rather than the old-fashioned curers' agreements with their fixed prices. The economics of scale in the supply of coal bunkers and water to such large numbers of vessels also dictated relatively few centres, and thus numerous small outlying stations soon declined and were closed. The failure of the West Side fishing from 1905 onwards also dealt a severe blow to the West Side and North Isles centres, and by 1914 the industry had become centred mainly on Lerwick, the number of stations in Lerwick and Bressay expanding rapidly between 1905 and 1914 (Fig. 47), while the harbour was dotted with coal hulks. The supply of coal was a considerable trade in itself, mainly in the hands of local firms such as Hay & Co. and J. W. Robertson.

The centralising forces apparent in the herring and haddock fishing were strongly reinforced by the development of communications on land and sea. The importance of land communications dated back to 1847-1851 when the main road arteries were built (Chapter 6), and the importance of the roads increased mainly as a result of the growth of livestock sales at various centrally located places throughout the countryside, including Ollaberry, Weisdale, Tresta, Mavis Grind, Voe, Scalloway and Dunrossness, as well as Lerwick.[176] This importance was recognised in the 1860s by the procurement of the Zetland Roads Act and the establishment of the Shetland Road Trustees in 1868 to maintain and improve the road network. However, township road construction did not receive a boost until the establishment of Zetland County Council in 1890 (Chapter 6). Steamship services were pioneered by the Shetland Islands' Steam Navigation Company's North Isles service begun in 1868, and the West Side service begun by the North Company in 1881, both of which took part in the herring carrying trade (Chapter 6).

Only two places really developed as central points providing a wide range of services with extensive retailing: Lerwick and Scalloway. This is strikingly demonstrated by the population trends, which parallel those for the developing fishing communities of Burra and Whalsay.[177] Meanwhile, the other trade points, both in the peripheral and central zones, tended to retain their importance as local centres with general merchants' establishments catering for retail needs and often buying local produce, such as fish, eggs, livestock and hosiery.

The dynamic aspects of location in the development of internal trade were parallelled in the external trade patterns after 1870. Shetland, in its competition with other fishing areas, had the advantage of being located centrally in the northern North Sea fishing grounds. This advantage was enhanced by the improved speed and reliability of the steamer services (Chapter 6).

In the case of the dried fish trade, the combination of changes from cod and haaf fishing aimed at the dried fish market to spring line and haddock fishing designed for the fresh fish market, plus the great swing from the traditional first two to the herring fishing, partly explains the declining competitiveness of Shetland in relation to the Faroe Islands. Faroe was of course nearer the principal cod fishing grounds, just as Shetland was in the centre of the haddock fishing grounds. This favoured the expansion of the Faroese industry, and Faroese dried salt cod succeeded in virtually ousting the Scottish product (a large proportion of which was derived from Shetland) from the traditional Spanish market in the early 1900s.[178] Meanwhile, the great development and prosperity of the herring industry tended to mask the basic weakness of the fresh fish trade. Whereas Faroe was really too far away from the markets for fresh fish in Britain, using sail-powered boats and in the absence of a regular steam service to this market, Shetland was just close enough, at least in good fishing seasons, to make the fresh fish markets an economic proposition in conjunction with the herring trade, despite the fact that the prices obtained in Shetland were only about one-third of those obtained in Aberdeen.[179] Also, with the advent of trawling, great line* fishing for the fresh fish market became uneconomic both in Faroe and Shetland. The haddock fishing was, as previously noted, not in direct competition with the trawling industry, and maintained its position, despite the alleged problems of destruction of haddock fishing grounds by trawlers.

The herring industry was also influenced by locational factors. The initial development of the industry was in large measure due to changes in the location of the herring shoals off the east coast of Scotland. During the 1870s in particular, there appears to have been a movement of herring offshore under the influence of physical factors,[180] which encouraged investment in larger boats capable of making longer voyages.[181] The first appreciable number of these Scottish craft fishing for Shetland herring appeared in 1875.[182] Once established as a herring cer ..e, the islands had the advantage of central location in the major herring fishing grounds of the British fleet, with the attendant economies. As in the other herring fishing areas, the Shetland industry had an extensive herring curing establishment, and almost all production was cured, especially during the early phase of development until the mid-1890s. However, its unfavourable location in relation to markets virtually excluded it from the fresh herring markets of Britain and the Continent until the early 1900s, when a regular service to Hamburg carrying roused herring* was instituted with great success in the summer months.[183] These lightly salted herring were generally canned on arrival in Germany.[184] The development of steam communications, while essential to the fresh herring market, was of limited benefit to the cured herring market, and sometimes compounded problems of oversupply of markets, as when several steamers arrived simultaneously in a continental herring port, leading to long delays in discharging and deterioration in the quality of the herring.[185]

The final important role of location was in the selection of Shetland as a base for the development of the Norwegian whaling industry[186] in 1903. In

P

that year two shore stations were set up at Ronas Voe, followed by two more, at Collafirth (Northmavine) and Olnafirth respectively in 1904. Altogether from eight to eleven whale-catching steamers fished from the stations in the pre-war period. The whales were processed immediately on being brought ashore by the catchers, and the oil and bone were shipped out mainly to Grangemouth and other British ports.[187] The islands were central to whaling grounds on the western and northern fringes of the continental shelf. Fishing began to the west and gradually moved closer to the shore and further round to the north and east in 1905 (the year the West Side herring fishing failed) and 1906 (when the Baltasound fishing failed).[188] The initial reasons for the establishment of the whaling bases in the islands were the shortage of whales on the Norwegian coast, and prohibition of whaling along long stretches of this coast by the Norwegian Government, partly at least because of protests by the Norwegian fishermen that whaling was damaging their fisheries. Similar protests by the Shetland herring fishermen about the failure of the early herring fishing evoked no similar response from the British Government, and there was consequently a great deal of political recrimination at local level.[189]

The improvement of communications had at first a relatively limited effect on Shetland trade. For example, in spite of the fact that steam services were introduced in the late 1830s, when the dry salt fish trade was still the staple of the trading economy, it did not have much effect as the carrying of this commodity was in the hands of Spanish shipowners to avoid differential duties, while the herring trade was in the hands of sailing vessels from Shetland and the east and west coasts of Scotland (Chapter 6). The first cargo of dried fish dispatched direct to the market by Spanish steamship was not until 1865,[190] and was, like most similar cargoes thereafter, a part-cargo picked up en route from Norway to Spain. The speed of communication made possible by steam did not make any material difference to this trade, as the product was designed to keep for long periods of time anyway, and speed was not essential. The takeover of the declining trade by the North Company in the late 1880s was a function of trade connections with the exporting houses rather than the influence of communications *per se*.

In the case of the fresh fish trade, although speed was absolutely essential for its long-term development, improved communications were para-doxically of limited importance in its early stages of growth. During the middle decades of the nineteenth century the great fisheries, apart from being geared to the dried fish trade, were also summer fisheries, and en-gagement in the fresh fish trade could thus be undertaken only in winter, when there was no steamer service. Even with the introduction of the winter service in 1866, there was no substantial development for over ten years. This can be traced in the first instance to the small-scale fresh fish trade, which had been developed using well-smacks* running direct to markets such as Grimsby or railheads such as Granton.[191] It is further evidence in support of the contention that the sudden rise of the fresh fish trade was like the growth of the herring industry in the late 1870s, which it parallelled almost exactly in time, rather than being the direct result of improved steam-ship services. The herring boats were used as fully as possible by engaging in the spring line fishing, and full use of labour in fishing on an annual basis undoubtedly encouraged the haddock fishing with open boats also. Never-theless, the haddock fishing was greatly aided by the development of steamer services which encouraged large-scale prosecution of this fishery, especially after the introduction of the West Side service in 1881, which fostered direct connection between the markets and the principal haddock fishing districts.

In contrast to the dried fish and haddock trades, the introduction of steam had immediate beneficial effects on the livestock trade as a direct result of speed, which enabled animals to arrive in a much better condition at market and fetch prices up to 50 per cent higher even as early as the 1840s.[192] Mean-while in all branches of trade, increased frequency and regularity of com-munication were at least as important for the transaction of business as for the carriage of goods, most of which, with the exception of fresh fish, did not have to be transported immediately. It is for this reason that so much emphasis was put on the improvement of the mail service from the 1890s onwards, not only for the sake of the fishing trades, but also for the hosiery and the general import trades, all of which could be conducted with greater ease.

Communities of Interest

The period beginning around 1870 marked the beginning of the end of the so-called 'traditional society', tied, in the Shetland case, not only to the land, but also the sea. It is apparent from the discussion so far that this slow dis-integration was accompanied by far-reaching developments in trade of a very different kind to those which had taken place in the period before 1870. It was a time of rapid change in comparison to previous periods, including rapid fluctuations in the quantities of exports and imports, the rapid rise and fall of new types of production, rapid effects of technological change, and increased mobility of labour in response to the relatively sudden creation of a wider range of economic opportunities, conveyed not least by the increasing speed and diversity of communications.

A characteristic theme which runs through these changes is that of increasing problems in island development as a whole, creating a situation in which it seems that the quick thinking and rapid decision-making, neces-sary in order to take advantage of opportunities, could not quite keep pace with the changes in trade which were taking place, notably in the forging of trade links and in the magnitudes of commodity flows. The end result was a certain lack of adjustment, periodic crises in the balance of supply and demand in the herring industry, for example, not to mention prolonged slumps in the knitwear trade, aggravated by the production of inferior

quality goods and competition from inferior products put on the market by
rival producers outwith the islands. These problems were associated with
increasing inadequacy of links between producers and markets, and the
setting up of producers' organisations to safeguard various interests, often
rather ineffectively.

Meanwhile, ordinary people were, by and large, little better off. Indeed,
the decline of the traditional haaf and cod fishing, and subsistence crofting,
had often left those on the land worse off. This curtailment of local 'economic
opportunity', with its problems of social and economic adjustment, is the
characteristic symptom of the 'stranded area'*.[193] In the Shetland case, the
situation was partly masked by the prosperity of the herring fishing, a 'substitute' industry, although it is worthy of note that earnings of Shetland-
owned herring boats tended to be lower than those of vessels from outwith
the islands, while concentration on the herring industry to the detriment of
the demersal fisheries meant that there was no ready alternative fishing, or
pool of experience of other fishings available when the herring industry
declined between the wars.[194] The weaknesses of the Shetland economy
were further obscured by the importance of the merchant service as an
employer, while the fresh fish, livestock and knitwear exports were of
sufficient importance to provide the degree of diversification necessary for
amelioration of these problems, at least in certain parts of the archipelago.

Despite the great and increasing flow of ideas with regard to the development of trade before 1870, it is apparent that many of these had a superficial
effect on trade at the time, and were often applied only after 1870. At this
stage in trade development perhaps the most effective impact of changing
ideas was at the level of the individual entrepreneur and business firms
generally, as they possessed the economic power to promote conscious
change, although it is arguable to what extent this power was exercised as a
conscious independent force, and to what extent it was the result of
economic and other pressures, such as changing conditions of competition
in the traditional markets for Shetland produce.

For the first time there were a real series of alternative ways of developing
production and trade, using the business firms which had evolved after
1840, in which an individual family business could transfer from one type of
business, such as cod fishing, to another, such as herring. To realise these
ideas meant appreciation of opportunity and an element of speculation. It is
perhaps the time taken for this to take place that explains the uncertainties in
trade development which characterise the 1870s. During this period,
although the cod fishing was in continuous decline, there was little or no
large-scale investment in other forms of production. In 1874, *The Shetland
Times* observed that 'There is still too much done in the old system here yet,
but we hope to see more emulation and enterprise shown by our capitalists
and business men ere long. The future prosperity of the islands demand
such'.[195] At all events there was little immediate acknowledgement of this in
the actions of entrepreneurs. The business firms tended to limit themselves

to the tried and proven, and supplemented locally caught supplies of cod and ling with substantial imports from Norway (Fig. 39) and continuing landings from English smacks (Fig. 26). Even speculative ventures followed this pattern. The most notable examples, the Shetland Fishery Company and the re-opening of the Sandlodge Mine, were destined to failure.

The observation of *The Shetland Times* on business enterprise comprised only one of many in that new newspaper at that period, ranging from the discussion of the feasibility of fish farming, to encouragement of new trials of the herring fishing, and the possibilities for the establishment of a fresh fish trade using the new all-year-round steam communication and rail transport.[196] Although the newspaper may well have had a beneficial effect in spreading these ideas, the establishment of the fresh fish and herring trades, discussed at the beginning of the decade but not implemented until its end, required a strong speculative element, as these trades were new and untried in an island context. When new investment took place, it was in the form of partnership between merchants and fishermen rather than in the paternalistic mercantile way characteristic of the earlier part of the century.

The element of speculation was no doubt encouraged by the large numbers of Scottish fishermen and curers arriving in the islands after 1880, although the fact that this was a seasonal influx may well have limited its impact. However, there was no waiting to see if these ventures were successful before taking up the herring fishing. This is apparent from the pattern of investment in the first-class boats in relation to the total numbers of boats fishing in Shetland (Fig. 42a, b). Finally, the elements of opportunity and speculation, in the export trades at least, must be viewed in the context of the increasingly wild economic fluctuations which took place, especially in the herring industry. Business under these new 'free trade' conditions was becoming increasingly hazardous, and casualties were by no means few in number.

Despite this reluctance to change in production and export trades, manifested by mercantile interests, there were notable ventures in tertiary economic activity, including the provision of local transport. In the agricultural field, for example, there was the import of ponies from Iceland and Faroe in the 1870s, to be re-exported after feeding.[197] Local cod production was supplemented by the import of wet salt cod, at first mainly from Norway (see above), and in the 1890s and early 1900s more from the Faroe islands (Fig. 39). Mercantile interest in provision of transport and trade facilities can be gauged in a number of ways. In 1885, for example, the first cargo of Welsh steam coal arrived, marking the new role of Lerwick as an occasional bunkering port on the Archangel trade route (Chapter 6). Bunkering facilities were greatly extended with the advent of the steam drifter after 1900. Speculation in trade was further demonstrated, for example, by Hay & Co.'s encouragement of steamer links with Faroe,[198] and the appearance of sailing vessels fitted out as travelling shops, for the selling, for instance, of shop goods in Faroe by Adie of Voe.[199]

It is clear, from the failure of business enterprise fully to grasp the new trade opportunities, that it cannot account for the changes taking place in trade after 1870, in the way its successful role can be used to explain certain characteristics of trade development in the late eighteenth and early nineteenth centuries. It is necessary, therefore, to look beyond the role of the individual to social and political factors. The role of political factors was largely indirect, and derived from Government legislation inspired by principles of social justice rather than economic efficiency. The first of these acts of Government was the investigation of the truck system in 1872, and the second was the granting of security of tenure to the crofters in 1886. Although the Crofters' Holdings Act was followed by a rather negative form of economic aid, through the institution of fair rents by which many of the crofters' rents were reduced and large amounts of arrears written off,[200] it could not get round the basic fact that crofting agriculture was increasingly uneconomic. If landowning was unprofitable in the middle of the nineteenth century (Chapter 4), it was even less so now. The best land was in the hands of farmers, and this small but important section of the community (still often landowners) constituted the driving force behind the expansion of livestock production and trade discussed above.

These politically inspired social changes, coupled with the developments of the haddock and herring fishings, would seem to have been the principal reasons behind the loss of initiative by the merchant class with respect to the island economy as a whole. The emergence of group interests, in contrast to previously communal ones, was demonstrated in two important respects in the mid-1880s, namely, the boldness with which evidence was given by the crofters to the Napier Commission in 1883 in contrast to the timid response to the Truck Commission in 1872;[201] and the successful challenging of the landowners' traditional right to one third of the proceeds of whale hunts by the crofters in the Hoswick Whale Case in 1888.[202]

And yet the pursuit of group interests in this fashion was no substitute for effective trading and economic development. On land, apart from the relatively vigorous farming community promoting agriculture, there was economic stagnation once the 'social rights' of the crofters had been established. Much larger holdings would have been required to make crofting economic, which social consideration had been the chief reason for safeguarding the security of tenure of the crofters. By 1888, when the depression in the herring fishing was biting hard into the economy, *The Shetland Times* estimated[203] that not less than 40 per cent of the crofter-fishermen would have been bankrupt had the merchants and curers demanded payment, and the class as a whole were worse off than twenty years previously, when earnings at the Greenland whaling were higher than in the then herring fishing, and when the women had been able to keep their families in provisions by their knitting, which was no longer possible. The reasons for this state of affairs were several, including the slump in the herring trade, a decrease in the price of livestock, failure of the Greenland whaling, and decline in the quality of Shetland hosiery and its market reputation, aggravated by the effects of the Truck Amendment Act of 1887.

In contrast to this deteriorating situation in crofting, there were signs of considerable vitality in the fishing industry. The decline of the traditional cod and haaf fisheries was accompanied by a new and previously unheard-of willingness by the fishermen to take up the herring fishing, which was not only yielding better returns and resulting in the formation of a separate class of full-time fishermen with the aid of the fresh fish trade developments, but also had the advantages over the Faroe fishing in particular of proximity to home and a better home life. This, no doubt, reinforced the outsiders' impression that the women who tended the crofts in the men's absence and were knitting continually, worked 'more consistently' than the men.[204] In the traditional haaf fishing and crofting sectors there was a good deal of mobility of employment between the herring fishing and the merchant service; in the full-time fishing sectors it was a mobility between different fishings. Fishermen engaging in the Shetland herring fishing sometimes carried on to the English or West Coast fishings (especially with the advent of the steam drifter and, after the war, the motor boat), and to the spring line and haddock fishings.

By the 1900s the fishermen were highly independent, so much so that there was vigorous protest against the whaling interests on the failure of the West Side herring fishing in 1905,[205] as the fishermen thought that the offal from the whaling stations was detrimental to the herring stock. There was a near riot in Scalloway the following year when fish buyers bought fresh fish from English boats in contravention of certain prior agreements between the buyers and the local haddock fishermen.[206] However, from a trade point of view, the fresh fish trade demonstrated the breakdown of the old and its inadequate replacement by the new. There was no proper agency system for disposing of the fish to southern markets, necessitating the formation of the Burra men's co-operative venture (see below), and in 1912 the Whalsay fishermen were complaining of the lack of haddock markets, brought about by their distance from the steamer terminals.[207]

The sense of insecurity engendered by the passing of the mercantile initiative was partly alleviated in the last two decades of the period by the creation of producers' organisations for the several commodity trades, in order to safeguard specific interests. However, in the main these were not inspired by a desire to expand trade but generally arose to ward off more immediate threats to production. Although mercantile interests were involved, these organisations were divorced from the practical commercial considerations, with resultant marketing problems and the absence of proper agency systems and trade links generally.

The earliest organisation was the Shetland Agricultural Society, founded in 1864, which, however, soon went into abeyance through lack of interest,[208] the only active agricultural society in the 1870s being that of Unst, started in 1870.[209] The Shetland Agricultural Society was resuscitated in 1892 at the instigation of the pony-breeding interests, concerned to export the best blood in view of the importance of the American market.[210] During the 1890s and subsequently, an increasing number of agricultural shows were held annually in various country districts such as Unst, Walls, and Tingwall,[211] spurred on by increasing interest in agricultural topics as the commercialisation of agriculture in general and stock production in particular gained momentum. In 1912 the Shetland Cattle Herd Book was established to protect the quality of the Shetland breed of cattle,[212] and by 1910 there was also talk of forming a Shetland Flock Book to safeguard the quality of Shetland wool,[213] which was then in great demand. However, the prime movers behind these new developments were the minority of farmers rather than the majority of crofters. During the period it was mainly sheep and lambs from the farm that were exported,[214] and as late as 1893 it was observed that a larger crofter membership of the Shetland Agricultural Society was necessary in order to improve the organisation.[215]

That the developments in agriculture preceded the developments in other branches of trade may appear surprising in view of the fact that agriculture at this time was, in the context of island trade as a whole, of less importance than the fisheries, and possibly even than knitwear. This seems to have been basically because of the threats posed by the market system to the singular character of Shetland livestock production. Ponies, cattle and sheep were all of distinctive breeds, the last producing a distinctive wool upon which the reputation of Shetland knitwear was based. It is perhaps a measure of the high esteem in which Shetland hosiery was held that there was no serious attempt to form a hosiery association despite the problems of underhand competition and indifferent quality control. It was 1907 before *The Shetland Times* advocated[216] the formation of a hosiery association to counter the effects of 'spurious' hosiery on the market, while there was a long discussion in the report on Highland Home Industries on the subject, with special reference to the means whereby quality might be protected by standardised trade marks.[217] In fact, the Shetland Woollen Industries Association, the first trade organisaton designed to foster and protect the hosiery trade, was not formed until 1921.[218]

As in the case of pony-breeding and knitwear, the fishermen and fish merchants were forced together by external threat rather than commercial farsightedness into forming fish producers' and fishermen's associations respectively in 1908 to deal with the problems arising from the introduction of whaling.[219] Only one organisation was formed for the furtherance of fishing interests by acting specifically as a trade link. This was Duncan & Co., a co-operative-type society formed in Burra to see to the selling of fish during the haddock season. They employed a man as clerk and manager who acted as a fish salesman and was otherwise employed during the herring fishing season.[220]

'The merchant,' wrote the Truck Commissioners in 1871, '. . . buys all that leaves the country, from a whale to an egg, and sells everything that the country people want, from a boll of meal or a suit of clothes, to a darning needle.'[221] This position did not change suddenly, and many merchants had stakes in several activities, from retailing, through herring and cod fishing, to agriculture, for a long time afterwards. Nonetheless the socio-economic changes which had taken place favoured specialisation in production, with external trade handled increasingly by agents only, while the means of production and internal trade was the preserve of the local merchants. The age of great men in mercantile development appeared to be at an end, and the market emerged as the primary governing force in the evolution of the island economy. The changing role of the individual in this new order is exemplified by the activities of John Walker, who, as factor on the Gardie estate, supervised the creation of sheep farms, and was instrumental, with a few others, in drawing the attention of the Truck Commission to the state of affairs in local trade. He also acted as the managing director of the Sandlodge Mine, and was a prime mover in the setting up of the Shetland Fishery Company to prosecute the cod fishing. Significantly, the first two ventures achieved concrete and lasting results, while the second two proved costly speculations destined to failure. Meanwhile, although the herring fishing increasingly overshadowed the trade of the islands, and although it was largely in the hands of Scottish curing firms, it was only partly an external influence, and the internal developments in boat-ownership and merchant participation indicate that there was also indigenous development.

It is apparent that there were two principal phases in the development of the trade economy as a whole, namely, before and after 1900. The first phase of expansion and construction of the herring industry demonstrates a relatively unchanging outlook. The herring fishing and the spring line fishing, and the haddock fishing, were added on to the existing economy. Although the cod and haaf fisheries declined greatly, they did not disappear, and the underlying resilience of the socio-economic structure was demonstrated by the resurgence of the cod fishing in the first half of the 1890s, with the great depression in the herring fishery. Dried fish production remained at a high level despite the decline in the traditional economy. The degree of this resilience is also illustrated by the remarks in *The Shetland Times*[222] to the effect that it was only the hope of better times that kept fishermen and fish curers going — neither fishcuring nor the fishing had paid either curers or fishermen for the four years prior to 1888, and continued to be unremunerative until the mid-1890s. Under these circumstances it is clearly not possible to explain changes merely by theories regarding prices and market competition.

Nonetheless the forces of market competition were present, and increasing. After 1900, these were brought into full play by the advent of technological change in the fisheries through the coming of steam, followed by motor power. The first manifestation of this was external in the form of the steam trawler, which for reasons already discussed undermined the spring line fishing in particular by its better access to the fresh fish markets from the early 1890s onwards. Of more crucial importance still was the advent of the steam drifter in the herring fishing after 1900. By 1906 as much herring was being landed by drifters as sailboats (Fig. 48b), and the advantages of speedier access ensured again that the value of the drifter catch was intrinsically higher. After 1905, the sailboat rapidly declined in importance, and the importance of the native Shetland sector of the herring industry declined along with it, as the fishermen rather than the merchants held the initiative in capital investment in boats, and the large amount of capital needed for drifters was beyond the reach of even some of the merchants who financed the fishermen's shares in boats to a large extent. By the end of the period fishing had become geographically as well as economically separated from agriculture to a considerable degree, and the fishermen were concentrating on acquiring decked boats for the haddock and herring fishing in the leading areas.

Meanwhile, the last of the sixerns disappeared in the early 1900s,[223] the last Shetland-owned Faroe smack sailed in 1906,[224] and the last recorded Dundee whalers to call at Shetland en route for the Davis Straits appear to have done so in 1911.[225] The traditional dried fish exports slumped sharply after 1900, and subsistence agriculture went into steeper decline while emigration probably accelerated. As early as 1892, Lawrence Williamson had observed[226] that the older order was passing away; by 1909 the new order had apparently come to pass, typified by the statement of *The Shetland Times* that 'We have but one string to our bow . . .' — in the shape of the herring fishing.[227] And yet there was a paradox. The year 1913 was one of the most prosperous ever for the Shetland economy,[228] but the system as a whole, let alone those parts of it constituting the trade links, existed rather in outward form than inward substance. The new fishermen's and agriculturalists' organisations were as yet hardly effective representatives of island trading interests in the sense that the nineteenth-century merchants were. Commercial initiative was lacking — the new generation of fishermen and farmers were not traders. In short, the 'stranded area' characteristics were present, and increasing in importance, although hardly appreciated. In these conditions of apparent stability, it was scarcely surprising that *The Shetland Times*,[229] while remarking that there was a growing tendency for the fishermen to 'put all their eggs in one basket', also observed that the haaf, whale, Faroe and spring fishings had come and gone: 'Yet Shetland has not suffered very much'. It must have seemed so, and the eruption of the Great War must have seemed correspondingly climactic.

6

The Traders and the Sea

Despite the use of steam propulsion in certain shipping sectors early in the nineteenth century, the sail was still very much in evidence until the early 1900s, both in the local fisheries and trade, and in the extensive international traffic which passed by Shetland shores. Locally, it was a world still very much dependent upon the sea for communications as well as sustenance, despite the building of the meal roads in the late 1840s. From the early eighteenth century until the mid-nineteenth century Shetlanders retained much of the initiative in providing shipping for Shetland trade, and this was indeed a significant measure of local independence in development, together with the provision of regular services for the carriage of mail. The importance of the sea was further highlighted by Shetland's central position on the major fishing grounds and seaways of northern Europe. From the days of the great Dutch herring fishery onwards this frequently proved to be a factor of some significance for the local economy and way of life and, together with its purely local importance, placed the sea at the centre of island consciousness.

The Days of Sail

For both open boats and decked vessels, there were a number of rules which had to be observed in making a journey. The vessel had to be overhauled and prepared for the journey or journeys which she had to undertake. A constant programme of maintenance was necessary. The hull had to be kept in order, which in the case of large sailing vessels meant careening on a suitable beach at least once a year to check the hull for rot, and making repairs if necessary, as well as cleaning the bottom. Then the vessel had to be rigged, a major task, usually undertaken at the beginning of the season. In the case of open boats it was relatively straightforward; in the case of trading vessels it meant frequent renewal of blocks and tackle, and other running rigging, often between voyages, with periodic renewal of standing rigging also. The masts and yard had to be varnished or painted, as did the topsides and other parts of the ship both above and below decks, while the decks themselves had to be maintained in a watertight condition by caulking as necessary. In practice, in a trading vessel maintenance went on continuously in port, and even at sea if weather conditions were suitable.[1]

The last job to be done to make a ship ready for sea was to load ballast. All sailing vessels required ballast, unless the weight of cargo was such that sufficient stability was ensured to the point at which ballast could be partly or wholly dispensed with. This operation, apart from working the cargo (see below), was one of those items which in trading voyages added to the considerable length of time taken to turn the ship round in port, and was a major factor governing the relationship between distance and travelling time. If the ship made a voyage in ballast, the ballast had of course to be discharged at the other end, thus adding to the time taken, and giving rise to the problem of ballast heaps in harbour, notably at Scalloway[2] and Baltasound,[3] where vessels sometimes grounded, and were damaged by sailing onto these uncharted hazards in shallow water.

The relationship between distance and sailing time depended on the design of the hull, the length of the ship and the rig. In practice, for any given vessel, by far the greatest influence on voyage times was, not surprisingly, the strength and direction of wind itself. A ship's speed under favourable wind conditions, in which the wind was blowing at an angle just forward of the beam*, at right angles to the path of the ship, or any angle abaft the beam to dead astern, increased until a certain strength of wind was reached, at which she was being driven at her maximum speed in relation to her length. When or before this speed was reached, depending on the vessel and the judgement of the skipper as to both the performance of the ship and the state of weather and sea, it was necessary to shorten or reduce sail either by taking in sail or reefing the sails.

Further increase in wind strength then had little effect on speed, but tended rather to reduce speed, as sea conditions were liable to be such as to slow the ship down through rolling and pitching, while under stormy conditions it became necessary to take in all sails and heave to. In very heavy seas it might be necessary to run before the wind and sea, the classic case of this being the colliers sheltering from a southerly gale at Great Yarmouth, which were forced to weigh anchor and run the whole way to Shetland. Thirteen of these arrived in the islands in the first week of January 1800, and two were wrecked.[4] When running before a heavy sea the great danger was that of broaching to, or being pushed side-on to the waves by the sea, or a combination of wind and sea. In common with fetching*, this was liable, in stormy conditions, to lay a sailing ship on her beam ends* or even capsize her, usually because cargo or ballast shifted. The great weight of the masts also acted as a turning moment on the hull. If the vessel was thus laid on her beam ends or nearly so, and could not be got up, the final desperate solution was to cut away the masts and rigging, thus lowering the centre of gravity and improving stability, unfortunately at the expense of manoeuvrability. By this time the vessel was likely to be waterlogged either through labouring or through the sweeping off of the hatch covers, deck-houses, bulwarks and other deck fittings by the sea. A large proportion of vessels wrecked or severely disabled in the Shetland area, particularly during prolonged gales from the south or south-east, were subjected to several or all of these conditions, and not infrequently arrived derelict*, and sometimes capsized, to be dashed to pieces on the rocky coastline.[5] Naturally, storm conditions, assuming that the vessel survived, tended to add to voyage times, as she was liable to be blown a long way off course and would probably have to seek shelter in a harbour far out of her original path, usually to undergo repairs and re-provisioning (Fig. 65).

The other major aspect of the wind was its direction in relation to the intended route. Under favourable wind conditions, sailing ships could make fairly good times and maintain steady speeds comparable, for example, to those of the steamships of the day. Under conditions of contrary winds*, however, a vessel could be delayed for long periods either beating about*, or sheltering. Thus, in her voyages to and from Shetland, the *Petrel's* voyage varied from under two days to as much as ten days over virtually the same route (Table 7).[6] On long voyages it became a case of 'working away' as much in tune with the elements as possible. In the case of the voyage of the *Janet Hay* to Bilbao, for example, she had to lie for a week in Longhope to await favourable winds, and anchored again on Belfast Lough for similar purposes. When she left, 'over 200 sail', also waiting, accompanied her. Again, crossing the Atlantic to the Davis Straits cod fishing took four weeks with the presence of contrary winds and calms, while she made the return journey in three weeks under favourable wind conditions.[7]

The problems of contrary winds were perhaps most potent in affecting accessibility, particularly at the local scale. Apart from hazards such as storms, leading to the loss of a vessel, there were others. One of these, which was especially dangerous for small open boats, was the sudden gust, or flan* of wind, which caught the sail and capsized the boat before the sheet could be let go. Such a flan of wind was responsible for the drowning of the laird of Muness and nine or ten others within sight of his house in 1699, for example.[8] Another hazard of particular danger was the presence of strong tidal streams, which could bring disaster either through the presence of broken water*, or by causing drifting on to the rocks, either through conditions of calm, or misjudgement of the strength and direction of tidal currents in relation to the wind when plotting courses. This latter misjudgement was responsible for the loss of several ships passing Fair Isle, which were driven on to the rocks in comparatively moderate weather conditions.[9] Broken water was especially dangerous for smaller craft, especially if aggravated by wind blowing in the opposite direction to the tidal current, Yell Sound being particularly dangerous in this respect. There is a record as early as 1620 of three men being drowned in Yell Sound.[10]

There was a maximum of shipping activity in the summer half of the year (March to October) in all the historical periods. In the era of itinerant merchants, the ships commonly arrived in May or June and left in August

Table 7. Log of Smack Petrel, 1874-1875

Note: The time taken for the voyages, in whole days (i.e. 24 hours from midnight to midnight) and hours (extra number of hours derived from the times of sailing and arrival recorded in the log). As arrival and sailing times are not always recorded in the log, the exact lengths of voyages in hours are consequently not always known.

Analysis:

Shetland to Scotland

Dates 1874	Times Whole days & hours	Hours (if known)	Voyage
25th Mar.-6th Apr.	9d. 15h.	231	Weisdale-Leith
23rd Apr.-25th Apr.	1d. 35h.	59	Hillswick-Aberdeen
9th May-11th May	2d. ?h.	?	Hillswick-Leith
30th May-4th June	4d. 27h.	123	Voe-Leith
30th June-5th July	5d. 10h.	130	Scalloway-Inchkeith
22nd July-25th July	2d. 26h.	74	Scalloway-Leith
10th Sep.-13th Sep.	2d. 9h.	57	Scalloway-Leith
19th Sep.-24th Sep.	4d. ?h.	?	Hillswick-Leith
21st Nov.-25th Nov.	3d. 19h.	91	Scalloway-Aberdeen
1875			
22nd Feb.-24th Feb.	1d. 13h.	37	Lerwick-Aberdeen
16th Mar.-19th Mar.	2d. ?h.	?	Weisdale-Burntisland

Scotland to Shetland

1874			
10th Apr.-15th Apr.	4d. 15h.	111	Leith-Voe
29th Apr.-3rd May	3d. 31h.	103	Aberdeen-Voe
15th May-22nd May	6d. 31h.	175	Leith-Voe
11th June-18th June	6d. 15h.	163	Leith-Scalloway
11th July-15th July	3d. ?h.	?	Leith-Scalloway
28th Aug.-30th Aug.	1d. ?h.	?	Leith-Scalloway
19th Sep.-22nd Sep.	2d. 12½h.	60½	Leith-Scalloway
1st Nov.-3rd Nov.	1d. ?h.	?	Leith-Lerwick
15th Dec.-17th Dec.	1d. ?h.	?	Leith-Scalloway
1875			
4th Mar.-5th Mar.	0d. 30h.	30	Aberdeen-Scalloway
16th Mar.-19th Mar.	0d. 35h.	35	Aberdeen-Lerwick

(Chapter 2). By the eighteenth century a change in the patterns of arrivals and sailings (Fig. 49) followed the practice of shipping out small quantities of fish, butter and oil from the previous year early in the season, and returning with meal, fishing necessaries and other goods in the early summer in time for the fishing. The peak of shipping activity took place in late summer and autumn, when the cured fish were ready for market.[11] Ships left as quickly as possible to catch the market. This pattern emphasises that in Shetland trade, geared to primary production, the pattern of seasonal shipping activity was governed primarily by the cycle of production, contrary to popular opinion, which held, and sometimes still holds, that ships did not travel much in

A: Foreign Trade ,1744 to 1768.

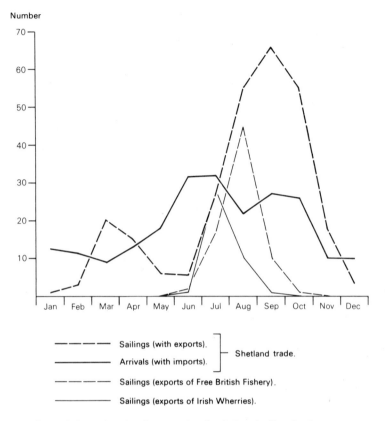

Number

Sailings (with exports). ⎤
Arrivals (with imports). ⎦ Shetland trade.

Sailings (exports of Free British Fishery).

Sailings (exports of Irish Wherries).

The statistics are based on the summation of arrivals and sailings for the years
1744 to 1755 , and 1757 to 1768 inclusive. The record of arrival and sailing
dates for 1756 is incomplete .

Source:Customs Quarterly Returns

Figure 49. Seasonal frequencies of arrivals and sailings

winter because of the greater hazards. This is borne out further by the substantial number of trucks which took place in the winter months at all
periods in history, demonstrating that appreciable trading continued in
winter. Again, the voyages of the *Janet Hay* (Fig. 58) illustrate that, in shipowning, trading continued all year round.

The requirements of the fishing industry continued to dominate the
seasonal pattern in the nineteenth-century cod-fishing era (Fig. 49b),[12] and
the cod smacks were used in trading at the beginning and end of the fishing
season, being in use from March until December, and often laid up in the
months of January and February, when refitting took place.

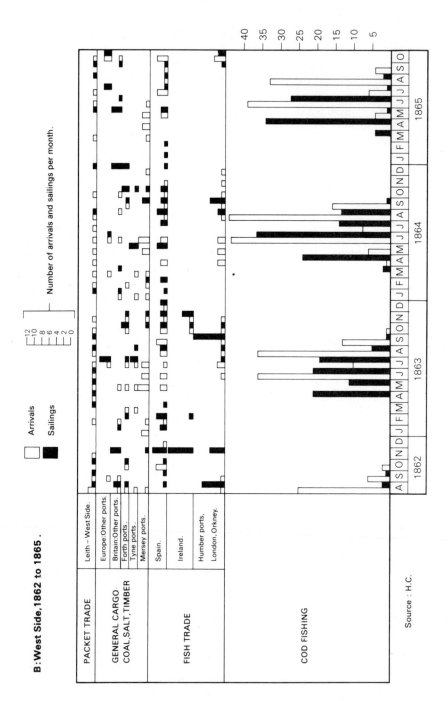

Figure 49. Seasonal frequencies of arrivals and sailings

Sea and Land

All the trading points, with the exception of Lerwick, owed their development to the geography of production in the fisheries, and generally became the site of a German merchant's booth, followed by a landowner's store and, in the nineteenth century, a leading merchant's shop and store. Notwithstanding the need for accessibility to the haaf stations, Lerwick and Scalloway owed very little of their growth to the geography of production. This was especially evident in the eighteenth century, when the Customs on more than one occasion endeavoured to make Lerwick the centre of landing and shipping of all cargo in Shetland.

Perhaps the strongest reason for the continuing separate existence of these trade points was the configuration of land and sea, which made for difficult communication between the East and West Sides. In the early 1700s, for example, a miscalculation regarding the degree of accessibility appears to have been at the root of the failure by English merchants to take over the fish trade in the wake of the German merchants' departure. It was later alleged that they sent only two ships, an insufficient number to travel round the numerous fishing localities, so that they often had to be dispatched without full cargoes.[13] Later, in 1723, during the establishing of Customs creeks for the landing and shipping of goods, it was pointed out that it was virtually impossible to have Lerwick as the only centre, as a fair wind on one side of the islands almost certainly spelled a contrary wind on the other, and that '. . . before any shipmaster will undertake this they will rather run straight south with those goods to any pairt in north Brittain and this may also be said of all the oyr. places named in the west side of Shetland'.[14] Such delays caused by inaccessibility of course aggravated the dangers of deterioration and damage of cargo, particularly fish, which was a special problem in Shetland export trading.

A further direct consequence of the configuration of land and sea was the suitability of the islands for smuggling, which could be readily carried out among the numerous voes and sheltering hills. This was a major reason for the first attempts of the Customs in the 1760s to have Lerwick erected as the only legal Customs creek, a move resisted strongly by the landowners, who advanced the same arguments against it as had been raised in 1723, and instanced examples of fish being damaged through being transported to Lerwick and thereby ruined by water when the ship encountered bad weather. It was noted that a six-day trip from Bergen to Hillswick had been lengthened to twenty-two days through the ship having to report at Lerwick for the landing of her cargo of wood goods, the trip from Hillswick to Lerwick having taken sixteen days because of adverse wind and weather conditions.[15] That there was a battle between the rival interests is evidenced by a process in the Sheriff court in which the Customs were indicted by the principal freighter and the skipper of the *Charming Babey* for failing to turn up to supervise the loading of a cargo of fish, with the result that the ship was likely to miss the market and considerable financial loss would be thereby incurred.[16] Further, the physical difficulties of catching smugglers were frequently emphasised by the Customs to their superiors in Edinburgh during the great smuggling era at the beginning of the nineteenth century[17] (Chapter 4).

Problems of cargo handling arose mainly from the effects of weather. The most important drawback was the impossibility of loading dry fish in damp and rainy conditions, which led to wetting of the fish. The problem was possibly less serious for those vessels which managed to leave reasonably early in the season. For those leaving in late autumn or winter, however, serious delays could ensue, and the numbers of vessels leaving in those seasons tended to increase after the cod fishing got under way.

A good example of the delays which were liable to occur is that of the loading of the *Janet Hay* with a cargo of fish for Bilbao at Scalloway in January 1863.[18] She arrived at Scalloway and dropped anchor at 0900 on Saturday 17th, and had to let go another anchor an hour later because of a north-west gale. From the following Monday until Wednesday was spent discharging ballast, and on the Wednesday twelve tons of fish were loaded '. . . being in a damp state for shipping which I cannot [be] accountable for not being responsible for quality of cargo; only for weight taken on board,' wrote the skipper in the log. From Thursday 22nd until Saturday 24th no fish were loaded because of the weather, and on Monday 26th anchor was shifted to be nearer the fish store. A period of uninterrupted loading took place from 27th until Saturday 31st January, during which the cargo appears to have been completed. However, from Monday 1st until Saturday 7th February a strong gale blew, at first from the south, then shifting round to the north, with heavy showers of hail, sleet and snow. Only after the storm abated was it possible to make the ship ready for the voyage, and she did not finally get under way for Bilbao until Wednesday 18th February, which was a full month after she had arrived in Scalloway.

There were other peculiarly local dangers. Perhaps the greatest of these, manifested by the numbers of vessels lost locally, was associated with anchorage in the harbours under stormy conditions, such as that described above in the loading of the *Janet Hay*. This may appear paradoxical in a place usually noted for the excellence of its natural harbours. However, some of the best of these, notably Lerwick, Scalloway and the voes in the central metamorphic rock area, are in fact the most dangerous. Parts of the floors of the voes do not provide good holding ground for anchorage, while the extensive reaches generate large waves which could prove damaging to vessels of from 40 to 80 feet overall, as were most of the cod fishing vessels and local traders in the nineteenth century. Thus a substantial number of wrecks of Shetland-owned vessels in Shetland itself took place in the 'sheltered' harbours under severe conditions (Fig. 67). The next most common causes of loss were running ashore through missing stays* when tacking*, and hitting submerged rocks.[19] Open boats were also liable to be blown away during storms, while hauled up on the beaches, and there is one attested case of this in the late eighteenth century.[20]

The development of communications at local level, by open boat, decked vessel and over land, exhibited certain factors common to all phases of historical development, with changing emphases according to the period in time. Broadly speaking, small-scale local journeys tended to be undertaken by open boats, while longer journeys became increasingly the preserve of decked vessels. This was perhaps more strongly influenced by economic than purely physical considerations. Thus in the case of open boats, use for transport was interchangeable between fishing and trade. For trade, flit-boats* ('great boats' in the seventeenth century, see below) were generally used for the various short sea crossings between the North Isles and the Mainland, and journeys across the voes and to and from the other islands, especially on the West Side in the vicinity of Scalloway. Sixerns or larger boats were used for the transport of fish from the stations to the trade points in both haaf fishing and cod fishing areas. The use of decked vessels in the coastal trade became more important as time progressed, particularly in the nineteenth century. The most important function of these vessels was usually connected on both eastern and western coasts with sailing among the several trade points with cargo to be landed or collected, as an extension of the coastwise trade between Shetland and Britain in which these vessels were generally engaged. There was, in addition, an important function in the transport of bulk goods, such as salt and barrels locally, especially in the servicing of the herring fishings.

Transport over land was of minimal importance, even for a considerable time after the coming of roads in the middle of the nineteenth century. The most important use was for the movement of livestock to and from the sales which grew up in the nineteenth century at certain central locations. The dangerous going in the peat-covered interior is often referred to by travellers, from the days of Brand onwards.[21] As late as 1859, after the first roads had been constructed, the Customs emphasised that '. . . the only possible means of travelling is by the trading packets, by hiring horses (native ponies) or boats or both'.[22] This was done frequently by the Customs officers themselves, particularly in the attendance of wrecks.[23] When supervising the loading and unloading of cargoes they usually travelled on the cargo vessel at the merchants' expense.

Despite the laying down of rates for both passenger transport and 'great boats' on established routes, there was little need for the former in a subsistence agricultural society, and the latter reflected the patterns of production fairly closely for obvious reasons (Chapter 2). There were no recognised services as such, as noted above, when the need for communications grew in the late eighteenth and early nineteenth centuries; the result was the possession of boats by merchants and shopkeepers. Unlike the external services, there was no need for mail to go by similar means of transport; it could go over land, and often did, ferries being hired where necessary. The first mail service of this kind, by post-runner, was established between Lerwick and the North Isles in 1821, and others to the North Mainland and West Mainland followed in the 1820s and 1830s.[24] Meanwhile, the patterns of transport of external trade commodities, as distinct from the local mercantile circulation of retail goods and production goods, was governed by the degree of accessibility of major trade points to external trade routes. When local packet services began to develop, therefore, these were often extensions of external routes under the same business management, although there were parallel, purely local developments also.

The beginnings of internally organised transport by decked vessels, as distinct from open flitboats, took place in the wake of the Napoleonic wars, demand increasing especially with the rise of the herring fishing in the late 1820s, which required the transport of salt, barrels, and herring to and from various stations. A good example was the voyages of the schooner *Mary* belonging to William Hay (Fig. 50).[25] Based on Lerwick, her job was to carry barrels and salt to the herring stations at Aithsvoe and occasionally Mid Yell, and return with herring to Lerwick. She was also engaged in carrying manure from Lerwick to the proprietor's house at Laxfirth, and in various other voyages. Another example of the use of coasting sloops at this time was the transport of lime from Girlsta to Uyea for the building of Thomas Leisk's mansion in Uyea in 1818[26] (Chapter 4); and carriage of granite from Stava Ness in Nesting to build the great house at Symbister in Whalsay around 1830.[27]

One of the first records of separate commercial organisation for local transport is of the North Isles Packet Company, in which the Hay family possessed shares in the 1820s.[28] This dates the first developments of this type of organisation parallel to that of the first mail services linking Shetland with the east coast of Scotland. The first proper service on the east side seems to have been inaugurated in the summer of 1839 using the sloop *Janet*, which sailed on the route from Lerwick to Unst.[29] Nonetheless, from around 1840 until the late 1850s on the East side, and as late as the 1880s on the West side, the sailing packets on the Shetland-Scotland run provided the main coastal service links within the archipelago as far as the carriage of goods, and to a lesser extent, passengers, were concerned.

Although there was talk of starting a local steam packet for Shetland in 1838,[30] at the time of the introduction of the service by the Aberdeen, Leith and Clyde Shipping Company, nothing was done until 1868, when the Shetland Steam Shipping Company Limited was established with a capital of £5,000 consisting of 500 shares of £10 each.[31] The setting up of the company was facilitated by the fact that the former owner of the ship used, the *Chieftain's Bride*, was a qualified shipmaster, and owned 200 shares. The Unst Shipping Company owned 50, and the rest were subscribed by most of the leading businessmen in the islands. Paid-up capital extended to a total of 438 shares. Although the calling up of capital proceeded cautiously at first, while the degree of success of the venture was assessed, the instigators need

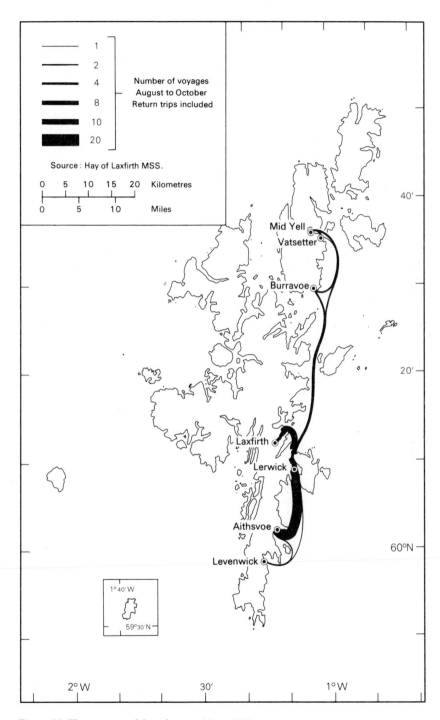

Figure 50. The voyages of the schooner *Mary,* 1829

not have worried unduly. The enterprise did fairly well, and by 1876, when the North Company had become the chief shareholder and the undertaking had acquired the name of the Zetland Islands Steam Navigation Company Limited, the North Company advised the purchasing of a new ship. The following year the first *Earl of Zetland* was acquired.[32] The *'Old Earl'*, as she was better known, served on the East side routes until 1946[33] (Fig. 51).

Business continued to expand under the influence of the herring industry and tourist trade,[34] and in 1881 the *Earl* was put on the run from Lerwick to Dunrossness as well as her usual North Isles runs. In 1885 the *Lady Ambrosine* was chartered to assist the operation of the service in summer. By 1887 the Leith-Aberdeen steamer was being put on the North Isles run in competition in peak summer and autumn periods, and the great depression in the herring trade finally hit the company in 1888. Two years later it was recommended that the firm be amalgamated with the North Company, and this was carried out in 1890. Meanwhile, the smacks trading between Leith and Shetland had been superseded on the West side also by the extension of the North Company's activities through the West side service in 1881. Thus both East and West sides of the archipelago were independently connected by sea to the south, and like external trade, internal services became virtually a monopoly of the North Company.

In spite of these developments in seaborne trade, the beginning of extensive use of the land for communication was also getting under way. The development of the road network in Shetland remained, until the close of the period, far behind that of communications by sea. Nonetheless there was some need, and a constant desire, for roads. As early as 1816, the Shetland Society recommended the setting up of a road committee and appointing a professional road surveyor,[35] and the desire was reiterated by the *Orkney and Shetland Chronicle* in 1825, who commented on the need for statute roads.[36] By 1833 roads committees had been set up in various districts, and the Commissioners of Supply* resolved that a fund be placed annually to each parish for the repair of bridges.[37] However, little in the way of roads was built, the only substantial one being that from Lerwick to Tingwall, completed in the late eighteenth century, which was virtually useless for horse-drawn traffic because of its steep gradients.[38]

The general lack of a pressing need for roads as a means of communication is most strikingly demonstrated by the fact that the major road network (Fig. 51) came into existence some time later, in the period 1849-1851 for the purposes of famine relief through the provision of employment (Chapter 4), rather than to promote better communication.[39] The only exception to this was the construction of the road from Lerwick to Scalloway between 1840 and 1847. The length of time it took to construct it suggests that the need for it was not pressing, although when the Scalloway Road Subscription Committee, set in train to supervise the building of it, ran out of funds in 1841, they emphasised its economic importance when applying for financial assistance to the Fishery Board for Scotland. Reference was made to the

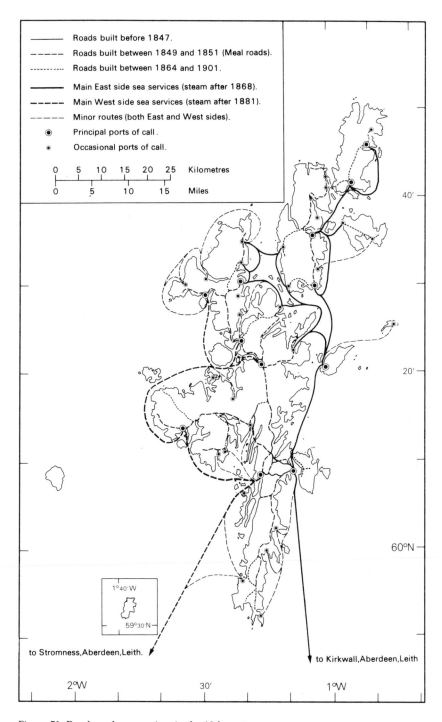

Figure 51. Roads and sea services in the 19th century

curers being '. . . obliged to transport their empty Barrels, Salt, Nets and provisions across the hills upon the backs, not only of Ponies, but of People, Women as well as Men . . .' It was further emphasised that the road would make it possible to transport herring to Scalloway to make up cargoes,[40] although it must be noted that at this time the herring fishing was in anything but a flourishing state (Chapter 4).

As regards the road network laid down in 1847-1851, it is significant that those parts not connected to the main network, such as North Roe and Ollaberry, Westsandwick in Yell, and in Sandsting, acted as extensions to the main sea-based communications network, while the first priority was generally to link up the major ports of the sea network as far as possible (Fig. 51). Just as the system of statute labour* was proved inadequate for the construction of the Scalloway road in 1846-1847, so it could not cope with the upkeep of the new road network or contribute to its extension and improvement. As early as 1852, the Commissioners of Supply sent a memorandum to the Commissioners of Highland Roads and Bridges requesting that they take the upkeep of the Shetland roads under their care,[41] and the following year it was resolved to take power from Parliament to maintain the roads by commuting the statute service to a rate levied on proprietors and tenants, and also carriages and carts.[42] This became more urgent as the 1850s and 1860s passed. Traffic on the roads increased greatly due to the use of the roads for movement of livestock and easier access from the nearer parts of Mainland to Lerwick.

Progress in implementing these decisions was slow; although the roads were being used increasingly for local trade, the sea service was still better for most purposes. Also much of the traffic, especially on the East side, was generated between Lerwick and the major islands which, with the exception of Yell, had no roads at this time. Delay was furthered in that, although the Commissioners of Supply had originally made the proviso that those who lived on roadless islands should not be subject to assessment for the upkeep of roads,[43] some proprietors in Mainland and Yell thought that the whole group should be assessed, it being pointed out in opposition to this proposal that '. . . it is almost solely from the North Isles that live stock is sent to the steamer, and it is found safer, more expeditious and cheaper, to send them by the numerous packets that ply to the stations of the steamer than across the many wide and dangerous firths, involving delays and risks, and an exhausting land journey'. Another reason given was the presence of livestock diseases such as scab (Chapter 4) on Mainland which was absent from the other islands.[44]

A Zetland Roads Act was finally passed in 1864, empowering the establishment of Road Trustees, and they were duly constituted in 1868, and a Road Surveyor appointed. Thereafter, the construction of more roads seems to have proceeded slowly and steadily, and most of the district roads constituting the missing links in the main network (Fig. 51) had been completed by 1890 and taken over by the Road Trustees.[45]

The completion of the network coincided with the economic development of the 1880s and 1890s, and increased the scope for the use of the roads, but by this time steam communication had become fully established on both East and West sides, and provided a much better service than could be maintained by the roads for transport of goods. The horse was no match for the steamer. Notwithstanding, there was substantial commercial development in the Lerwick and Scalloway area, notably the growth of the firms of R. D. Ganson in Lerwick, which by the 1890s had 36 horses,[46] and in the 1880s and 1890s sometimes imported cargoes of fodder from abroad,[47] and James Johnston in Scalloway, whose coach house was destroyed by a disastrous fire in 1909.[48] The principal use of the roads in the central area was to supplement the sea transport system's role in the commodity trades, and there are frequent examples of transporting cartloads of fresh haddocks to Scalloway to catch the steamer. In one day in February 1897, 190 boxes were taken to Scalloway for shipment in 35 carts, causing *The Shetland Times* to remark: 'Let us hope that the curers still have a margin of profit. They deserve it'.[49]

Unlike the external communications, which had been in part developed in order to improve the mail service and communications *per se*, the reverse had been the case with the road network. By the early 1900s, with the major roads practically complete (Fig. 51), the mail was carried by mail gig and ferries to the North Isles.[50] Nonetheless the desire for the benefits of communication conferred by roads remained strong, and after the County Council was formed in 1890, it was inundated with petitions for the construction of township roads connected to the main network.[51] However, the roads could not compete with steam until the advent of motor transport. The first car did not appear in Shetland until 1906,[52] and the age of the motor car and lorry lay beyond 1914.

As a postscript to the account of the development of internal communications by land and sea, it is fitting to consider the development of port facilities as the link between the two. It is in some respects a striking fact that port facilities were not more widely developed in Shetland, bearing in mind the dangers and heavy losses incurred by Shetland craft in the nineteenth century and that the natural harbour qualities of the voes and sounds are deceptive — witness the most intensive proper harbour development in Bressay Sound itself. Very small docks were in fact built at Uyeasound, Busta, Urie in Fetlar,[53] and Symbister in Whalsay in the days of open boats, landowners and merchants in the eighteenth and nineteenth centuries. However, the first harbour — indeed the only one to parallel the great harbour-building era on the east coast of Scotland — was the Freefield and Garthspool docks built in the 1820s and 1830s[54] (Fig. 52). The piers and basin built at Scalloway in the days of the cod smacks are the only other example of notable harbour development. Thereafter, the only demand was for the building of piers, almost entirely in connection with the herring fisheries. Such piers, which could be used for loading and unloading at herring stations, were requested as early as 1826 from the Fishery Board, to be

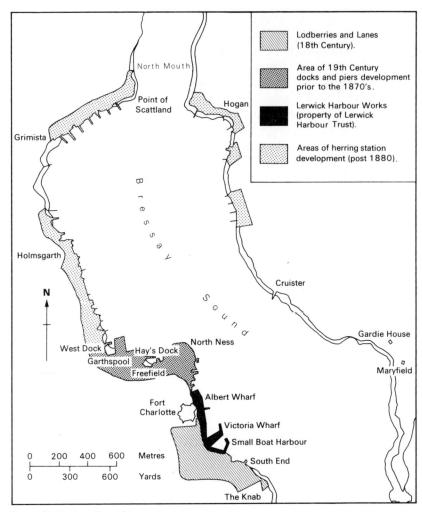

Figure 52. Bressay Sound

erected at Sandsayre, Cumlewick and Aness, but the petition was un-successful.[55] Most of the piers, including practically all those built at the sites of the herring stations (Fig. 47), appeared in the period 1880-1900, with the exception of the great complex of piers along the shores of Bressay Sound, a large proportion of which belong to the post-1905 period in which the herring fishing became centred on Lerwick (Chapter 5, Fig. 52).

The only really major harbour development was that at Lerwick itself, in the area below the Fort and stretching southwards to the South End (Fig. 52). The development of a harbour at Lerwick was urged by *The Shetland Times* in 1874,[56] and the Lerwick Harbour Trust was set up by Act of Parliament in 1877 for the purpose.[57] Any shipowner having at least 20 tons of shipping registered in the port of Lerwick was qualified to vote in the appointment of

Trustees, but the organisation was run on commercial lines, charging dues to provide for expenses, and was empowered to borrow money for improvements. The first major scheme, the building of the Albert Wharf and Victoria Pier, was undertaken immediately, the former being completed in 1884 and the latter in 1886, enabling steam ships to come alongside for the first time. The second phase of expansion of the harbour coincided with the peak of the herring fishing and its concentration on Lerwick after 1900, and included a new extension in 1904, new quays and the deepening of the basin in 1908, extension of Victoria Pier coupled with other improvements in 1912, and the building of the small boat harbour just before World War I.[58] The building of the harbour works converted the port from a lighter* — or more correctly 'boater'* — to one which could cater adequately for the new steamers, followed by the herring drifters.

Shetland Shipping and Trade

Before the middle of the eighteenth century local transport was separate from outside links, the emphasis being on trade, which was why communications were difficult. Open boats were the main means of transport, the situation being well described by Brand, writing in 1700, who remarked: 'And indeed, the easiest and safest way of Travelling is by Sea in Boats about the skirts of the Isles which also is not without danger'. He thereupon proceeded to recount the tragedy involving the Laird of Muness. As early as 1604, the boats of Burra were instructed to wait on Earl Patrick Stewart while he was in residence in Scalloway Castle, and the Burra people were to raise money for a ferry-boat for this purpose.[59] The earliest attempt at regulation on a large scale seems to have been in 1615, when a series of standard fares were laid down on main routes among the islands, mainly for 'the service of His Majesty's leiges' rather than transport as such. These included links between all the major islands and Mainland.[60]

The most complete account of statutory links dates from 1733.[61] Again, it consisted of 'ferry freights', and from this record it is possible to reconstruct a detailed pattern of transport links, with standard rates for four- and six-oared boats respectively, and an additional set of rates for long-distance 'great-boat' routes (Fig. 53). The 'great boats' were, as far as can be ascertained from rather sparse evidence, the equivalent of the type of craft later called a flitboat, being boats the size of sixerns or even larger. These craft probably carried most of the cargo, both on the routes illustrated in Fig. 53 and on the shorter routes connecting fishing stations to trade points (Chapters 3, 4). Robert Sinclair of Burgh (Chapter 2) had such a craft at the time of his death in 1616, and Sinclair of Quendale hired his great boat to the Dundee merchants for passage between Fair Isle and Dunrossness in 1695 (Chapter 2).

There were many connections across the voes and sounds, especially on the East side, with no outstanding focal points except, possibly, Burravoe in

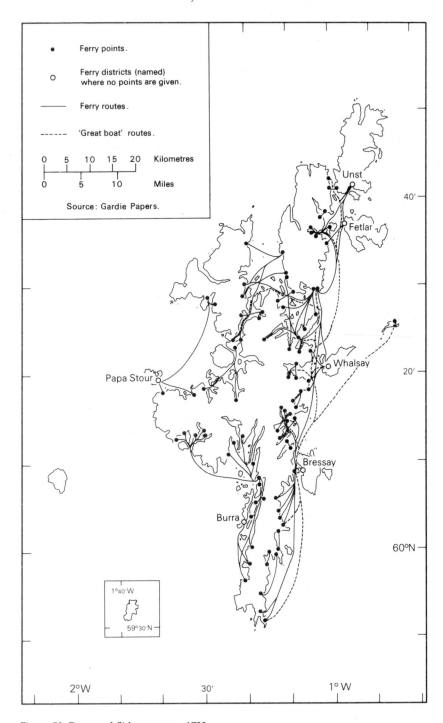

Figure 53. Ferry and flitboat routes, 1733

Yell. This, in common with the pattern of fishing trade points in the six-teenth and seventeenth centuries (Chapter 2), is a reflection of the dispersed settlement pattern and the absence of pre-eminent trade points. Thus routes were followed which to modern eyes appear strange. For example, in 1576 it is recorded that three lasts* of butter and other goods were taken from Bressay to Sumburgh, while the Bishop's and King's rents (Chapter 2), which were paid in kind, were transported to Laxfirth, thence overland to Scalloway. The inhabitants of Delting and Scatsta also had been used to pay their rents at Laxfirth, but had been subsequently ordered by Lord Robert Stewart to take the rents to Northmavine for reception and packing, fol-lowed by transportation to Laxfirth.[62] The general flexibility of the system from the individual point of view is further illustrated by the perambulations of the Customs officer in the early 1670s. For example, in the summer of 1672 he travelled from Orkney to Scalloway, and thence in turn to Bressay Sound, Whalsay, Burravoe (Yell), Unst, Northmavine, Papa Stour, Walls, Burra, and Dunrossness.[63]

Apart from their use in Shetland, a large class of open boat was used in the extensive trade and communication with Orkney (Chapter 2), the difficulties of which were frequently emphasised, being highlighted, for example, by the high costs of transporting small quantities of goods seized or poinded* in cases of debt, which in the early seventeenth century had to be brought to Scalloway.[64] Again, in the early 1650s, it was requested that Shetland be allowed to pay its superior duties direct to Scotland, which was more con-venient than carrying these goods to Orkney.[65] When Charles II was engaged in raising a militia force in Scotland in the early 1680s, it was emphasised locally that problems of distance among the islands and between Orkney and Shetland were such as to preclude a rendezvous more than once a year.[66] It was in an open boat 'of about sixty meils' that Brand had to travel from Orkney to Shetland in 1700, arriving after considerable delays, due to the weather, along a rather tortuous route from Kirkwall via Sanday, Eday, and Stronsay to Lerwick. The journey took from 27th April to 18th May to complete. They were detained in Sanday from 27th April to 9th May awaiting a fair wind, and had to put into Calf Sound, Otterswick and Stronsay because of the weather, after leaving Eday originally on 13th May. The final leg from Stronsay to Lerwick under fair wind conditions took only 20 hours, while the return journey, again with a fair wind, took only 15 hours from Lerwick to Kirkwall.[67] Such open boats remained in use until the middle of the eighteenth century at least, and one such from Sanday is recorded as having landed two cargoes of timber from Norway in Shetland in 1749.[68] Even at the end of the eighteenth century, it was still common, especially in cases of emergency in wartime, to send mail by 'barge' or open boat to Orkney and thence overland through Scotland.[69]

It is probable that the Orkney shipping link was the last surviving element of the medieval system, in which open boats of various kinds were used in all external trade. In the Shetland case, where the only link seems to have been with western Norway generally (Chapter 2), and Bergen in particular, it is likely that this vessel would have been the cargo-carrying variant of the original Viking longship and her descendants. The other major ship type in northern Europe was the cog*, a partly-decked vessel with forecastle and sterncastle, which was used in the Hanseatic spheres of influence in the southern North Sea, the Baltic and southern Norwegian coastal waters.[70] This type of vessel was unsuitable for prolonged sea voyages in the open sea in which bad weather was likely to be encountered, as its sea-keeping* qualities were not of comparable standard to the northern ship, although it probably excelled in cargo-carrying capacity. In practice, this did not matter greatly so long as the Hanseatic merchants maintained their commercial power through the Bergen kontor (Chapter 1).

At all events, the perfection of the fully decked ocean-going vessel in the fifteenth century was an absolute precondition for the establishment of trade links of a direct nature between north Germany and Shetland, as it was for the comparable Iceland trade of the Germans and the English, not to mention the fifteenth and early sixteenth-century development of the cod fisheries in these waters (Chapter 2). The technology of sailing during this era was unremarkable; the vessels probably had a single mast with a large square sail and a foresail, carrying capacity (deadweight tonnage)* being from 30 to 40 lasts* (60-80 tons), which was from a third to half the size of German vessels engaged in the Iceland trade.[71] This was of the same order of size as most of the eighteenth-century Shetland trading vessels.

As noted in Chapter 3, perhaps the most significant aspect of the itinerant merchant trade system was that the merchant owned and travelled on his ship and personally supervised and was otherwise acquainted with every aspect of his trade. Apart from the Orkney and Norway vessels, these north German traders were the only major means of communication with the islands, and bearing in mind the summer nature of the trade (Chapter 2), it is hardly surprising that it should have been remarked on more than one occasion by Scottish Customs officials that there was virtually no communication to be had with the islands in winter.[72]

The element of local shipowning implied by the landowners' trading activities provided the local basis, albeit tenuous, for the trade system involving agents and merchant houses. Throughout the seventeenth century, information on locally owned shipping is sparse, but approximately ten vessels can be traced, mainly through name or other specific indications of ownership. As early as 1588, for example, it is recorded that Andrew Umphray of Berry carried the survivors of the *El Gran Grifon* (the supply ship of the Spanish Armada wrecked on Fair Isle) to the Fife coast in his own ship.[73] Robert Sinclair of Burgh owned at the time of his death the ship *Swanne*, valued at £2,000 Scots, and there were others[74] (Chapter 2).

After the demise of the itinerant merchant, the basis of the trade link became the ship and her crew, with which the landowner or merchant generally travelled as supercargo. Indeed, in the early days of the merchants, between 1790 and 1820, notably in the smuggling trades, it was common for the merchant to supervise operations in this way, a classic case being the smuggling voyages of James Hay (Chapter 4). In some of the external smuggling activities, the supercargo was, strictly speaking, the person placed in charge of the cargo and superintending all the commercial transactions of the voyage, rather than the owner of the vessel.

More commonly in Shetland trade as a whole, indeed as with shipping in the whole trading area of western Europe, the skipper of the ship was the business manager of all things pertaining to the vessel, including engaging and paying off the crew, paying the crew's wages, provisioning, maintaining the vessel herself, and supervising the commercial dealings in connection with the cargo. This included the payment of port charges such as warehousing duty, lighterage* (commonly necessary when many goods from butter to fishing lines were packed in barrels — Chapter 3), weighing of cargo, receiving and collecting money including demurrage*, port dues, customs duties and insurance, all of which had to be arranged on the typical trading voyage. Supervision of loading and discharging the cargo itself was generally the responsibility of the mate, or 'meeresman' as he was known in northern and eastern European continental ports,[75] the ships of which carried a significant proportion of Shetland trade in the eighteenth and early nineteenth centuries. The mate kept an exact tally of every article taken on board, according to which account the captain signed the bill of lading, which contained the full list of cargo items. Thus, for example, on a voyage to Hamburg in the *Clara Margareta* in 1746, Robert Gifford, who was travelling on the ship as supercargo, was instructed by his father Thomas Gifford to attend the sales of the fish and see them carefully delivered. Robert was also to give the mate 20 ling for taking care of the fish and 'telling' (i.e. counting) 14,600 of these aboard the ship at Shetland and ashore again in Hamburg.[76]

In the fish trade, it was common for a vessel to have several points of loading (Chapters 3, 4), and the Customs officers who, until the early nineteenth-century advent of the Fishery Board, were responsible for weighing fish for the bounty as well as jerking* the ship, had consequently to travel round the coast with the vessel. The expense of this travelling was payable by the consignee of the cargo, at standard rates laid down as early as 1723.[77] Meanwhile, the merchant or his agent had to make an entry at the Custom House regarding the quantity and quality of fish exported, where the duty paid on the salt used in curing the fish was debited on his separate salt account.[78] Dry fish required careful stowage, and apart from the need for dry weather conditions in loading, which often caused considerable delay, it was necessary to have timber for dunnage*, and 'Russia mats'*. The former was used for stowage of the cargo, and the latter, which were specially imported for the purpose, for spreading over the cargo to protect against water from above.[79]

The full complexity of the supercargo's business is particularly well illustrated in the record of James Hay's trading voyages in the *Catharine* in 1814.[80] Hay of course tended to conduct all his merchant business, as well as perform the agency-type function of the supercargo. Thus he commonly wrote by ship letter* to his next port of call to arrange freights in advance, kept a tally of prices of commodities, and organised the timing of his voyages so that these did not clash with the herring and cod fisheries in which his vessels were also sometimes engaged. The importance of personal contacts in this system is exemplified in his arrangement of insurance at Leith, also via ship letter, in which he remarked by way of justification of his selection of Leith insurers that '. . . the Leith underwriters are better acquainted with our ships and shipping than those of London are . . .' He had also to form judgements on the difficult trading conditions in Norway on the cessation of the blockade, including mastery of current exchange rates and freights, had to establish personal contacts for possible future trade commitments, such as buying meal for export from the lanndowner on Sanday, and generally had to keep up to date with the economic complexities of international seaborne trade.

After 1820, and the secure establishment of the business firms (Chapter 4), it was more common for the skipper to conduct the day-to-day operations of the trade link. Undoubtedly the best record of this is to be found in the log of the *Janet Hay* which contains in one book a record of most of the major commodity trades in which nineteenth-century Shetland shipping was engaged.[81] She was at the outset engaged in cod fishing, with a crew of twenty-two. After returning from the Davis Straits and discharging her cargo of wet salt cod at Scalloway, and taking in herring from Hamnavoe in Burra, she proceeded round to Lerwick to prepare for trading. This involved paying off the fishing crew and signing on the trading crew, which for Shetland trading vessels in the eighteenth and nineteenth centuries was commonly four or five men. Getting the ship ready for trading included the usual maintenance, heaving ballast, getting stores, and loading a cargo of 952 barrels of herring for Stettin. The several voyages thereafter illustrate the variety of problems with which a skipper had to contend in the course of trading voyages. In Stettin the ship was towed from Swinemunde Roads to the harbour boom* by steam tug, contrasting sharply with conditions in Bilbao, where the ship was towed up river by bullocks, and where the crew, having begun to take in ballast out of a lighter after discharging the cargo, were '. . . obliged to knock off by orders of the harbour-master [it] being a holy day'. In Vadso it was decided to haul the ship 'on ground' and clean and paint the bottom, which was very dirty. After loading a cargo of pitch and tar at Archangel, the skipper discovered that the ship was down by the head, and he refused to sail, thereby incurring the displeasure of the shippers. The dispute was settled on the skipper's initiative in calling in a marine surveyor, who confirmed his judgement, and the cargo was trimmed accordingly. Apart from such problems, the master was totally responsible for all the multitude of decisions necessary for the navigation of the vessel, of which the log is a priceless record. All in all, the skipper's role was a crucial and challenging one. The essential difference between the itinerant merchant system compared to that of the agency network was that the business of transport of goods and communication of information (including payments) became a separate *commercial* undertaking, with a distinct and independent business organisation, which branched out into shipowning, engaging particularly in the import trade (Chapter 3). However, there was one function largely absent, that of finance and marine insurance, which was largely the preserve of the British-based merchant house, situated at the market end of the chain.

The growth of the British merchant house can really be traced back to the commercial revolution of the late seventeenth century, which introduced the mechanism of credit into the market place, especially in the days of slow communications. Apart from this, the merchant houses also acquired by degrees agency work and became shipowners, by a process similar in kind to that taking place on a•much smaller scale in Shetland (Chapter 3). In function, the merchant house was an extension of the old factor system, but from the intermediate locations of the large British ports it operated a shipping network which extended to gradually take over most of the Shetland export trade. It seems likely that the crucial element in the development of this pattern was the provision of trading finance and connections in the market areas, as Shetland did not assert itself in its own freight market until the establishment of the first and last local merchant, that of Hay and Ogilvys (Chapter 4).

The size of vessel used in Shetland trade after 1707 appears to have been of the same order as those in use by the German merchants, or possibly slightly smaller. For example, in 1741, Robert Dick of Fracafield is recorded as buying '. . . a good england built ship . . . about 80 tons'.[82] However, in general, information on tonnages is sparse, and it is probable that in the eighteenth century there were two sizes of vessels, corresponding to the frequent mention of sloops* and brigs* respectively in the records.[83] The sloop was a simple fore-and-aft rig favoured for smaller craft up to perhaps 40 tons, such as those trading to Scotland, while the brig was usually in fact a brigantine* rig, favoured on many of the ships trading to Hamburg, Bergen and the Iberian Peninsula such as the *Elizabeth* of Yell[84] and the *Dolphin* of Scalloway.[85]

In the nineteenth century, when mercantile shipowning expanded, there was still a tendency to have two basic sizes. The sloop of from 15 to 40 tons was most common in the trade to Scotland and round the islands, although it is worthy of note that many of the early merchants' ventures — not least those of James Hay (Chapter 4) — were undertaken in sloops. These sloops were also the basis of the cod fishing during the pre-1850 phase of development, and were generally built locally or in ports on the east coast of Scotland, whence second-hand vessels were acquired. In contrast, the second class of vessel was generally built to English designs and acquired

R

second-hand from English ports (Fig. 54). This type ranged upwards in size from 50 to well over 100 (120-150) tons, and was mainly ketch-rigged*, the largest being rigged as brigantines and topsail schooners. The schooner rig was more manageable than the brig and brigantine, a few of which remained among the largest trading vessels until the 1840s.[86] During the first half of the nineteenth century, the majority of these large vessels were engaged for most or all of the time in trading. However, after 1850, and in parallel with the second phase of expansion of the cod fishing, the number of vessels in the 50-100 ton class greatly increased. These were the legendary smacks*, more generally known as 'Faroe smacks', through association with the main cod fishing grounds in the vicinity of the Faroe Islands (Fig. 62). Ketch-rigged for the most part, these vessels were large enough for trading also, and the period from 1850 until 1880 was the heyday of the fishing/trading combination in the use of shipping.

Throughout the greater part of the eighteenth century, the number of ships owned in Shetland appears to have been low, probably around five to ten at most at any given time. In 1784, for example, there is reference to only 'five or six small coasting barks'.[87] The numbers increased fairly dramatically in the course of the 1790s, partly as a result of Shetland merchants acquiring prizes brought to the islands in the first of the Napoleonic Wars.

Table 8. Vessels Registered in Lerwick

Year		Number	Total Tonnage	Number Men in Crews
1789	(foreign trade)	5	250	25
	(coastwise trade)	1	41	4
	(total)	6	291	29
1794	(foreign)	5	258	18
	(coastwise)	3	131	10
	(total)	8	389	28
1800	(total)	17	552	56
1801	(total)	14	460	45
1802	(total)	15	419	50

In 1809, Edmondston records[89] that there were 10 vessels of 768 tons engaged in the foreign trade, which he averred was the highest number ever. From the 1820s onwards the shipping industry expanded more or less in parallel with the cod fishing, revealed by the number of vessels registered* (Fig. 26). Most vessels were registered, as even the smaller cod sloops engaged in some trading activity. The numbers fluctuated from as low as the mid-40s to the 70 to 80 range.

There were five phases of development (in the development of the traffic pattern generated by shipping and the carrying trades), beginning in the

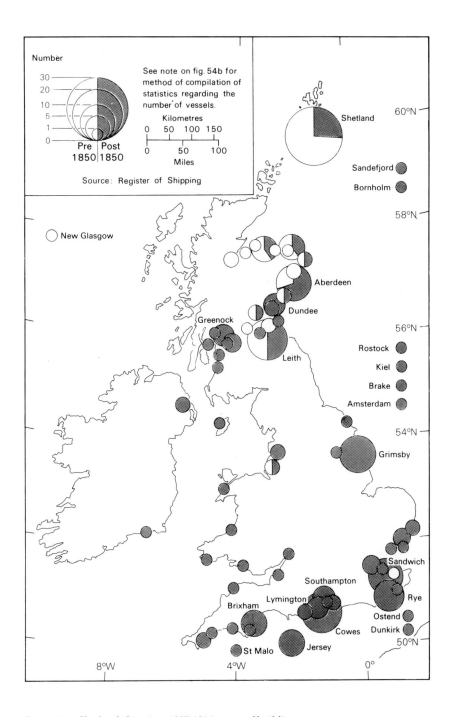

Figure 54a. Shetland shipping, 1837-1914: ports of building

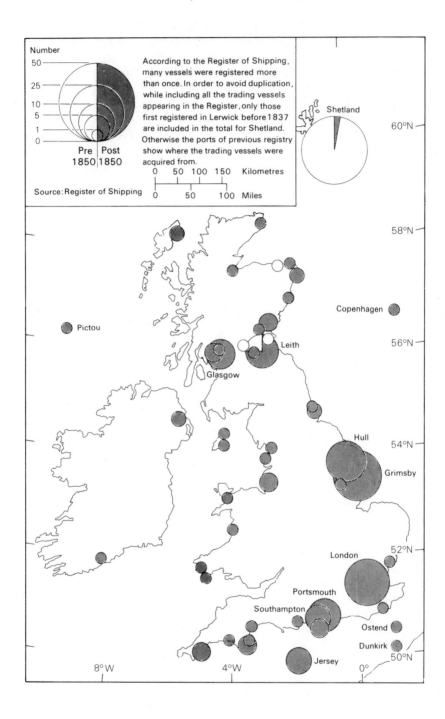

Figure 54b. Shetland shipping, 1837-1914: ports of previous registry

eighteenth century. The first period, until around 1760, corresponds with the phase of 'landmaster-trader' development and covers the first part of the beginning of division of labour in the running of the landowners' businesses. During the following phase, until 1820, the merchants established themselves as shipowners, culminating in the phase of merchant house domination in shipowning in the form of Hay and Ogilvys in the period 1820-1840. These three phases represented the building up and culmination of local commercial power. In the final two phases of development, discussed in the next section, a new shipping system evolved, in which shipping became a business undertaking removed from finance and sometimes even agency work.

The method of analysis of the several periods is based on the analysis of traffic flows and ports of registry*, which reveal respectively the patterns of use of shipping in the sea trades of Shetland, and the nature of the trade link connections on which these commodity trades were based. The analysis is derived from information in the Customs Quarterly Returns up to 1829,[90] and, in the case of the nineteenth century, export statistics from 1821 onwards were obtained from the Fishery Board records.[91] The two major gaps in the material concern coastwise trade statistics at all periods, of which a qualitative picture only can be gained, and the foreign trade imports after 1829, to which the same remark applies. After the middle of the nineteenth century, detailed tonnage statistics relating to both the foreign and coastwise trade exist,[92] but it is not possible to ascertain cargo details or ports of registry from these.

Throughout the eighteenth century, the principal export commodity trade was of course dried fish, while imports consisted mainly of timber, fishing necessaries and foodstuffs (Chapter 3). Thus it is hardly surprising that traffic flows reflect the changing locations and relative importance of different markets. Meanwhile, as the port of registry was almost invariably that of ownership of the vessel, it tends to reflect the influence of trade links in determination of these markets.

Information for the first half of the eighteenth century is of course incomplete, but two important features stand out (Fig. 55a). The first was the predominance of Shetland vesssels in both import and export trades, coupled with a relatively high proportion of continental shipping, especially from the Bergen and Altona areas, which corresponds with the close links forged by the factors in Bergen and Hamburg respectively. There was also an appreciable number from the Forth ports, signifying the general coastal trade links and their interaction with the foreign trade. The coastwise trade itself seems to have been of least importance at this time, the principal element being the meal trade from Orkney (Chapter 3), together with similar links with ports on the east coast of Scotland, such as Leith and Montrose. The second feature of the commodity trades was the importance of London and Southwold vessels in the export trade, due to the export of herring to Hamburg for the Free British Fishery, and to the large number of

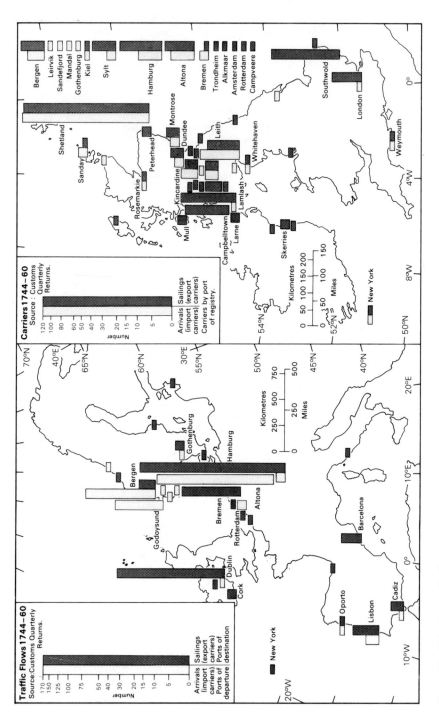

Figure 55a. Shipping traffic flows and carriers, foreign trade

vessels hailing from ports round the Clyde and Solway estuaries and Ireland, consequent upon the fishing activities of the Irish wherries.

On the whole, it was an era when the landowners' ships ventured on all trade routes, exporting to north Germany and the western side of the Iberian Peninsula, and engaging in the import trades from north Germany, western Norway and the east coast of Scotland. Few of the landowners wholly owned their ships, with the exception of large operators such as Thomas Gifford of Busta, and John Bruce Stewart of Symbister (Chapter 3). More commonly, there was a share system, such as that between Robert Blellock and the Unst landowners in 1716 (Chapter 3). With the exception in which Nicolson of Lochend and one or two others engaged in cod fishing using their trading ships (Chapter 3), they were generally unenterprising in the realms of shipowning as such, and appear to have seen it as merely a necessary means to an end of fostering trade.

The short period from 1761 to 1768 (records for 1770 to 1779 are unfortunately incomplete — Chapter 3) demonstrated well the shape of things to come in the new order of the agent-merchant house system (Fig. 55b). It was notable for the concentration of the import trade from Bergen and Hamburg-Altona, and shows the expanding Spanish and Italian trades and declining Hamburg trade in the export sector. Although the remnants of the Free British Fishery and the Irish wherry trades were still evident, the rise of the new set of English ports, and of Leith and Glasgow was the result of the new merchant house activity. During and immediately following the 1760s, the merchants of course established their shipowning businesses, and this helps to account for the continuing importance of Shetland shipping in the carrying trade, although it possessed a relatively smaller share than previously. In the 1770s, it is apparent from the Customs Returns that the Shetland merchants concentrated on the development of the import trade, which could be carried on at less capital risk using smaller craft. This of course included interests in smuggling, especially from the Dutch ports (Chapter 3).

This basic pattern continued into the 1790s (Fig. 55c), although the increased importance of Bergen and Christiansand reflects changes in the timber trade, while the pre-eminence of Barcelona and Dublin likewise reflects the concentration of the fish export trade on these ports. However, as previously pointed out (Chapter 3), the business connections with Scotland were by this time beginning to occupy a leading role, and this is exemplified by the strong rise of Scottish-registered vessels, especially in the export trade. Leith and Greenock were of course the leading merchant house connections, along with Liverpool, where the firm of Sellar and Henderson were engaged in exporting Liverpool salt to Shetland. Thus the coastwise trade increased considerably also, and part of this is recorded for the commodity trades in coal and stone, which were required to pay duty.

It may seem paradoxical at first sight that the tonnage of locally owned shipping should rise dramatically just at the end of the 1790s, when the

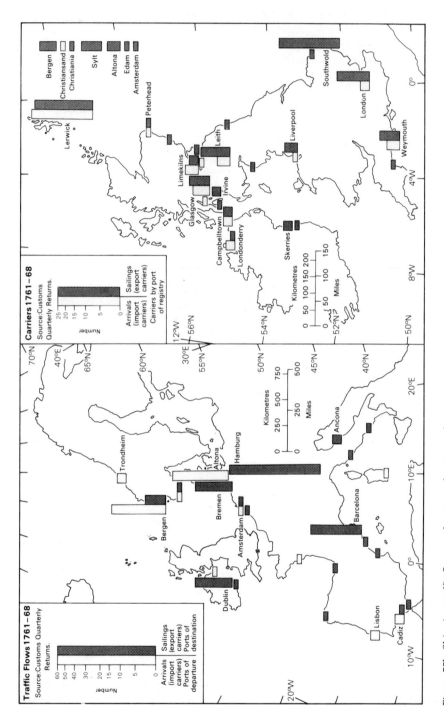

Figure 55b. Shipping traffic flows and carriers, foreign trade

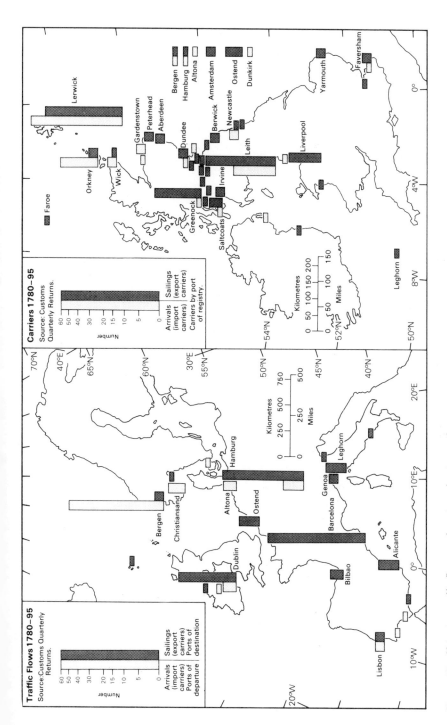

Figure 55c. Shipping traffic flows and carriers, foreign trade

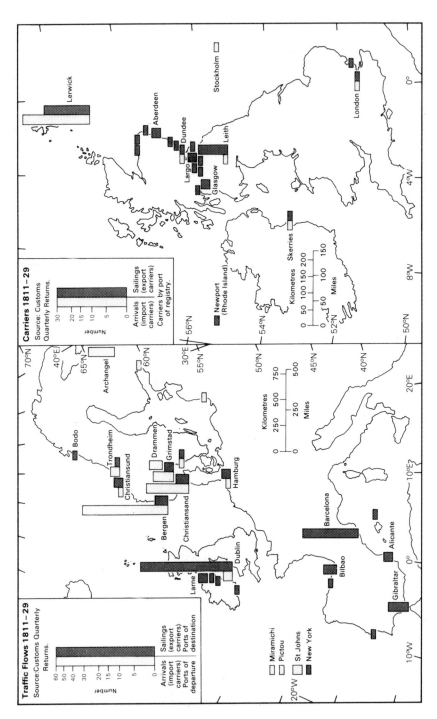

Figure 55d. Shipping traffic flows and carriers, foreign trade

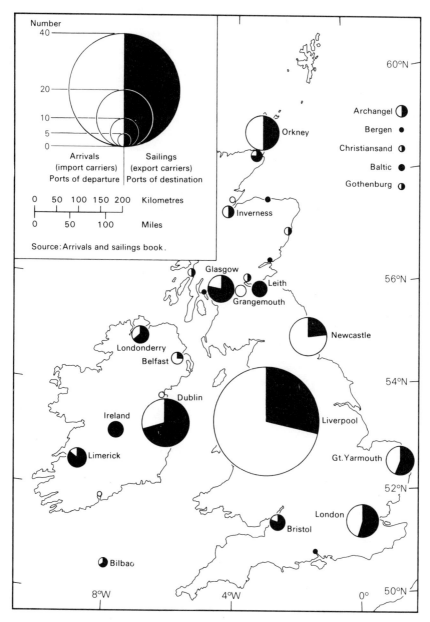

Figure 56. The voyages of Hay & Ogilvy's ships, Jan. 1840 - Sept. 1842

Spanish market was cut off virtually for the duration of the Napoleonic Wars, and other shipping links curtailed (Chapter 4). However, the wars were in many ways a blessing in disguise for the up-and-coming Shetland merchants. The great reliance on the home market for fish put them in a favourable position as carriers, while the need for the merchant houses' foreign connections and trade facilities was extinguished. Ships were also easier to acquire, due to the substantial number of captures of enemy merchant shipping in the sea round Shetland. Thus the merchants were enabled to build up their shipping business, and the coastwise trade expanded greatly along with it. By 1816, over 3,000 tons of shipping were engaged in the export trade coastwise,[93] and by 1819 the Customs remarked that '. . . the trade of this country is almost wholly confined to the coasting trade . . .'[94]

However, by the mid-1810s, the foreign trade links were being re-established and trade was on the increase. The growth of the merchants' shipowning activities was such that for the first time the largest operators were in the position of being able to set up their own merchant house organisation, Messrs. Hay and Ogilvys. The pattern which persisted from around 1820 until the bankruptcy of Hay and Ogilvys in 1842 was thus characteristically different from the preceding patterns, while being at the same time the culmination of the development of the merchant house system in a Shetland context. Despite some overlap between the two periods in the records, which extend from 1811 to 1829, the shape of the pattern is clearly distinguishable. Between 1820 and 1840, Hay and Ogilvys succeeded in building up a virtual monopoly of the external freight trade of the islands, the only notable incursion upon their power before 1830 being participation of vessels from the east coast of Scotland (Fig. 55d). Ships belonging to the company ranged as far afield as Jamaica in the herring trade,[95] and the Maritime Provinces in the timber trade.[96] There were also new patterns in the shipping trades, notably a great emphasis on the Irish market compared to the Spanish for fish (Chapter 4), and the diversification of the timber trades. Although Bergen remained the centre for boats, important new links, based on the timber trade, developed with south-eastern Norway, the Baltic, Archangel and the Maritime Provinces (Fig. 55d). In the 1830s the pattern of foreign trade freights was complicated by the takeover of the Spanish trade by Spanish vessels, while a substantial number of Irish and West of Scotland vessels had a share in the herring trade.

This expansion in the foreign trade was parallelled by even greater expansion in the coastwise trade. In 1832, this trade involved entering and clearing about 70 to 80 vessels yearly; by the mid-1830s, under the influence of the expanding herring market and the consignment of all fish to Britain and Ireland, the numbers increased still further (Chapter 4) (Table 9).[97] Even after they lost the Spanish trade in 1838 and the herring trade virtually collapsed in 1840, Hay and Ogilvy still had by far the greater share of the coastwise trade, and the pattern of their trade for 1840-42 is virtually that for Shetland as a whole (Fig. 56). The most important links were to Liverpool or Irish ports with fish, and back from Liverpool with salt; to Leith, Yarmouth and London with general exports, cattle and fish, and back with general goods or coal from Newcastle.[98]

Table 9. Shipping Movements, 1835-1837

	1835	1836	1837
Foreign Trade			
Vessels with cargoes inwards	28	27	6
Vessels with cargoes outwards	20	6	1
Coastwise Trade			
Vessels with cargoes inwards	174	182	175
Vessels with cargoes outwards	161	153	157

It is this interest in shipping, together with the expansion of the cod fishery, which was responsible for the building of Hay's Dock at Freefield (Fig. 52). In December 1832, for example, 11 sloops, 9 'big' boats (flitboats larger than sixerns), and 7 sixerns were hauled up at Freefield, while another 10 sloops and an unspecified number of boats lay in the dock.[99] Apart from 16 shares in the Shetland New Shipping Company and a half interest in the Union, Leith and Shetland Shipping Company, the firm had at the date of their bankruptcy in 1842 two-thirds shares* in 7 large vessels in the brig, brigantine and schooner class, and in 11 sloops; half-shares in 2 sloops, one-third in one sloop, and one-sixth each in a sloop and a smack.[100] This effectively represented about one-third of the total number of vessels in the islands, most of which were cod sloops engaging little in outside trade, and virtually all the external trade tonnage. Their shipping interest also securely established a shipbuilding industry in Shetland (Fig. 54a), which was responsible for practically all the vessels built in the islands during the 1820s, 1830s and 1840s, and included vessels as large as the 300-ton barque* *North Briton*, launched in 1836.[101]

From the early 1840s until around 1880, shipowning was based on the use of the large smack class of vessel, which was generally 60 to 80 feet overall and from 50 to 100 tons register*. The main period of investment in these vessels began in the late 1840s, with a peak in the late 1850s and early 1860s, and again in the early 1870s, when a number of well-smacks* were acquired, principally by the Shetland Fishery Company (Chapter 5). Unfortunately, shipping statistics are incomplete for this period, and limited mainly to exports in the foreign trade, although the tonnages of import and export traders in the foreign and coastwise trades are available from 1855.[102]

In the export trade, external non-commercial factors began to play a significant role in the patterns of the carrying trade, principally through the ruling of the Spanish Government that goods imported into Spanish ports by Spanish ships would obtain a more favourable rate of duty than those imported in foreign bottoms. Coming into force in 1838, this ruling coincided with the re-opening of the Spanish market to Shetland dried fish, and did not have a great effect on the shipping of the islands from an economic point of view, as it was at that time primarily engaged in the herring trade and Irish dried fish trade (Fig. 57a). In the case of the herring

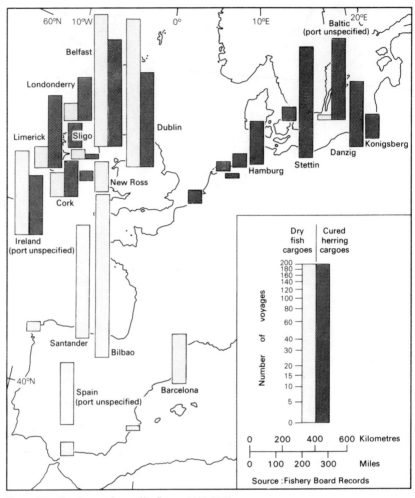

Figure 57a. Foreign trade, traffic flows, 1835-1875

trade, which fluctuated with the scale of the herring fishing itself, peak periods such as the late 1850s required as much tonnage as the dried fish trade. Shetland vessels had the largest share, although there was a marked shift in location of ports of registry of the external carriers from the west coast to the east coast and continental ports in sympathy with the shift from Ireland to the Continent of the main herring market (Fig. 57a). The position regarding the timber import trade is less clear, although it appears that an increasing amount of Norwegian tonnage participated in this trade.[103]

The role of Shetland shipping in the coastwise trade, built up in the 1820s and 1830s, continued in this period, notably in the use of the smacks for carrying fish to Liverpool and Ireland, and returning with cargoes of salt from Liverpool, and coal from the Tyne ports. The coastwise trade expanded

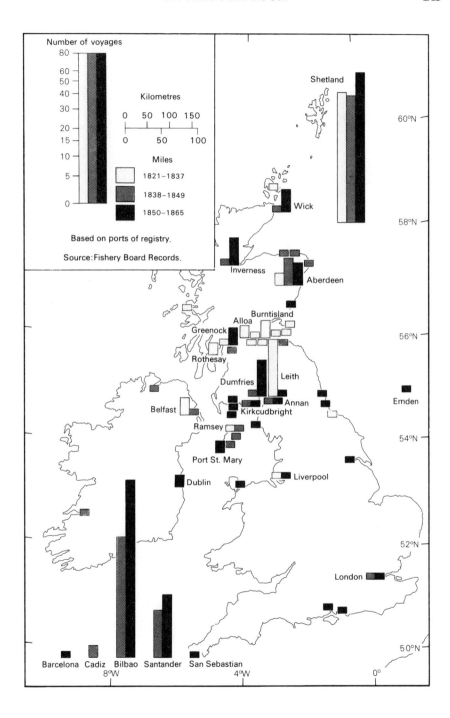

Figure 57b. Export carriers, fish, 1821-1865

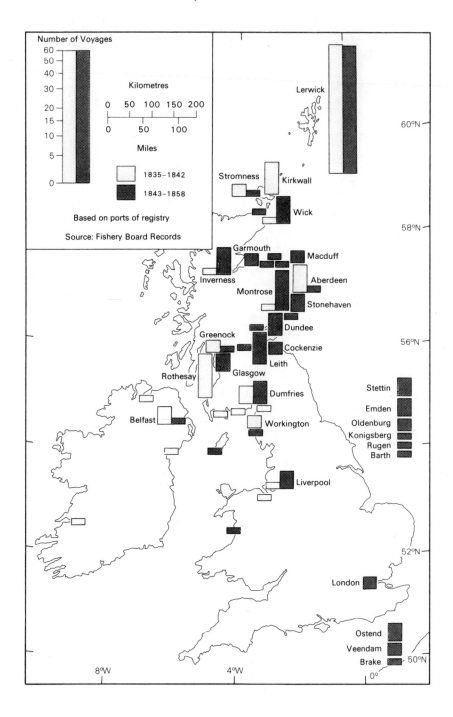

Figure 57c. Export carriers, herring, 1835-1858

VOYAGE	DATES		FROM	TO	CARGO
1	1862	29/5 to 26/6	Lerwick	Davis Strait	Ballast
2	"	26/8 to 16/9	Davis Strait	Scalloway	7,854 Cod
3	"	20/9 to 22/9	Scalloway	Lerwick	Ballast, Some Herring
4	"	7/10 to 16/10	Lerwick	Stettin	Herring
5	"	14/11 to 23/11	Stettin	Fraserburgh	Timber
6	"	8/12 to 10/12	Fraserburgh	Newcastle	Ballast
7	"	27/12 to 29/12	Newcastle	Lerwick	Coal
8	1863	16/1 to 17/1	Lerwick	Scalloway	Ballast
9	"	18/2 to 27/3	Scalloway	Bilbao	Dry Salt Fish
10	"	10/4 to 25/4	Bilbao	Cardiff	Ballast
11	"	3/5 to 9/5	Cardiff	Liverpool	Coal
12	"	21/5 to 26/5	Liverpool	Vadsö	Salt
13	"	16/7 to 26/7	Vadsö	Archangel	Ballast
14	"	13/8 to 28/9	Archangel	Liverpool	Tar
15	"	21/10 to 30/10	Liverpool	Lerwick	Salt

Figure 58. The voyages of the *Janet Hay*, 1862-1863

S

considerably with increased prosperity in the 1850s and 1860s. However, shipowning activity other than in fishing appears to have been of reduced importance, and only pursued on an appreciable scale by Hay & Company,[105] the descendants of Hay and Ogilvy. The most complete account of the activities of a Shetland trading vessel in the mid-nineteenth century is to be found in the log of the *Janet Hay*, summarised in Fig. 58. The principal cargoes carried were coal, salt, timber, herring and dried fish, and it was tried as far as possible to obtain back-freights and intermediate freights on journeys commencing with Shetland export cargoes.[106] In short, it was participation in the tramp shipping trade within Europe as a whole. One interesting small-scale development towards the end of this period was the introduction of the travelling shop. For example, T. M. Adie of Voe sent vessels to Faroe with general cargoes for salt in 1872, portions being disposed of, while the rest was brought back to Voe along with ponies.[107] The use of ships in such commercial undertakings is an important indication of ideas on commercial opportunities.

Table 10. Entries and Clearances[104]

		1856		1857	
Coastwise Trade					
Inwards		139 ships	16886 tons	148 ships	24871 tons
Outwards		123	15961	120	22767
Foreign Trade					
Inwards	(cargo)	19	1419	23	2525
	(ballast)	10	640	12	615
Outwards	(cargo)	21	1452	33	2306
	(ballast)	15	818	9	613

The period from 1880 to 1914 was remarkable for the great expansion in shipping activity associated with the development of the herring trade and greatly improved steamship services, and the changed structure of the transport system due to the replacement of sail by steam and the taking over of the coastwise trade to a large extent by the North Company, based in Aberdeen and Leith. The complexity of the system was made greater by the changes taking place in the commodity trades due to market forces, which had arguably become for the first time more powerful than the system of trade links, and also because the system of trade links was by this time based on shipping agencies, import-export agents, and banks, which were separate business organisations.

The principles of competition inherent in the market system operated no less in the freight markets in the post-navigation laws era.[108] The carrying trades, which consisted largely of herring exports and timber, barrel and salt imports were shared among ships of several nations. There were substantial elements of Norwegian, Swedish, German, Russian and other European nations involved which it is difficult to analyse in detail because of the absence of detailed statistics on ports of registry, and the non-distinction in some of the statistics between foreign-registered trading vessels and fishing vessels (especially Swedish, Danish and Dutch) belonging to the same countries (Fig. 59b). [109]

Under such circumstances, the local shipping fleet, which was declining, was placed in a disadvantageous position in relation to the great expansion in shipping activity, although the participation of many smacks in the coastwise and herring trades probably means that the decline was less sharp than that of numbers engaged in the cod fishing (Fig. 26). The reasons for this included the structure of the herring industry itself, in which transport of fishing stock* and herring was organised in such a way that a continuous circulation was taking place among stations where vessels might pick up or unload several part-cargoes for a curer who had stations scattered over several localities. This is illustrated by the pattern of shipping movements sailing from Ronas Voe[110] (Fig. 60), one of the leading early herring fishing localities (Chapter 5). A second reason for the decline of local shipowning was the lack of investment in steamships, which in the herring trade, as well as in other trades, were rapidly supplanting the sailing ship from the 1880s onwards, although there was a temporary increase in sailing tonnage after 1880 due to the high demand for freight imposed upon a shipping market in which steam was still only being developed (Fig. 61). Most of the Shetland business firms were either herring curers, hiring or owning vessels like other curers, or still engaged in the cod fishing and hiring their smacks out to curers for coasting work among the stations, for example. A final reason was the predominance of the North Company in the coastwise trade, which implied the use of steam all year round on all services, and the advantages of scale of company organisation, and which signified the merging of the business of communications with that of trade, through the carriage of mails.

Sea Services

Unlike the development of shipping and sea trade, communications were often improved for social purposes, and economic consequences were therefore indirect, as was the case with passenger transport. This goes far to explain their separate business organisation to begin with, and the peculiar difficulties of the development of sea services associated with what must now be regarded as mythical tales about the remoteness and inaccessibility of Shetland throughout the several historical periods. Notwithstanding, the fostering of trade was undoubtedly one of the principal reasons behind the inauguration of the mail service, and transmission of information on war situations a strong reason for its maintenance.

Apart from the requirements of the itinerant merchants, both externally

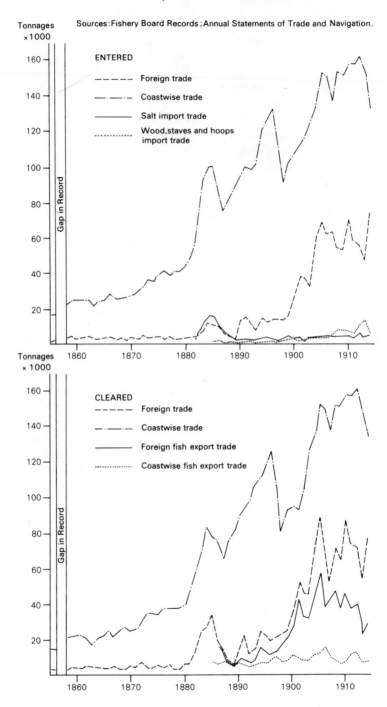

Figure 59. Shipping traffic, 1855-1914

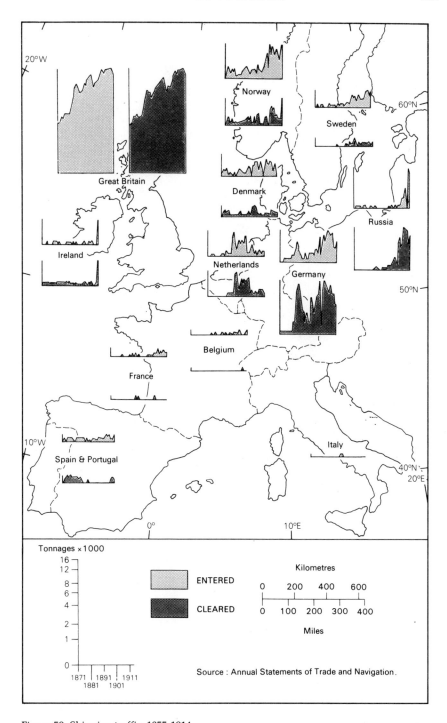

Figure 59. Shipping traffic, 1855-1914

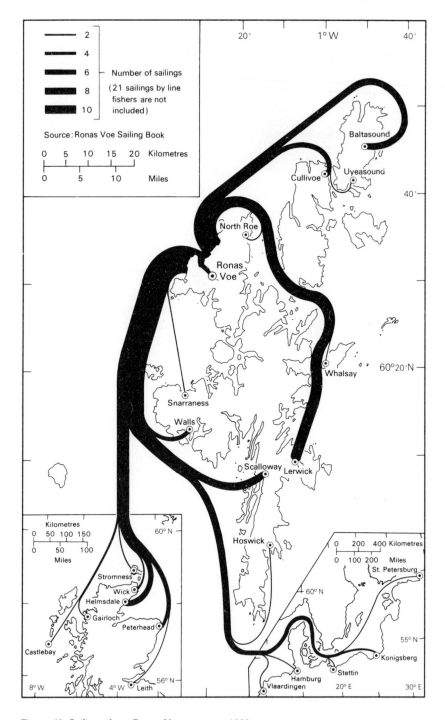

Figure 60. Sailings from Ronas Voe, summer 1900

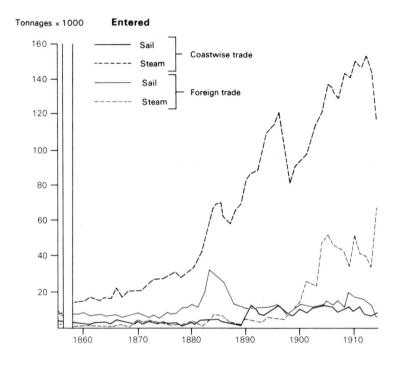

Source: Annual Statements of Trade and Navigation

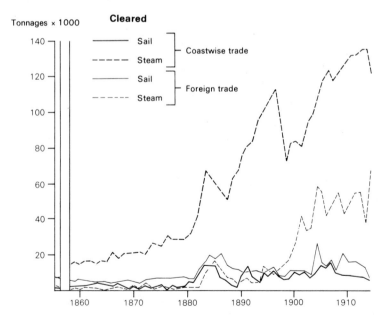

Figure 61. Sail and steam power in external trade, 1855-1914

and internally, the need for communications was minimal in early times, and until the middle of the eighteenth century it was limited mainly to travelling by government and church officials. It was largely for this purpose that the ferry freights and routes were stipulated in the early seventeenth century, and again in the 1730s. Another example of this type of communication was the perambulation of the Customs officers, recorded around 1670, and their observations that it was impossible to get to Shetland except during a few months in the summer. Contrary to popular opinion, the reason for this difficulty of communication was not the remoteness of the islands and the danger of storms, but simply that there was little need to communicate outwith the requirements of trade. However, it was the *idea* that the islands were remote that proved influential. One suspects that this was the case with Brand, who was sent by the Church of Scotland to investigate and ensure change in the local churches after the Revolution Settlement of 1688. It was 1700 — no less than twelve years later — before Brand made the journey, and only he among the Church Commissioners was prepared to face up to the real and imagined dangers of the voyage from Orkney to Shetland, on which he dwelt at considerable length in his writings.[111]

The casual organisation in personal transport in those days continued for some considerable time after the advent of the first packet service. It was common, as the Rev. John Mill did on occasion,[112] to travel on trading ships when necessary, and even the packet was noted for its dilatory progress and lack of organisation. However, the system was in many respects more flexible from the individual point of view than later organisations. For example, Thomas Mouat, in his account of his journey to London in 1775,[113] noted that on the first leg of the trip on the packet from Lerwick to Leith, he left the ship and went ashore at Cellardyke to explore and make contacts along the coast in the vicinity, before boarding a vessel from Anstruther to Leith. Again, on the journey from Leith to London by packet, he left the vessel on another unscheduled stop at Great Yarmouth, and proceeded on the remainder of the journey overland through East Anglia. To this characteristic of flexibility in individual movement was added another, often inconvenient, one for passengers, that of flexibility of time taken to complete voyages, usually because of unfavourable weather conditions. Charles Ogilvy (later of Hay and Ogilvy — Chapter 4) records taking twelve days on the packet from Leith to Lerwick in 1815. They left Leith on 27th April and put back to Burntisland Roads on 1st May, leaving again on the 4th and arriving in Lerwick on the 9th.[114] His experience was by no means uncommon.

As with personal transport, the carriage of mail depended almost entirely on the passage of trading ships, and it is from trading interests that the first pleas come for an improved mail service linking the islands with Scotland. One of the first requests for an independently operated mail service dates from 1757, when it was proposed that a Post Office be established in Lerwick. The main reasons given were that it would eliminate the increasing inconvenience encountered in the pursuit of trade, and also provide a better and more reliable means of communication of intelligence regarding shipping movements, especially in wartime.[115]

Although there is a reference to a regular trade contact being established between Shetland and Leith as early as 1736 by William Farquhar,[116] one of Shetland's leading skippers in the mid-eighteenth century, it is probable that no mail service as such was inaugurated till the late 1750s, at the time of the Post Office proposal. This first packet, the *Isabella*, began running between Leith and Lerwick in the spring of 1758,[117] but seems to have been discontinued soon after, and only re-established after the Seven Years' War in 1763 or 1764 when a Post Office was established. It ushered in what may be termed the first period of development of communications links *per se* with the 'south', which lasted from the 1760s until the 1820s. The period was dominated by the uncertainty of communication and the organisation of the service to run from Leith or Aberdeen rather than Shetland.[118] In 1763, the postal rate was fixed at 6d a letter and the Post Office paid £60 a year to a firm of Leith merchants (almost certainly one of the merchant houses) towards the cost of a sloop making the passage five times a year. This organisation proved inadequate, as the service was secondary to the carriage of goods, which in a Shetland context meant irregularity in sailing times due to seasonality of supply and demand factors, resulting in general lack of dependability with periods of up to five months without a packet. Sending of mail by trading vessels was thereby encouraged, which made the operation of the packet for the carriage of mail increasingly uneconomic. By the late 1780s John Bruce of Sumburgh remarked forcibly that '. . . the Packet Boat . . . is positively, *on its present establishment* a perfect nuisance, an Interruption of all Information and a ruin to the Trade, Commerce & even Credit of this Country'.[119]

This state of affairs led to the petitioning of Lord Dundas (the Earl of Zetland, Chapter 4), and the Government, with only limited success. In 1789 an Aberdeen firm offered to run an Aberdeen-Lerwick service twelve times a year for £60, which offer was accepted, but this venture appears to have come to nothing, and the former Leith arrangement was resorted to. It is likely at this time that Leith was a more satisfactory base, as most of the trade and general financial connections were with merchant houses and banks in Leith or Edinburgh (Chapter 4). That there was inefficiency on the Post Office side also is apparent from a memo of the merchant house involved, Robert Strong & Co. of Leith, that the Post Office were three years in arrears with their payment to the contractor.[120] Meanwhile, it was common to send mail by open boat to Orkney and thence overland. Much of the naval intelligence reached the ears of Government this way. Alternatively, such missives might be dispatched by visiting British warships, which in wartime could be safer, as the packet, in common with other trading vessels, was liable to be intercepted by enemy warships and privateers. This happened on more than one occasion as, for example, in 1798[121] and 1799.[122]

The situation with regard to the packet appears to have improved somewhat in 1802, when the Government, with Admiralty help, agreed to a contribution of £120 a year for ten trips annually, although Shetland tried unsuccessfully to secure a more frequent service. From then on, little was heard of the packet until 1812, when Shetland wanted the contribution increased from £120 to £300'per annum, whereupon the Post Office pointed out that the total annual revenue from Shetland letters was only £75, and suggested that all letters be sent as ship-letters.[123] The packet continued on this irregular footing for the remainder of the decade and during the early 1820s. In 1819 the Customs remarked on '. . . the irregularity of our packets . . .',[124] and commented in 1822 that sometimes there was no packet for many weeks together, followed by a series in successive weeks.[125]

The provision for the mail service continued to be inadequate for some time after 1820 — indeed in the eyes of many it was always inadequate. However, after 1820, more systematic organisations appeared to develop sea services, principally for the transport of goods, but catering also for the mails. In general it is possible to detect the importance of the coast trade itself in the operation of the packet service; for example, in 1825, the vessel carrying the mail sailed for Montrose with a cargo of cattle.[126] The trade link to Leith was of greatest importance. As early as 1809 it was noted that 'for long' the trade had been considerable, employing two 70-ton sloops which made an average of seven voyages a year each,[127] probably largely as a consequence of the home market for dried fish (Chapter 4).

The problem always revolved round the impossibility of providing an economically viable service free of trade requirements, and from the early 1820s the emphasis shifted from the provision of services for the carriage of mails to services catering for the needs of the commodity trades. The 1820s were of course a good time for the provision of an organised cargo service, as the coastwise trade was expanding rapidly because of the increased importance of the home fish market relative to foreign markets (Chapter 4), and a general increase in trade as the economy expanded after the Napoleonic Wars.

These services were based in Shetland, rather than in Aberdeen or Leith. The first attempt was in 1823, when the Contract of Co-partnery of the Leith and Shetland Shipping Company,[128] to remain effective for 25 years, was signed. With a capital stock of £4,000, subscribed by six small-scale Lerwick merchants, a Lerwick lawyer and an Edinburgh merchant, the company put the 87-ton schooner *Norna* on the Lerwick-Leith run. The vessel seems to have run fairly regularly. In 1828-29, for example, a schedule approximating to six weeks for the round trip was adhered to.[129] The *Norna* was lost in 1839 on the Blue Mull of Unst while on passage from Baltasound round to Cullivoe with a cargo of Christmas stores,[130] and was replaced by a smaller vessel of the same name.[131] Thereafter, the history of this undertaking is obscure, but the principal link seems to have been that provided by the second company incorporated to provide a cargo service. This was the

Zetland New Shipping Company, established by another group of Lerwick merchants in 1829 with a capital of £2,400.[132] This company acquired the brand-new 110-ton schooner *Magnus Troil,* which operated throughout the 1830s and early 1840s, being replaced in 1847 by the 107-ton clipper-schooner *Matchless.* The *Matchless* was built by the famous clipper builders, Alexander Hall and Company of Aberdeen, on the lines of the *Scottish Maid* class, built to compete with steamships on routes from Scottish ports to London.[133] She successfully competed with the steamships of the North Company till 1881, although the trade became unremunerative after the transfer of the North Company's headquarters from Granton to the more accessible Leith in 1879.[134]

Meanwhile, the standard of the mail service did not improve, and was subject to constant complaints in the 1820s, culminating in a petition to Government in 1833 for a new mail vessel.[135] Whether this petition was directly successful or not is not clear, but in 1833 a third shipping company was established on the relatively small capital of £1,000. The Zetland Union Shipping Company, as it was known,[136] was also backed by a small group of Lerwick merchants, with the stipulation that one of the directors was *always* to be one of the partners of Hay and Ogilvy. At all events, the ships of Hay and Ogilvy seem to have run an improved mail service connecting with Peterhead[137] until the commencement of the operations of the Aberdeen, Leith and Clyde Shipping Company in the late 1830s using steamships.

The activities of the Aberdeen, Leith and Clyde Shipping Company ushered in a new era in Shetland shipping and communications, through the coming of steam and the application of large-scale business organisation to the provision of shipping links. The service hinged, however, not on the transport of goods, which was already being catered for by the 'sail' shipping services, and by other vessels on a more casual basis, but on the provision of a mail service. In this context, therefore, the impetus for development was the same as it had been during the period from the middle of the eighteenth century until the early 1820s. Under these circumstances, bearing in mind the continuing uneconomic proposition of running a mail service only, the first result of the pressure for improved services led to the introduction of the s.s. *Sovereign,* a paddle-steamer making a once-fortnightly call at Lerwick in summer only, on her run from Leith via Aberdeen and Wick to Kirkwall, in the summers of 1836 and 1837.[138]

In 1838, after much wrangling between the Commissioners of Supply representing Shetland interests, the Post Office and the shipping company, it was agreed to provide, on contract, a weekly mail service in summer, and to run less frequently in the winter months also. This system ended in disagreement in February 1839, as the shipping company had not sufficiently established their carrying trade to make the running of the service economic. They then applied to the people of Lerwick to use their influence with Government to limit the service to eight months per annum, apparently reinforcing the request with the threat of withdrawing from the contract altogether if their demands were not met. As this was the only steamship company likely to operate in the area at that time, their request was acceded to, and thereafter for two decades the mail service was operated using steamships for six months of the year and a succession of sailing packets in the winter months,[139] these being the *Aberdeen Packet* (1838/39-1847/48), the *William Hogarth* (1848/49-1851/52, when she was lost on passage from Aberdeen to Shetland), and the *Fairy* (1852/53 to 1860/61).[140]

Not surprisingly, the sailing packet was often delayed in winter by contrary winds or bad weather, causing frequent delays reminiscent of the pre-steamship era which ended in the 1830s. Thus there was a continuous pressure for further improvements, especially the desire to have all-year-round steam communication. In 1844, the Commissioners of Supply appointed a committee to investigate this possibility,[141] and petitioned the Government for such a service in 1851.[142] However, it was not until the winter of 1858-59 that their wishes were realised, in the shape of a fortnightly steamer service in winter, which operated for two years in conjunction with the *Fairy*.[143]

Meanwhile, the weekly summer service had been maintained, and about the time the *Fairy* was withdrawn this was extended to a weekly winter service as well in the winter of 1860-61, although at first not on a regular basis.[144] The improvements in the steam service in the late 1850s and early 1860s were undoubtedly related to that increasing prosperity in the island economy which became evident from the late 1850s onwards (Chapter 4). How much it contributed to that prosperity is, in the absence of detailed records, a debatable point. What seems likely is that by this time the company had succeeded in establishing a secure footing in the carrying trade despite competition from the other carriers. In the export of agricultural produce in particular, such as livestock and eggs, steam communication was much more suitable than sail, and this sector of the economy derived substantial benefit from its introduction (Chapter 4). However, the shipping company had little or no share in the fish and herring export trades, and the problem that little export cargo was available to match the capacity of the steamer services tended to remain until and even during the expansion of the herring fishing.[145]

Notwithstanding the greatly improved services, the pressure for further elaboration continued unremittingly, particularly in relation to mails. Thus, in 1862, the *Shetland Advertiser* was advocating[146] a bi-weekly mail in summer, which desire was fulfilled in the summer of 1866.[147] This event possibly marked the end of the phase in which the balance of power between the local community in Shetland and the company altered from the former to the latter. Until this time, constant pressure was kept up to get improved services from a company which had only a limited share in the carrying trade, and for which the mail contract alone was an uneconomic proposition. After 1870, and particularly after 1875, when the name of the company was changed to the North of Scotland and Orkney and Shetland Steam

Navigation Company,[148] the element of decision-making exercised by the company enters much more into the scene. Transmission of information had again become of less importance in relation to goods services, and the separate business organisation of communications assumed the initiative in developing sea services.

The new pattern which evolved after 1870 was commercially organised and commercially viable, based on a near-monopoly of large sections of the coastwise trade by the 'North Company', as the North of Scotland and Orkney and Shetland Steam Navigation Company was generally known. The main implication of this new situation was the introduction of company, as distinct from individual, decision-making on a large scale into Shetland shipping links with Britain.

The North Company at the time of its change of name was, with minor exceptions, such as the Shetland Fishery Company and the Sumburgh Mining Company, the only company of any size connected with Shetland trade which was not a family business. Even the great joint-stock concern of Hay and Ogilvys had been in many respects a family concern, and its successor Hay and Company, although ultimately a limited liability company from the legal point of view, was still basically a family interest at this time. In 1878 the North Company had 30,000 shares belonging to several hundred shareholders, mainly from Aberdeen and the North-East of Scotland. Only a very few had holdings amounting to over 100 shares, the bulk of the share capital being subscribed by the great majority of small shareholders.[149] Thus the weight of investment — and the decision-making — was extended to Shetland. The growth of the company can perhaps best be assessed from their ability to provide shipping services, measurable by the number of ships they had. In 1878 there were four steamships; by 1896 there were ten, not counting the vessels belonging to the Kirkwall and Leith Shipping Company, taken over in 1884, and the Shetland Islands Steam Navigation Company, absorbed in 1890.[150]

The processes of company decision-making emerge most clearly in their policy for the provision of services, and the reaction of the island community to these, which was particularly bound up with the carriage of mails. In some respects the observation of action and reaction between the company on the one hand, and the Shetland community on the other, is liable to result in sterile arguments as to which led the way and was responsible for economic developments in general and the fostering of trade in particular. A more detailed study of the available evidence shows that, although expanding economic conditions encouraged the establishment of steamer services, implementation of new services remained essentially a company decision. The process can be observed most clearly at the beginning of the great herring fishery (Chapter 5). In 1880, for example, it was observed that the success of the herring fishery in Leith, Caithness and Shetland (where this was the first year of major herring landing) had greatly augmented freight receipts, and the following year the company decided to introduce the West Side service.[151] The introduction of this service cannot, however, be seen in a Shetland context only. It must also be viewed in relation to events in Orkney and Caithness, where the herring fishing was of considerable importance in the 1880s. The service linked Leith and Aberdeen with Stromness and Scalloway, with various extensions to other ports on the South Isles of Orkney and West Side of Shetland, and increased the frequency of links to Shetland from the winter:summer ratio of 1:2, established in the late 1860s, to 2:3. The move, combined with the withdrawal of the *Matchless,* gave the company a virtual monopoly of the coastwise trade,[152] although complete monopoly was prevented for some time by the operations of a few of the schooners and occasionally other steamship companies.

Throughout the 1880s and 1890s, in spite of variations in timetabling, there was a tendency to increase the frequency of services, due partly to pressure for improved mails and partly to commercial decisions by the company. The introduction of the West Side service in 1881 was accompanied by the hope, expressed in the Annual Report to shareholders, that passenger traffic (especially tourists), and the development of the fishings, would add to the freights obtainable on this route. The great expansion of the herring fishery until 1886 was certainly instrumental in the creation of renewed pressure in the islands for still more services. In 1887, for example, there was a local lobby emphasising the need for daily steam communicaton with the south, and *The Shetland Times* regretted the refusal of the company to do anything about the fresh fish trade,[153] which of course it would have been impossible to develop without steam communication (Chapter 5). One of the complaints was that the terminal on the West Side service in winter was Scalloway, thus placing the haddock fishermen on the West Side north of Scalloway at a severe competitive disadvantage by virtue of inaccessibility (Chapter 5).

Continued pressure, this time by the newly created Zetland County Council and Lerwick Town Council,[154] emphasised the importance of direct communication between Lerwick and Aberdeen for the benefit of the fresh fish and livestock trade, and that this would also confer the benefits of a better mail service. In the same year, 1891, the direct Aberdeen-Lerwick service was inaugurated on a weekly basis,[155] bringing the total number of weekly connections to three in winter and four in summer. The management replied that the Aberdeen-Lerwick routes already possessed too much capacity, but there were further complaints in the late 1890s about the fish service and the mails.[156] There was a persistent call for a daily mail service, and it was pointed out that this service would increase the value of the fisheries, presumably through better contact with the markets. The situation appears to have remained more or less static until 1906, when a further petition was sent to the company from the County Council requesting one additional mail between Aberdeen and Lerwick, principally for the convenience of the hosiery trade, now on the increase after the advent of the parcel post. It was also hoped to ensure a more steady fish market, as better mail communications could avoid the placing of all the Shetland fish on the market at the same time in the week, causing potential gluts.[157] From the period 1909-1914, Shetland had the best steamer service it has ever possessed at any time before or since, with five summer services connecting to Aberdeen and Leith in summer, and four in winter.[158]

The greatest encouragement to the development of shipping services between 1880 and 1914 was the growth of the herring industry and all the ancilliary trade which arose out of it. Despite the large foreign tonnage engaged in the import of fishing stock and the export of herring, there was still ample scope for the North Company, especially in the transport of herring coastwise to the home market and for re-export from Leith. The industry also contributed to a large seasonal passenger traffic in the movement of thousands of herring shore workers (gutters and packers) between Shetland and the east coast of Scotland. However, the herring industry was limited mainly to summer and autumn as far as the carrying trade was concerned, and even allowing for one service a week less in winter, there was still spare capacity on the routes. The situation was in practice ameliorated by the increase in livestock exports, and by the rise of the fresh fish trade. In addition, in the late 1880s, the company succeeded in acquiring most of the declining dried fish trade, the fish being in the first instance transported on the West Side route to Stromness, and transferred to Langland's steamer (see below) for the passage to Liverpool, whence they made their way to Spain.

Although the conflicts between the North Company and Shetland interests would suggest that the company was doing the minimum to encourage the commodity trades' development, this was not so. There was one field in which the company went to great lengths to encourage development, namely the tourist trade. The initial growth of the tourist industry in Shetland is rather obscure, as tourists, in common with other travellers, used any ship available. Perhaps the best-known early tourist was Sir Walter Scott, who made his journey to the islands in 1814 in the vessel of the Northern Lighthouse Commissioners.[159] Thereafter there was a series of nineteenth-century visitors, many of whom left written accounts of their visits. However, large-scale tourism does not seem to have gained a footing until the late 1860s and early 1870s, presumably coinciding with the provision of improved steamer connections. In August 1872, it was noted that the *Chieftain's Bride* was crowded with tourists, and the great development of the trade by the North Company followed in the 1880s. It was of course conducted with reference not only to Shetland, but to the whole area of the company's operations. However, Shetland derived substantial benefits, one of the reasons for the introduction of the West Side steamer service being the encouragement of the tourist trade, while in 1885 special excursion fares were introduced on the normal services. In 1887 the first *St. Sunniva* was acquired specially for that tourist trade, and in subsequent years during the

1880s, 1890s, and 1900s was engaged in running cruises to the fjords of western Norway (inaugurated in 1886), some of which called at Shetland, as well as cruises round Britain, and occasional charter work to the Baltic and Mediterranean.[160] A new boost was given to the industry by the opening of the company's St. Magnus Hotel at Hillswick in 1902, at the summer terminus of the West Side service route, coupled with the introduction of inclusive holidays, the cost of which covered fares and hotel accommodation.[161]

The activities of the North Company dominated the business of communications and most of the coastwise trade of Shetland between 1870 and 1914. As might be expected in an age of rapid economic development, however, there were other companies, and other routes were pioneered. The first of these was largely a speculative venture establishing Lerwick as a port of call on the route linking Denmark, Granton, Faroe and Iceland. As early as 1855, there is mention of a regular trader which carried the mails between Faroe and Shetland,[162] but the continuance of any such further links is obscure until 1870, when Hay and Company, in conjunction with the Danish Government shipping company, arranged for Lerwick to be made a port of call in summer on this route, carrying general cargo, mails and passengers.[163] However, in the words of the Customs, 'The encouragement the vessel has received in the way of trade at this port, has not realised the sanguine expectations entertained by the agents'.[164] In an age of speculation this did not necessarily deter further trials, and in 1872 a link from Bergen to Iceland calling at Lerwick and Faroe was advertised.[165] The most successful enterprise in this field seems to have been the summer trade conducted by the Aberdeen, Leith and Clyde Shipping Company in the early 1870s, between Granton and Iceland, using the *Queen*, which sometimes carried Iceland ponies to Shetland (Chapter 5).[166]

The second notable shipping link was that between the east and west coasts of Scotland operated by Langland's of Glasgow. This service appears to have commenced by calling at Stromness weekly, beginning in 1874, and intermediate links between Glasgow and Dundee included Oban and Aberdeen.[167] The date of extension of the service to Shetland is uncertain, and it seems to have been irregular, being determined mainly by commodity trade requirements in the 1880s. Thus, for example, in September 1885, Langland's steamer arrived from Glasgow with a large general cargo including the remainder of the gasholder being erected at Lerwick.[168] This service also took away livestock, and in the late 1880s became the means whereby dried fish was sent to Liverpool for export via the North Company to Stromness. In November 1888 the largest dried fish consignment to date, consisting of 1,400 packages, was dispatched by this link.[169]

There were other notable attempts to establish links. In 1877, the Caledonian Steam Navigation Company advertised a weekly service leaving Lerwick for Aberdeen and Newcastle, while in 1880 it was emphasised that the company's links with Leith, Middlesbrough, Stockton and Hull facilitated the consignment of cargo through Leith to continental ports.[170] This was no doubt aimed at the growing herring trade. Finally, in 1882, the Napier Shipping Company of Glasgow proposed the opening up of trade between Glasgow, Thurso, Kirkwall and Lerwick.[171]

Despite competition between shipping interests and the fostering of new trade links, practically all of the competition in external trade appears to have been eliminated in the course of the 1890s, with the exception of the carrying trade in the herring industry, in which the North Company had a share. By the early 1900s, the company had established a virtual monopoly in the operation of Shetland's external shipping links, as by then even the smacks had largely disappeared from trade, outside the herring industry, where most of those remaining had been absorbed. It is at this point that the last shipping development of interest prior to 1914 occurred, namely, the incorporation of the Shetland Islands' Steam Trading Company Limited in the winter of 1902-03, founded with the avowed intention of 'breaking the monopoly' of the North Company in island trade links.[172]

In January 1903, 25 per cent of the capital was called up to charter a ship for operation on the Leith-Aberdeen-North Isles route, and in June of the same year the service was commenced using the *Minnie Hind*, renamed *Norseman*. The immediate reaction of the North Company to this competition on the same route was to make substantial reductions in freight rates.[173] By the end of 1904 the new company was in a weak financial position, but it persevered, and in 1905 acquired the *Norseman*. However, the position continued to deteriorate. By June 1907, the debit balance in the company's accounts stood at £6,000, and it ceased operations later in the same year.[174] To compete successfully, the Shetland company would have required a vastly greater capital stock. It is doubtful if such an undertaking could have succeeded in the long term, given the dominant position of the North Company in relation to the total volume of available trade, especially as it made little effort to branch out into the continental herring trade, for example. The lack of ability to influence North Company decisions or to run an independent company from the Shetland end emerges clearly in the political arguments conducted at the time the Shetland company was set up. Apparently Shetlanders had never invested to any great extent in the North Company, which might have given them a say in company policy in relation to the island services. One writer in January 1904 estimated[175] that the amount invested by Shetlanders in both companies was approximately the same, being of the order of a mere £5,000 in each.

Commercial interests played a leading role in the improvement of the mail service from its inception in the 1750s until the campaigns for a daily mail service in the 1880s. As for the telegraph, the measure of its value is apparent in that, when a meeting of Lerwick burgesses was held in 1869 to consider a guarantee required by the Orkney and Shetland Telegraph Company before laying a cable north to Shetland from Orkney, £400 was subscribed there and then in the meeting room.[176] Again, the leading role of commercial interests

T

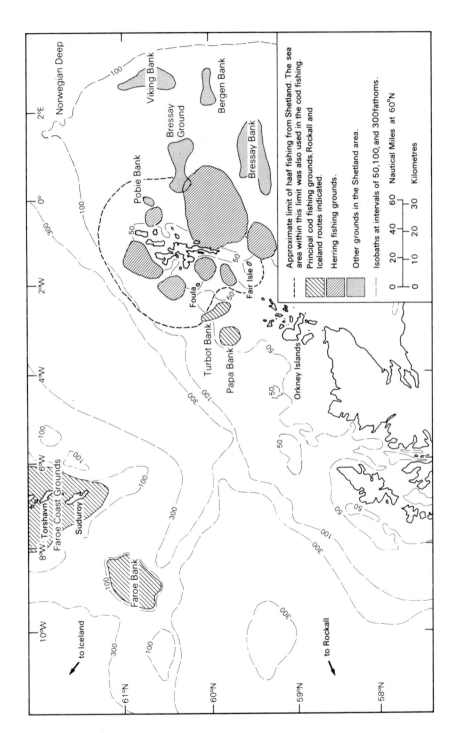

Figure 62. Fishing grounds

emphasised the importance of this new form of communications link, and the frequent breakages in the cable which occurred in the early 1870s caused considerable annoyance and equally frequent demands that the Post Office should take over the cable, which was done in the late 1870s.[177] When the herring fishing got under way in the early 1880s, the curers pressed to have extensions to all the outlying stations, and lines of telegraph poles soon appeared along the new road network, while a new and more reliable cable was laid direct from the Scottish mainland by the Post Office.[178] In 1872, laying of the Faroe and Iceland cable commenced,[179] while work began on a new Iceland cable in 1905.[180] By 1898 the Aberdeen Telephone Company was endeavouring to establish a telephone exchange in Lerwick,[181] a task finally accomplished by the Post Office in 1907.[182] The era of instant communication had arrived.

The precise effects of the improved mail services and the telegraph are of course difficult to gauge (Chapter 5). In 1892, *The Shetland Times* remarked, by way of proof, that the coming of steam and the parcel post were destroying local monopolies in Shetland,[183] which no doubt referred to the hosiery trade in particular. The telegraph was regarded by the herring curers as 'the very sinew of war', just as the mail had been looked on as absolutely necessary for business in the days of the merchant houses and the dried fish trade, and was so regarded by those involved in the haddock trade in the days of steam communication. The basic reason for all this was the requirement of speed in communication, so well expressed by John Bruce, writing in 1786 about the flurry of letter-writing at the last minute which always preceded the departure of the packet. 'The reason for this is,' he stated, 'that People are willing to give *the latest* information to their correspondence & others, upon business or any thing else.'[184] The prime requirement at all times had been for the producer to know as soon and as accurately as possible the state of the markets. It avoided as far as possible excessive speculation, which might otherwise have been necessary in the fresh fish and herring trades. The coming of 'instant' communications emphasised what had been true all along, that, in spite of being an island group, Shetland was very much in the mainstream of European trading developments prior to 1914.

The Seaways of Europe

The location of Shetland in relation to the lands and seas of Europe had two characteristics. First was its central position in relation to the major fishing grounds of the northern half of the continental shelf lying west of the Norwegian Deep (Fig. 62). Second was the close proximity of the islands to several of the major European trade routes (Fig. 65). These two characteristics pertained essentially to the large, external scale, and not to the indigenous development of trade described in the preceding chapters. Nonetheless both the importance of externally based fishing and the position on the trade routes had various repercussions on the island economy.

The economic importance of the external fisheries is difficult to assess. On the whole it seems likely that the sum total of their effects in promoting trade was greatest in the seventeenth century, under the influence of the Dutch herring fishing, and this is the reason for including the development of this fishing and its effects in the discussion of the trade system of the seventeenth century (Chapter 2). However, there were other fisheries of importance in the sixteenth and seventeenth centuries. For example, the Dutch also fished for cod and ling in Shetland waters, using 'hookers'*, throughout the period of the great herring fishery. Perhaps more important than the Dutch fishery was the English fishery for cod and ling, which in the later sixteenth and early seventeenth centuries was sometimes connected with trading ventures of the kind pursued by the German merchants. As in the case of the Dutch hooker fishery, the most important fishery area seems to have been Iceland, at least in the later part of the sixteenth and seventeenth centuries. In the early part of the sixteenth century, there were about 80 English vessels fishing in the Shetland area, and 120 at Iceland.[185] By mid-century, this had dropped to 10 and 43 respectively.[186] The frequent unsuccessful attempts at expanding the English fisheries in the seventeenth century are further evidence of decline. The growth of the Dutch fisheries may have aided the decline also.[187] It is likely that from the mid-seventeenth century onwards, the English fishing vessels entered the general traffic past Shetland, as, for example, in 1655 when a man o' war convoying seven ships from Iceland stated that all was well in Shetland when he went past it.[188]

The Scottish fishery in the Shetland area was based on cod, ling and possibly some herring fishing. The principal bases were the fishing burghs on the Fife coast of the Firth of Forth, and Dundee. Both in the 1580s and 1610s there are several references to the arrival of shiploads of herring and dried fish at Dundee from Shetland.[189] As in the case of the English fishings, this is difficult to disentangle from the trading activities (Chapter 2). Unlike the fisheries of England, the Scottish fisheries thrived until the 1630s, but declined thereafter. Brand, writing as late as 1700, attributed the decline of herring fishing off Shetland by the Scots to 'the death of so many Enster men in the battle of Kilsyth'[190] (fought in 1645). By the end of the period there was some revival, although it is not clear how this applied to Shetland. Brand's remark suggests that it did not.

External fisheries in the eighteenth century opened on a low key after the disaster which overtook the Dutch in 1703 (Chapter 2). These fisheries, although never assuming the importance they had enjoyed in the seventeenth century, were nevertheless extensive, and were arguably at least as important as local trade in the development of Lerwick, until the supplanting of the landowners by the merchants as leaders in trade. Thus in 1733, for example, Gifford remarked that Lerwick had declined since the burning of the Dutch busses,[191] but Low, writing in 1774, noted that the

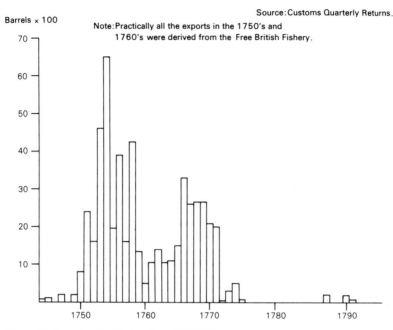

Figure 63. Exports of white herring, 1744-1795

annual fair in June was still taking place in Lerwick, on the usual basis of bartering fresh provisions and woollen stockings for brandy and tobacco.[192] A lot of petty smuggling took place, and also some large-scale smuggling under cover of fishing, particularly by the Danish fishing company vessels in the 1770s (Chapter 3).

The dominant feature of eighteenth-century external fisheries development was the setting up of companies to prosecute the herring fishing, following the example of the Dutch. The most noteworthy of them was the Free British Fishery, which was a company established by Royal Charter. It commenced operations in 1751,[193] using Shetland as a base to some extent, at least for export agency work,[194] although, in common with other herring fisheries, the herring was cured at sea. The fishing was encouraged by a bounty system based on the tonnage of the vessels employed, so that by the 1770s, when market conditions were unfavourable, the vessels were evidently being sent to sea to collect the bounty rather than to fish for herring.[195] The great phase of expansion of this fishery took place in the 1750s, and was severely curtailed by the Seven Years' War. It enjoyed renewed activity on a smaller scale in Shetland waters in the 1760s, but became extinct in the early 1770s. Most of the exports (Fig. 63) were directed towards Hamburg and Bremen, using yagers* after the Dutch fashion.

A second venture, which resulted in a certain amount of agency work, and almost certainly was the means of establishing permanent contact with the

Irish dried fish market, was the arrival of Irish wherries* in Shetland waters in 1751. These vessels fished mainly off the West Side from a base in Walls,[196] and their presence was resented by many of the landowners and fishermen, who blamed them for an alleged decline in the fisheries in the late 1750s and early 1760s.[197] Whatever may have been the truth of this contention, they succeeded in obtaining an order prohibiting the operation of these vessels in 1763. This was achieved by arguing that the wherries were using British salt, which had not paid duty, for salting fish for export to Ireland.[198] Most of the exports to Ireland in the 1750s (Figs. 14b, 16) were derived from this source.

By the 1780s, there were two to three hundred Dutch herring busses, and thirty to forty French herring busses, operating out of Dunkirk, with similar numbers from Emden and Denmark, while the Swedes sent about half that number after the failure of the Gothenburg herring fishery, and a few even came from Hamburg. In addition there were from 60 to 100 Dutch cod fishers engaged mainly in the Iceland fishery, up to one-third of which might remain in Shetland for the whole season if the fishings were favourable, operating out of Quendale Bay and other localities, whence fresh provisions and water could be obtained.[199] During the Napoleonic Wars most fishing activity ceased, and the next period which can be distinguished lasted from around 1815 until the great herring fishing of the 1880s and after. The external fisheries were definitely of little importance in local trade, although the French and Dutch cod fishers, calling at the islands en route for Iceland in the spring, often smuggled spirits and tobacco. Their example was followed by the Dutch herring fishermen who, it seems, were much poorer than they had been in the eighteenth century.[200] The·number of busses seldom amounted to more than one or two hundred.

The period after 1880 witnessed the influx of large numbers of vessels from outside the islands, in which English, Scottish and Dutch predominated, using the islands as a fishing base and service centre. The Dutch were by far the most important foreign contingent, amounting to as high as five or six hundred boms* in number.[201] This of course contributed substantially to the use of Lerwick as a base for provisioning, and petty smuggling probably increased substantially. There was also a resurgence of highly organised, Dutch-based smuggling activity in the 1880s, carried on mainly at sea by vessels which were at first sight indistinguishable from fishing craft, but were in fact 'travelling shops' (Chapter 5). The shiploads of spirits, tobacco and sweetened spirits* were seized at sea in 1886 and both vessels and cargoes forfeited. The smugglers had been going among the huge herring fleet of Shetland, Scottish, English and Dutch boats selling their wares.[202]

The close proximity of the islands to several major trade routes led to considerable use being made of island facilities by trading vessels not directly involved in island trade, and the disruption of these trade routes (and to some extent external fisheries also) by piracy and war. Another consequence of nearness to trade routes was shipwrecks. In the course of ordinary trade, it was common for vessels to call for water and provisions, be detained by contrary winds in Shetland, or call for smuggling purposes. For example, in 1831, 33 vessels from Great Britain were forced to put in by contrary winds on their outward voyages.[203] During the great smuggling era of the early nineteenth century (Chapter 4) Shetland's position on the trade routes between Norway and Ireland and between Holland and Faroe rendered it a suitable port of call for smugglers. As in the case of the fisheries, all these functions had generally beneficial effects in a subsistence community, in that a barter trade with the natives could be carried on.

However, there could be harmful consequences too. For example, as early as 1630 an order was issued by the Privy Council stating that ships arriving in Scotland from Bordeaux, Denmark, Sweden, France, Orkney and Shetland were to be quarantined because of disease in these areas.[204] This indicates the importance of Shetland as a staging point even at this early date, and it is almost certain that disease had been carried to the island by ships stopping over for one of the above reasons. During the great cholera epidemic in Europe in the early 1830s, the islanders lived in fear that cholera might be introduced by passing ships. In 1831, four ships put in from Russia flying the yellow flag, and there were fears that the epidemic might be imported from Rothesay on vessels engaged in the herring trade.[205] When a man travelling from Leith to Shetland on the packet *Magnus Troil* died of the disease, the magistrates ordered that he be taken out and buried in as deep water as possible and that the ship be fumigated.[206] By 1833, the effects seem to have extended to trade generally, judging by references to the great loss incurred by merchants and shipowners through strict observance of the cholera regulations, which necessitated lengthy periods of quarantine for vessels coming from infected areas.[207]

The disruption of trade and fisheries resulting from piracy and war was potentially damaging to Shetland trade itself until the beginning of the nineteenth century, as well as to trade and fisheries in the vicinity. The problem of piracy seems to have been at its height in the final three decades of the sixteenth century. In the 1570s especially, it was pursued under cover of fishing in the same types of vessels, and this seems to have been the kind of piracy in which Lord Robert Stewart was implicated (Chapter 2). Piracy as such seems to have been of little consequence beyond the first quarter of the seventeenth century, however. It may be that the substitution of privateering* in the many wars of the period covered up what amounted to piracy in reality. Such an example was murderous raids carried out by 'one Potts, a privateer' in Faroe in the 1780s.[208] At all events, one of the last references to pirates in the sea areas to the north of Scotland was as late as 1728, when the pirate Gow was captured in Eday in Orkney.[209]

The effects of war stemmed mainly from Shetland's strategic location in the north-west approaches to the North Sea from the Atlantic, resulting in direct disruption of local trade, and direct attack (Chapters 2, 3, 4). The full importance of the islands in wartime can be appreciated by considering the series of wars from the first half of the seventeenth century until the beginning of the nineteenth.

During the seventeenth century, the main pre-occupation of the English was Shetland's strategic position in relation to the Dutch fisheries and Dutch trade routes. The importance of the islands first became apparent during the short interlude in the Thirty Years' War in which Charles I became involved, and a direct attack was made on property in Shetland. Meanwhile, later in the Thirty Years' War, Bressay Sound was the scene in 1640 of a full-scale naval engagement between ten Dunkirk privateers and four Dutch warships, ending in the destruction of the four Dutchmen.[210] However, the supreme importance of the islands dates from the period of the Anglo-Dutch wars. In the first, from 1652 until 1654, Cromwell's troops garrisoned Scalloway Castle, and some start on the fortifications of Fort Charlotte may have been made.[211] At least fifty Dutch herring busses were captured off Fair Isle, and a major action between the Dutch fleet under van Tromp and the English fleet under Blake in the Fair Isle area was cut short almost before it began by a sudden storm from the north, from which a large section of the Dutch fleet sheltered in the Scalloway area, at least four ships being lost in the vicinity of Burra.[212] In both this war and that of 1665-67 the English fleet anchored in Bressay Sound,[213] while in the second war the fortifications later to be name Fort Charlotte were constructed.[214] In the final war of 1672-74, the Dutch succeeded in striking the first blow, and burnt the fort and Lerwick.[215] In the continuation of the war with France, the French captured several busses in Bressay Sound in 1677,[216] but the *coup de grâce* for the Dutch fisheries was administered soon after the outbreak of the War of the Spanish Succession in 1703, when the French burnt in the region of 150 busses in Bressay Sound (Chapter 2). Most of these actions arose from the importance of the herring fisheries, but the Dutch fleet was also anxious to protect its trading ships, and in 1667 there is a record of Dutch warships cruising in Shetland waters awaiting the arrival of their East India fleet, and using the islands as a base for obtaining water and provisions,[217] just as they were to do over a hundred years later in the war of 1780-82 (Chapter 3).

The wars of the eighteenth century and against Napoleon seem to have had less effect in terms of direct attack than those up to and including the War of the Spanish Succession, although disruption of markets and trade routes was serious problem on occasion (Chapters 2, 3, 4). However, Shetland's position in the north-west approaches was again of importance, although possibly less so due to the relatively small scale of the Dutch fisheries and the fact that, with the exception of 1780-82, the principal antagonists were Britain and France, with the consequence that the major theatres of war were usually elsewhere. In the war of 1780-82 against Holland, a memorandum[218] was sent to the Board of Customs enumerating the dangers of the war for Shetland and emphasising the strategic importance of the islands for British and Dutch trade and fisheries. It was probably instrumental in the repairing and re-garrisoning of the fort at Lerwick,

named Fort Charlotte in 1781. During all these wars privateers cruised in
Shetland waters, intercepting shipping bound to and from America and
various ports on the North Sea, Baltic and Archangel sea routes. In 1779, for
example, the legendary John Paul Jones was narrowly prevented by a
sudden squall from entering Bressay Sound and burning Lerwick to the
ground. [219]

After the Napoleonic wars there was a century of peace, until the islands
again became of key importance for defence and preying on enemy shipping
in the First World War. However, it is worth noting that the Crimean War
seems to have acted as an encouragement in the provision of lighthouses, [220]
and that the Lerwick Customs suspected a French warship which anchored
in Bressay Sound during the Franco-Prussian War of 1870 of lying in wait for
Prussian and other German vessels passing Shetland on their way to
America. [221]

The subject of shipwrecks throws much light upon Shetland life and the
role of Shetland in the seaways of Europe. The principal list of Shetland
wrecks, upon which the work of O'Dell [222] and the writings of Bruce [223] were
based, contains a list of between 500 and 1,000 wrecks, compiled mainly
from manuscripts and verbal information supplied to Bruce by numerous
local people. [224] Perhaps not surprisingly, information on many of the wrecks
is incomplete, and the problem is complicated by the fact that Bruce did not
consistently reference his work, and his source material is consequently not
fully known and categorised.

The procedure adopted in this study, therefore, was to begin by isolating
as far as possible the trading vessels, which meant compiling a list which
excluded all the flitboats* and fishing craft. Then there is the problem of
defining a wreck. Bruce recorded many strandings which resulted in vessels
being refloated and repaired; he also included collisions which admittedly
were not common in the days of sailing ships engaged in trade, although
there were numerous such instances (sometimes with dire consequences)
among the sailboats in the great herring fishing era after 1880. Again, in a
substantial number of cases, it is not clear whether the vessels were lost or
not. In cases of serious damage to ship or cargo, protests against wind and
weather were commonly registered in the sheriff court [225] at the end of the
eighteenth and in the first part of the nineteenth centuries. In the later
decades of the nineteenth century entries were made in the Depositions
before the Receiver of Wreck [226] in similar manner, but in both cases many of
the entries signified damage only, not resulting in total loss.

In view of these complexities, the remaining list was subdivided into three
sections containing, respectively, lists of ships which were certainly
wrecked, those in which wreck was uncertain, and those in which wrecks
occurred offshore, for example by foundering, and which appear in
Shetland records usually because the islands were the place where the
wrecks were reported through the landing of survivors or the driving of
wreck wood. The result of this sifting was the compilation of the following

table, subdivided on the basis of time periods adopted in the study as a whole. Further discussion of wrecks was then based on the certain category. It will be noted that the number of uncertain wrecks is a much higher proportion in the earlier periods, which might be expected from the quality of historical records.

Table 11. Shetland Wreck Statistics

	Totals	Certain Wrecks	Uncertain Wrecks	Offshore Wrecks
1550-1710	71	28	39	4
1710-1790	134	78	53	3
1790-1870	234	159	45	30
1870-1910	124	102	5	17
Grand total	*563*	*367*	*142*	*54*

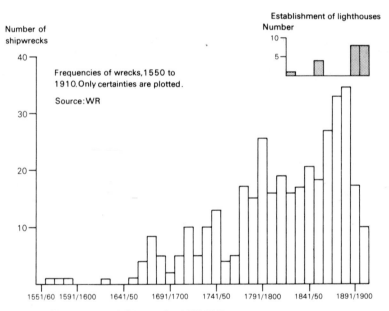

Figure 64. Frequencies of shipwrecks, 1550-1910

As a preliminary to the discussion of the character of the trade routes as depicted by the wreck records, it is of value to note the obviously increasing frequency of wrecks with time, more fully illustrated in Fig. 64, which is based on the number of certain wrecks. Although it has been suggested that the better quality of records may go a long way to explain this increasing frequency,[227] it is much more likely that the rise is due chiefly to the great increase in traffic in the eighteenth and nineteenth centuries, which indeed reflects the growth of the Shetland economy and that of Europe as a whole.

A further striking fact is that the numbers of wrecks continued to increase despite the provision of lighthouses at Sumburgh in 1821, and at Muckle Flugga, Skerries and Bressay in the 1850s.[228] It remains, of course, a moot point how far the lighthouses lessened a frequency of wrecks which might well have been even higher without them. However, the large number of wrecks which were unavoidable due to dragging of anchors in semi-exposed locations, such as the wide bays of Unst and Dunrossness, or being driven ashore in a disabled condition, decreases in the 1890s and 1900s, when the supremacy of sail was rapidly being supplanted by that of steam in sea trade. In such circumstances, the presence or otherwise of a lighthouse made little practical difference.

Broadly speaking, there were four categories of trade routes. The first passed immediately to the south of the islands in the vicinity of Fair Isle, carrying ships to and from the ports round the North Sea and the Baltic into the Atlantic, and connecting with routes leading to the western coasts of Britain, Ireland, the Atlantic coasts of Iberia and France, the Mediterranean, the Atlantic coasts of Canada and the United States of America, the West Indies, and ports in the Indian Ocean and China seas. The second route connected the port of Archangel and ports on the Norwegian coast north of Bergen with ports on the eastern and western coasts of the British Isles. Third was the route connecting Greenland, Iceland and Faroe with North Sea ports. Fourth, there were a substantial number of wrecks of vessels blown a long way off course, the largest numbers of these undoubtedly being those bound between the eastern and western shores of the southern half of the North Sea (Fig. 65).

Although the nature of the trade passing along these routes varied with historical periods, some broad generalisations can be made which are of significance in a Shetland context. First, ships bound to or from the great ports of continental Europe tended to be involved in the colonial trade along the first trade route, the principal ports involved being Gothenburg, Hamburg, Bremen, and Amsterdam, many of the ships from which are recorded as having departed from the Texel (Fig. 65). A number of general cargo ships also left from London and Leith. The majority of these ships were outward bound and caught in spring gales, and this category tended to contain the richest cargoes, irrespective of destination. Included, for example, are the four Dutch East India Company treasure ships, the *Lastdrager*,[229] wrecked at Cullivoe Ness in 1653; the *Kennemerland*,[230] lost at Skerries in 1664; the *De Liefde*,[231] also at Skerries in 1711; and the *Rijnenburg*, lost at Mu Ness in 1713 (Fig. 66). These treasure ships were undoubtedly at the root of the great interest of the landowners and others in wrecks in the seventeenth and early eighteenth centuries, establishing strong traditions which lasted virtually until the end of the period. Other notable ships were the *Wendela*, the 'silver ship' of Fetlar, wrecked in 1737 outward bound from Copenhagen; and the *Concordia*, wrecked at Helliness in Cunningsburgh in 1786 (Fig. 66). Both these ships belonged to the Danish East India Company. Then there was the

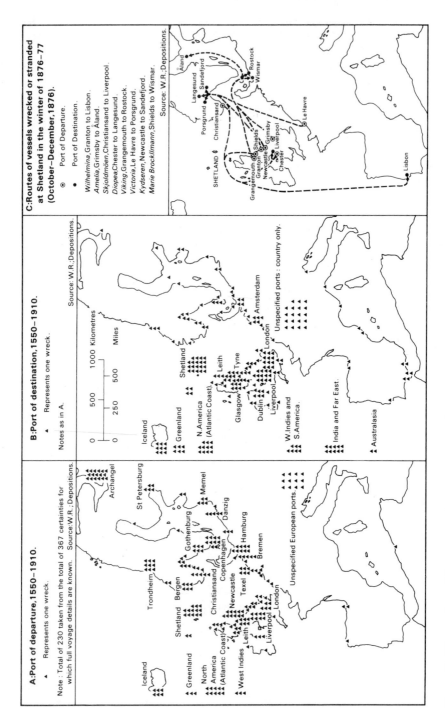

A:Port of departure,1550-1910.

▲ Represents one wreck.

Note : Total of 230 taken from the total of 367 certainties for which full voyage details are known.   Source:W.R.;Depositions.

Iceland
Greenland
North America (Atlantic Coast)
West Indies
Trondheim
Shetland Bergen
Christiansand
Newcastle
Texel Hamburg
Leith Bremen
Liverpool
London
Gothenburg
Copenhagen Danzig
Memel
Archangel
St Petersburg
Unspecified European ports.

B:Port of destination,1550-1910.

▲ Represents one wreck.

Notes as in A.   Source:W.R.;Depositions.

0 250 500   1000 Kilometres
0   500   Miles

Iceland
Greenland
N.America (Atlantic Coast)
Shetland
Glasgow
Dublin Leith Tyne
Liverpool London
Amsterdam
W.Indies and S.America.
India and Far East.
Australasia.
Unspecified ports : country only.

C:Routes of vessels wrecked or stranded at Shetland in the winter of 1876-77 (October–December,1876).

◉ Port of Departure.
● Port of Destination.

Wilhelmina,Granton to Lisbon.
Amelia,Grimsby to Åland.
Skjoldmöen,Christiansand to Liverpool.
Diopea,Chester to Langesund.
Viking,Grangemouth to Rostock.
Victoria,Le Havre to Porsgrund.
Kydseren,Newcastle to Sandefjord.
Marie Brockllmann,Shields to Wismar.

Source: W.R.;Depositions.

Åland
Langesund Sandefjord Rostock
Porsgrund Christiansand Wismar
SHETLAND
Grangemouth Shields Grimsby
Granton Newcastle Liverpool
Chester
Le Havre
Lisbon

Figure 65. Shipwrecks and European trade routes

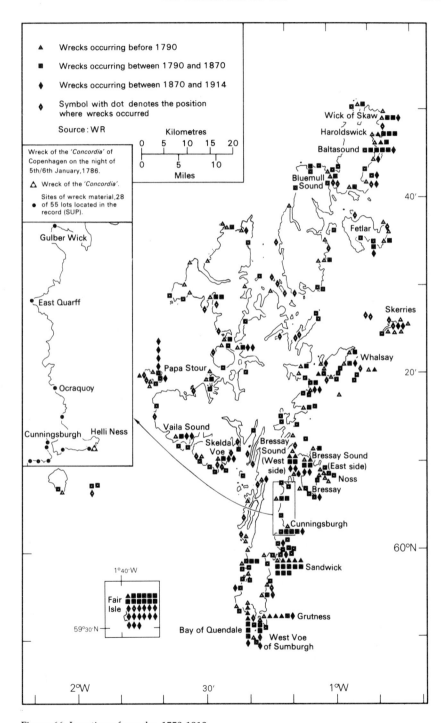

▲ Wrecks occurring before 1790

■ Wrecks occurring between 1790 and 1870

♦ Wrecks occurring between 1870 and 1914

◊ Symbol with dot denotes the position
   where wrecks occurred

Source : WR

Kilometres

Wreck of the 'Concordia' of
Copenhagen on the night of
5th/6th January,1786.

△ Wreck of the 'Concordia'.

● Sites of wreck material, 28
  of 55 lots located in the
  record (SUP).

Gulber Wick

East Quarff

Ocraquoy

Cunningsburgh   Helli Ness

Wick of Skaw
Haroldswick
Baltasound
Bluemull
Sound
Fetlar
Skerries
Whalsay
Papa Stour
Vaila Sound
Skelda
Voe
Bressay
Sound
(West
side)
Bressay Sound
(East side)
Noss
Bressay
Cunningsburgh
Sandwick
Fair
Isle
Bay of Quendale
Grutness
West Voe
of Sumburgh

Figure 66. Location of wrecks, 1550-1910

remarkable double disaster of 12 January 1745 when two ships of the Swedish East India Company, the *Stockholm* and the *Drottingen af Sverige*,[232] both outward bound from Gothenburg for Canton, were lost in the same day. A large consignment of lead was among the salvaged materials. Not surprisingly, the numbers of rich cargoes of this kind were largely confined to the seventeenth and eighteenth centuries. Later, the improvement of the commercial system — in particular the removal of the necessity of carrying large amounts of precious metals (Chapter 2) — militated against such windfalls.

The second group of wrecks were those outward bound with cargoes of timber. The most important single port of departure was Archangel (Fig. 65); the other major ports involved were Bergen and Trondheim, the ports of south-eastern Norway, and the Baltic ports of St. Petersburg, Memel and Danzig. A substantial number of vessels bound from south-eastern Norway and the Baltic were blown off trade routes in the southern North Sea. Those from Bergen, Trondheim and Archangel were generally on the first and second trade routes respectively, detailed above. The main destinations of these ships were the east coast of England (especially the Tyne ports and London), Liverpool, Ireland and the Mediterranean ports. Some of the Baltic and Archangel ships carried large quantities of tallow and flax, while those from western Norway sometimes had cargoes of stockfish bound for the southern European ports. The timber trade ships helped to maintain the local interest in wrecks among merchants and tenants alike in the eighteenth and nineteenth centuries, as the cargoes not only possessed a value heightened by the high duty on timber products, but could also be put to immediate practical use.

The third important group of wrecks represented the coal trade from the Tyne and the salt trade from Liverpool, usually bound along the timber trade routes in the reverse direction, and of least potential value as only the remains of the ships could be salved and not the cargoes. The coal trade in particular was at its height in the closing decades of the nineteenth century. Meanwhile, the vessels on the Faroe, Iceland and Greenland routes were generally whalers and fishing vessels, with a few general traders.

To appreciate the reasons why a high number of ships sailing on routes in the fourth category (those remote from the islands) were lost at Shetland, it is necessary to investigate the role of wind and sea conditions. Although the lack of detailed reliable statistics and the nature of the source material, discussed above, are disadvantages, a fairly accurate picture of causes of wrecks can be gained from the study of the certain category. It is possible to be more specific concerning the weather situation. Undoubtedly by far the most hazardous conditions were created by the prolonged south or south-easterly gale, not infrequently lasting for several weeks without any real abatement. This caused the driving of many vessels from the southern parts of the North Sea, as well as from the south-eastern coasts of Norway. Classic examples of this condition, which tend to correlate with those years in which the largest number of wrecks were recorded, include the first week of January in 1800, when several colliers were forced to run all the way from Great Yarmouth before the gale; the winter of 1817-1818, when four out of nine ships lost were outward bound from the Baltic; the winter of 1847-1848, when a large amount of timber came to the islands (see below); and the winter of 1876-1877, illustrated in Fig. 65.[233] It is worth noting in this last case that only half the ships wrecked would have passed anywhere near Shetland under normal circumstances. There were, of course, gales from every conceivable direction. Although, of these storms, perhaps westerly to northerly gales were most severe in terms of high winds coming in the wake of deep depressions, these were associated with fewer wrecks, as there were no major trade routes to the west and north of the islands.

The location of the wrecks in Shetland highlights a third set of physical factors. A glance at Fig. 66 confirms that by far the greater number of wrecks in the certain category took place on the east coast, which is a direct consequence of the relation of the islands to the trade routes described above, supplemented by the importance of southerly and south-easterly gales. There were particular concentrations in Fair Isle, Dunrossness, Bressay, Whalsay, Skerries and Unst, corresponding to those locations where the first lighthouses were sited. However, a closer inspection of the map reveals that by far the greater proportion of losses did not take place on completely exposed coasts, but rather in bays (notably Haroldswick, Sandwick, West Voe of Sumburgh and Quendale Bay), and even in harbours such as Baltasound and Bressay Sound. In the case of losses in harbours, this was generally the result of dragging anchor in severe weather. In the larger category of wrecks in bays, the usual cause was 'stranger' ships anchoring in areas with as much sea-room as possible for manoeuvre, or making the land under bad conditions and having to make the best effort possible to save ship and crew, often at night with a vessel severely disabled through loss of some or all of rudder, masts, spars, sails or rigging. The concentration of bay wrecks at the extremities of Unst and Dunrossness indicates attempts to clear the islands at the last moment on passage from the east, and failing by a narrow margin.

The location of so many wrecks in bays greatly increased the possibilities of salvage of the cargoes, which was one of the principal economic repercussions of wrecks. Much of the cargo, especially in the case of timber, could be readily used locally. Other cargoes, such as the valuable general cargoes, were salvaged and eventually re-entered trade, an example being the wreck lead mentioned above, which was shipped to Amsterdam. Of economic importance also was the loss of locally owned vessels.

The loss of a ship was of course a serious business, and of frequent occurrence. Bruce's records show that at least eight Shetland vessels were certainly totally wrecked in Shetland in the eighteenth century and, judging by later proportions, this was probably not much more than half of the total number lost, to which must be added several taken by privateers in the eighteenth century and especially in the Napoleonic Wars. The most accurate measure of the importance of losses of locally owned shipping may be gained from analysis of the extant Register of Shipping from 1837 until 1914.[234] Of 223 separate trading vessels registered between those dates, no fewer than 75, or almost exactly one-third of the total, were lost through total shipwreck. Of this 75, 38 were lost locally, at least half of them actually in harbour, usually through dragging anchor in severe gales (Fig. 67). Twenty-six of the remainder were lost on trading and fishing voyages outwith the islands (Fig. 67), while the location of the wrecks of the remaining eleven is not certain. The consequences of the loss of locally owned vessels fell at first mainly on the landowners, and later upon the merchants.

In the case of wreck cargoes, the economic repercussions were potentially wider and could result in gain for all. It is difficult to assess the relative importance of cargoes in offsetting the loss of locally owned shipping. Such an assessment is liable to be meaningless anyway, and a better idea of the effects can be gained from historical events. The most certain return at all periods, in the days of wooden ships, was the driving ashore of large quantities of wreck timber, masts, spars, and rigging of the ships themselves, which were well worth getting hold of even if, as was often the case, the ship was 'smashed to pieces'. One of the best recorded wrecks of this kind was that of the *Concordia* of Copenhagen, mentioned above. The ship went ashore in a storm in the middle of the night, and the crew were lost. Although there was a valuable general cargo, most of the remains recovered consisted of wreck wood and materials of the ship herself. It is important to note that under such conditions the wreck was liable to be scattered over a wide area of coast, and the *Concordia* was no exception (Fig. 66). As was common practice, the wreck material was sold by lots where it lay (in this case no less than 55) and bought up mainly by the rising class of merchants[235] (Chapter 3).

Among the most valuable cargoes were the general colonial ones, and interest in the treasure ships in particular persists to this day, with diving taking place on the sites of the losses of the *Lastdrager* and *De Liefde* among others, in the last case with considerable success in terms of several thousand coins recovered. As early as 1665 there is a reference to 'a (Holland) ship in Zetland . . .' from which had been recovered three chests of gold worth upwards of £10,000 sterling, in addition to a shipload of other cargo which was transported to Leith, and included 'two great brass guns', gems, cables, iron, wine, French brandy, and 136 tuns of sugar casks of which 20 were empty.[236] In the late eighteenth and nineteenth centuries, the most valuable cargoes were undoubtedly timber. In exceptional cases, the supply of wreck timber made import unnecessary. For example, in 1848 practically no timber was imported thanks to two full wreck cargoes of Canadian timber from the *Agenoria* and *Clarendon*.[237]

There was, of course, every conceivable type of cargo to be found at one time or another, from casks of spirits to tallow, linen and even palm oil and

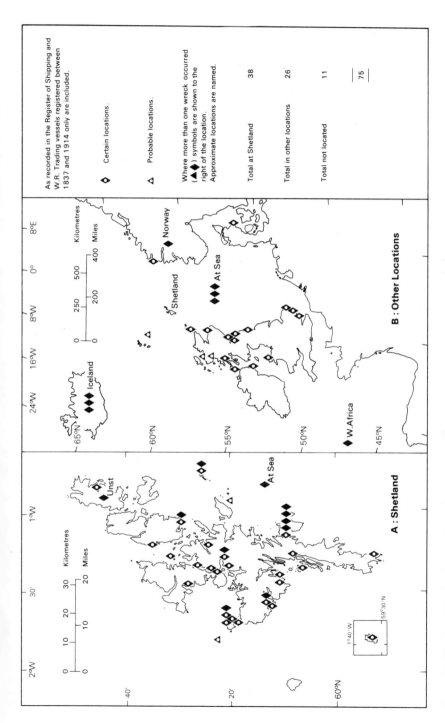

As recorded in the Register of Shipping and W.R. Trading vessels registered between 1837 and 1914 only are included.

◆ Certain locations.

△ Probable locations.

Where more than one wreck occurred (◆◆) symbols are shown to the right of the location. Approximate locations are named.

Total at Shetland 38

Total in other locations 26

Total not located 11

75

B : Other Locations

A : Shetland

Figure 67. Wrecks of Shetland-owned vessels, 1837-1914

earthenware, all of which could be made use of by the inhabitants if only it could be got hold of and subsequently kept clear of the Customs. Notwithstanding the plundering of wrecks, it was common for the level of receipts of the Customs to be primarily determined by the quantity of wreck brought ashore. In 1845, for example, it was recorded that '. . . the trade of the port has increased in receipts from £135 in 1843 to £463 in 1844 . . . chief cause . . . was the accidental circumstances of a wreck . . .'[238] — in this case the wreck at Easter Quarff (Fig. 66) of the brig *Jessmond* of South Shields, on passage from Archangel to Hull with a valuable cargo of linseed, battens, flax and mats, most of which was salvaged.

The handling of salvage demonstrates the economic importance of wrecked ships and cargoes. Two periods can be distinguished, before and after the middle of the eighteenth century, the change corresponding more or less with that from landowners to merchants in the trade system as a whole (Chapter 3). The conflict at all times was essentially between the principle of salvage enunciated as early as the reign of Edward III of England, to the effect that wreck goods should be restituted to their rightful owner with a share deducted for the benefit of the salver, and the local attitude to wreck, epitomised by the remark of the Customs in 1828 regarding driftwood: '. . . there is a general and we may say hereditary feeling in the country that such drifts should be considered Godsends'.[239] It is therefore hardly surprising that dealings between opposing sides were often contentious.

Before the middle of the eighteenth century, the principles of mercantilism are perhaps nowhere better illustrated than in the attitudes and machinations of the landed gentry, high and low, with respect to wrecks, an attitude much encouraged by the potentially high gains to be had from the rich colonial cargoes. The legal custody of wreck was vested in the power of Admiralty*, which was a feudal jurisdiction, the granting of which lay ultimately with the reigning monarch. The importance which the feudal superior attached to the right of Admiralty is evident from a representation of the Earl of Morton to the Crown just before he regained the Earldom through feudal purchase in 1706 (Chapter 2), to the effect that Queen Anne had wrongfully granted the Admiralty to the Duke of Lennox, and pointing out that it belonged to him by virtue of his Earldom.[240]

In practice, of course, responsibility for the supervision of the right of Admiralty had to be delegated, generally to a leading local landowner, who became Admiral Depute. By a tradition which extended not only to shipwrecks but also to the stranding of whales (Chapter 4), the Admiral was entitled to one-third of the proceeds of wreck, with one-third going to the owner of the shore on which the wreck occurred, and the remaining third going to the salvers, who were usually the tenants. In addition, the Admiral had the right to the 'best anchor and cable' of any ship wrecked, which was often an item of high value. A good early example of the procedure in operation is to be found in a contract drawn up between Sir John Mitchell of

Westshore, the Admiral Depute, and William Henderson of Gardie and James Mitchell of Girlsta (Chapter 2), whereby John Mitchell disponed* to the other two his one-third share of wreck of the *Good Friend* of Amsterdam, then lying at Leira Voe in Bressay, and a one-fifth share of dry wheat saved from her. Also covered by the contract was the best anchor and cable of the *Rey Flower* of the island of 'Skelling' in Holland, wrecked at Otterswick (in Yell) in November 1711.[241] The landowners often went to great lengths to secure wreck material, which could of course be sold. Sinclair of Quendale (Chapter 2) was accused of pressing his tenants by searching their houses for wreck,[242] and in 1729 and 1730 considerable effort was expended in financing a diving expedition in Skerries to attempt recovery of treasure known to lie there, but without much success.[243]

After the middle of the eighteenth century, the treatment of wreck, although still strongly influenced by the desire for gain, was more fully governed by commercial procedures. Thus, for example, the wreck of the *Concordia*, discussed above, was subject to sale by roup*, under the supervision of the Sheriff and Admiral Depute, and much of the material was in fact bought by the up-and-coming class of merchants. The clash between the feudal and commercial systems came during the decades between 1790 and 1840, as it did in the case of the land through valuation of teinds and the breaking of the hold of fishing tenures. In 1797, the Customs were emphasising to their superior in Edinburgh that '. . . in the cases of shipwreck . . . it is perfectly necessary that a good understanding subsists betwixt the Admiral, the Gentlemen of the Country, and the Revenue Officers, and altho' considerable embezzlements always take place when shipwrecks happen, they certainly would be greater, the revenue & unfortunate proprietors would suffer more if that understanding was once broken'.[244] By 1809, however, Lord Dundas, as Vice-Admiral of Orkney and Shetland, had clashed in court with the Board of Customs and Excise over the rights to wrecks: '. . . his Lordship has been in use to delegate his authority to two deputies, with whom unfortunately the officers of the Revenue in Orkney and Shetland have had frequent disputes by whom they have been for a considerable time past uniformly opposed, when endeavouring to take possession, for the security of the Revenue, of the materials and such parts of the cargoes as have been saved from ships driven on shore, or stranded upon the coasts of these islands'.[245]

In the 1810s and 1820s the conflict became one between commercial interests (usually landowners on the one hand and merchants on the other) for the possession of agencies for the disposal of wreck goods. In 1819 the Customs observed that '. . . it is notorious that very incorrect notions on the law of salvage obtain in this country as well as subjects connected with the Revenue. Although much thwarted and calumnated we have strenuously endeavoured to introduce a new and better order of things and we shall persevere therein, notwithstanding we have little expectation of doing much good, so long as the society here is constituted as it is'.[246]

This was a far cry from the 'understandings' of 1797, and the change becomes even clearer in 1825 in the battle between lairds and Customs over the wreck of the brig *Resolution* of Hamburg, bound from Hamburg to New Orleans with a valuable cargo. The *Resolution* came to grief at Haroldswick in Unst, and the cargo, including 42,000 yards of linen, was extensively plundered by the local inhabitants, while the local landowners seem to have assumed the agency rightfully belonging to the agent appointed by Lloyds as insurers of vessel and cargo.[247] Thomas Leisk of Uyea referred in his diary to the 'godless multitude of Unst' plundering the ship, in spite of the fact that a large proportion of the crew had been tragically drowned.[248] The *Orkney and Zetland Chronicle* saw the situation more clearly, however, deploring those who bought the cargo cheap, and considering the action of the country people excusable in view of the 'sharks' of wreck agents.[249] Clearly, wrecks could be a valuable adjunct to trading activities. As for the tenant population, their attitude throughout the nineteenth century remained that of the woman who came down to salve oats from the wreck at Cunningsburgh of the schooner *Janet Gibson* of Kincardine, bound for Archangel to London: '. . . the wreck was given or thrown on the island by the Almighty as a boon for them,' she stated to the skipper of the Revenue cutter, but '. . . the Devil had sent his servants [in this case the crew of the Revenue cutter] to take it from them . . .'[250]

7

The Old Rock

The Legacy of Time

By many people in many fields, 1914 has been regarded as the end of an era.[1] Indeed at the time it seemed so. The sheer magnitude and enveloping horror of the 'Great War' alone ensured that.[2] On a European scale it signalled the virtual end of all the remaining continental empires, two to be replaced by totalitarian regimes and the third fragmented into an explosive combination of new nation states. The old empires of the west, dependent upon sea-based links, weakened and were eventually to disappear, their demise hastened by the economic calamities of the 1920s and 1930s which again, at the time, seemed climacteric to many.

The Shetlanders, despite their small numbers, were very much part of all these events. Large-scale emigration had begun in the 1860s and 1870s, and accelerated in the hard times of the 1920s and 1930s, so that there were substantial communities of Shetlanders in many of the great British ports,[3] as well as in Canada, the United States of America, Australia and New Zealand. But the largest and most important community of all was that of the seamen manning British ships engaged in nearly all the trades in the world. Countless numbers were shipmasters.[4] Many settled elsewhere, notably in Leith and Edinburgh, and on Tyneside, notably in South Shields. The others kept their crofts, but spent most of their time away. There were whole families of seamen, extending from generation to generation.

And yet Shetland's economy still depended upon herring and haddocks, livestock and hosiery. Although truck waned and security of tenure stabilised the crofting situation, credit was still necessary for many down to the 1930s. The economic decline, and increasingly violent economic cycles, encouraged emigration not only to sea, but also to other occupations. Young single women obtained jobs in service, and whole families emigrated. Ideas for re-organisation of economic activity and for government help to stem the decline were there, but never really proved fully effective. For example, the fishermen's co-operative set up in Burra did not last, and the formation of the Shetland Woollen Industries Association did not really co-ordinate all the hosiery interests, although the establishment of the flock and herd books was significant. Nationally the herring industry was most important, but by the time the Herring Industry Board was established in 1934, the herring industry was well into decline, with the Russian market permanently gone. It was facing competition from other European producers despite technical modernisation in conversion of the fleet from sail to motor.[5] The by now fully developed specialisation of communities persisted even in decline, with Burra and Whalsay as leading fishing centres, for example, while Scalloway and Lerwick remained the main centres for sea-based communication, itself being undermined by the roads and motor transport. Thus the period between the World Wars was one of continuity in an organisation of society and economy going back to the 1870s. Shetland remained a land of fishermen and crofters, and thousands of Shetlanders were scattered to the ends of the earth.

The period of the Second World War itself was associated with the working out of ideas for large-scale practical state intervention in both economy and society, which led to the extensive legislation of the late 1940s, establishing the welfare state, consolidating secondary education, nationalising the public utilities and certain old 'industrial revolution' industries such as coalmining, establishing a physical planning system, and assisting the development of industry. Although the precedents for these ideas stretched back to the beginning of the century, the initiative was only fully assumed by the state in the 1940s. But it was an initiative organised on a national, rather than a regional, scale. Its consequences for Shetland were profound, though it would be unwise, especially in the absence of detailed historical analysis, to ascribe the course of events entirely to the state. Local economic and political influence had arguably been declining since the collapse of Hay and Ogilvy in 1842, but it was nonetheless present in considerable measure, most notably in areas where the opportunities were greatest such as the service industries, including retailing and transport, in knitwear manufacture, and in fish processing.[6]

The place of the old in the new is somewhat problematical. At the production level, the post-war fisheries were but a shadow of the past.[7] While there was still a herring fishing until the mid-1960s, it remained small and was declining further. The fisheries were really restructured with the advent of the widespread use of the seine net and a combination of dual purpose MFV*-type fishing craft, some inherited from the Second World War, and a class of smaller inshore 'white fish' boats using the seine net only, with forays into line fishing from time to time. In the course of the later 1960s and 1970s this pattern was replaced by the emergence of a new and more specialised fleet including multi-purpose steel purse-netters, more advanced middle-range boats, and small craft concentrating on the lobster, crab, and scallop fisheries. Investment in the fishing fleet was aided at first by the financial assistance of the White Fish Authority established in 1952, and later by the Highlands and Islands Development Board (HIDB), set up in 1965.[8] The chief role of the latter, however, was in the financing of modern fish processing plants in the late 1960s and early 1970s, which were crucial in maintaining the small-scale fishing economy.

On the land also, the development of production was aided by Government initiative, notably through the reconstituted Crofters Commission of 1956 and the agricultural extension service operated by the North of Scotland College of Agriculture, and later by the considerable investment of the Highlands and Islands Development Board in knitwear factories.[9] Thus considerable land improvement occurred in the crofting areas under the apportionment schemes which involved fencing and reseeding hill land, and a substantial modern production of livestock and knitwear was built up. These industries were also very different in production characteristics to what they had been prior to 1939.

The expansion of markets in the traditional industries was a notable feature of the 1960s and 1970s, reflecting the role of local initiative aided by Government finance in the expanding world economy. Thus the processed frozen fish market was opened up by direct exports to North America and Europe, as well as via more traditional U.K. outlets. Despite trade mark and associated copying problems, Shetland knitwear enjoyed an international reputation with markets to match, notably in Europe. In most of these developments local initiative was crucial in taking advantage of Government finance. When recession set in in the 1970s and early 1980s it became even more important, underlain by increasing awareness of the practical economic and political consequences of maintaining a regional identity even on such a small scale.

It may be tempting to ascribe the resurgence of regional interests to reactions against big government, or a pre-occupation with a Shetland identity harking back to the period before the great emigration commenced in the 1870s, as distinct from a more remote Viking past, in an age when so much education was, inevitably, 'for export'.[10] No doubt these factors were of significance especially at intellectual and political levels, although detailed historical analysis is required to ascertain their precise role. But the essence of the focus on a Shetland outlook was above all practical. First, it was a reaction to the need for a regional approach to economic development in the 1960s, exemplified by the role of the HIDB, coupled nonetheless with a reaction against centralising government tendencies in the re-organisation of local government. These changes were both amplified and somewhat obscured by the coming of oil in the 1970s, leading to the Zetland County Council Act of 1974[11] aimed at strengthening local control over oil industry developments. Politically it was reflected in the late 1970s growth of the Shetland Movement, the assertion of Shetland's position at the EEC fishing negotiations complete with a local fishing plan,[12] and the demands for at least administrative devolution and the role of the new Shetland Islands Council in financing local industry.[13] By the early 1980s the initiative in economic development thus seemed to be shifting towards local sources once again. But this initiative was not confined to a single group such as the merchants: it was in all the groups involved — local government, industry and the fishermen.

In these recent events, the coming of oil is worth a special mention for its apparently cataclysmic aspect — a break in the order of development, as it were, bringing in its wake the problems of urban society to a rural environment. Although the outward manifestations are real enough in the form of the Sullom Voe Terminal and the service bases, the employment changes and social problems, these may also be seen as part of a European, if not global, movement in the exploitation of energy resources offshore. In social and economic terms this is not dissimilar from the assault on the pelagic fish stocks at the end of the nineteenth century. The great difference is the massive authority of the corporate state and companies responsible for the development. The Shetland response may, however, prove to have been similarly corporate, with influence from outside perhaps greater than that from within, as historical analysis of the evidence progresses. Outwardly it may seem so even now.

The Shetland Traders

It is in the field of initiative, the adoption of new ideas, that the key to certain periodic changes in the pattern of Shetland's social and economic development would appear to lie. At the centre of these changes has been the successive emergence of new social groups who have eventually assumed the initiative in economic development, thus producing a sequence of change which can be traced particularly clearly from the eighteenth century onwards, although there are almost certainly ramifications extending further back in time, and perhaps more truly defining the 'modern' period in history.

The assumption of initiative is particularly striking in its pattern and, together with the changing social groupings, has lent cohesion to the patterns of change. Thus the landowners assumed the initiative in the 1710s, principally through taking over external trade from the German merchants. The Shetland merchants took over from the landowners by the 1790s in a less obvious way, when the combination of internal and external trade links including shipping was run by them. In the 1870s the decline of truck, and the decline of the old staple industries and emigration, combined with the improvement in communications brought about by the penny post, steamships, the telegraph and newspapers, were decisive in the fishermen and crofters branching out into various activities both in Shetland and beyond. The assumption of initiative by central Government, first through specific economic sectors and later through regional development measures, dates from the 1940s, and may yet bring a greater role for local initiative via the local authority.

The emergence of social groups to occupy dominant positions is to some extent problematic in that all groups have been present throughout — landowners, merchants, tenants and fishermen. Their appearance tends to be consolidated roughly halfway through each of the 'initiative periods' identified above. Thus the merchants became a major force in the system in the 1760s, though they did not effectively direct the course of the economy until the 1790s, building up into a peak in the activities of the business firms of the 1820s and 1830s led by Hay and Ogilvy and the Shetland Bank, who wielded enormous influence until the collapse of 1842. The 1840s arguably saw the passing of much initiative beyond Shetland, despite a regrouping of business interests, and the tenants and fishermen struck out in new directions within the earlier economic framework. The role of local initiative continued to drain away especially after 1870 when people 'voted with their feet'. From the early 1880s to the 1900s the influence of the state may be discerned in early social and economic welfare arrangements, above all the Crofters Act of 1886 and ensuing legislation culminating in moves such as the setting up of the Herring Industry Board in 1934. But the emphasis was on regulating, rather than initiating, new development. Local social re-organisation and political awakening arguably belongs to the late 1970s and early 1980s, in the shape of institutions such as the Shetland Fishermen's Organisation, fish producers' co-operatives and the Shetland Movement. On the basis of the patterns of the past, the harvest of these changes may not become apparent until after 2000, when the role of local enterprise could conceivably again be paramount in local development, as in the period between 1820 and 1840 under the influence of the mercantile capitalists.

The social changes are in significant respects more clearly visible on the ground than the dominant initiative changes. Thus, for example, the land-owning group of families who took over trade in the 1700s had become increasingly influential from the post-Restoration economic recovery of the 1660s and 1670s, and continued to be so until at least the 1740s and 1750s, being replaced by a new generation of landowners and smaller merchants by the 1760s. Their influence was also probably diminished to some extent by the abolition of Heritable Jurisdictions in 1747. A mercantile organisation subsisted from the 1760s until the 1840s associated with fundamental changes in external marketing arrangements. From the collapse of the 1840s to the collapses of the 1920s and 1930s a system of landowning and non-landowning business firms, tenants and fishermen existed. Since then a combination of state agencies and local producer groups has existed, and may now be transformed as more co-ordination of regional economic interests at local level become apparent.

It is both tempting and perhaps of some value to extend the analysis back-wards in time, despite the inevitable problem of lack of data. The beginning of the end of the Middle Ages in Shetland was arguably the taking over of the Norway trade by the German merchants and their direct trade with the north German ports from the 1410s or 1420s.[14] It is open to question whether they gained control of Shetland trade by mid-century, though they almost certainly had by the time of the pledging in 1469, which was followed in the 1470s and 1480s by the first notable influx of Scottish landowning families, particularly the Sinclair group from the north of Scotland.[15] It may well be to this fifteenth-century period that we must look for an understanding of the large estates amassed under the udal* system of land tenure.[16] From the 1490s to the 1560s the new Scottish landowners seem to have existed side by side with older udal families and to have adopted the Old Norse landowning traditions. The revolution came in the 1570s,[17] when a new wave of Scottish landowning families came into conflict with both the Crown in the shape of Lord Robert Stewart and his son, Earl Patrick, and with the people, finally assuming the initiative in the 1610s, and being leaders in island affairs until the upheavals of the mid-century revolution. These, together with the earlier family groups, were the ones who began to be eclipsed after the Restoration, and were sometimes in dire straits by the early eighteenth century.

The initiatives for trade were throughout this whole early modern period largely external. From the mid-fifteenth century until the 1530s the German merchants expanded and consolidated their trade, and the Baltic ports led by Lübeck were probably of significance. From the 1540s until the 1620s the focus was upon Hamburg and Bremen, accompanied by the rise to a peak of the Dutch herring fishery. From the 1630s until the 1700s there was a pattern of stable Hamburg and Bremen trade with some competition from the Scots and English, together with the Dutch herring fishing, and with the Norway trade in the hands of the local landowners. The 1610s-1630s, and 1660s-1680s were periods of economic expansion, with the late sixteenth century, the mid-seventeenth and the late seventeenth as periods of depression. This system retained its stability despite these fluctuations and the constant hazards of naval warfare and the revolution in England.

Shetland and the Sea

The patterns of initiative and social change were thus the outcome of the interplay of internal and external forces acting in concert. And yet Shetland has a clear, island identity which, although stemming from its distinctive environment of land and sea, and a highly misleading 'isolation' probably better described as island distinctiveness, is based upon recognisable local environmental, social and economic, political and cultural factors which have also had distinctive relationships with the trades and traders.

Compared to the changes of history, the islands and the surrounding sea appear unchanging. It is indeed striking that the pattern of townships established in the early Middle Ages continued to evolve throughout the modern period. The economic and cultural unity binding land and sea represented by the townships finally faltered and disintegrated in the 1870-1940 period, although the landscape still represents the old pattern in many places, especially where post-1840 depopulation occurred.

The physical contrast of the central voes and hills on the one hand, and the outlying exposed cliffs and beaches on the other, is both remarkable in itself[18] and as mirroring economic and social change, especially since the early eighteenth century. This began with the far haaf fishing, dependent upon accessibility of the ground to the far-flung stations with their stony beaches. The cod fishing, farming improvements and growth of Lerwick and Scalloway of the nineteenth century produced a contrasting shift towards the voes and valleys of the centre which were more suited to the operation of decked boats. In the early years of the late nineteenth-century herring fishery, outlying harbours found favour. The post-1945 economy has again favoured Lerwick, Scalloway and the fishing communities of the centre, with the outlying areas without good land or mineral resources in continuous decline, from the 1840s in a number of cases.

The variability of the environment is also an important consideration, especially as the period spanned coincides to a considerable extent with the 'Little Ice Age' climatic deterioration. The frequency of poor harvests and fishings, often occurring simultaneously for two or three years at a stretch at intervals of twenty or thirty years, was probably greater between the late sixteenth and late nineteenth centuries than either before or after. By the late seventeenth century this climatic deterioration had progressed far enough, possibly in association with land use activities, to precipitate erosion in the major sandy coastal areas, especially in the South Mainland.[19] Fish stocks and fisheries were also probably affected, although available evidence could be profitably extended to further substantiate this.[20]

The variability of the seasons was more striking than these longer-term changes, in the immediate onset of dearth in many years before the 1850s. There were many poor seasons on land and sea, although, as Adam Smith observed, the fisheries were certain enough in the long run.[21] In the long run also, there were successive periods of economic expansion and depression which, in general, form part of the wider national and European trends, although significantly affected before 1850 by the local variations in productivity characteristic of the dependence upon the produce of land and sea.

An Unfinished History

Probably Shetland's economic development should be seen as part of social change, rather than the other way round, so that each distinctive social period had characteristic economic attributes and impact upon land and sea. The reason for this is the clear influence of enterprise in guiding development. Thus, until the early eighteenth century, the main local economic initiative was in land ownership, with overseas trade ideas coming from the markets of Europe. From the early eighteenth century until the late nineteenth the initiative in all areas was primarily local, passing from one social group to another, although the ideas underlying the initiative often came from outside. From the late nineteenth century, with the Crofters' Act and emigration, initiative passed increasingly to the state, and to the individual.

Behind the initiatives, of course, is the role of ideas. The influence of these, and often their national — Scottish or British — provenance, may be most clearly seen in the period from the 1700s to the 1860s. The successful innovations were those which could be economically developed under Shetland conditions. In this the limits to the initiative of successive social groups were undoubtedly crucial in the transfer of that initiative to the next group. This is particularly striking in the transfer from the landowners, who would not risk much capital in trading, to the merchants in the late eighteenth century; and again, less obviously perhaps, from the business firms to the fishermen and crofters, and thus often out of the islands altogether, in the 1870s and 1880s.

The role of the groundswell of ideas emerged above all in local legal and political conflict which tended to climax in periods of transfer of initiative. This was evident in the battle between the local merchants and landowners from the 1780s into the early nineteenth century,[22] evidenced in legal documents and in the largely Edinburgh-based political pamphlets aimed at undermining the landowners' influence. Again a similar sequence occurred in the battles between Arthur Anderson and the local establishment in the 1830s and 1840s,[23] also a time of social change. Yet again political influences may be discerned in the coming of the Truck Commission into Shetland in 1872.[24] By the time of the Napier Commission in 1884, and after, social conflict and the interplay of ideas may often be more clearly followed in Parliamentary Papers and related Government reports, in the local press, and in local literature.

These conflicts were instrumental in forming a constantly strengthening Shetland dimension — a Shetland identity[25] evident less in the economic realm than in local politics, and above all in literature. This reached its full expression in the years before 1914, not least under the influence of intellectuals such as Jakob Jakobsen the scholar, Gilbert Goudie, Haldane Burgess, and Lawrence Williamson. There was emphasis on the continuity of culture from Old Norse times as against the cataclysms of Victorian change. But there was also the contemporary and enduring image of the Old Rock, the point of departure and sometimes return of the thousands of ordinary emigrants and seamen.

The Old Rock itself implied the surrounding sea. To those non-Shetlanders beyond, particularly those who lived in the cities of Scotland and England and who took an interest in Shetland, albeit often romantically or politically biased, the sea and the distance separating the islands from them seemed a barrier. The islands were regarded as remote and perhaps peculiar, with a Viking image cultivated by the intellectuals, and lairds' and tenants' conflicts cultivated by the politicians. To the Shetlanders themselves living in the islands or looking back to the Old Rock, the sea was more of a bridge, a link to the world beyond, the world of ships, distant ports, seamen, trade, politics and war. The sea was all around and its imagery ran deep, as a provider and highway, and as a foundation of Shetland life itself.

It is thus important to appreciate that Shetland was and remains in reality far from remote in the context of things British and European. It has European roots — a sea centre of communications in the Middle Ages which led to enduring cultural foundations and overseas links — which have led some authors to believe that Shetland — and indeed Scotland — did not emerge from the Middle Ages until 1707! On the contrary, the beginning of the early modern period was marked by the shift in initiative in trade from Norway to the Hanseatic towns, while the transfer to the centres of Scotland and Britain in the early eighteenth century merely marked the end of this early modern phase. The rapid cultural development of Europe and Britain, and the political turbulence associated with it, was ever in front of the Shetlanders, generally on their doorstep in the form of pirates, privateers and straightforward naval warfare, as well as in the numerous personal and trade contacts, and in the sad procession of wrecks. The titanic struggles of Britain and France between 1756 and 1815 in particular were directly responsible for the indelible imprint of the press gang both then and long afterwards.

The nineteenth century saw the expansion of the strongest maritime links of all, with the communities of Shetlanders at sea, and overseas. These communities have maintained their links with the Old Rock and sometimes with one another in expatriate societies scattered across the globe, their importance shown by the Hamefarin of 1960 and by the constant stream of visitors looking for their forebears. The full story of this great migration has still to be written, but the Shetland identity has certainly remained alive overseas as well as at home.

The forging of the regional identity of Shetland is a subject which has still to be fully researched, and the story of the Shetland traders and the sea cannot be fully understood without it. Much of the raw material lies in the field of language and literature, and in oral history. When the Shetland identity is fully understood, then the long and difficult voyage through modern history may be at an end.

Notes and References

Abbreviations used in the Notes and References

APS   Acts of the Parliaments of Scotland
CLB   Letter Books, Collector to Board (Lerwick Outport Records — SA, CE85)
CQR   Customs Accounts, Quarterly Returns Shetland (Lerwick) (SRO, E504/32)
ERS   Exchequer Roll of Scotland
HC   Hay & Company Records
HL   Hay of Laxfirth MSS
LUE   Library of the University of Edinburgh
NS   North of Scotland Orkney and Shetland Shipping Company Limited Records
NSA   The New Statistical Account of Scotland
OSA   Statistical Account of Scotland (The Old Statistical Account)
PRO   Public Record Office
RFB   Annual Reports of the Fishery Board for Scotland
RPC   Register of the Privy Council of Scotland
SA   Shetland Archives
SRO   Scottish Record Office
ST   The Shetland Times
WR   Wreck Records compiled by R. Stuart Bruce, in Tom Henderson Collection.

Shortened literature references are by author and date of publication, with the exception of a few early references referred to by author and shortened title.

Chapter 1

1. For the early history of Up-Helly-Aa see: Mitchell, C. E., *Up-Helly-Aa, Tar Barrels and Guizing* (Lerwick, 1948). Most notable was the choice of the Old Icelandic motto of Lerwick Town Council: 'Med logum skal land byggia' — 'With laws shall the land be built up'.

2. The central academic work was that of Jakobsen (below). However, there were considerable contributions of varying quality by others, both within and beyond Shetland. For early writing on the tings see e.g. Hibbert, S., 'Memoir on the tings of Orkney and Shetland', *Archaeologia Scotica, 3* (1831), 103-210.

3. Jakobsen, J., *The dialect and place-names of Shetland* (Lerwick, 1897); *An etymological dictionary of the Norn Language in Shetland* (London and Copenhagen, 1928-32); *The place-names of Shetland* (Lerwick, 1936). Note, however, the Lowland Scots influence noted by Fenton, A., 'Northern links', *Northern Studies, 16,* 15-16; Nicolaisen, 1983, 69-85.

4. Seton-Watson, 1977.

5. Small, 1967-68, 145-155.

6. See particularly Jakobsen, note 3 above; also Fenton, 1978; Hamilton, J. R. C., *Excavations at Jarlshof, Shetland* (Edinburgh, 1956); Small, A, 'Excavations at Underhoull, Unst. Shetland', *Proc. Soc. Antiquaries Scot.,* 98 (1964-66), 225-248; Small, 1981.

7. Smith, B., 1980, 22-27.

8. Miller, J. A., Flinn, D., 1966, 95-116; Flinn, 1980, 31-58.

9. Small, notes 5 and 6 above.

10. Lamb, H. H., 'Our changing climate, past and present', *Weather, 14* (1959), 299-318; Lamb, 1982.

11. Smith, B., 1979, 12; Crawford, 1978a, 5, 9.

12. Brøgger, 1929, 7.

13. Donaldson, 1958, 73, 135-136.

14. Lythe, 1960, 1-23.

15. Thowsen, 1973, 5-6.

16. Gade, 1951, 9.

17. Thowsen, 1969, 145.

18. Goodlad, 1971, 75-78.

19. *Ibid.*, 68-78.

20. *Ibid.*, 82-83.

21. Gade, 1951, 31.

22. Crawford, 1967-68, 156-176.

23. Goudie, 1904, 97-104.

24. Bugge, A., *Norges Historie* (Kristiania, 1916), Vol. II, 3-4.

25. Friedland, 1973, 78.

26. Dollinger, 1970.

27. Gade, 1951, 9.

28. *Ibid.*, 48-70.

29. *Ibid.*

30. *Ibid.*

31. *Ibid.*, 106-108; Dollinger, 1970, 242-243.

32. Gade, 1951, 48-70; Thowsen, 1973, 5-6.

33. Gade, *ibid.*

34. Friedland, 1973, 67, 73.

35. Gade, 1951, 48-70.

36. Friedland, 1973, 68-69.

37. Crawford, 1969, 35-53; Crawford, 1983, 42-43.

38. Donaldson, 1983, 8-9.

39. Carus Wilson, E. M., 'The Iceland trade'. In: Power, E., Postan, M. M. (eds.), *Studies in English trade in the fifteenth century* (London, 1933), 155-182.

40. Donaldson, 1983, 8-16.

41. Gade, 1951, 116.

42. *Ibid.*, 9.

43. *Ibid.*

44. Koenigsberger, H., *Europe in the sixteenth century* (London, 1968), 22-32.

45. Kranenburg, 1983, 98-99.

46. Beaujon, 1883, 35.

Chapter 2

1. Friedland, 1973, 69-70.

2. *RPC*, 1st Ser., Vol. 14, 267-271. See also: Tait, E. S. R., *Some notes on the Shetland Hanseatic Trade* (Lerwick, 1955), 11.

3. MacDonald, Sir George, 'More Shetland tombstones', *Proc. Soc. Antiquaries Scot.*, *69* (1934-35), 27-48.

4. Friedland, 1973, 72.

5. Balfour, David, *Oppressions of the Sixteenth Century in the Islands of Orkney and Shetland*, Abbotsford and Maitland Clubs *31* (Edinburgh, 1859).

6. Buchanan, George, *Rerum Scoticarum Historia* (Edinburgh, 1582), trans. I. Aikman (Glasgow, 1827), *Vol. 1*, 61.

7. Acts and Statutes within the Lawting, etc., within Orkney and Shetland, 1602-1640. *Maitland Club, 51, Misc. 2, Part 1* (Edinburgh, 1840). Barclay, R. S. (ed.), *The Court Book of Orkney and Shetland, 1612-1613* (Kirkwall, 1962). Barclay, R. S. (ed.), *The Court Book of Orkney and Shetland, 1614-1615,* Scott. Hist. Soc., 4th Ser., Vol. 4 (Edinburgh, 1967). Donaldson, Gordon (ed.), *The Court Book of Shetland, 1602-1604* (Edinburgh, 1954).

8. SRO, CC17, Commissariot Records of Orkney and Shetland. Dr F. J. Shaw kindly provided extracts from these, from which the present references are drawn. See also: Shaw, F. J., *The Northern and Western Islands of Scotland: their economy and society in the seventeenth century* (Edinburgh, 1980), 173 ff.

9. Rentals and Accounts of the Lordship of Zetland for various years, SA and Orkney Archives, GD150/2015-2026, Morton Papers; Gardie Papers, Bressay; SRO, RH9/15, Orkney and Shetland Papers.

10. SRO, E72/17 Exchequer Records, Customs Books, 1669-1673.

11. Dollinger, Phillippe, *The German Hansa* (London, 1970), 272-273.

12. Friedland, K., personal communication.

13. E.g. Boece, H., *The History and Chronicles of Scotland, written in Latin by Hector Boece and translated by J. Bellenden,* 2 vols. (Edinburgh, 1821), *Vol. 1,* p.81; also: Smith, Capt. John, *England's Improvement Revived. Vol. VI* (London, 1670), reprinted in *MacFarlane's Geographical Collections, Vol. III,* 60-65, Scott. Hist. Soc. (Edinburgh, 1908). The exact number of Lübeck merchants is unknown, as relevant records are held in the German Democratic Republic — Friedland, K., personal communication.

14. Bang, Nina Ellinger, and Korst, Knud, *Tabeller over Skibsfart og Varestransport gennem Øresund, 1497-1783* (København og Leipzig, 1906-53).

15. Donaldson, 1954, 28, 64; SRO, CC17, Commissariot Records of Orkney and Shetland, note 8 above.

16. Friedland, personal communication.

17. Baasch, Ernst, 'Hamburgs Seeschiffahrt und Waarenhandel vom Ende des 16. bis zur Mitte des 17. Jahrhunderts', *Zeits. des Vereins für Hamburgische Geschichte, 9* (1889), 312, 323-332; also: Ehrenberg, R., 'Aus der Hamburgischen Handelsgeschichte', *Zeits. des Vereins für Hamburgische Geschichte, 10* (1899), 18-20; Friedland, 1973, 73.

18. Gardie Papers, 1684. Inventor of the Dutchmens' Bonds granted to them for the Buter & oyll duty. for the Crop 1683 payable 1684. do. Crop 1684 payable 1685.

19. Friedland, 1973, 71-72.

20. *Ibid.,* 73; Donaldson, Gordon, *Shetland Life under Earl Patrick* (Edinburgh, 1958), 60-62; Brill, E. V. K., 'Whalsay and the Bremen connection', *Shetland Life No. 17* (1982), 11.

21. Donaldson, 1954, 153-154, 46.

22. *Ibid.,* 65, 80.

23. SRO, CC17, Commissariot Records.

24. SRO, RH9/15/173, Orkney and Shetland Papers, Copy Rental of the Lordship of Zetland Crop 1656, Accompt of Tollis recd. from the Dutch merchandis & others, 1656; do., 1657.

25. SRO, E72/17, Exchequer Records, note 10 above.

26. Gardie Papers 1684, note 18 above.

27. SA, D12/110/9, Neven of Windhouse Papers, Nott of fish put in to Otta Macke. Ane nott of geir taikin out from Otta Macke 1653.

28. SRO, E72/17, Exchequer Records, note 10 above.

29. Ibid.

30. Gardie Papers 1684, note 18 above.

31. SRO, E72/17, Exchequer Records, note 10 above.

32. Brand, *Brief Description,* 200.

33. Baasch, 1889, 312.

34. Friedland, 1973, 76 and personal communication.

35. Brill, E. V. K., 'More Bremen connections with Shetland', *Shetland Life No. 30* (1983), 36-37, 45; Donaldson, 1954, 9-10, 14, 16-17, 28, 39, 62, 69, 80, 93-95. See also: Tonkin, J. W., 'Two Hanseatic houses in the Shetlands', *Hansische Geschichtsblatter 94* (1976), 81-82.

36. SRO, CC17, Commissariot Records.

37. Ibid. Also: NLS, 13.2.8. Leigh, Mr. Hugh, A Geographical Description of the Island of Burray 1654, 64-74.

38. SRO, CC17, Commissariot Records.

39. Friedland, 1973, 74-75.

40. SRO, E72/17, Exchequer Records, note 10 above.

41. SA, SC12/53/1, Sheriff Court Records, Suspension & Relax. Henrick & oyrs. contra Cockburn & oyrs. 1681.

42. Friedland, 1973, 76.

43. Brand, *Brief Description*, 199.

44. SA SC12/53/1, note 40 above.

45. Ibid., 339-340. Contract, 1709.

46. Donaldson, 1954, 94-95, 153-154.

47. Friedland, 1973, 74.

48. *Ibid.*, 76.

49. Balfour, 1859, 41, 63-64.

50. Donaldson, 1954, 93-94; Friedland, 1973, 77.

51. Donaldson, 1954, 16-17.

52. SRO, CC17, Commissariot Records.

53. Balfour, 1859, 63-64; Friedland, 1973, 77.

54. Donaldson, 1958, 89-94, 106ff.

55. NLS, 13.2.8, A description of Dunrossness by Mr. James Kay, Minister thereof, 22.

56. Ibid., 54.

57. Brand, *Brief Description*, 200.

58. SRO, RH9/15/173, note 24 above.

59. Lordship rentals, note 9 above.

60. Gardie Papers 1682, Memorial for Andrew Mouat, by David Murray of Clerdone, 1682.

61. Hay & Company Records, Rental of the Lordship of Zetland, Crop 1772.

62. SA, SC12/53/1, note 45 above.

63. Ibid., note 44 above, 1695.

64. Gardie Papers 1682, note 60 above.

65. Gardie Papers, Account Current, Westshore and Gardie, 1703-1708.

66. *WR*, Unst.

67. Friedland, 1973, 75-76.

68. Brand, *Brief Description*, 199.

69. Note 27 above.

70. The Customs Books (note 10 above), Smith (note 13 above), and Brand, *Brief Description* are the principal sources for details of import commodities. See also Friedland, 1973, 75-77.

71. Friedland, 1973, 76.

72. *Ibid.*

73. SRO, E72/17, Exchequer Records, note 10 above.

74. Brand, *Brief Description*, 200.

75. *Ibid.*

76. Donaldson, 1954, 112.

77. Balfour, 1859, 15-16, 19, 41-42, 115-116; Johnston, A. W. & A. (eds.), *Orkney and Shetland Records* (Edinburgh, 1907-42), *Vol. 1*, 178-192; Adamsone, Johne, Minister of Nesting, The Parish of Nesting. In: *Reports on the state of certain parishes in Scotland made to his Majesty's Commissioners for plantations of Kirks, etc. in pursuance of their ordinance date April 12th, 1627* (Edinburgh, 1835), 224-232; Donaldson, 1958, 89-90.

78. Balfour, 1859, 37-38; *RPC*, 1st Ser., Vol. 9, 247-248.

79. SRO, RH15/101/5, Pyper MSS. Scheme of a voyage from Edinburgh to Hitland wt. pryces current. See also: Smout, T. C., *The Shetland News*, 11th November, 1958.

80. SA, SC12, note 45 above. Also: Lane, F. C., 'Tonnages: medieval and modern', *Ec. Hist. Rev., Second Ser.*, 17 (1964-65), 213-233.

v

81. Brand, *Brief Description*, 195.
82. Friedland, 1973, 78-79.
83. Lordship rentals, note 9 above.
84. Brand, *Brief Description*, 165-166.
85. Barclay, 1967, 64-65.
86. Brian Smith, personal communication based on examination of: SA, GD150/2015/B/1, Morton Papers, In nott of the dewties receaved at Skalloway Banks, begining the 14 of September 1653, owt of the parochins of Gulbervikk and Tingwall off the crope 1651; Goudie, 1904, 177-183.
87. Friedland, personal communication.
88. Smith, note 13 above.
89. *ERS*, 21, 325-327.
90. Smith, note 13 above.
91. Leigh, note 37 above.
92. Friedland, 1973, 75.
93. Johnston, 1907-42, Vol. 1, 218.
94. Donaldson, 1954, 106, 16-17.
95. NLS, 13.2.8, A geographical description of the Island of Bressay, 1684, 74.
96. Donaldson, 1954, 94-95, 153-154.
97. *Calendar of State Papers, Domestic Series, Vol. CLII*, 67.
98. *APS, Vol. 4*, 234-238.
99. Smith, note 13 above.
100. *RPC*, 1st Ser., Vol. 2, 272-273.
101. Millar, A. H. (ed.), *The Compt Buik of David Wedderburne merchant of Dundee, 1557-1630, together with the Shipping Lists of Dundee, 1580-1618*, Scott. Hist. Soc. (Edinburgh, 1898).
102. *RPC*, 1st Ser., Vol. 8, 647-650, 660.
103. Millar, 1898.
104. Goudie, 1904, 174, quoting from a document in the Sumburgh Papers.
105. Peterkin, Notes, 90.
106. *RPC*, 1st Ser., Vol. 14, 732.
107. SRO, CC17, Commissariot Records.
108. *APS*, Vol. 7, 409.
109. *RPC*, 3rd Ser., Vol. 1, 182.
110. *APS*, Vol. 7, 64, 81, 102-103.
111. *Ibid.*, 103.
112. Kay, note 55 above.
113. Ibid.
114. Lordship rentals, note 9 above; SA, D13/389/81, Midbrake Papers.
115. *Calendar of State Papers, Domestic Series, 1678*, 123-124.
116. Sibbald, *Description*, 24-25.
117. Note 79 above.
118. Brand, *Brief Description*, 205.
119. Smout, T. C., *Scottish Trade on the Eve of Union, 1660-1707* (Edinburgh, 1963), 24-25.
120. Orkney Archives, GD150, Morton Papers, Charter, 1706.
121. SA, D12/101/5, Neven of Windhouse Papers, The Rt. Hon. the Earl of Morton his 13 Queries anent the state of Zetland, answers thereto by Thos. Gifford of Busta (Copy, watermark 1811).
122. Lythe, S. G. E., 'The Dundee whale fishery', *Scott. J. Pol. Econ.*, 11 (1964), 158-160.
123. Note 45 above.
124. SRO, CC17, Commissariot Records.
125. Gardie Papers, Lordship Rentals, note 9 above.
126. Kay, note 55 above; Sibbald, *Description*, 22.
127. Kay, note 55 above.
128. Sibbald, *Description*, 12.

129. Fea, 1775, 108.

130. Brand, *Brief Description*, 110-111.

131. Kranenburg, 1983, 97-100. See also: Michell, A. R., 'The European fisheries in early modern history'. In: Rich, E. E., Wilson, C. H. (eds), *Cambridge Economic History of Europe, Vol. V: the economic organisation of early modern Europe* (Cambridge, 1977), 148-153; Beenhakker, A. J., *Hollanders in Shetland* (Lerwick, 1973).

132. *Acts of the Lords of Council in Public Affairs, Scotland: 1501-1554*, 497.

133. *Ibid.*

134. Beaujon, 1883, 28.

135. *Ibid.*, 35.

136. Goodlad, 1971, 84-85.

137. Beaujon, 1883, 63-66.

138. Ferguson, James, *Papers illustrating the History of the Scots Brigade in the Service of the United Netherlands, 1572-1782*, Scott. Hist. Soc. (Edinburgh, 1899), *Vol. 1*, 166.

139. Barclay, 1967, 65.

140. MacGillivray, Evan, 'Description of Shetland, Orkney and the Highlands of Scotland, by Richard James (1592-1638)', *Orkney Misc.*, 1 (1953), 50.

141. Barclay, 1967, 65; SRO, SC10/1/4, Sheriff Court Book of Shetland, note 7 above.

142. Beaujon, 1883, 63-66.

143. Brand, *Brief Description*, 134.

144. Gifford, *Historical Description*, 5.

145. Beaujon, 1883, 77.

146. Kranenburg, note 131 above, and quoted in Michell, 1977, 134, 148-149; Beenhakker, 1973, 2-3.

147. *Calendar of State Papers, Domestic Series, 1653, Vol. XXXVI*, 15.

148. Beaujon, 1883, 72-76.

149. *Ibid.*

150. SRO, RH9/15/138, Orkney and Shetland Papers, Memorial from Capt. Dick anent the Admiralty of Orkney & Zetland & his being Capt. of a fort at Brasey Sound & the Customs of Zetland to be allowd for his incuragement, 1689.

151. Note 95 above.

152. Beaujon, 1883, 77-78.

153. Gifford, *Historical Description*, 5-6; Gifford quotes 1702 in error. *Calendar of Treasury Books and Papers, Vol. 23, Part II*, 195-196; Beenhakker, 1973, 3 mentions the 1722 attack.

154. Hay, D. (ed.), *The Letters of James V* (Edinburgh, 1954), 408.

155. Note 138 above.

156. *RPC*, 1st Ser., Vol. 11, 605-606.

157. Gentleman, Tobias, *England's Way to Win Health* (1614), 12-14.

158. Barclay, 1967, 65.

159. Acts and Statutes within the Lawting, etc., note 7 above.

160. *RPC*, 2nd Ser., Vol. 1, 147-148.

161. Beaujon, 1883, 52; Michell, 1977, 149, 152.

162. Goodlad, 1971, 83.

163. *Ibid.*, 85-86.

164. Kay, note 55 bove.

165. Brand, *Brief Description*, 199.

166. Copy Rental, note 24 above.

167. *Calendar of State Papers, Domestic Series, Vol. 24*, 255.

168. Brand, *Brief Description*, 199-200.

169. Gifford, *Historical Description*, 5.

170. *Ibid;* also: *Calendar of Treasury Books and Papers*, note 153 above.

171. Donaldson, 1983, 12; Shaw, 1980, 177.

172. SRO, CC17, Commissariot Records, note 8 above.

173. Ibid.

174. Acts and Statutes within the Lawting, etc., note 7 above; Barclay, 1962, 20; Barclay, 1967, 23.

175. Donaldson, 1983, 11-13.

176. Grant, Francis J., *The County Families of Zetland* (Lerwick, 1893).

177. But see, e.g., Shaw, 1980, 34.

178. Saint-Clair, Roland W., *The Saint-Clairs of the Isles* (Auckland, N.Z., 1898).

179. Donaldson, 1983, 11-12.

180. Hay & Company Records, Rental of the Lordship of Zetland, Crop 1772.

181. Lordship rentals, note 9 above.

182. *RPC*, 2nd Ser., Vol. 5, 219-221.

183. SA, D8/10, Sumburgh Papers, List of goods and gear spoiled from Wm. Bruce of Simbister by Patrick, Earl of Orkney 1609. See also: A Decreit of Spulzie, granted by the Lords of Council to William Bruce of Symbister in Zetland, against Patrick, Earl of Orkney, 4th of February 1609. Communicated with remarks by David Laing, Esq., Treasurer. *Arch. Scotica 4* (1857), 385-398.

184. *RPC*, 1st Ser., Vol. 14, 732.

185. Gardie Papers (small bound volume), Holograph Signatures compiled by Thos. Mouat of Garth. collected AᎾ 1812.

186. Goudie, 1904, 117-124; Naes, And., 'Skottehandelen på Sunnhordland', *Sunnhordland Tidss.*, 7 (1920), 41-42.

187. *Calendar of State Papers relating to Scotland and Mary, Queen of Scots, Vol. 10*, 503-504. No. 553: Andrew Mouatt to Queen Elizabeth.

188. SRO, CC17, Commissariot Records, note 8 above.

189. Note 183 above.

190. Note 187 above.

191. Thowsen, 1969, 145.

192. *Ibid.*, 148.

193. Terry, C. Sanford, *The Cromwellian Union*, Scott. Hist. Soc. (Edinburgh, 1902), 125.

194. Sibbald, *Description*, 24.

195. Thowsen, 1969, 150-151.

196. *Ibid.*, 151-153.

197. *The Shetland News*, 8th May, 1947.

198. Terry, note 193 above; Marwick, Hugh, *Merchant Lairds of Long Ago* (Kirkwall, 1939), Part II, 43-80.

199. Tveite, Stein, *Engelsk-Norsk Trelasthandel, 1640-1710* (Oslo, 1961), 574-578.

200. Nicolaysen, N., 'Tabel, uddragen af foranstaaende lensregnskab, over skibe ankomne til Bergen fra 1 Mai 1577 — 1 Mai 1578 samt over de ind- og udforte varer', *Norsk Magasin II* (1868), 81.

201. Terry, note 187 above.

202. Bugge, A., *Den Norske Traelasthandels Historie* (Skien, 1925), *Vol. II*, 247.

203. *The Shetland News*, note 197 above.

204. Nicolaysen, note 200 above: 'Tabel over Skibe, som ladede i Søndhordland 1566-1567, samt over hvad de udførte'.

205. Thowsen, 1969, 150.

206. Bugge, 1925, 247.

207. Naess, 1920, 46. Table 2 is from p.33.

208. Thowsen, 1969, 151-153.

209. Friedland, personal communication.

210. Smith, note 13 above, quotes 1633 prices; 1733 prices are referred to by Gifford, *Historical Description*, 21-26, 50-53.

211. Barclay, 1967, 64-65.

212. Note 86 above.

213. Smith, note 13 above.

214. *Exchequer Rolls of Scotland*, various, especially Vol. 21, 325-327.

215. Balfour, 1859, 15-16, 34, 53.

216. *Ibid.*, 63-64.

217. Lythe, 1964.

218. *RPC*, 2nd Ser., Vol. 2, 605.

219. NLS, 13.2.8, Description of Zetland, by M.T.V.

220. Brand, *Brief Description*, 122-124; SRO, E217, Exchequer Records: Declared Accounts of Geo. McKenzie of Stonehyve and related papers: Double Bill of Suspension at the instance of Sir. Alexander Brand against Geo. MacKenzie; SRO, E41/24/36, Exchequer Records: Instructions from the heritors of the cuntrey of Zetland to Allexander Brand stewart & justiciar of Orkney & Zetland for representing ther conditione to the Lords of His Majesties Councill and Thesaurie, subscrivit the 22 of Augues 1696; Gardie Papers, Memorabilia Zetlandica.

221. Edinburgh University Library, Laing MSS, Gilbert Neven to Col. William Sinclair, Vol. 1, 361-362.

222. Lordship rentals, note 9 above.

223. SRO, RH9/15/215, Orkney and Shetland Papers, Committee of War to Baillie (blank).

224. *RPC*, 3rd Ser., Vol. 15, 338-339; SRO, E41/24/36, note 220 above.

225. Note 223 above.

226. Gifford, *Historical Description*, 4-7.

227. Supple, B. E., 'Currency and commerce in the early seventeenth century', *Ec. Hist. Rev., Ser. II, 10* (1957), 239-245.

228. Sperling, J., 'The international payments mechanism in the seventeenth and eighteenth centuries', *Ec. Hist. Rev., Ser. II, 14* (1961-62), 446-468.

229. Hinton, R. W. K., *The Eastland Trade and the Common Weal in the seventeenth century* (Cambridge, 1959).

230. *WR*, Sandwick.

231. Note 224 above.

232. *Calendar of Treasury Books and Papers, Vol. 23*, note 152 above.

233. Balfour, 1859, 39-42.

234. SRO, RH9/15/173, Orkney and Shetland Papers, Copy Rental, note 24 above.

235. *RPC*, 3rd Ser., Vol. 3, 65.

236. *RPC*, 1st Ser., Vol. 9, 247-248.

237. Friedland, 1973, 78.

238. *APS*, 5 Anne c. 48.

239. *RPC*, 3rd Ser., Vol. 1, 182.

240. *APS*, Vol. 7, 409.

241. Kay, note 55 above.

242. Note 238 above.

243. Note 232 above.

244. Marwick, J. D. (ed.), *Extracts from the Records of the Convention of Royal Burghs of Scotland, Vol. 4*, 408.

245. Note 232 above.

246. Flinn, 1977, 130.

247. *RPC*, 2nd Ser., Vol. 5, 659-660.

248. Renwick, R. (ed.), *Extracts from the Records of the Royal Burgh of Stirling: 1519-1666*. The Glasgow, Stirlingshire and Sons of the Rock Society (1887), Glasgow, 1635, 1st June.

249. Peterkin, 1822, 150-151.

250. Lordship rentals, note 9 above; Thomson, 1983a, 156-157.

251. Smout, 1963, 245-249; Lamb, 1982.

252. SRO, E217, Declared Accounts, note 220 above: The State of the Crown Rents, Excyse, Customes, Pole Money, Land tax and Hearth money of Orkney and Zeatland from the year 1688 being the year of the revolution to the Union in the year 1707.

253. SRO, PA7/16/72, Supplementary Parliamentary Papers, Petition for Mr. Wm. Craigie of Gairsie, the oyr, Heretors within the Stewartrie of Orkny & Zetland Unto His Grace His Majestie's High Commissioner And the Right Honourable Estates of Parliament; see also: SRO,

E41/24/36, Exchequer Records, note 220 above.

254. Brand, *Brief Description*, 106-109, 124-129.

255. Grant, 1893, 'The Sinclairs of Brew'; Kay, note 55 above.

256. SA, GD150/1704, Morton Papers, Decreet Absolvitor: The Earl of Morton against Rbt. Sinclair of Quendale. 1718.

257. Kay, note 55 above.

258. Ibid.

259. Ibid. Also: Description of Zetland by M.T.V., ibid; Instructions, note 220 above.

260. Brand, *Brief Description*, 193-195; note also SRO, E41/24/36, Exchequer Records, note 220 above. See also Lamb, 1982, 207-210.

261. Brand, *ibid.*, 193-194.

262. Note 180 above.

263. Smout, 1963, 19-20.

264. Gardie Papers, Copy Instructions for Thos. Leslie Commissary of Zetland and Jas. Kinnaird, relating to their commission given them for fewing of the Kings Tacks & Udal lands; O'Dell, 1939, 247-263.

265. *Calendar of State Papers, Domestic Series, 1675-1676*, 130-131.

266. Balfour, 1859, 15-16, 34, 53.

267. *RPC*, 1st Ser., Vol. 13, 400-401.

268. Goudie, 1904, 165-171; note 61 above.

269. Note 86 above.

270. Balfour, 1859, 123; Lythe, 1960, 101-102.

271. Gardie Papers, 1776. A view of the Payment of the Crown Rents in the Ldp. of Zetland from the year 1643 to this date 1776.

272. Smith, B., 1979, 13.

273. *RPC*, 1st Ser., Vol. 14, 267-271. For discussions generally see Anderson, 1982, 88-90, 118-125.

274. *RPC*, 1st Ser., Vol. 2, 222-223.

275. *Calendar of State Papers relating to Scotland and Mary, Queen of Scots*, Vol. 5, 205-210; Anderson, 1982, 118-128.

276. *Calendar, ibid.*, Vol. 10, 503-504.

277. *RPC*, 1st Ser., Vol. 9, 240-241.

278. Smith, note 13 above; Smith, B., 1979, 13.

279. Sibbald, *Description*, 17; Shaw, 1980, 1.

280. Lordship rentals, note 9 above.

281. Note 61 above.

282. Ibid; Lordship rentals, note 9 above.

283. Ibid.

284. SA, GD150/2024, Morton Papers, Accounts of ley lands in Zetland, crops 1712-1719 and miscellaneous rental accounts of same date.

285. Ibid.

286. Ibid.

287. Holograph signatures, note 185 above.

288. SRO, PA7/16/72, Supplementary Parliamentary Papers: The Petition of Captain Andrew Dick, sometime Stewart of Orkney, 1700.

289. Note 284 above.

290. Memorabilia Zetlandica, note 220 above.

291. Gifford, *Historical Description*, 4-7.

292. Smith, B., 1979, 14.

293. Holograph signatures, note 185 above.

Chapter 3

1. Smout, 1963, 279-280.
2. Goodlad, 1971, 90-128.
3. Thowsen, 1969, 166-208; Bruce, 1914, 289-300.
4. Thowsen, 1969, 168, 193; Henderson, 1945; Goodlad, 1971, 57, 104, 115, plate facing p.92; Osler, 1983.
5. Thowsen, 1969, note 3 above.
6. Goodlad, 1971, 105-106, quoting Edmondston. The similarity of Shetland and Norwegian etymology for sails and rigging indicates the use of sails much earlier than the eighteenth century. See Thowsen, 1969, 200.
7. Gardie Papers, 1764. Answers to Queries respecting Shetland, 1764.
8. Goodlad, 1971, 107-110.
9. SA, AF29, Department of Agriculture and Fisheries, Lerwick Fishery Office Records, Abstract Books; *OSA, 12*, 360.
10. SA, D12/110/18, Memorandum on Curing Fish in Zetland, by Thomas Leisk of Uya. June 1824; Low, *Tour*, 120-121.
11. Ibid.
12. Memorandum, note 10 above.
13. Ibid.
14. Ibid.
15. Low, *Tour*, 120-121.
16. Memorandum, note 10 above.
17. Low, *Tour*, 137.
18. Gardie Papers, 1723. Resolutions: The Heritors and Gentlemen of Zetland — Anent Several Grievances of the Country. With the Stewart Depute his Act and Authority Interponed thereto, 1733.
19. Edmondston, 1809, *2*, 298.
20. Gardie Papers, Scroll Answer to the Shetland Paragraph in the *Edinburgh Advertiser* of 4th January, 1785.
21. Goodlad, 1971, 110-118.
22. *Ibid.*
23. *OSA, 12*, 351.
24. Low, *Tour*, 95, 102.
25. Edmondston, 1809, *1*, 288.
26. SRO, CE1, Scottish Board of Customs, Minute Books. Vol. 1, Friday 13th December, 1723.
27. *OSA, 7*, 588-589; *1*, 387; *21*, 280.
28. *OSA, 7*, 593.
29. *Ibid.*
30. Grant, 1893.
31. *Ibid.*, the Mitchells of Girlsta, the Scotts of Melby.
32. Gardie Papers, Memorabilia Zetlandica.
33. Tait, 1934, 60.
34. SA, GD144, Symbister Papers, Box 18: Memorial for John Bruce Stewart of Simbister Esq., Relative to his fishing at Skerries in Shetland.
35. Hay and Company Records, Rental of the Lordship of Zetland, Crop 1772.
36. Ibid.
37. SA, D8, Sumburgh Papers, Mr. Scott to Mr. Anderson, 11th May, 1799.
38. J. J. Graham, personal communication.
39. Gifford, *Historical Description*, 54-55; Answers to Queries, note 7 above; Rental, note 35 above.
40. Smith, Adam, *The Wealth of Nations, Vol. 1*, 223, quoted by Thomas Mouat in his Notebook (Gardie Papers); Gardie Papers: Observations on & causes of the particular connections that subsist betwixt the Landholders of Shetland and their Tenants or Fishers, 1785.

This appears in: Third Report from the Committee, appointed to enquire into the State of the British Fisheries, and into the most effectual means for their Improvement and extension, 1785. Appendix. *Reports of Committees of the House of Commons, Vol. 10;* Scroll Answer, note 20 above; evidence that rents were paid in fish right from the beginning of the period, in 1712, is apparent from — SA, GD144/7, Symbister Papers, Rental of Quendail's lands and corn teind in the parishes of Dunrossness, Sandwick and Conisburgh, 1712 (drawn to my attention by Mr. Brian Smith).

41. Edmondston, 1809, *2,* 294-337.

42. SA, D8, Sumburgh Papers, Memorial for John Bruce, Collector of Customs at Lerwick, 1782; Observations, note 40 above.

43. Edmondston, 1809, *1,* 314-317.

44. SA, D8, Sumburgh Papers, Letter Book: John Bruce to Charles Innes, 27th August, 1786; — do. —, 23rd December, 1786.

45. Gardie Papers, Zetland Product, 1778-1818. Statistical extracts compiled by Jonathan Wills.

46. SA, D1/37, Day Book of Thomas Gifford.

47. Gifford, *Historical Description,* 25-26.

48. Smith, Capt. John, *England's Improvement Revived* (London, 1670). Reprinted in: *MacFarlane's Geographical Collections,* Scott. Hist. Soc. (Edinburgh, 1908), *Vol. 3,* 60-65.

49. *OSA, 12,* 359.

50. *OSA, 7,* 593.

51. SA, D8, Sumburgh Papers. A Sketch of a Computation upon the Quantity of Victual Necessary to maintain the Inhabitants of Shetland for a Twelvemonth, & by what means they have been maintained from July 1784, to July 1785. Being the third year of Famine in these Islands. n.d. with related papers.

52. Resolutions, note 18 above.

53. Rental, note 35 above.

54. Ibid; Edmondston, 1809, *2,* 297-298.

55. The late G. M. Nelson, personal communication.

56. Sketch, note 51 above.

57. Shand, J., Foreign Coin in Shetland. *Old Lore Misc., 6* (1913), 37-40.

58. *Ibid.*

59. Resolutions, note 18 above.

60. See note 40 above.

61. Scroll Answer, note 40 above.

62. O'Dell, 1939, 302-303.

63. Resolutions, note 18 above.

64. O'Dell, 1939, 308.

65. Gardie Papers, Scroll Answer to the Queries of Sir John Sinclair for Unst, 1791.

66. *OSA, 20,* 99; O'Dell, 1939, 23.

67. Answers to Queries, note 7 above; Scroll Answer, note 40 above.

68. *OSA, 7,* 589.

69. *Ibid.*

70. Gifford, *Historical Description,* 4-7.

71. Answers to Queries, note 7 above.

72. Low, *Tour,* 66.

73. Brand, *Brief Description,* 129-130.

74. *OSA, 3,* 418.

75. Scroll Answer, note 40 above.

76. Gardie Papers, Contract, Urie, 30th October, 1716.

77. Gardie Papers, Contract, Bressay, 2nd February, 1721.

78. Gardie Papers, Contract, Lerwick, 30th May, 1727.

79. Bruce, 1922, 48-52; 1931, 356-376.

80. Memorabilia Zetlandica, note 32 above.

81. Smout, 1963, 77-78.

82. NLS, 31.2.9, Letter Book concerning the Earl of Morton's Affairs in Zetland (1715-1721, 1730-1736).

83. Gardie Papers, Memorial. Thos. Gifford of Busta to Arthur Nicolson of Lochend & Magnus Henderson of Gardie, 31st May, 1722.

84. Rental, note 35 above.

85. Letter Book, note 44 above: John Bruce to Charles Innes, 20th August, 1785.

86. SA, GD144/Box 7: Rental of Busta's Estate in the West Side of the Parish of Northmavine and the Island of Papa Stour Including such lands he has in Tack from the Earl of Morton and Sir And. Mitchell of Westshore within the said West side, 1758.

87. Ibid.

88. Gardie Papers. Holograph Signatures, compiled by Thos. Mouat of Garth, collected A⁰ 1812.

89. Goudie (ed.), 1889, *Mill's Diary*.

90. Low, *Tour*, 50.

91. Edmondston, 1809, *1*, 17, 25.

92. Gray, 1957, 12-13, 26-29.

93. SA, D12/101/5. Neven of Windhouse Papers. The Rt. Hon. the Earl of Morton his 13 Queries anent the State of Zetland with answers thereto by Thos. Gifford of Busta, n.d.

94. SA, GD144/Box 7: Symbister Papers, Wm. Hogg & Son to Thos. Gifford, 29th December, 1753.

95. SA, GD144/Box 7: Symbister Papers, Miscellaneous accounts and invoices.

96. Grant, 1893, Bruce of Symbister, Whalsay.

97. SRO, E504/32. Customs Accounts, Quarterly Returns Shetland (Lerwick) (henceforward cited as CQR), 1740s.

98. Ibid., 1760s.

99. Gardie Papers, Contract, Lerwick, 21st September, 1752; Contract, Lerwick, 29th January, 1754.

100. Gardie Papers, Contract, 2nd July, 1763.

101. Sandison, 1934.

102. Scroll Answer, note 40 above.

103. Ibid.

104. Smout, 1963, 96-99.

105. Gardie Papers, Memorial and Queries for the Fish-curers of Zetland, Edinburgh, 28th February, 1776; note also Smout, 1963, 97.

106. Scroll Answer, note 40 above; Hibbert, 1822, 506-507.

107. Information on Sellar and Henderson of Liverpool supplied by Dr. R. Mooney, personal communication. See also, e.g., John, A. H., 'The London Assurance Company and the marine insurance market in the 18th century', *Economica New Ser., 20* (1953), 126-141.

108. SRO, GD9, British Fishery Society, Letter Books, Vol. 4, 8-11: William Stratton to George Fowler, Carthagena, 5th January, 1788.

109. R. Mooney, personal communication.

110. CQR.

111. Gardie Papers, Vade Mecum.

112. Ibid.

113. Minute Books, note 26 above. 24th December, 1723.

114. SRO, RH20, Treasury Records Accounts Scotland, Vol. 13. An account of the quantity of British Herrings and cod exported from Scotland from Christmas 1750 to Christmas 1782 distinguishing each year and the ports from whence exported.

115. Low, *Tour*, 191; Memorial and Queries, note 105 above.

116. Goodlad, 1971, 162-171.

117. Vives, 1969, 483-485.

118. Memorial and Queries, note 105 above.

119. Goodlad, 1971, 92.

120. Memorial for John Bruce Stewart, note 34 above; Scroll Answer, note 20 above; Memorial and Queries, note 105 above.

121. SRO, NG1, Records of the Board of Trustees for Fisheries and Manufactures in Scotland, Vol. 20, 228.

122. Memorandum on curing fish, note 10 above.

123. SRO, E502, Customs Cash Accounts, 1708-09 — 1720-21.

124. *OSA, 12,* 359.

125. Low, *Tour,* 191.

126. *OSA, 12,* 367.

127. *The Diary of the Rev. John Mill,* June, 1791.

128. Scroll Answer, note 20 above.

129. Ibid.

130. Vilar, 1962, *3,* 66-142.

131. Scroll Answer, note 20 above; Observations, note 40 above.

132. Memorial and Queries, note 105 above.

133. Goodlad, 1971, 92-93.

134. O'Dell, 1939, 305.

135. Memorial and Queries, note 105 above; Scroll Answer, note 20 above.

136. William Stratton to George Fowler, note 108 above; *OSA, 3,* 190-191.

137. Scroll Answer, note 20 above; Vilar, 1962, *3,* 128.

138. Memorial and Queries, note 105 above.

139. Gardie Papers, Account Ct., Capt. Jas. Moodie of Melsetter & Magnus Henderson of Gardie.

140. David Anderson, personal communication.

141. Vives, 1969, 601.

142. Ibid.

143. Vilar, 1962, 117, 121.

144. *Ibid.,* 128.

145. *Ibid;* O'Dell, 1939, 305.

146. Scroll Answer, note 20 above.

147. Ibid.

148. MS Letter Book of Thomas Gifford of Busta, in possession of the late T. Henderson, quoted in O'Dell, 1939, 304-307.

149. CQR.

150. Ibid.

151. Third Report from the Committee, note 40 above, Appendix 10.

152. Edmondston, 1809, *1,* 287; *OSA, 3,* 415-416.

153. CQR.

154. Resolutions, note 18 above; Gifford, *Historical Description,* 22.

155. The late G. M. Nelson, personal communication.

156. NLS, 31.2.9, note 82 above: Letter to Patrick Gifford, 7th April, 1735.

157. Ibid.

158. Resolutions, note 18 above.

159. Rental of the Lordship of Zetland, note 35 above.

160. SA, D6/1/18, E. S. Reid Tait Collection. ? Thorton to Rbt. Neven, 13th July, 1765.

161. Rental of the Lordship of Zetland, note 35 above.

162. Edmondston, 1809, *1,* 297-298.

163. The late G. M. Nelson, personal communication.

164. Sinclair, Sir John, Anderson Dr., *Report of the Committee of the Highland Society of Scotland, to whom the subject of Shetland Wool was referred* (Edinburgh, 1790).

165. SA, GD144, Symbister Papers, Box 7. Account, Foreign Salt, 1737; Scroll Answer, note 20 above; Vade Mecum, note 111 above, 17-19.

166. Memorandum on Curing Fish in Zetland, note 10 above.

167. SA, D12/64/3, Neven of Windhouse Papers, Thomas Gifford to William John Neven,

23rd March, 1743.

168. CQR.

169. Ibid.

170. Vade Mecum, note 111 above, 17; Memorandum on Fish Curing in Zetland, note 10 above.

171. Note 151 above.

172. Bridbury, 1955; Adams, 1965, 153.

173. CQR.

174. Resolutions, note 18 above.

175. CQR.

176. Vade Mecum, note 111 above, 17-19; *Statutes at Large,* 5 Geo. I c.18; for the suggested role of the salt duties in precipitating the demise of the German merchants and the corresponding rise of the lairds in trade, see Gifford, *Historical Description,* 25; Hibbert, 1822, 245-6; Tudor, 1883, 129-130.

177. SA, CO1/1/4, MSS. Minutes of the Commissioners of Supply. Memorandum on the depressed condition and peculiar burdens of Shetland. to Govt. and both Houses of Parliament, 1851.

178. CQR.

179. Thowsen, 1969, 150-153.

180. *Ibid.,* 155.

181. CQR.

182. Bruce, 1931, 364-365.

183. SA, SC12/6/160, Sheriff Court Records, Petition by Arthur Nicolson, merchant in Lerwick, 1742.

184. Gardie Papers, Journal of a Jaunt to London in 1775, by Thos. Mouat, yr. of Garth.

185. *Chambers' Twentieth Century Dictionary.*

186. *Calendar of Treasury Papers, Vol. CVI, 60* (1708-1714, 29-30), Comrs. of Customs (Scotland) to Wm. Lowndes, Esq., 17th April, 1707/8.

187. SA, GD144/Box 7, Symbister Papers, Invoice of goods shipt at Hamburg pr. the *Sibella,* 2nd October, 1752.

188. SRO, CE1, Scottish Board of Customs, Minute Books, Vol. 4, Tue. 6th July, 1742.

189. SRO, RH/20, Treasury Records Accounts Scotland, Vol. 13, Pt. 6, An account showing the variations on the Duties of Customs upon Rum, Foreign spirits, wine, tobacco, and other principal articles imported, mentioned in the preceding account from 1769 to the present time, 11th December, 1783.

190. Gardie Papers, Arthur Nicolson to Wm. Mouat, 15th August, 1765.

191. Gardie Papers, Copy petition & presentation in the name of the whole inhabitants and merchants of Zetld. — to Comrs. of Customs in Scotland, 31st December, 1765.

192. *The Diary of the Rev. John Mill,* note 89 above, 1771, 37.

193. Gardie Papers, Copy Draft Memorial for Zetland, from Wm. Mouat to Thos. Dundas, October, 1769.

194. *Calendar of Home Office Papers, George III, 1770-1772.* Doc. 32: Thos. Bradshaw to Richard Sutton, Esq., 31st January, 1770, 7. Doc. 56: Thos. Bradshaw to Richard Sutton, Esq., 28th February, 1770, 14.

195. *The Diary of the Rev. John Mill,* note 89 above, 1776, May.

196. *Ibid.,* 1774, August 1775, December 1777 (52-53).

197. SRO, E510, Collectors' Incident Accounts, Christmas Quarter, 1780.

198. Letter Book, note 44 above: John Bruce to Charles Innes, 17th September, 1786.

199. SA, D8, Sumburgh Papers, Walter Scott of Scottshall to (?), 24th April, 1792.

200. Edmondston, 2, 16-17.

201. The Rt. Hon. the Earl of Morton his 13 Queries, note 93 above.

202. CQR.

203. Sandison, 1934, 63.

204. Low, *Tour,* 80.

205. *OSA, 1,* 403.

206. Thomson, 1983a, 156-158.

207. *The Diary of the Rev. John Mill,* note 89 above, February, 1783, 69.

208. Scroll Answer, note 20 above; A Sketch of a Computation upon the Quantity of Victual, note 51 above.

209. Scroll Answer, note 20 above.

210. Ibid.

211. SRO, CE1, Scottish Board of Customs, Minute Books, Vol. 4, Wed. 29th April, 1741; *The Diary of the Rev. John Mill,* note 89 above, 24; Edmondston, *2,* 138.

212. A Sketch of a Computation upon the Quantity of Victual, note 51 above.

213. *The Diary of the Rev. John Mill,* note 89 above, September, 1778, 54-55.

214. Arthur Nicolson to Wm. Mouat, note 190 above.

215. CQR.

216. *OSA, 5,* 194-195.

217. Gifford, *Historical Description,* 26.

218. NLS, 640f 187, Melville Papers, 92, 189: Memorial for the fish curers on the Coast of Scotland, particularly those in the Shetland Islands, relative to an act passed the 10th of May last, imposing an additional duty on salt, 1798.

219. Edmondston, *1,* 288.

220. Memorial for the fish curers, note 218 above.

221. Edmondston, *1,* 240.

222. Journal of a Jaunt to London in 1775, note 184 above; SA, D8, Sumburgh Papers, State or View of the Money owing to Robert Hunter in October, 1794; Checkland, 1793.

223. Bruce, 1922, 1931; Gifford, *Historical Description;* numerous documentary references inc. notes 82, 83, 93, 95 above; Cowie, 1874, 267; Smith, B., *Introduction* (to facsimile reprint of *Historical Description*), 1976.

224. Memorial for John Stewart of Simbister, note 34 above.

225. SA, D8, Sumburgh Papers, Proposals for furnishing the English Greenland Fleet with Men from the Islands of Shetland, n.d; Observations: Effect of the Dutch War on Shetland from which J. Bruce's Representation to the Board of Customs was taken. January, 1781.

226. Edmondston, *2,* 139.

227. Gardie Papers, Copy Letter (?) to Sir John Inglis, 6th January, 1785.

228. The Rt. Hon. the Earl of Morton his 13 Queries, note 93 above.

229. Sinclair, Sir John, Anderson, Dr., note 164 above.

230. The Rt. Hon. the Earl of Morton his 13 Queries, note 93 above.

231. Copy Letter to Sir John Inglis, note 227 above; Scroll Answer, note 20 above.

232. SRO, GD9, British Fisheries Society, Letter Books, Vol. 1, 35-38: Wm. Cobb to Duke of Argyll, 17th September, 1773.

233. Copy Draft Memorial for Zetland, note 193 above.

234. Edmonston, 251-252; SA, D12, Neven of Windhouse Papers, Comparative statements on fishing with sloops and boats, n.d.

235. Mason, John, *A history of Scottish experiments in rural education from the 18th century to the present day* (London, 1936), 26-28.

236. Low, *Tour,* 188.

237. The Rt. Hon. the Earl of Morton his 13 Queries, note 93 above.

238. Low, *Tour,* 162.

239. Orkney Archives, GD150/2519, Morton Papers, Indenture, between James, Earl of Morton and The Governor and Company for smelting down lead with pit salt and coal salt, 7th July, 1709; Copy Letter of Attorney by Jas., Earl of Morton authorising his attorney to cancel Indenture between said Earl & the Governor & Company for smelting lead in Orkney and Shetland, 20th April, 1714.

240. SA, SC12/6/170, Contract and agreement betwixt Jo. Leslie of Ustaness and Rbt. Dick of Fracafield, 1740.

241. Bruce, 1912-13, 157-159.

242. Answers to Queries, note 7 above.

243. Third Report from the Committee, note 40 above. Appendix.

244. SA, D12/64/3, Neven of Windhouse Papers: William John Neven (?) to Anthony Simpson, n.d; Thos. Gifford to William John Neven, 25th November, 1743.

245. Bruce, 1922, 51-52; Smith, B., 1976.

246. The Rt. Hon. the Earl of Morton his 13 Queries, note 93 above.

247. Records of the Board of Trustees, note 121, Vol. 7, 48, 58.

248. Ibid., 138.

249. Ibid., Vol. 6, 140; Vol. 18, 78; Vol. 20, 15, 43, 51.

250. SA, GD150/2518B, Morton Papers. Proposal: Robert Dick of Fracafield to the Rt. Hon. the Earl of Morton, 8th March, 1741/2.

251. Scroll Answer, note 20 above.

252. CQR.

253. Scroll Answer, note 20 above.

254. Hamilton, 1963, 134-149; Gray, 1957, 124-141.

255. Records of the Board of Trustees, note 121 above, Vol. 6, 111, 153-154, 169; Vol. 18, 117; Vol. 19, 20, 40; Vol. 21, 44-45.

256. Edmondston, 2, 3-4; Records of the Board of Trustees, note 121 above, Vol. 19, 119; Vol. 20, 44-45.

257. Gardie Papers, Copy Letter: Sir John Mitchell & other members of Comrs. of Supply to Messrs Gibson and Balfour, 22nd December, 1770.

258. Edmondston, 2, 4.

259. Willis, Douglas P., The Changing Cultural Landscape of Orkney, 1750-1900 (M.Litt. Thesis, University of Aberdeen, 1967, Unpubl.).

260. Edmondston, 2, 5.

261. *Ibid; OSA, 1,* 390; *2,* 416.

262. Gardie Papers, Notebook.

263. Low, *Tour,* 50.

264. Memorial for John Bruce, note 42 above; Observations, note 40 above.

265. Edmondston, *1,* 314-317.

266. The Rt. Hon. the Earl of Morton his 13 Queries, note 93 above.

267. Gifford, *Historical Description,* 4-7.

268. SA, GD150/2518B, Morton Papers: Memorial for the Rt. Hon. the Earl of Morton on behalf of the Gentlemen Heritors, Merchants, and other Inhabitants of the Islands of Zetland, 14th August, 1756.

269. Proposals for furnishing the English Greenland Fleet, note 225 above. See also Jackson, 1978, 89.

270. CLB, Collector to Board, 1817 No. 21.

271. Memorial for the Rt. Hon. The Earl of Morton, note 268 above.

272. Gardie Papers, Draft Letter: John Bruce Stewart *et al* to Capt. Napier or Officer superintending the Impress Service of the North east Coast of Scotland, 21st April, 1777.

273. Memorial and Queries for the Fish-curers of Zetland, note 105 above.

274. *OSA, 1,* 396.

275. Copy Letter (?) to Sir John Inglis, note 227 above.

276. Memorial for the Rt. Hon. The Earl of Morton, note 268 above.

277. The Rt. Hon. the Earl of Morton his 13 Queries, note 93 above.

278. NLS, MS354, Melville Papers, 71, fo. 35-41, Representation. John Bruce, Collector of Customs at Lerwick in Shetland to the Honable. The Commissioners of H.M. Customs at Edinburgh, n.d. ca. 1800; Copy Letter (?) to Sir John Inglis, note 227 above.

279. Thomson, 1983a, 150-162; Flinn, 1977, 185.

280. Brand, *Brief Description,* 106-109.

281. Edmondston, 84-87.

282. Gardie Papers, Vade Mecum, note 111 above.

283. Thomson, 1983a, 154-156.

284. Hamilton, 1963, 13-17; Gray, 1957, 63-64, 90.

285. Low, *Tour*, 50.

286. *OSA, 5*, 182-202; Brian Smith, personal communication on research into Sheriff Court Records (SA, SC12/6/5253).

287. NLS, MS5575, Liston MSS., Letter (?) to Mr. Liston, 30th April, 1774.

288. Third Report from the Committee, note 40 above.

289. *OSA, 5*, 182-202.

290. Proposals for furnishing the English Greenland Fleet, note 225 above.

291. Ibid.

292. Answers to Queries, note 7 above.

293. Copy Letter (?) to Sir John Inglis, note 227 above; Scroll Answer, note 20 above.

294. See, e.g., Wills, 1974, Chapters 2 and 3; Memorial for Mr. Peter Innes for the use of his friend at Edinburgh, 22nd May, 1776 (photocopy in SA).

295. Copy Letter (?) to Sir John Inglis, note 227 above.

296. Smout, 1964, 214-234; Rymer, L., 'The Scottish kelp industry', *Scott. Geog. Mag.* 90(3) (1974), 142-4; Thomson, 1983b, 'Kelp-making in Orkney'.

297. Rostow, 1960, 23-24.

Chapter 4

1. CQR.

2. CLB, Collector to J. Westgarth & E. Cunningham, 8th February, 1814; Crawford, Rev. James, *The Parish of Lerwick, 1701-1901* (Lerwick, 1901).

3. CQR.

4. Ibid.

5. NLS, MS640, Melville Papers, 72: Memorial for the fish curers on the Coast of Scotland, particularly those in the Shetland Islands, relative to an Act passed the 10th of May last, imposing an additional duty on salt. 1798.

6. SA, D13/387/15, Midbrake Papers, Jas. Linklater to Jas. Irvine of Midbreck, 7th November, 1795.

7. Ibid., 387/16, Jas. Linklater to Jas. & Geo. Irvine, 25th September, 1797.

8. CQR.

9. SA, D13/387/33, Midbrake Papers, Wm. Henderson (of Bardister) to Jas. Irvine, 13th May, 1813.

10. Memorial for the fish curers, note 5 above; HC, Mr. Hay's Private Ledger from 1819 to 1829.

11. Edmondston, 2, 43-44.

12. SA, D6, E. S. Reid Tait Collection, Articles of Lerwick United Trades Society, Est. 1809.

13. SA, D4/10, Hay of Laxfirth Papers, Thos. Williamson to Jas. Hay, 23rd November, 1814; (Jas. Hay?) to Thos. Williamson, n.d.

14. Mr. Hay's Private Ledger, note 10 above.

15. CLB, Board No. 16, 9th March, 1821.

16. *ST*, 18th November, 1876; Jackson, 1978, 70-90, 117-131.

17. Lythe, 1964, 158-159; Michie, 1979.

18. NLS, 81.9.2, Chalmers MSS, Bound Volume, 304.

19. Ibid., 81.9.1, 62.

20. Ibid., 69.

21. Edmondston, 2, 18.

22. SA, D4/8, Hay of Laxfirth Papers, Letter Book (of Jas. Hay), n.d.

23. CLB, Board No. 9, 25th February, 1808.

24. SA, D8, Walter Scott of Scottshall to (?), 24th April, 1792.

25. Board No. 9, note 23 above.

26. Edmondston, 2, 61.

27. CLB, Board No. 40, 10th May, 1825.

28. *NSA.*, 52.

29. Edmondston, *2*, 17.

30. CQR; CLB, Board No. 23, 15th August, 1800.

31. SA, SC12/6/5547, Petition of Rbt. Robertson of Gossabrough, etc., *contra* Rbt. & Wm. Pole, *et al.*

32. SA, D8, Sumburgh Papers, Matthew Thomas to John Bruce, 12th February, 1802.

33. Edmondston, *2*, 17.

34. Cowie, 1874, 159.

35. Letter Book, note 22 above; CLB, various letters, 1814; Nicolson, 1982, 2-3.

36. CLB, Board No. 62, 17th November, 1852.

37. Letter Book, note 22 above.

38. CLB, Board No. 68, 11 December, 1810; Board No. 80, 19th August, 1814.

39. CLB, Board No. 40, 24th April, 1818; Board No. 76, 15th June, 1818; Board No. 120, 9th October, 1818.

40. CLB, Board No. 40, 24th April, 1818.

41. Ibid.

42. CLB, Board No. 34, 9th April, 1819.

43. Ibid.

44. The late G. M. Nelson, discussion.

45. CLB, Board No. 108, 20th November, 1819.

46. CLB, Board No. 34, 13th April, 1822; Board No. 40, 10th May, 1825; Board No. 56, 9th August, 1826; Board No. 8, 25th January, 1827.

47. CLB, Board No. 7, 17th February, 1797.

48. CLB, Board No. 12, 24th March, 1798.

49. CLB, Board No. 34, 13th April, 1822.

50. CLB, Board No. 9, 25th February, 1808; Board No. 54, 11th April, 1816.

51. CLB, Board No. 34, 13th April, 1822.

52. CLB, Board No. 51, 25th October, 1822.

53. CLB, Board No. 34, 13th April, 1822.

54. Ibid.

55. CLB, Board No. 51, 25th October, 1822.

56. Ibid.

57. CLB, Board No. 57, 30th June, 1823.

58. CLB, Board No. 51, 2th October, 1822.

59. CLB, Board No. 61, 9th November, 1831.

60. Mr. Hay's Private Ledger, note 10 above.

61. SA, D6, E. S. Reid Tait Collection, Articles of Agreement for the cod fishery, 1824; sloop *Anne;* CLB, Board No. 39, 6th May, 1826.

62. Mr. Hay's Private Ledger, note 10 above.

63. *The Shetland Journal*, 1837.

64. *Minutes of Evidence taken before the Poor Law Enquiry Commission for Scotland*, 17th-20th July, 1843, 182-221.

65. SA, D6, E. S. Reid Tait Collection, Small Bound Volume, Contracts of Co-partnery.

66. SRO, CS285/52, Court of Session Records, Petition & Complaint for William Irvine in sequesn. of the Shetland Banking Co., June, 1843.

67. Gray, 1967, 187-216; Gray, 1978, 27-57.

68. Ployen, *Reminiscences*, 171; Minutes of the Directors of the Royal Bank of Scotland, Vol. 27, 83-84.

69. CLB, Board No. 9, 10th January, 1843.

70. Petition & Complaint for Wiliam Irvine, note 66 above; Nicolson, 1982, 4-7.

71. CLB, Board No. 21, 27th February, 1824; Hibbert, 1822, 287; Catton, 1838, 66.

72. CLB, Board No. 16, 9th March, 1821.

73. SA, D8, Sumburgh Papers, Sir Wm. Forbes, Jas. Hunter & Co. to John Bruce, 8th February, 1817.

74. SA, D6, E. S. Reid Tait Collection, Bound Vol. of Shetland Society Reports, Fourth Annual Report of the Shetland Society, October, 1818.

75. Ibid., Fifth Annual Report of the Shetland Society, October 1820.

76. Petition & Complaint, note 66 above; ibid., Answers for Archibald Horne, Trustee in the sequd. Estate of Hay & Ogilvy To Petition and Complaint for William Irvine, 1843.

77. Ibid.

78. Hamilton, 1963, 294-305, 314-327, 330-339; Checkland, 1973, 91-462 esp. 315; Munn, 1981, 73, 201.

79. *The Orkney and Shetland Journal,* 1st June, 1838.

80. *Poor Law Enquiry Commission,* note 64 above; The Shetland Bank to John Thomson, note 68 above.

81. Answers for Archibald Horne, note 76 above.

82. SA, SC12/6/2580-2800, Sheriff Court Records, Bill Protests.

83. The Shetland Bank to John Thomson, note 68 above.

84. *NSA,* 31; Henderson, 1980; Coull, 1983, 123-126.

85. Minutes of the Directors of the Royal Bank of Scotland, Vol. 27, note 68 above, various letters.

86. SRO, CS279/1089, Court of Session Records, Inventory of Concurrences; for background and comments on the failures see also: Munn, 1981, 88-89; Nicolson, 1982, 14; Checkland, 1973, 413.

87. Petition & Complaint for William Irvine, note 66 above; Answers for Archibald Horne, note 76 above.

88. Inventory of Concurrences, note 86 above.

89. CLB, Board No. 8, 10th January, 1844.

90. *Poor Law Enquiry Commission,* note 64 above.

91. Edmondston, 1820.

92. Hibbert, 1822, 521-522.

93. Edmondston, 1809, *1,* 289.

94. CLB, Board No. 33, 25th June, 1811.

95. Tait, 1947, 87-91.

96. Edmondston, 1820.

97. Edmondston, 1809, *1,* 289.

98. *The Orkney and Shetland Chronicle,* 28th February, 1825.

99. CLB, Board No. 12, 21st February, 1834; HC, Large volume, Arrivals and Sailings, 1834-1837; Tudor, 1883, 142-145 gives 1832 or 1833 as the date.

100. Arrivals and Sailings, 1834-1837, note 99 above.

101. *ST,* 8th February, 1876.

102. Ployen, *Reminiscences,* 29.

103. *Report of the Commissioners appointed to enquire into the Sea Fisheries of the United Kingdom,* 1866, *Vol. 2, Minutes of Evidence,* 709; CLB, Board No. 6, 16th January, 1860; Goodlad, 1971, 137; Nicolson, 1982, 64-70.

104. Goodlad, *ibid.,* 141-144.

105. CLB, Board No. 7, 19th March, 1869.

106. CLB, Board No. 15, 25th May, 1866.

107. *Second Report of the Commissioners appointed to enquire into the Truck System (Shetland),* 1872, *Vol. 1, Report and Appendix,* 38.

108. Edmondston, 1809, *1,* 244.

109. *NSA,* 78.

110. Goodlad, 1971, 124; *NSA,* 30.

111. *Sea Fisheries Report,* note 103 above, 711.

112. *NSA,* 96.

113. Cowie, 1874, 94.

114. HC, Miscellaneous Scalloway Fish Ledgers, Account of haddocks bought, 1861-1869; Nicolson, 1982, 82-83.

115. CLB, Board No. 39, 22nd August, 1794.

116. Edmondston, 1809, *1*, 279; Letter Book, note 22 above.

117. Edmondston, 1809, *1*, 278-283.

118. Tom Henderson, personal communication; see also Coull, 1983, 123-140: provides a detailed account of all aspects of the herring fishery at this time.

119. SRO, AF38, Department of Agriculture and Fisheries Records, Harbour files, Petition: John Bruce of Sumburgh to Has. Dunsmure, Secretary, Commissioners of the British White Herring Fishery, 5th April, 1826.

120. CLB, Board No. 54, 27th July, 1827.

121. *NSA*, 134.

122. *Truck System (Shetland) Report, Vol. 1*, note 107 above, 39.

123. Gardie Papers, Draft Agreement: Jas. J. Hanna of Belfast, mcht., & Wm. Mouat Cameron & Wm. Mouat of Garth.

124. Tom Henderson, personal communication and 1980; SA, D4, Hay of Laxfirth Papers, Dundas to William Hay, 19th November, 1840; *ST*, 22nd July, 1876.

125. *The Orkney and Shetland Journal and Fishermen's Magazine*, 1st March, 1839.

126. *Ibid.*, 1st May, 1839; see also, Gray, 1978, 139.

127. SA, AF29/18, Department of Agriculture and Fisheries Records, Shore-Curing Book; for further discussion of post-1840 herring fishing, see: Nicolson, 1982, 75-82.

128. Edmondston, 1809, *1*, 190-204; see note 74 above: Second Annual Report of the Shetland Society, 1816.

129. Cowie, 1874, 171, 182.

130. Note 74 above, Fifth Annual Report of the Shetland Society, October, 1820.

131. Duncan, *Zetland Directory and Guide, 2nd Edition*, 125-126, 133.

132. *Ibid;* Ployen, *Reminiscences*, 144.

133. Duncan, note 131 above, 125-126.

134. Cowie, 1874, 309.

135. LUE, Laing MSS, III, 352.1, Unto the General Assembly of the Church of Scotland, the petition & representation of the Pisbitery of Zetland, 12th May, 1790.

136. Edmondston, 1809, *1*, 222.

137. *NSA*, 65.

138. SA, D8, Sumburgh Papers, Sandlodge Mine File, Robert Bruce to John Bruce, 28th October, 1802.

139. Ibid., Michael Linning, Secretary, Scottish National Mining Co. to John Bruce, 12th January, 1826.

140. Edmondston, 1809, *2*, 201-202.

141. Jameson, 1798, 21.

142. Edmondston, 1809, *2*, 201-202.

143. *Ibid.*

144. Sandlodge Mine File, note 138 above.

145. Ibid.

146. Hibbert, 1822, 257-258; Edmondston, 1809, 201-202.

147. *NSA*, 45.

148. Hibbert, 1822, 591-592; Boud, 1978.

149. Cowie, 1874, 231-232; Gardie Papers, Copy Agreement, Heritors of Baliasta Scattald & Wm. Mouat.

150. Cowie, *ibid;* Ployen, *Reminiscences*, 177.

151. Mr. Hay's Private Ledger, note 10 above; *NSA*, 29.

152. SA, D12, Neven of Windhouse Papers, Haaf Gruney Chromate Quarry Documents, 1854-1869.

153. *NSA*, 103.

154. O'Dell, 1939, 171-172.

155. SA, D12/111, Neven of Windhouse Papers, Diary containing the state of the wind, weather and occurrences, also state of the Thermometer at noon, continued from old book by

Tho. Leisk at Lunna.

156. Cowie, 1874, 204.

157. Tom Henderson Collection, Arrivals and Sailings of Vessels, 1840-1842; Nicolson, 1982, 34.

158. *NSA*, 134; Gray, 1957, 155-158.

159. Duncan, note 131 above, 13.

160. *NSA*, 148.

161. Edmondston, 1809, 2, 14-15.

162. *NSA*, 4; O'Dell, 1939, 163; *ST*, 30th March, 1874.

163. Mr. Hay's Private Ledger, note 10 above; Arrivals and Sailings, 1834-1837, note 99 above; see Nicolson, 1982, 33 for boatbuilding in the 1850s.

164. Goodlad, 1971, 129-159 describes the cod fishing in detail.

165. Flinn, D., 1964, 321-339.

166. SA, AF29, Coast Fishery and Shore Curing Books, 1820s and 1830s.

167. Ibid., 1850s, 1860s, 1870s.

168. SRO, AF38, Harbour Files, George Henderson to Laurence Lane, 31st August, 1852.

169. Ibid., Alex. Millikin to Secretary, Fishery Board, Edinburgh, 5th November, 1885.

170. CLB, Collector to J. Westgarth & E. Cunningham, 8th February, 1814.

171. Edmondston, 1809, 2, 31-32; 1, 311-312.

172. Note 74 above, Third Annual Report of the Shetland Society, October, 1817.

173. SRO, RH9/15/209, Orkney and Shetland Papers, Copy translation of the Great Seal Charter, erecting Lerwick into a Burgh of Barony, 1818.

174. CLB, Board No. 56, 24th June, 1822; Report of Collector of Customs, Lerwick on petition of John Mouat of Garth; CLB, Board No. 14, 4th February, 1824; Board No. 21, 27th February, 1824; Nicolson, 1982, 5.

175. CLB, Board No. 16, 16th March, 1832.

176. Ibid.

177. CLB, Board No. 14, 4th February, 1824.

178. Catton, 1838, 66.

179. SA, D4, Gavin Colvin to Wm. Hay, 31st December, 1832.

180. HC, Arrivals and Sailings from West Side, 1862-1870.

181. Mr. Hay's Private Ledger, note 10 above; Scalloway shop Account starts in 1831; CLB, Board No. 30, 10th October, 1833.

182. *Poor Law Enquiry Commission*, note 64 above.

183. CLB, Collector to Marine Department, Board of Trade, 22nd August, 1863.

184. CLB, Board No. 16, 6th April, 1857.

185. CLB, Board No. 66, 22nd October, 1856; Board No. 27, 12th November, 1867.

186. CLB, 1850s, various.

187. Catton, 1838, 67.

188. *NSA*, 81.

189. *NSA*, 137-138.

190. *Shetland Advertiser*, 31st March, 1862.

191. *Truck System (Shetland) Report, Vol. 1*, note 107 above, 18-19.

192. Edmondston, 1809, 1, 326-327.

193. *Ibid.*, 304.

194. *Ibid.*, 300-301.

195. *Ibid.*, 155-156.

196. J. J. Graham, personal communication.

197. Edmondston, 1809, 1, 299, 328.

198. SA, D8, Sumburgh Papers, Letter Book, John Bruce to Harry Davidson, 5th May, 1785.

199. Gardie Papers, Memorabilia Zetlandica.

200. *NSA*, 63.

201. Note 198 above, John Bruce to Chas. Innes, 12th October, 1786.

202. Edmondston, 1809, 2, 142.

203. SA, D12/97/7, Neven of Windhouse Papers, Thoughts on the comparative value of fish and cattle, etc., in Shetland, for Busta's and Mr. Arthur Cheyne's consideration and amusement, by Thos. Leisk, 1814.

204. SA, SC12/6, Summonses of Removal.

205. Thoughts on the Comparative value, note 203 above.

206. Shirreff, 1814, 77-99.

207. Catton, 1838, 102.

208. *Ibid.*, 78.

209. SA, CO1/1/4, Minutes of the Commissioners of Supply, Memorandum on depressed condition & peculiar burdens of Shetland, to Government and Both Houses of Parliament, 1851.

210. Discussions with the late G. M. Nelson and W. P. L. Thomson.

211. Summonses of Removal, note 204 above; J. J. Graham, discussion; Cowie, 1874, 309.

212. SA, D13/394/3, Midbrake Papers, Excerpts from Sir Edward Coffin's final reports on the effects of the late measures for the relief of the distressed districts of Scotland, and on their existing state.

213. *Truck System (Shetland) Report, Vol. 1,* note 107 above, 5.

214. Brian Smith, personal communication, based on Sheriff Court Records research (SA, SC12/6).

215. SA, SC12/6, Sheriff Court Records, Petitions for breach of fishing contracts, various.

216. Edmondston, 1809, *2,* 142.

217. Catton, 1838, 65.

218. *NSA,* 158.

219. SA, D12/101/8, Neven of Windhouse Papers, Thomas Leisk to Sir Arthur Nicolson Bart., 8th March, 1832.

220. *NSA,* 160-162.

221. *Shetland Advertiser,* 7th July, 1862.

222. Cowie, 1874, 128.

223. *Truck System (Shetland) Report, Vol. 1,* note 107 above, 17.

224. *Ibid.,* 22.

225. Vives, 1969, 603.

226. Memorial for the fish curers on the Coast of Scotland, note 5 above.

227. Vilar, 1963, *3,* 561.

228. LUE, Laing MSS, Dk. 6.253, Capt. J. J. Stuart to C. Stuart, 8th February, 1803.

229. CQR.

230. Shirreff, 1814, Appendix 10, 51-53.

231. Edmondston, 1809, *2,* 23.

232. *Ibid.*

233. Shirreff, 1814, 102.

234. *Ibid;* CQR.

235. Shirreff, 1814, Appendix 10, 51-53.

236. *Ibid.,* 87.

237. Edmondston, 1809, *1,* 258-259.

238. Edmondston, 1820.

239. CQR.

240. Edmondston, 1820.

241. *Ibid.*

242. SA, D13, Midbrake Papers, William Henderson (of Bardister) to Jas. Irvine, 13th May, 1813.

243. Hibbert, 1822, 527.

244. SA, D12/101/8, Neven of Windhouse Papers, Thomas Leisk to Commissioners of Supply, 26th January, 1824.

245. Goodlad, 1971, 170.

246. *The Shetland Journal,* 1st July, 1837.

247. *NSA*, 171.
248. Anderson, 1845.
249. Ployen, *Reminiscences*, 49.
250. Anderson, 1845.
251. *Ibid.*
252. *Sea Fisheries Report, Vol. 2*, note 103 above, 708.
253. Anderson, 1844.
254. SA, AF29/52-56, Exportation Books, 1821-1865.
255. Anderson, 1845.
256. Nicolson, 1932, 58-59.
257. SA, CO1/1/4, Minutes of the Commissioners of Supply, 14th October, 1846.
258. Ibid.
259. Ibid., 30th April, 1850.
260. *Sea Fisheries Report, Vol. 2*, note 103 above, 714-715.
261. Exportation Books, note 254 above; Nicolson, 1982, 70-75.
262. *Sea Fisheries Report, Vol. 2*, note 103 above, 708.
263. Duncan, *Directory to Zetland*, 23.
264. CLB, Board No. 24, 29th April, 1850; Nicolson, 1982, 67-68.
265. CLB, Collector to Seizures Branch, 9th January, 1858.
266. Vives, 1969, 693-695.
267. Tom Henderson Collection, Minute Book: The Directors of the Zetland North Sea Fishery Company, 7th September, 1869.
268. *The Orkney and Shetland Journal and Fishermen's Magazine*, 1st March, 1839.
269. Gray, 1967, 191-192; Coull, 1983, 137-139.
270. *The Orkney and Shetland Journal and Fishermen's Magazine*, 1st March, 1839.
271. *Ibid.*, 1st May.
272. SA, AF29/26-27, Herring Exportation Books, 1835-1858; AF29/62-65, Abstract Books, 1836-1876; Nicolson, 1982, 77-82.
273. *Sea Fisheries Report, Vol. 2*, note 103 above, 715.
274. Goodlad, 1971, 15-18; Lamb, 1982, 207-210 discusses long-term fluctuations.
275. *Ibid.* See also: McIntyre, A., Ruddiman, W. F., Jantzen, R., 'Southward penetrations of the North Atlantic polar front: faunal and floral evidence of large-scale surface water mass movements over the last 225,000 years', *Deep Sea Res. 19*(1) (1972), 61-78.
276. Edmondston, 1809, *1*, 183-184; *NSA*, 84; SA, D13/378/78, Midbrake Papers, Thomas Irvine to Daily Review, 15th April, 1870; Diary containing the state of the wind, note 155 above.
277. Lythe, 1964, 162-163; Jackson, 1978, 126-130.
278. Thomson, 1983a, 156-159; Graham, 1983, 228-229.
279. SA, SC12/6, Summonses for the Division of Runrig.
280. Note 74 above, First and Second Annual Reports of the Shetland Society, 1815 and 1816.
281. Edmondston, 1809, *1*, 225.
282. *ST*, 1870s, various; Cowie, 1874, 187, 209-211.
283. Shirreff, 1814, 58-59.
284. CLB, Board No. 21, 19th March, 1817.
285. Mr. Hay's Private Ledger, note 10 above.
286. CLB, Board No. 12, 21st August, 1865.
287. Cowie, 1874, 176; Nicolson, 1982, 49-50.
288. Edmondston, 1809, 2, 20-23.
289. Note 74 above, Second Annual Report of the Shetland Society, 1816.
290. Mr. Hay's Private Ledger, note 10 above.
291. *NSA*, 29.
292. Edmondston, 1809, 2, 224.
293. *Ibid.*
294. *The Shetland Journal*, 31st October, 1837.
295. Cowie, 1874, 184-187; Standen, 1845.

296. *Truck System (Shetland) Report, Vol. 1,* note 103 above, 45.

297. Cowie, 1874, 184-187.

298. Ibid., 97.

299. SA, D28, G. M. Nelson Collection, William Hay to (?), 1841; Nicolson, 1982, 34, 56.

300. Cowie, 1874, 131.

301. *Shetland Advertiser,* 30th March, 1863; see also Nicolson, 1982, 56.

302. Mr. Hay's Private Ledger, note 10 above.

303. Edmondston, 1809, *1,* 184.

304. Mr. Hay's Private Ledger, note 10 above.

305. See, e.g., Lawton, R., 'Historical Geography from the coming of the Anglo-Saxons to the Industrial Revolution'. In: Watson, J. Wreford and Sissons, J. B. (eds.), *The British Isles: a systematic geography* (London, 1964).

306. Dr. R. Mooney, personal communication.

307. Ployen, *Reminiscences,* 173.

308. CQR.

309. CLB, Board No. 36, 27th August, 1839.

310. Thowsen, 1969, 156-157.

311. Duncan, 1861, 66; see also Nicolson, 1982, 32-33.

312. Thowsen, 1969, 155-156.

313. CLB, Board No. 85, 23rd December, 1844.

314. Thowsen, 1969, 156-157.

315. SA, CO1/1/4, Minutes of the Commissioners of Supply, 3rd May, 1844.

316. CLB, Board No. 9, 16th February, 1859; see also Nicolson, 1982, 33-34.

317. Edmondston, 1809, *2,* 24.

318. *The Shetland Journal,* 1st May, 1837.

319. CLB, CE85/4/20, Collector to Seizures Branch, 9th January, 1858.

320. *Truck System (Shetland) Report, Vol. 1,* note 103 above, 23.

321. *Poor Law Enquiry Commission,* note 64 above.

322. Goodlad, 1971, 154; Nicolson, 1982, 70 refers to steam drying; CLB, Board No. 11, 9th March, 1860 states only one Shetland-owned well-smack. Board No. 7, 19th March, 1869 notes that some Shetland owners were introducing well-smacks.

323. Gray, 1967, 191-192; Gray, 1978, 58-63.

324. Duncan, 1861, 43.

325. Minute Book, note 267 above, same date.

326. *Shetland Advertiser,* 30th March, 1863.

327. Letter Book, note 198 above, John Bruce to Chas. Innes, 10th March, 1787.

328. Edmondston, 1809, *1,* 253-258; SA, D12/97/9, Neven of Windhouse Papers, Comparative statements on fishing with sloops and boats, n.d., watermark 1810, in Thomas Leisk's hand; SA D13/389/89, Midbrake Papers, Sketch of a plan for an improved & more extensive mode of fishing on the coast of Zetland, 1814.

329. *ST,* 8th February, 1876.

330. *NSA,* 172.

331. SA, D13/387/42, Midbrake Papers, J. Irvine to Messrs Wilkinson & Rowlett, 14th November, 1816.

332. *The Shetland Journal,* 1st February & 1st September, 1837. See also, Nicolson, 1982, 82-83.

333. Account of haddocks bought, note 114 above; Nicolson, 1982, 82-83.

334. *Shetland Advertiser,* 29th December, 1862.

335. SA, D13/387/11, Midbrake Papers, Prospectus for a shipping company to be called the Zetland Whale Fishing Company, 1853. Hay & Co. took shares in whalers in the 1860s — see Nicolson, 1982, 45.

336. *Orkney and Zetland Chronicle,* 28th February, 1825.

337. SA, D12/96, Neven of Windhouse Papers, History and Laws of the Iberian Patriotic Society — with observation and instructions. by Thomas Leisk of Uya, February, 1809.

338. Note 74 above.

339. SA, D12, Neven of Windhouse Papers, Shetland Agricultural Society: Agricultural Meeting and Show of Livestock, &c. at Lerwick, 9th August, 1864. (Programme).

340. CLB, Board No. 33, 21st October, 1793.

341. Memorial for the fish curers on the Coast of Scotland, note 5 above.

342. SA, SC12/6, Sheriff Court Records, Processes, 1308, 1618-1620, 2012-2013, 2289, 3724, 4176, 4486.

343. Edmondston, 1809, 2, 20-23.

344. CLB, Board No. 56, 11th April, 1816.

345. *Orkney and Zetland Chronicle,* 31st March, 1825.

346. CLB, Board No. 16, 9th March, 1821.

347. *The Orkney and Shetland Journal,* 1st July, 1838.

348. Lythe, 1964, 162-163.

349. CLB, Board No. 75, 30th July, 1847; Board No. 26, 7th July, 1851; Board No. 25, 10th May, 1852; Board No. 8, 8th January, 1853; Duncan, 1861, 43.

350. Cowie, 1874, 96.

351. CLB, Board No. 8, 8th January, 1853.

352. Duncan, 1861, 43.

353. Graeme, 1953.

354. Note 74 above, Fifth Annual Report of the Shetland Society, October, 1820.

355. *The Orkney and Shetland Journal,* 1st June, 1838.

356. Nicolson, 1932.

357. Simpson, 1983, 137-140.

358. Ibid.

Chapter 5

1. *ST,* 18th May, 1874.

2. *Second Report of the Commissioners appointed to Enquire into the Truck System (Shetland) together with Minutes of Evidence* (Edinburgh, 1872), *Vol. 1, Report and Appendix,* 11.

3. *Ibid.,* 51-56; Smith, H. D., 1978, v-viii.

4. 33 & 34 Vict. cap. 105.

5. *Report of Her Majesty's Commissioners appointed to Enquire into the condition of the crofters and cottars in the Highlands and Islands of Scotland* (Edinburgh, 1884), *Vol. 2, Minutes of Evidence,* 1203-1434, henceforward cited as: *Napier Commission.*

6. 30 & 31 Vict, cap. 46; *ST,* 14th May, 1887.

7. *ST,* 2nd January, 1908.

8. *ST,* 30th September, 1872.

9. *RFB,* 1894, 172; Goodlad, 1971, 182-183.

10. *Napier Commission,* note 5 above, *Vol. 1, Report,* 48.

11. Cowie, 1874, 96.

12. *Truck System (Shetland) Report,* note 2, *Vol. 1,* 44.

13. CLB, Board No. 32, 1st May, 1858.

14. *ST,* 20th April, 1874.

15. *ST,* 15th October, 1881.

16. Findlay, J. R., *A history of Peterhead* (Peterhead, 1933), 237.

17. *ST,* 27th August, 1892.

18. *ST,* 15th April, 1911.

19. *ST,* 13th September, 1888; 28th December, 1889.

20. *RFB,* 1895, ix.

21. *ST,* 18th May, 1874.

22. Cowie, 1874, 108.

23. *Truck System (Shetland) Report, Vol. 1,* 40.

24. *ST,* 18th May, 1874.

25. Duncan, 1854, 23.

26. *ST*, 15th April, 1911.

27. *Report of the Commissioners appointed to enquire into the Truck System* (London, 1871), *Vol. 2, Minutes of Evidence*, 882.

28. *ST*, 22nd July, 1876.

29. CLB, Board No. 8, 10th January, 1844; Gray, 1978, 139; Coull, 1983.

30. *RFB*, 1882, xiii.

31. Duncan, 1854, 23.

32. *RFB*, 1894, xvi.

33. NS, News Cuttings.

34. CLB, Board No. 11, 9th April, 1860.

35. Halcrow, 1950, 120.

36. CLB, Collector to Assistant Secretarial Branch, 4th October, 1871.

37. *ST*, 18th November, 1872.

38. CLB, Collector to Assistant Secretarial Branch, 7th October, 1872.

39. Halcrow, 1950, 75-80, 169-178.

40. *ST*, 31st December, 1904.

41. *ST*, 29th December, 1900.

42. *ST*, 19th April, 1903.

43. Custom House, Lerwick Records, Register of Shipping.

44. Goodlad, 1971, 157-159.

45. Vives, 1969, 710-711.

46. *ST*, 26th August, 1882.

47. *RFB*, 1882, xxxv; 1885, iv; 1886, lix; 1891, xxxviii.

48. *ST*, 20th August, 1881; *RFB*, 1901, xii; Nicolson, 1982, 139.

49. *RFB*, 1901, xii.

50. *RFB*, 1905, 242.

51. *ST*, 1st November, 1879.

52. *RFB*, 1882, xxxvi.

53. *ST*, 17th December, 1887.

54. *ST*, 10th December, 1892; 6th October, 1894.

55. *ST*, 2nd June, 1894; 6th October, 1894; 9th November, 1895, and others.

56. *ST*, 1st January, 1909.

57. *RFB*, 1908, xlvi.

58. *ST*, 31st December, 1910.

59. *ST*, 19th June, 1886.

60. CLB, Collector to 3rd Division, 14th May, 1887.

61. *ST*, 21st November, 1885.

62. *Napier Commission Report, Vol. 2*, 1283.

63. *ST*, 31st December, 1904.

64. *ST*, 25th June, 1898.

65. Goodlad, 1971, 157.

66. O'Dell, 1939, 120; Nicolson, 1982, 111-113, 136-137.

67. Goodlad, 1971, 221-222.

68. *ST*, 6th July, 1874.

69. Halcrow, 1950, 135.

70. SA, AF29, Lerwick Fishery Office Records, Abstract Book (Herring Curing Tables); Nicolson, 1982, 101-107.

71. Ibid., Abstract Book; Gray, 1978, 63-72, 151-153.

72. *ST*, 19th June, 1886; *RFB*, 1892, v.

73. *ST*, 26th September, 1885.

74. *RFB*, 1887.

75. *RFB*, 1894, 172.

76. *RFB*, 1900, 253.

77. Halcrow, 1950, 148-151.

78. Abstract Book, note 70 above; *RFB*, 1905, 212-213.

79. Goodlad, 1971, 208, 213-215; *ST*, 29th December, 1906.

80. *ST*, 28th December, 1907.

81. Information on the European market is derived at first hand from *RFB*. See also: Stewart, 1930, 219-227; Gray, 1978, 58-63, 146-148.

82. *RFB*, 1907, xlii-xliii; 1908, 252-282.

83. *RFB*, 1896, v; 1900, xxxiv.

84. *RFB*, numerous references; Gray, 1967, 187-216.

85. Abstract Book, note 70 above.

86. *RFB*, numerous references.

87. *RFB*, 1906, 1.

88. *RFB*, 1907, 302-320.

89. *RFB*, 1907-1909.

90. Stewart, 1930; *RFB*, numerous references.

91. Stewart, 1930, 224-226.

92. *RFB*, 1908, 252-282.

93. *RFB*, various years.

94. *RFB*, 1895, iii-iv.

95. *RFB*, 1906.

96. *RFB*, 1908, 252-282.

97. *RFB*, 1907, 302-320.

98. *RFB*, 1905, iii.

99. *RFB*, 1906.

100. *RFB*, 1907, 302-320.

101. *Ibid*.

102. *RFB*, 1885, liii-liv; 1887, lvii; 1890, xxiii-xxiv; 1894, xii; 1900, xxxiv; 1910, xlvi; 1912.

103. *RFB*, various references.

104. *RFB*, 1896, xxi.

105. *RFB*, 1907.

106. Halcrow, 1950, 151-156.

107. H. A. J., 'Snapshots of yesterday', *The New Shetlander No. 99* (1972), 16; Nicolson, 1982, 116.

108. *Report of the Scottish Departmental Committee on the North Sea Fishing Industry* (London, 1914), 212-213; Goodlad, 1971, 219.

109. *RFB*, 1894, xvi.

110. PRO, Customs 23, Abstracts of Imports under Ports, 1873-1899.

111. CLB, numerous references; Abstracts of Imports, note 110 above. See also: Hoel, Werenskiold, 1962, 103; Proctor, 1981, 31-42.

112. *RFB*, various.

113. *Napier Commission Report, Vol. 2*, 1214.

114. *ST*, 31st December, 1898.

115. SRO, AF39/23, Board of Agriculture and Department of Agriculture and Fisheries Records, Agricultural Census, Orkney and Shetland, 1866-1914.

116. SA, D13/387/78, Midbrake Papers, Thomas Irvine to *Daily Review*, 15th April, 1870.

117. *ST*, 30th September, 1872.

118. *ST*, 24th October, 1885.

119. Cowie, 1874, 108.

120. *ST*, 1904.

121. Evershed, 1874, 210-211.

122. *ST*, 22nd June, 1874.

123. *Napier Commission Report, Vol. 2*, 1302.

124. *ST*, 1880s.

125. *ST*, 12th October, 1912.

126. O'Dell, 1939, 83-84.

127. Skirving, 1874, 246.

128. *ST*, 20th October, 1873.

129. O'Dell, 1939, 85.

130. *ST*, 20th October, 1873.

131. *ST*, 17th June, 1872; 22nd September, 1873; Evershed, 1874, 187, 209-211.

132. *ST*, 27th December, 1913; O'Dell, 1939, 16-17.

133. Evershed, 1874, 210-211.

134. *ST*, 30th December, 1905.

135. *ST*, 17th June, 1872; 30th September, 1872.

136. Adams, Ian H., A Directory of Former Commonties in Scotland (unpubl., 1967); SRO, RHP, Plans of Division of Commonties, various.

137. Ibid; *ST*, 31st December, 1892; 31st December, 1910; 3rd October, 1914.

138. *Report to the Board of Agriculture for Scotland on Home Industries in the Highlands and Islands* (London, 1914), Cmnd.7564, 36.

139. *Truck System Report*, note 27 above, Vol. 2, 882.

140. *Truck System (Shetland) Report*, Vol. 1, 50-51.

141. *Home Industries Report*, note 138 above, 83-84.

142. *ST*, 2nd January, 1897.

143. *Home Industries Report*, note 138 above, 87.

144. *ST*, 10th March, 1888.

145. 45 & 46 Vict. c. 74; SA, D4, E. S. Reid Tait Collection, Memorandum of Zetland County Council, Unto the Rt. Hon. Sir Henry Campbell-Bannerman, First Lord of His Majesty's Treasury, The Rt. Hon. John Sinclair, His Majesty's Secretary for Scotland and the Rt. Hon. Sydney Charles Burton, His Majesty's Post-Master-General, 1906.

146. *Home Industries Report*, note 138 above, 91.

147. *ST*, 2nd January, 1897.

148. SA, D8, Sumburgh Papers, Sandlodge Mine File, Account of ore shipped from Sandlodge Mine by Mr. John Walker.

149. Ibid., The Sumburgh Mining Co. Ltd., Report c. 1880.

150. Ibid.

151. Ibid., Report by Francis F. Oats, 18th May, 1924; Memorandum on Sandlodge Mine . . . by Geological Survey of Great Britain (Scottish Office) for the Ministry of Munitions Committee on Iron and Steel in Scotland, 1914.

152. O'Dell, 1939, 171-173.

153. *ST*, 10th March, 1888.

154. O'Dell, 1939, 174.

155. *ST*, 5th September, 1885.

156. T. Donnelly, personal communication; *ST*, 1st November, 1890.

157. *ST*, 1st November, 1890.

158. Discussion with H. Smith, Berry Road, Scalloway.

159. *ST*, 16th May, 1872.

160. *Home Industries Report*, note 138 above.

161. *Ibid*.

162. *ST*, 6th & 13th August, 1898; 30th June, 1900; various, 1901.

163. *Truck System (Shetland) Report*, Vol. 1, 16.

164. *Report of the Departmental Committee*, note 108 above, 212-213.

165. *Manson's Almanac*, 1891 *et seq* contains lists of boats and owners, including places of residence of owners.

166. SA, AF29, Abstract Book, State of the Fisheries at each creek.

167. *ST*, 10th March, 1888; 31st December, 1904; *RFB*, 1905, 213.

168. Goodlad, 1971, 222-223.

169. *ST*, 4th October, 1884.

170. *ST*, 31st December, 1910; *RFB*, 1909.

171. CLB, Collector to Third Division, 29th July, 1890; SA, CE85/4/6, Ronas Voe Sailing Book, Part 1: Sailings from Mid Yell.

172. Sandison, Charles, *Unst; my island home and its story* (Lerwick, 1968).

173. Goodlad, 1971, 179-185.

174. *Ibid.*, 182-187.

175. *RFB*, 1900, 255.

176. *ST*, 1897.

177. Barclay, R. S., 'The population of the parishes and islands of Shetland, 1755-1961', in: Cluness, A. T. (ed.), *The Shetland Book* (Lerwick, 1967), 52-53.

178. *RFB*, 1905, 242.

179. *ST*, 25th June, 1898.

180. Gray, 1967, 188, 208, 212-213.

181. *Ibid.*

182. Goodlad, 1971, 178-179.

183. *RFB*, 1905, 212-213.

184. *RFB*, 1913.

185. *ST*, 13th September, 1890.

186. O'Dell, 1939, 140-143.

187. Ronas Voe Sailing Book, note 171 above.

188. SA, D4, E. S. Reid Tait Collection, Memorandum of Zetland County Council to Rt. Hon. H. H. Asquith, Prime Minister.

189. Ibid; *ST*, 2nd August, 1908.

190. HC, Arrivals and Sailing from West Side, 1862-1870.

191. *ST*, 21st October, 1872; 30th November, 1874; 4th October, 1879.

192. *NSA*, 29.

193. Hoover, E. M., *The Location of Economic Activity* (New York, 1963), 196-200.

194. Goodlad, 1971, 202-203.

195. *ST*, 23rd March, 1874.

196. *ST*, 7th July, 1873; 6th July, 1874; 13th April, 1874.

197. Skirving, 1874, 246; *ST*, various, 1872-73.

198. CLB, Board No. 6, 2nd February, 1870; Board No. 16, 27th May, 1870.

199. *Ibid.*, Board No. 16, 8th May, 1871; Board No. 21, 18th July, 1872.

200. 49 & 50 Vict. c. 29; *ST*, 6th November, 1886; 24th October, 1889.

201. Graham, 1983, 230-232.

202. *ST*, 15th September, 1888; 3rd November, 1888; 2nd June, 1889.

203. *ST*, 10th March, 1888.

204. *Home Industries Report*, 142. For a recent consideration of the position of women, and the oral history of fishing communities in Shetland and elsewhere, see Thompson *et al*, 1983.

205. Memorandum to Rt. Hon. H. H. Asquith, note 188 above.

206. *ST*, 1906.

207. Report of the Departmental Committee, note 108 above, 213.

208. *ST*, 27th August, 1892.

209. Evershed, 1874, 220.

210. *ST*, 27th August, 1892.

211. SA, D4, E. S. Reid Tait Collection, Agricultural Shows Programmes.

212. *ST*, 4th May, 1912.

213. *Home Industries Report*, 82-83.

214. *ST*, 30th December, 1905.

215. *ST*, 26th August, 1905.

216. *ST*, 30th April, 1907.

217. *Home Industries Report*, 95-102.

218. O'Dell, 1939, 159-162.

219. *ST*, 11th & 18th April, 1908.

220. *RFB*, 1911, 218-221; *Report of the Departmental Committee*, note 108 above, 212-213.

221. *Truck System (Shetland) Report, Vol. 1,* 20.
222. *ST,* 10th March, 1888.
223. Goodlad, 1971, 124.
224. *Ibid.,* 158.
225. *ST,* 15th April, 1911.
226. Graham, 1983, 226.
227. *ST,* 1st January, 1909.
228. *ST,* 27th December, 1913.
229. *ST,* 15th April, 1911.

Chapter 6

1. HC, Log of the *Janet Hay,* 26th May 1862 - 31st October, 1863.
2. CLB, Collector to Marine Department, Board of Trade, 22nd August, 1863.
3. Ibid., Collector to Marine Department, Board of Trade, 16th October, 1863.
4. WR.
5. Ibid; SA, CE85/4/10-11, Lerwick Outport Records, Register of Examinations on oath concerning wrecks and casualties on the coasts of the United Kingdom, by the Receiver of Wreck. Henceforward cited as Depositions.
6. HC, Log of the Smack *Petrel* of Lerwick, 25th March, 1874 - 31st August, 1875.
7. Log of the *Janet Hay,* note 1 above.
8. Brand, *Brief Description,* 122-123.
9. WR; Depositions, note 5 above.
10. *RPC,* 1st Ser., Vol. 12, 270-271.
11. CQR.
12. HC, Arrivals and Sailings from West Side, 1862-1870.
13. SA, D12/101/5, Neven of Windhouse Papers, Copy: The Rt. Hon. the Earl of Morton His 13 Queries anent the State of Zetland with answers thereto by Thos. Gifford of Busta. n.d., watermark 1811.
14. SRO, RH9/15/208, Orkney and Shetland Papers, Memorial for the Earl of Morton and the Heritors of Zetland, 1723
15. Gardie Papers, Copy petition & presentation in the name of the whole inhabitants and merchants of Zetlnd. to Comrs. of Customs in Scotland, 31st December, 1765.
16. Gardie Papers, Copy Protest: John Thomson, mcht., Edinburgh to Andrew Henry, master, 4th September, 1767.
17. CLB, Board No. 54, 11th April, 1816; Board No. 34, 13th April, 1822.
18. Log of the *Janet Hay,* note 1 above.
19. WR; Brand, *Brief Description,* 122-123.
20. Gardie Papers, Thomas Mouat to Robert Hunter, 17th March, 1785.
21. Brand, *Brief Description,* 112.
22. CLB, Board No. 50, 2nd August, 1859.
23. Ibid., Board No. 36, 26th May, 1848.
24. *The Orkney and Shetland Journal,* 1st March, 1838; Mackay, 1979.
25. SA, D4, Hay of Laxfirth MSS, Journal of the *Mary* (Schooner) 1829.
26. SA, D12/111, Neven of Windhouse Papers, Diary, containing the state of the wind, weather and occurrences, also the state of the Thermometer at Noon, continued from an old book by Tho. Leisk at Lunna.
27. Cowie, 1874, 204.
28. HC, Mr. Hay's Private Ledger, 1819-1829.
29. Donaldson, 1978, 63.
30. *The Orkney and Shetland Journal,* 1st June, 1838.
31. SA, D13/387/117, Midbrake Papers, Prospectus: Shetland Steam Shipping Company Ltd., 1868.

32. SA, D6, E. S. Reid Tait Collection, Shetland Islands Steam Shipping Company Limited. Annual Reports, 1877-1890.

33. Donaldson, 1978, 65-75; Robson, 1982.

34. Annual Reports, note 32 above.

35. SA, D6, E. S. Reid Tait Collection, Second Annual Report of the Shetland Society.

36. *The Orkney and Zetland Chronicle*, 31st March, 1825.

37. SA, CO1/1/3, Minutes of the Commissioners of Supply, Vol. 3, 2nd May, 1833.

38. Note 35 above, Second Annual Report of the Shetland Society.

39. Shetland Islands Council, Department of Construction, MSS Maps, Map of Shetland from the survey by Lieut. Thomas, R.N., showing the roads constructed by the Edinburgh Section of the Central Board for Relief of Highland Destitution. In co-operation with the Proprietors. During the Years 1849, 1850 & 1851. Under the Superintendence of Captain Craigie, R.N. Inspector Genl. & Captain Webb R. Engineers.

40. Reid Tait, 1946, 18-79.

41. Minutes of the Commissioners of Supply, note 37 above, 24th February, 1852.

42. Ibid., 4th May, 1853.

43. SA, D12/155/1, Neven of Windhouse Papers, Memorial relative to claim by certain proprietors in Zetland for an Act to assess the whole group . . . to maintain and extend roads in two of their number, 1861.

44. Ibid.

45. SA, CO2/1/5, Minutes of Zetland Road Trustees, 1868-1890.

46. The late G. M. Nelson, discussion.

47. *ST*, 24th October, 1885; 28th January, 1899.

48. *ST*, 9th October, 1909.

49. *ST*, 25th February, 1897.

50. SA, D6, E. S. Reid Tait Collection, Petition of Zetland County Council Unto the Rt. Hon. Sir Henry Campbell Bannerman, First Lord of His Majesty's Treasury, The Rt. Hon. John Sinclair, his Majesty's Secretary for Scotland, and The Rt. Hon. Sydney Charles Burton, his Majesty's Postmaster-General, 25th June, 1906.

51. *ST*, 9th August, 1894

52. *ST*, 1906.

53. Laurenson, J. J., 'Owre da hills ta Urie', *The New Shetlander, No. 58* (1961), 21-23.

54. Gardie Papers, Maps: Mr. Mouat's Park and Dry Harbour at Freefield, 1822; Garth's Pool, 1832; Nicolson, 1982, 5.

55. SRO, AF38/115, Fishery Board Records, Petition: John Bruce of Sumburgh to James Dunsmure, Secretary, Commissioners of the British White Herring Fishery, 5th April, 1826.

56. *ST*, 9th March, 1874.

57. SA, D6, E. S. Reid Tait Collection, Lerwick Harbour Trust Papers; Nicolson, 1975, 22-30.

58. Lerwick Harbour Trust Papers, note 57 above; Nicolson, 1975, 31-91.

59. Donaldson, 1954, 114.

60. Barclay, 1967, 70.

61. Gardie Papers, Copy: Regulation anent the Rates of the Ferry Freights & Passages st. in the Country of Zetland and Wages to be paid to Such as serve on board of Great Boats within the said Country, 1733.

62. Balfour, 1859, 59-62.

63. SRO, E72/17/1-3, Exchequer Records, Customs Books, 1669-1673, Discharge, 1st November, 1671 - 1st November, 1672.

64. *RPC*, 2nd Ser., Vol. 5, 122-123.

65. Terry, C. Standford (ed.), *The Cromwellian Union* (Edinburgh, 1902), Scottish Hist. Soc., 125-126.

66. *RPC*, 3rd Ser., Vol. 8, 132.

67. Brand, *Brief Description*, 7-16.

68. CQR.

69. SA, D8, Sumburgh Papers, John Bruce to Sir. Robert Harris of London, 28th June, 1780;

Additional Copy Letter to the Commissioners, 30th June, 1780.

70. Dollinger, 1970, 24, 141-142, 372; Unger, 1980, 201-250.

71. Friedland, 1973, 73-74.

72. Report by Thomas Tucker upon the settlement of the revenues of Excise and Customs in Scotland, 1656. *Misc. Scott. Burgh Records Soc.* (1881), 25.

73. WR.

74. Tom Henderson Collection, Shetland Shipping Lists, compiled by R. Stuart Bruce.

75. CLB, Board No. 40, 14th May, 1821.

76. SA, GD144/Box 18, Symbister Papers, Instructions to Robert Gifford from Thos. Gifford, 2nd August, 1746.

77. SRO, CE1, Scottish Board of Customs, Minute Books, Vol. 1, Fri. 13th December, 1723.

78. Gardie Papers, Vade Mecum.

79. CLB, Board No. 27, 22nd June, 1807.

80. SA, D4/8, Hay of Laxfirth MSS, Letter Book of James Hay, n.d.

81. Log of the *Janet Hay*, note 1 above.

82. Gardie Papers, Robert Dick of Fracafield to Henry Rose, Collector at Lerwick, 9th May, 1741.

83. Shetland Shipping Lists, note 74 above.

84. SA, D12, Neven of Windhouse Papers, various references, 1740s.

85. SA, D8, Sumburgh Papers, Copy Proceedings in the Admiralty Court of Shetland relating to the sale of the Brigantine *Dolphin*, November, 1772.

86. Mr. Hay's Private Ledger, note 28 above; SRO, CS279/1089. Court of Session Records, Inventories of the Estates Real and Personal of Hay & Ogilvy and the Shetland Bank as given up by them to the Interim factor on their Sequestrated Estate; Custom House, Lerwick, Register of Shipping, 1837-1914 (2 vols.).

87. Gardie Papers, A.B. to Charles Dundas, 5th (?), 1784.

88. NLS, 81.9.1, ff.62, 69; 81.9.2, f.304, Chalmers MSS.

89. Edmondston, 1809, 2, 18.

90. CQR.

91. SA, AF52-56, Exportation Books, 1821-1865; AF26-27, Herring Exportation Books, 1835-1858; AF62-65, Abstract Books, 1846-1876.

92. *Annual Statements of Trade and Navigation of the United Kingdom* (London, 1855-1914).

93. CLB, Board No. 21, 19th March, 1816.

94. Ibid., Collector to E. Earl, Chairman, Consolidated Board, 27th August, 1819.

95. HC, Arrivals and Sailings, 1834-1837.

96. WR.

97. CLB, Board No. 4, 5th January, 1837.

98. Tom Henderson Collection, Arrivals and Sailings of Vessels, 1840-1842.

99. SA, D4/54, Hay of Laxfirth MSS., Gavin Colvin to William Hay, 31st December, 1832.

100. Inventories of the Estates Real and Personal, note 86 above.

101. Arrivals and Sailings, 1834-1837, note 95 above.

102. *Annual Statements of Trade and Navigation*, note 92 above.

103. CLB, Board No. 9, 16th February, 1859.

104. CLB, Collector to Assistant Secretary's Branch, 9th January, 1858.

105. HC, Ships' Books; Nicolson, 1982, 85-99.

106. Log of the *Janet Hay*, note 1 above; Tom Henderson Collection, Minute Book: The Directors of the Zetland North Sea Fishery Company, 1863-1871.

107. CLB, Board No. 21, 18th July, 1870.

108. 12 & 13 Vict. c. 29 repealed the Navigation Laws in 1849. The repeal procedure was extended to the coastwise trade in 1854.

109. *Annual Statements of Trade and Navigation*, note 92 above.

110. SA, CE85/4/6, Ronas Voe Sailing Book, 1887-1910.

111. Brand, *Brief Description*, 7-16.

112. *The Diary of the Reverend John Mill*, 2, 7, 29-30.

113. Gardie Papers, Journal of a Jaunt to London in 1775 by Thos. Mouat, yr. of Garth.

114. SA, D12, Neven of Windhouse Papers, Charles Ogilvy to (?), 9th May, 1815.

115. SA, GD150/2521, Morton Papers, Proposal for establishing a Post Office at Lerwick, 1757; see also Mackay, 1979.

116. NS, Scrapbook (from a newspaper cutting, *ST*, 1892).

117. Note 88 above, 81.9.2, f.301; see also Mackay, 1979.

118. Haldane, 1971, 172-174; Mackay, 1979.

119. SA, D8, Sumburgh Papers, Letter Book, John Bruce to Charles Innes, 6th February, 1787.

120. Haldane, 1971, 173.

121. CLB, Board No. 40, 1st August, 1798.

122. CLB, Board No. 30, 17th December, 1799.

123. Haldane, 1971, 174.

124. CLB, Collector to E. Earl, Chairman, Consolidated Board, 31st July, 1819.

125. CLB, Board No. 32, 6th April, 1822.

126. CLB, Board No. 44, 24th May, 1825.

127. Edmondston, 1809, 2, 18, 21.

128. SA, D6, E. S. Reid Tait Collection, Contract of Co-partnery of the Leith and Shetland Shipping Co., 1823.

129. Donaldson, 1978, 5.

130. WR.

131. Donaldson, 1978, 8.

132. SA, D6, E. S. Reid Tait Collection, Contract of Co-partnery of the Zetland New Shipping Co., 1829.

133. Donaldson, 1978, 8-9.

134. *ST*, 10th September, 1881.

135. SA, CO1/1/3, Minutes of the Commissioners of Supply, Vol. 3, 2nd May, 1833.

136. SA, D6, E. S. Reid Tait Collection, Contract of Co-partnery of the Zetland Union Shipping Co., 1833.

137. Arrivals and Sailings, 1834-1837, note 95 above.

138. Donaldson, 1978, 18.

139. Ibid., 19-20.

140. *Ibid*.

141. Minutes of the Commissioners of Supply, note 135 above, 13th November, 1844.

142. Ibid., Memorandum for all-year-round steam packet, 13th March, 1851.

143. Donaldson, 1978, 20.

144. *Ibid*.

145. Scrapbook, note 116 above, 28th November, 1891.

146. *Shetland Advertiser*, 21st April, 1862.

147. Donaldson, 1978, 22.

148. *Ibid.*, 15.

149. NS, North of Scotland and Orkney and Shetland Steam Navigation Company Annual Reports, 1877-1896.

150. Ibid., 1884, 1890.

151. Ibid., 1881; Donaldson, 1978, 22-23.

152. *ST*, 10th September, 1881.

153. *ST*, 19th November, 1887.

154. Scrapbook, note 116 above, 28th November, 1891.

155. Donaldson, 1978, 30-31.

156. *Ibid; ST*, 25th January, 1896; 17th December, 1898.

157. Petition, note 50 above.

158. Donaldson, 1978, 34-35.

159. Simpson, 1983, 137.

160. Annual Reports, note 149 above.

161. Donaldson, 1978, 86-87.
162. CLB, Board No. 44, 6th July, 1855.
163. CLB, Board No. 6, 2nd February, 1870.
164. CLB, Board No. 16, 27th May, 1870.
165. *ST*, 17th June, 1872.
166. *ST*, 15th September, 1873; Scrapbook, note 116 above, 1870.
167. Donaldson, 1978, 24; *ST*, 5th September, 1885.
168. *ST*, 10th October, 1885.
169. *ST*, 3rd November, 1889.
170. Scrapbook, note 116 above, 1877, 1880.
171. Ibid., 2nd November, 1882.
172. NS, News Cuttings, 1903-1907, 28th February, 1903.
173. Donaldson, 1978, 24-25.
174. *Ibid.*
175. News Cuttings, note 172 above, 22nd January, 1904.
176. HC, Large Bound Volume, Arrivals and Sailings.
177. *ST*, 24th June, 1872; 18th May, 1874.
178. *ST*, July, 1885.
179. *ST*, 17th June, 1872.
180. *ST*, 26th May, 1905.
181. *ST*, 6th August, 1898.
182. *ST*, 28th November, 1907.
183. Scrapbook, note 116 above, 1892.
184. Letter Book, note 119 above, John Bruce to Mr. Davidson, 16th September, 1786.
185. Fulton, 1911, 89-90.
186. *Ibid.*
187. *Ibid.*, 87.
188. *Calendar of State Papers, Domestic Series, 1655*, 524.
189. Millar (ed.), 1898, 231, 237, 262, 296; *RPC*, 1st Ser., Vol. 4, 665-666.
190. Brand, *Brief Description*, 31; Smout, 1963, 220-223.
191. Gifford, *Historical Description*, 4-7.
192. Low, *Tour*, 63-74.
193. CQR.
194. Ibid.
195. Edmondston, 1809, *1*, 265-267.
196. Low, *Tour*, 94-95.
197. SA, GD150/2518B, Morton Papers, Memorial for the Rt. Hon. the Earl of Morton on behalf of the Heritors & Merchants in the Country of Zetland, n.d.
198. Ibid; Edmondston, 1809, *1*, 252-253.
199. SA, D8, Sumburgh Papers, Observations on the probable effects of the present Dutch War, upon the Islands of Shetland and its Fisheries, January, 1781.
200. CLB, Board No. 80, 30th October, 1829.
201. O'Dell, 1939, 129.
202. CLB, Board No. 30, 14th August, 1886; Board No. 31, 16th August, 1886; SRO, CE85/4/20, General Register of Seizures, 1860-1918.
203. CLB, Board No. 61, 9th November, 1831.
204. *RPC*, 2nd Ser., Vol. 3, 353-354, 386.
205. CLB, Board No. 61, 9th November, 1831; Board No. 29, 26th April, 1832.
206. CLB, Board No. 48, 17th July, 1832.
207. CLB, Board No. 19, 25th March, 1833.
208. SA, D8, Sumburgh Papers, Walter Scott to (?), 27th May, 1781.
209. Peterkin, 1822, 212-224.
210. WR; NLS, 13.2.8, Sibbald MSS, A geographical description of the Isle of Bressay, 1684.
211. Firth, C. H. (ed.), *Scotland and the Commonwealth*. Scott. Hist. Soc. (Edinburgh, 1895),

xlix-l, 278; *Scotland and the Protectorate*, Scott. Hist. Soc. (Edinburgh, 1899). See also Ball, 1965, 5-25.

212. Sibbald MSS, note 210 above, A Geographical Description of the Island of Burray 1654 by Mr. Hugh Leigh.

213. A geographical description of the Isle of Bressay, note 210 above.

214. Sibbald MSS, note 210 above, Description of Zetland by M.T.V., n.d; *Calendar of State Papers, Domestic Series, 1664-1665*, 316, 344-345, 534; *1666-1667*, 201; *RPC*, 3rd Ser., Vol. 2, 366-367.

215. Description of Zetland by M.T.V., note 214 above.

216. SRO, RH9/15/138, Orkney and Shetland Papers, Memorial from Capt. Dick anent the Admiralty of Orkney & Zetland & his being Capt. of a fort at Brasey Sound & the Customs of Zetland to be alloed for his incuragement, 1689.

217. LUE, II421.2, Laing MSS, Gilbert Neven to Col. William Sinclair, Governor of Shetland, 11th July, 1667.

218. Observations on the probable effects of the present Dutch War, note 199 above.

219. Ibid.

220. O'Dell, 1939, 23.

221. CLB, Board No. 34, 25th August, 1870.

222. O'Dell, 1933, 137-145; 1939, 5-10.

223. Bruce, 1907-12, *Old Lore Misc.*, 1, 35-42, 123-128, 176-178, 217-220, 281-284, 308-309; 2, 31-33, 101-104; 3, 34-35, 164-165; 5, 20-24, 73-78; numerous newspaper articles.

224. WR.

225. SA, SC12/6, Protests against Wind and Weather, 1785-1810.

226. Depositions, note 5 above; WR.

227. O'Dell, 1939, 7-8.

228. *Ibid.*, 22-25.

229. Stenhuit, 1974, 213-256.

230. Aston University Sub-aqua Club, 1974; Forster, Higgs, 1973, 291-300; Muckelroy, 1976, 280-290; Price, Muckelroy, 1974, 257-268; 1977, 187-218; 1979, 311-320; 1980, 7-25.

231. Bax, Martin, 1974, 81-90.

232. Dowle, Martin, *The Scotsman*, 5th August, 1980.

233. Depositions, note 5 above; WR.

234. Custom House, Lerwick, Register of Shipping, 1837-1914 (2 vols.).

235. SA, D8, Sumburgh Papers, Articles and Conditions of Sale of Such Parts of the Wood of the Wrecked Ship *Concordia* of Copenhagen, 1786.

236. NLS, 7033, ff. 31-36, Yester MSS, Papers concerning a ship in Zetland, n.d.

237. CLB, Board No. 2, 6th January, 1849.

238. CLB, Board No. 6, 10th January, 1845.

239. CLB, Board No. 14, 22nd February, 1828.

240. SRO, RH9/15/141, Orkney and Shetland Papers, Representation for The Earl of Morton, Mr. Robert Douglas his brother & Sir Archibald Stewart Anent the Admiralty of Orknay & Zetland, 1705.

241. Gardie Papers, Contract: John Mitchell and Wm. Henderson & Jas. Mitchell, 16th February, 1712.

242. SRO, RH9/15/142, Orkney and Shetland Papers, Memoir for the Earl of Morton with respect to the admiralty of Orkney & Zetland, 1720.

243. SA, GD150/2609B, Morton Papers, Contracts granting privileges for diving and recovering all Gold, Silver & other metals & good which have been wrecked in Orkney & Shetland & relative papers, 1721-1731.

244. CLB, Board No. 58, 11th December, 1797.

245. SRO, RH9/15/143, Orkney and Shetland Papers, Information for the Hon. the Comrs. of H.M. Boards of Customs and Excise in Scotland . . . in the Process of Declarator & Delivery against the Rt. Hon. Thomas, Lord Dundas, Vice-Admiral of Orkney & Zetland & now Depute Vice-Admiral of Orkney, Defenders, 29th June, 1809.

246. CLB, Board No. 42, 20th April, 1819.

247. CLB, Board No. 52, 28th June, 1825.

248. Diary containing the state of the wind, weather and occurrences, note 26 above.

249. *The Orkney and Zetland Chronicle*, 28th February, 1825.

250. CLB, Board No. 62, 17th November, 1852.

Chapter 7

1. For recent statements see, e.g., Galbraith, 1977, 133-160; Pollard, 1981b, 61.

2. *ST*, 1914.

3. See, e.g., Gregson, 1981, 29-37.

4. The shipping columns of *The Shetland Times* for the period provide ample evidence of this.

5. Goodlad, 1971, 203-225.

6. Smith, H. D., 1977, 69-71; Donald, 1983, 198-213.

7. Goodlad, 1971, 227-319.

8. Grassie, 1983.

9. Ibid; Highlands and Islands Development Board, *Shetland Woollen Industry: planning for progress* (Inverness, 1970).

10. Smith, H. D., 1977, 66-68.

11. 74 Eliz. II c.8.

12. Goodlad, J. H., 'Shetland fisheries — conservation and development', *Marine Policy* 4(3) (1980), 244-245; Coull, J. R. Goodlad, J. H., Sheves, G. T., *The fisheries in the Shetland area: a study in conservation and development* (Aberdeen, 1979).

13. Note in this context: The Nevis Institute, *The Shetland Report: a constitutional study* (Edinburgh, 1978), and the work of the Montgomery Commission (1982-83).

14. Friedland, 1973.

15. Saint-Clair, 1898; Grant, 1983; Crawford, 1978.

16. Smith, B., 1979; Crawford, 1978, 5, 9.

17. Smith, B., 1975, 1979.

18. Flinn, 1964; 1980. For human geography regionalisation see Heineberg, 1969.

19. Smith, H. D., Scotland and the sea in early modern times. Paper delivered at 9th Biennial Conference of the Scottish History Society, 'Scotland and the sea', Dundee, 10-12 September, 1980.

20. Ibid.

21. See above, Chapter 3, note 262.

22. See above, Chapter 3, notes 293, 294, 295.

23. See above, Chapter 4, notes 248, 253, 255, 256, 356.

24. See above, Chapter 5, notes 1, 2.

25. For discussion of periodicities and problems of interpretation, see e.g. Galtung, J., *et al*, 1979, 318-361; the importance of identity in social and national terms is discussed in Seton-Watson, 1977, 480-1; Thomas, 1979, 617.

Glossary

Admiralty	Jurisdiction of the High Court of Admiralty of Scotland, abolished in 1830. Jurisdiction, delegated to Admiral-deputes in various specified areas, extended to all maritime causes. In a Shetland context this was mainly concerned with salvage from shipwrecks, and stranding of whales.
ad valorem	According to value. Duty on wood goods was commonly levied as a proportion of its value, hence the term.
angel	An old English gold coin, originally called *angel noble,* having as its device the archangel Michael and the Dragon. Its value varied from 6s 8d to 10s.
anker	A cask or keg holding ten old wine or eight and one-third imperial gallons. Equivalent to one-third of a *barrel,* q.v. Also used as a dry measure in Scotland for e.g. potatoes.
ayre	A shingle or stony beach. Occasionally applied also to tombola structures forming a neck of land with water on both sides.
bailing	The process of ladling water out of an open boat.
balk ropes	The ropes by which herring nets were fastened to one another in a fleet, used before the advent of the *bush rope,* q.v.
bark	The covering of the trunk or branches of a tree. Oak bark was used for *tanning* (q.v.) lines and nets.
barque	A three-masted vessel, square-rigged on the fore- and mainmasts and fore-and-aft rigged on the mizzen mast.
barrel	A dry measure varying in different localities and with different goods. A cask or keg holding a barrel measure. The herring barrel was generally of capacity 32 imp. gals., while ½, ¼ and ⅛ barrels were respectively of 16, 8 and 4 gallon capacity. The Scots barrel of 24 imp. gals. replaced the Orkney barrel of 27 imp. gals. in the early 18th-century measurement of rent commodities, e.g. butter.
batten	A piece of sawn timber used for flooring, support of laths, etc. Also a piece of sawn timber used to fasten down hatches on board a ship.
baukt	A single length of line, used in *long line* fishing, q.v. In the haaf fisheries it was generally 50 fathoms, with hooks spaced at regular intervals of 3½ to 5 fathoms. In the haddock fishing, it was 60 fathoms, with 100 hooks similarly spaced.

bawbee	A coin of six pennies Scots struck in base silver by James V and Mary, and in copper by Charles II, William and Mary, and William III. Although issued as sixpenny pieces, the bawbees of base silver were 'cried down' to threepenny pieces by an Act of James VI.
beam-ends	Of a ship, the laying of a vessel on her beam-ends implies that she is lying at an angle in the water so that the ends of the beams are level with or below the water surface, and she is in danger of capsizing. This often happened to sailing vessels in bad weather, due to heavy sea conditions and/or shifting of ballast and/or cargo.
beating about	Sailing backwards and forwards in an attempt to make headway against the wind.
bere	A kind of barley, hardier than the ordinary kind, but of inferior quality. Bere has generally 4 rows of grain on the head, while ordinary barley has 2.
blaand	Whey mixed with water.
bloom	See *pining*.
boater	This term was used in Lerwick for the men who ferried goods between ships and shore in small boats in Bressay Sound, before the construction of Lerwick Harbour in the 1870s. The Lerwick boaters were among the objectors to the proposed harbour scheme at that time.
boll	A measure of capacity for grain, etc. In Scotland, usually equal to six imperial bushels.
bom = bosmschuit	A bluff-bowed fishing boat, the successor of, and similar in size to, the *buss*, q.v. Boms were the usual type of fishing vessel used by the Dutch during the 1880-1914 phase of herring fishery development.
bootikin	A knitted legging with feet, worn by children.
bounty	Payment made by government to exporters to encourage the fish trades. Assessed by weight of dry fish, barrels of herring, or tonnage of vessels engaged in fishing. The bounty on the export of dry fish was fixed in 1718 at 3/- per cwt. dry ling and cod (5 Geo. I cap. 18), and remained until 1830, although detailed modifications regarding specification of degree of salting, etc. were made thereafter. Bounties assessed on the tonnage of vessels engaged in the fisheries were payable in the Free British Fishery, and by an Act of 1808 (48 Geo. III c.110) in the herring fishing; and in the cod fishing. All bounties on fish exports were abolished in 1830.
brands	Trade-marks adopted in the herring fisheries in Europe generally, to signify quality and origin of cured herring by means of marks applied to the herring barrels using hot branding irons. In Scotland, responsibility for ensuring quality rested with the Fishery Board for Scotland. Fishery Board inspectors checked full herring barrels before export, and marked these according to quality. The several brands included: *Crown Brand:* for top quality herring only. *Large:* for extra-large herring.

	Mattie: for young herring with the milt or roe not fully developed, first cured separately in Scotland in 1849. *Full:* for herring just before spawning, with fully developed roe. *Spent:* for herring which had spawned and were of poor quality. A common end of season product. In addition to these Fishery Board brands, the curers had their own marks.
brandy	Originally *brandywine*, from the Dutch *brandywijn*, to burn, plus wine (see Table 1). An ardent spirit, distilled from wine or grapes, but also a name for other similar spirits. *cognac:* Strictly speaking, brandy from the Cognac region of France, legally defined in 1909. Probably generally used in Shetland to refer to any expensive brandy of French origin, drunk by the upper classes. *corn brandy:* Distilled from rye, and imported from Hamburg. The drink was used extensively by the haaf fishermen at sea in the 18th and 19th centuries, together with *blaand,* q.v.
brig	Shortened from *brigantine,* q.v.
brigantine	A two-masted vessel, square-rigged on the foremast and schooner-rigged on the mainmast.
broken water	Extremely choppy sea, with short, breaking waves, common in strong tidal streams, especially when the tidal current is running in the opposite direction to the wind.
bush rope	(occasionally, *buss rope*): The single heavy rope to which a fleet of herring nets are attached. It was adopted in Shetland to replace the *balk ropes,* q.v., from the late 1890s onwards, in association with the steam capstan. When hauling the nets, the bush rope was led through a block to the steam capstan and down into the rope room forward, where 'the boy' (usually the cook) coiled it down ready for the next shooting of the nets.
buss	A two- or three-masted vessel of various sizes, used especially in the Dutch herring fishery. Generally from 50-100 tons in Shetland waters, in the 17th and 18th centuries, bluff-bowed and possessing a large carrying capacity relative to her length.
caain' whales	Pilot whales, so called in the Shetland dialect from the practice of driving or *caain'* schools of these whales on shore in the voes, where they were slaughtered for their meat, bone and especially blubber, which could be rendered into oil, a valuable export commodity. This was a common practice in Shetland in the 18th and 19th centuries, but an absolute decline in numbers took place at the same time as the landowners' rights to one-third of the proceeds of these hunts were successfully contested by the crofters in the Hoswick Whale Case of 1888-1889.
carding	The process of teasing wool, whereby the fibres were separated in preparation for spinning.
castin and raisin peats	Cutting peats and erecting these in small clumps for drying.

Cavendish tobacco	Tobacco which has been softened, sweetened and pressed into cakes. An important commodity of later 19th-century smuggling into Shetland.
central place	A settlement which provides service for a population outside the built-up area of the settlement itself. In a Shetland context, applies particularly to the points at which the retailing of goods and services is concentrated.
chapmen	Pedlars.
c.i.f.	Cost, insurance, freight. A method of quoting commodity prices, such as that of cured herring, at the market, signifying that transport costs were included in the quoted price, as distinct from *f.o.b.*, free on board, in which transport costs were not included.
coastwise trade	Trade among ports within a country, and therefore not generally subject to duty, so that much of it in early times went unrecorded. In Shetland's case coastwise trade was mainly with the east coasts of Scotland and, to a lesser extent, England.
cog	An early medieval form of ship, broadly built, with a roundish bow and stern. Often only partly decked, with a single mast and square sail. The provenance of the cog was the southern North Sea and Baltic, where it was the basic type of ship used by the traders of the Hanseatic League until the 15th century.
cognac	See *brandy*.
coinage	See under: *shilling* (Danish); *bawbee, groat, mark* (Scots); *angel, angel noble* English; *stiver, zopindale* (German).
comforter	A long, woollen scarf, worn round the throat.
Commissioners of Supply	Local government officers, first appointed in the time of Charles II. The predecessors of the County Council, they were replaced by the Local Government (Scotland) Act of 1889. They were responsible for collection of local taxes, such as window tax and cess, in the 18th century; making up the valuation roll (from the 1860s onwards); and after about 1830, looking after problems of general economic and social welfare, such as famine relief, mail service provisions, and customs duties on Shetland import and export trades.
commonty	A Scottish term, meaning much the same as the Shetland *scattald*, q.v., although the scattalds were common grazings attached to a specific district rather than to an estate. Before divisions began (below), commonties were not enclosed in any way, but delimited by division lines based on landmarks.

Processes for the division of commonty began to be raised in Shetland in substantial numbers in the late 19th century, as the landowners' attention turned increasingly from the laying out of arable farms, by then virtually complete, to the laying out of sheep farms, using this poor hill land. This involved surveying the scattald and dividing it up among the several land-owners who had shares in the township to which it pertained. The several sections might then be enclosed by fences. The division of commonty was still far from complete by 1914. |

The division of commonty is, strictly speaking, a legal process, not to be confused with the regulation of stock on the scattalds, covered by the Crofters' Holdings Act of 1886, and also beginning to be put into effect before 1914. However, both processes were ultimately directed towards the same end, namely, the improvement of livestock husbandry on the hill land principally by prevention of overstocking, which was the major impediment to agricultural improvement in this area in the 19th century.

contrary winds   Head winds relative to a vessel's voyage direction or directions.

corn brandy   See *brandy*.

country   1. A colloquial term applied in Shetland to rural areas outwith Scalloway and Lerwick.
                      2. A common 17th and 18th century literary usage referring to Shetland as a whole.

croft   A smallholding containing arable land. In Shetland, these became the focus of attention in the course of the 19th century, being created with the division of runrig into separate holdings, and attention culminating in the Crofters' Holdings Act of 1886, which granted security of tenure, among other things, to the crofters.

Crown Brand   See *brand*.

Crown rents   These were originally rents paid to the Norwegian Crown from Royal estates in Shetland, which were relatively small, but were added to in various ways over the centuries (notably by the acquisition of the Bishopric estate in 1614), and were referred to collectively as the *Lordship estate*, q.v. In addition the Norwegian kings collected scats or taxes from all lands in the islands. After 1469 these rents and duties passed to the Kings of Scotland, and were generally held by Scottish nobles, notably Robert Stewart (d. 1593) and his son Patrick (d. 1615). From 1643 onwards the Earls of Morton received various grants of the estates, culminating in an irredeemable grant to the 14th Earl in 1742. In 1766 Morton sold the lands and duties to Sir Laurence Dundas of Kerse, whose family still possesses the remnants.

                      By 1766 substantial parts of the estate had been feued off to local landholders, notably in 1589 and 1664, and the residue was referred to as the 'property lands of the Lordship'; in the second decade of the 19th century Dundas allowed Shetland proprietors to redeem the scats payable by them as well. At various times from the 16th to the 19th centuries the rents and duties were paid in skins, cloth, butter and oil, and constituted a substantial item of trade. See also *Lordship estate*.

cure   A colloquial expression referring to the quality or time of curing of herring.

currency   See *pound Scots; dollar*.

cutter	A small vessel with one mast, a mainsail, a forestaysail and jib. Any *sloop*, q.v., of narrow beam and deep draught.
deadweight tonnage	See *tonnage.*
deals	Standard size fir or pine boards.
deal ends	Short sections of deals.
debenture	A certificate given to an exporter of imported goods on which a drawback is allowed, certifying that the holder is entitled to an amount therein stated. In the Shetland case, debentures were payable in respect of foreign salt imported and used in curing fish for export during the 18th century. Foreign salt was thus in practice admitted duty free, so long as it was used for fish for export only. In England, considerable restrictions were placed on the import of foreign salt in 1701 and 1703 (1 Anne c.21, 2 & 3 Anne c.14), which applied to Scotland after the Union in 1707 and which remained throughout the 18th century, but the superior quality of this salt ensured a continuing import trade, and the continuing of the payment of debentures.
	This payment of drawback is not to be confused with the payment of bounties, also by debenture. In this case, a debenture was simply a voucher certifying that a sum of money was owing to the person designated in it.
delve	(Shetland: *dell*): To dig and turn over the ground with a spade.
demersal	Fish which feed and live on or near the seabed. Important commercial species in Shetland during the period covered by this book were successively ling, cod and haddock.
demurrage	Charges payable for undue delay of a vessel.
deputation of Admiralty	An appointment by the Admiral, holding the office of *Admiralty*, q.v. The Admiralty was in the nature of a feudal sinecure, and the responsibility for the execution of the office was delegated to leading figures in the several parts of Scotland. In Shetland, the right of admiralty was vested in the *Lordship estate*, q.v., and one or more admiral-deputes were appointed by the Earl of Orkney from the ranks of the local landowners, and later merchants, who supervised the legal aspects of salvage operations in cases of shipwreck, and disposal of the produce of *caain' whale* hunts, q.v., the admiral being entitled to one-third of the proceeds of such hunts.
derelict	Of a ship, abandoned; with no crew on board.
dispone	In Scots law, to convey legally.
dogger	A two-masted sailing fishing vessel, of Dutch provenance.
dollar	English name for the German *thaler;* also of the *rigsdollar* of Denmark, etc.— see *rixdollar.*
dunnage	Light materials, such as mats, or timber, stowed among and beneath the cargo of a vessel to keep it from injury by chafing or wet. In the Shetland

export trade, it was particularly important to protect dry fish in this way. See *Russia mats*.

early herring   In a Shetland context, this referred to herring caught on the *West Side* grounds, q.v., mainly in June and early July; see *early herring fishing*.

early herring fishing This was the June and early July fishing for the Atlanto-Scandian stock of herring on the grounds to the west and north-west of Shetland (Fig, 62).

English herring   In Shetland, this commonly referred to the East Anglian herring fishing,
fishing   carried on from October to Christmas. Shetland boats participated in this fishery more extensively after the advent of the steam drifter, especially after the First World War.

factor   (landowning) The factor was someone employed by a landowner to conduct the business of the estate, especially the financial business, such as rent collection. Not to be confused with the *tacksman*, q.v.

factor   (trade) The factor in the case of Shetland trade was usually a Scots resident in overseas ports frequented by Shetland export and import traders, in the 18th century. He was responsible for acting as middleman or agent between the shipmaster, supercargo or landowner on the one hand, and the dealers in Shetland export and import trade commodities on the other. He also commonly supervised all customs and docking and harbour arrangements, and acted as a general adviser on trade conditions.

Fair Isle &   *Fair Isle* is a term applied to the complex traditional patterns of Shetland
Spaniards   knitwear, employing a variety of colours and forms. Traditionally, the patterns are held to have originated in Fair Isle as a consequence of the wreck of the Spanish Armada store ship *El Gran Grifon* of Rostock, in 1588. The islanders allegedly were taught the patterns by the Spanish sailors. Hence the apparent incongruity of selling Fair Isle patterned knitwear to Spanish buyers in London in the 19th century.

Faroe fishing   The colloquial name in 19th-century Shetland for the smack cod fishery, which was concentrated mainly on the Faroe Bank (Fig. 62) and along the coast of the Faroe Islands.

fetching   Sailing into the wind.

fifie   A type of *herring boat*, q.v., with vertical stem and stern posts, common in the second half of the 19th and early 20th centuries on the east coast of Scotland, probably so called from having been first built and used on the Fife coast. The majority of the *luggers*, q.v., and many later, larger herring boats possessed this hull form.

finnan haddocks   Haddocks cured with the smoke of green wood, peat or turf.

fish vat   A large wooden tub in which cod and ling were soaked in brine before drying.

fishing lodge   A small, drystone-built, turf-roofed dwelling, built at the *haaf* fishing stations, in which the fishermen stayed while ashore during the haaf fishing season. They often went home at weekends.

fishing necessaries	An 18th-century Shetland colloquialism applied to hooks, lines, bark, pots, kettles, corn brandy, and other articles required for the *haaf* fishing.
fishing stock	A name applied to cargoes of barrels, staves, hoops and salt required for the herring fishing, particularly after 1880.
flakes	Flat pieces of wood upon which fish were placed for drying, rather than drying them upon beach stones.
flan	A sudden strong gust of wind, often associated with hilly areas in Shetland, and a particular danger for open boat sailing in the *voes,* q.v.
flitboat	A boat used for conveying goods in Shetland. Usually an open boat. The word came into use in the 19th century. Also applied to a similar boat used for conveying passengers and goods between steamer and shore.
foud	An official, originally of the Norwegian Crown, whose duty was to preside at the tings or local councils, and to collect taxes, etc; under the Scottish feudal regime, to carry out the functions of sheriff. The Great Foud fulfilled the function of chief administrator before the advent of Lord Robert Stewart in 1581 (see *Crown Rents*), and had subordinate under fouds responsible for individual parishes. The office of foud disappeared with the abrogation of the Norse Law in 1611.
fourern	An open boat, rowed with four oars. The boats were generally double-ended, clinker-built and about 14 feet of keel, being used mainly in near shore fishing.
full herring	See *brands.*
geneva	A spirit distilled from grain, flavoured with juniper berries, made in Holland, and also called *Hollands,* formerly *Hollands geneva.*
gin	Abbreviation of *geneva,* q.v. In the form *gin,* the name denotes a spirit of British manufacture, usually flavoured not with juniper, but with some substitute, but sometimes, as in 18th century Shetland, *gin* and *geneva* were used indiscriminately. Often *Dutch gin* was used.
great line	Also *long line,* q.v. The name applied to long lines used for fishing large fish species, such as cod, ling, hake and halibut.
groat	An English coin long current in Scotland; value about 14d.
gutters	The girls and women employed on the herring stations to remove the entrails from the herring prior to salting. After landing, the herring were placed on long troughs called farlins, at which the gutters worked. A single quick movement with the gutting knife was sufficient to remove the entrails, and the herring were then passed to the *packers,* q.v.
haaf	1. The deep or open ocean, as opposed to coastal waters. Cognate of Norwegian *hav* — ocean. 2. The long line fishing using open boats, in the 18th and 19th centuries.

haddock boats	Open, four-oared boats of 14 to 18 feet of keel, used at the haddock fishing between 1880 and 1914. Similar to the earlier *fourern*, q.v., imported from Norway, but distinguished by being built in Shetland on the lines of a *Shetland model*, q.v.
haddock line	1. A colloquial expression for the haddock fishing. 2. A haddock line consisted generally of 6 *baukts*, q.v. (occasionally 5), each 60 fathoms long with 100 hooks. Each man had 3 such lines, and each haddock boat was crewed by 4 men. Thus a boat carried 12 lines.
half-catch	Originally, a system whereby the proceeds of the fishing were divided up so that half went to the owners and half to the crew, after expenses had been deducted. In practice, a variety of financial arrangements of a more complex kind applied, and continue to apply, in the several Shetland fisheries.
half-decked boats	Boats of various sizes, probably mainly 20 to 30 feet of keel, decked forward only, used in the Shetland herring fishing from the late 1820s until the early 1840s. Most of these boats were imported from the east coast of Scotland, although a number were built by Hay and Ogilvy.
hap	A wrap, similar to a shawl, worn by Shetland women outdoors as a protection against inclement weather.
harrowbills	A kind of hard wood imported into Shetland from Norway in the 18th and 19th centuries, used in the manufacture of harrows.
hatch covers	The covering of a vessel's hatches, designed to make these secure and watertight; usually composed of wooden planks laid close together, covered by a tarpaulin and battened down.
hazel cuts	Hazel branches and twigs imported into Shetland from Norway for use in threshing grain, and for making walking sticks.
herring boat	A fishing boat designed primarily for the drift-net herring fishing, and used solely or mainly for that purpose. Before 1914, most were *fifies* or *zulus*, q.v., and *lug-* or *smack*-rigged, q.v.
herring brands	See *brands*.
hooker	A two-masted Dutch coasting or fishing vessel.
in ballast	A term originally applied to a sailing vessel laden with ballast only, and carrying no cargo.
inoculation	Impregnation of a person with the virus or germs of a disease, specially for the purpose of inducing a milder form of the disease and rendering the subject immune. John Williamson, better known as 'Johnnie Notions' (see *The New Shetlander*, No. 47, 1958, 15-16), applied serum containing smallpox as a protection against smallpox itself, using a small knife, followed by a dressing consisting of a piece of cabbage leaf. His efforts were in large measure responsible for the decline in the virulence and scale of smallpox epidemics in Shetland from the 1770s onwards.

iron man	The hand-operated predecessor of the seam capstan, used in hauling herring nets.
jerking	Checking or searching a ship for contraband.
ketch-rigged	Two-masted, fore-and-aft rig, with jib, foresail, mainsail and mizzen.
kishie	A straw basket, used to carry peats, etc., usually by slinging across the back.
knee	Oak knees, shaped like a bent knee, were used in boat and ship construction.
kontor	A trading post in a foreign country run by a group of German merchants belonging to the Hanseatic League.
large herrings	See *brands*.
last	1. A commercial denomination of weight, capacity or quantity, varying for different goods and localities. As a weight it is estimated at 2 tons or 4,000 lb. A last of cod and herrings is 12 barrels. See *tonnage*.
late herring fishing	The colloquial Shetland reference to the herring fishing to the east, south-east and south of the islands from mid-July onwards. To distinguish it from the *early herring fishing*, q.v.
lathwood	Thin, narrow, flat pieces of wood, used to form a groundwork for slates, tiles or plaster in house-building.
leases, short, for tenants	The tenants in Shetland before the Crofters' Holdings Act were subject to eviction on 40 days' notice, which amounted in practice to no security of tenure at all. In reality, for a variety of economic reasons, few evictions took place until the 1840s.
ley land	Land which was unworked, and presumably therefore untenanted. It increased greatly in quantity after the 1690s, probably because of the smallpox epidemic of 1700, and famine (Chapter 3), and was recorded in the rentals by virtue of the fact that ley lands were not liable to payment of *scat*, q.v. The quantity of ley land remained high throughout the 18th century, no doubt partly because of continuing famine and smallpox, and latterly apparently as a device for avoiding the payment of *superior duties*, q.v.
lighter	A boat used for ferrying cargo between ships anchored offshore and the shore.
lighterage	Charges for transporting goods by *lighter*, q.v.
lispund	A measure of weight, originally used in the Baltic region and thence adopted in Shetland and Orkney, especially for weighing grain, malt or butter. The measure seems to have been about 12 lb. Scots (16.3 lb. avoirdupois), but from its frequent use in weighing rent in kind payable to landowners, it was gradually increased to 30 lb. Scots or more by the 18th century, partly as a means of extortion, and partly due to devaluation.

lodberry	A store built out into the sea, at which goods can be directly transferred to or from vessels or boats. Peculiar to the South End of Lerwick.
long hundred	Usually 120, and a common measure for quantities of wood goods, such as deals, spars counted in hundreds (i.e. = 120) and quarters (= 30).
long lines	The long line consisted of a series of *baukts*, q.v., tied together as the lines were laid, and held in position at either end by stone sinkers attached to surface marker buoys by buoy ropes. It ranged in length from 40 to 120 baukts (2 to 6 miles).
Lordship estate	See *Crown Rents* for its origins. In the 18th century, this was the estate belonging to the Earl of Zetland. It was granted by Queen Anne to the Earl of Morton in 1706 for an annual payment of £500 sterling. The Earl of Morton sold his rights in 1766 to Lord Dundas of Kerse, and Lord Dundas disposed of most of the duties of the estate in 1812. It was one of the largest estates in 18th-century Shetland, although very scattered.
lug-rigged	See *lugger*.
lugger	A lug-rigged vessel, carrying a lugsail or lugsails, with one, two or three masts. A number of the Dutch smugglers of the early 19th century were of this type. The first herring boats in the 1880s phase of herring fishing development were often rigged in this way.
mark, Scots	also *merk*: 1. Originally a certain weight of gold and silver estimated in money terms and used as a money of account from early times, with the value of two-thirds of the *pound Scots*, q.v., or 13 shillings 4 pence Scots, which by the 18th century was equivalent to 13 and one-third pence sterling. A silver coin of this denomination was coined at intervals from the reign of James VI, in 1578, to that of Charles II. As a money of account, the name persisted into the 18th century, frequently as a collective plural. In Shetland, the merk was originally the slightly lighter Norwegian màrk, and the calculations of land values therefore were on that basis. 2. In Orkney and Shetland, a division of land, being the area of land originally having the capital value of one merk, on its arable part, and subdivided into 8 ures. The exact extent of the area involved varied considerably according to the district and quality of the soil. 3. As a dry measure, one twenty-fourth part of a *lispund*, q.v.
mart	also *mert:* An ox or cow, fattened for slaughter, and usually killed at the end of the year, around *Martinmas*, q.v., to provide salted meat for a family.
Martinmas	The feast day of St. Martin, 11th November.
mead	An alcoholic liquor made by fermenting a mixture of honey and water.
merchant house	In the 18th and early 19th centuries, applied to a business undertaking, often initially of a family variety, partnership, or joint-stock arrangement, generally specialising in import-export trading in certain specific commodities (such as dried fish), together with finance and shipowning.
MFV	Motor fishing vessel. A term applied to a specific set of designs of fishing vessel, initially built for the Admiralty in World War II.

missing stays	Failing to come round from one course to another while *tacking*, q.v.
mother sloops	*Sloops*, q.v., used as floating bases from which *sixerns*, q.v., were operated. The boats were tied up alongside or astern of the sloop when not in use, and returned to discharge their catches aboard the sloop instead of at the fishing station.
mum beer	A kind of beer, originally brewed in Brunswick.
'Ness yoal	An open boat of the form of the *sixern*, q.v., or *fourern*, q.v., but with a much narrower beam, suitable for working in strong tidal streams. Peculiar to the Dunrossness area.
outsets	Smallholdings created by enclosing parts of the hill land beyond the hill dyke (Fig. 1). Many of these came into being during the period of population expansion, notably in the late 18th century.
packers	The women and girls (mainly) engaged in putting gutted herring (see *gutters*) into herring barrels. After the herring left the hands of the gutters, they were lightly salted and packed in barrels. After settling for a day or two the barrels were repacked at least once, and perhaps oftener, before being finally sealed for export.
pining	The process of causing fish to shrink by drying in the process of curing. When all the fish were equally dried, or pined, this was known by the salt appearing on the surface in a white efflorescence called *bloom*.
plaid	A long piece of woollen cloth.
plantie-crub	A small drystone-walled enclosure used for growing vegetables, particularly cabbage or kale.
plough timber	Assorted pieces of wood used in the construction of agricultural ploughs.
poinded	A Scots legal term meaning 'impounded'.
port of registry	The port at which a vessel is registered under the merchant shipping acts of 1786, 1854, 1894, etc. The whole of Shetland constituted the Port of Lerwick for this purpose. Usually, the port of registry was the area of residence of the vessel's owners.
pound Scots	Originally the same as the English pound sterling, it was at the Union of the Crowns equal to one-twelfth of a pound sterling, being divided into 20 shillings each of the value of an English penny.
privateer	A merchant ('private') ship commissioned to seize and plunder enemy shipping. These were often the chief danger to shipping in wartime in Shetland waters in the 17th and 18th centuries.
registered tonnage	See *tonnage*.
rivlins	A type of footwear made of hides.

rixdollar	A silver coin and money of account from c. 1600-1850 in various European countries; the value varied from about 4s 6d to 2s 3d. It stood at around 4s-4s 10d in the late 17th and early 18th century Shetland trade.
roup	An auction.
rouped	Sold by auction.
roused herring	Lightly salted herring, destined eventually for use in a virtually 'fresh' state, as distinct from cured. Much roused herring was exported to Hamburg in the early 1900s for canning.
runrig	A form of land use in which arable land was held in common, and the several farmers had different ridges or strips of land allotted to them in different years.
Russia mats	Matting manufactured in Russia from the inner bark of the linden. Used as *dunnage*, q.v., to cover dry fish, being specially imported for the purpose.
sailboat	A general term applied to the sail-powered *herring boats*, q.v., of whatever hull design or rig, from the 1880s onwards.
scaap	Shellfish beds. Usually mussels or oysters.
scat	Scats were taxes paid from all lands in the islands, and originated during the period of the Scandinavian settlement, when they were payable to the Norwegian kings. When the Scottish Crown acquired these rights in 1472, subsequent to the pledging or pawning of Orkney and Shetland, scat continued to be collected by the Scottish earls and donatories. In the later 17th century, it was paid mainly in butter and oil. See also *Crown rents*.
scatlands	Those areas under the Crown of Norway liable to the payment of *scat* to the Norwegian Crown in the later Dark Ages and early Middle Ages; included, at various times, Shetland, Orkney, Faroe and Iceland.
scattald	This was originally a neighbourhood district, dating from the period of the Scandinavian settlement. For the past two centuries it has meant a common pasture shared by a specific group of *townships* (see *township*). For a full discussion see also: Smith, Brian, 'What is a scattald? rural communities in Shetland, 1400-1900', in: Crawford, Barbara E. (ed.), *Essays in Shetland History* (Lerwick, 1984).
scoops	Concave wooden vessels used for *bailing* out open boats.
sea-keeping quality	The degree of ability possessed by a vessel, by virtue of her design, to handle and behave well at sea, especially under adverse conditions, with high waves.
set (lines)	To lay lines, particularly long lines, haddock lines.
set (tacks)	Letting or leasing of an estate, farm, fishing station.
settling	The annual, end of season squaring of accounts by fishermen, particularly applicable to the close of the herring season, when the expenses of the

fishing were set off against the proceeds in a meeting between individual boat's crews and curers.

Severra frocks   Origin uncertain. Severra appears to be a geographical name; therefore, probably a style of woollen frock named after a particular locality.

shares   1. Fishing boats were normally divided into 6 shares, which might be held by a single owner, or by several, either shore-owners or fishermen.
2. Vessels registered under the merchant shipping acts as ships were divided into 64 shares. Again, these were commonly apportioned among several owners. In both cases, the profits were divided out according to the ratio of shares possessed by each owner, after expenses had been deducted from the gross earnings of the boat or vessel.

Shetland cattle   A breed of cattle peculiar to Shetland, much smaller than other cattle breeds, and capable of grazing on poor, heather-covered hill land in summer.

Shetland model   A double-ended hull form, similar to the open boats imported from Norway. The term seems to have originated in both Shetland and Norway in the 19th century, after boatbuilding on a large scale was undertaken for the first time. Many of these Shetland-built boats were larger and had other hull form modifications relative to earlier *fourerns* and *sixerns* (q.v.). After 1900, fully decked boats of 30 to 50 feet overall were built to this type of design, and used in haddock, herring and halibut fishing.

Shetland pony   A breed of pony peculiar to Shetland. It is much smaller relative to most breeds of horse. Between 1850 and 1910, Shetland ponies were used extensively for pulling wagons in the coal mines, and from 1870 onwards were bought as pets.

Shetland sheep   A breed of sheep peculiar to Shetland. Much smaller than most sheep breeds, it possesses very fine soft wool, known as Shetland wool, which is the basis for the reputation of Shetland knitwear.

shilling, Danish   A silver coin, at the beginning of the 17th century equal to 24s Scots, or two English shillings.

ship letter   A letter sent by ship, rather than by a postal service. This was the main means of transmission of letters by sea out of Shetland before the advent of the postal service.

sixern   An open boat rowed with six oars. The boats were double-ended, clinker-built, and about 18 feet of keel, used mainly for offshore fishing. Later 19th century sixerns tended to be larger, over 20 feet of keel and up to 30 feet overall, being often used as *flit-boats*, q.v.

sloop   A one-masted cutter-rigged vessel, having a fixed bowsprit and pro-portionately smaller sails.

smack   A decked, *ketch-rigged*, q.v., vessel, used for both fishing and trading.

small lines   Often virtually synonymous with *haddock lines*, q.v., used in haddock fishing in a Shetland context. Long lines for catching small fish, such as haddock, whiting, in distinction to *great lines*, q.v.

sound	A fish's swimming bladder.
spars	A general term for timber shaped for masts, yards, booms, gaffs, etc.
spent herring	See *brands*.
spinning	The process of manufacturing woollen thread into *yarn*, q.v., after *carding*, q.v. Traditional spinning was done using a spinning wheel.
staples, also *steeples*	A heap or stack of fish laid crosswise in a pile to dry, especially for *pining*, q.v.
stations	The localities used as shore bases in the fisheries. In the *haaf* fishing, this was commonly a stony beach. The cod fishing required a landing place for vessels with shelter and deep water access. Curing was carried out partly on the station, and often largely on nearby beaches used also in the open boat fisheries. Herring stations had similar requirements to cod stations, while curing was carried out at the point of landing.
statute labour	Compulsory labour on roads.
steam drifter	A wooden or steel-hulled vessel powered by a steam engine. These were introduced into the herring drift net fishery in the 1890s.
steam drying	A process for drying fish using pipes heated by passing steam through them. First used in Shetland in the mid-19th century for drying cod and ling.
stiver	1. A small, originally silver coin, of the Low Countries. 2. A type of coin of small value, e.g. German stivers.
stranded area	An area which has suffered a rather rapid absolute curtailment of local economic opportunity, posing the problem of adjustment to at least temporarily lowered incomes. In Shetland, this was brought about by the decline of the *haaf* and cod fisheries, Greenland whaling and subsistence agriculture, so that by the 1880s the crofters were less well off than they had been in the 1860s. It was only those areas where the haddock and herring fishings became effective substitute activities that the problems were alleviated; other districts continued to decline as people moved away, either by emigration, or seeking employment in the merchant service.
stranger boats	A colloquial Shetland expression referring to fishing boats from outwith the islands, especially Scots, English and others engaged in the herring fishing.
superior duties	An alternative name for the rents payable to the *Lordship estate*, q.v., including *scat*.
Swedish	Norway and Sweden were politically united until 1905, but geographical distinction is consistently made between Norwegian and Swedish vessels and ports in British shipping records.
sweetened spirits	Perfume or scent, smuggled by the Dutch herring fishermen in quantity in the 19th century.

tack	1. The leasehold tenure of an estate, land, fishing station, with rights to collect the revenues in return for payment of a sum of money, commonly known as tack duty, to the proprietor.
	2. A piece of land held on lease.
tacking	Sailing to and fro on courses against the wind, turning into the wind, at each change of course.
tacksman	One holding property in *tack*, q.v.
taft	A narrow plank in an open boat used for sitting on while rowing.
tanning	The process of immersing lines or nets in a solution of *bark*, q.v., in order to preserve them against the effects of immersion in salt sea water.
teinds	Tithes. Until the early 19th century these were generally paid in kind, hence the demand for valuation, so that these could be converted into money payments.
tilfers	Flat boards laid in the bottom of an open boat, to act as flooring.
tom	A short piece of line attaching the hook to the *baukt*, q.v. See *long line (great line)*.
tonnage	Varying measure of the size of a vessel.

lastage (see *last*): The last is taken as 2 tons, when used as a measure of carrying capacity of a ship, which it was in the Baltic and southern North Sea coastlands in the Middle Ages and early modern times, as late as the 18th century.

deadweight tonnage: The difference of a vessel's displacement when loaded and light; therefore, equal to the weight of the cargo she can carry. In common use for the measurement of cargo vessels.

displacement tonnage: The weight of water displaced by ship; therefore equal to the weight of the ship. Used for measuring warships.

gross tonnage: A measure of the cubic capacity of the ship, less machinery space and other deductions, arrived at according to specified formulae.

register tonnage: A similar measure to gross tonnage, although changes were made from time to time in the formulae. Thus the rules in the merchant shipping act of 1786 were changed in the similar act of 1854, for example. As a sailing ship has no machinery space, the register tonnage is the same as the gross tonnage, although in the later 19th century, it may not be quite the same due to minor regulations regarding the inclusion or otherwise of deckhouses, crew space, etc.

tons burden: A term used for a ship's carrying capacity, in common use until the 18th century, and calculated in many ways, often directly related to the type of cargo, salt, wine, etc. she was carrying, especially before the advent of standard formulae. This applies particularly to *lastage* (above), as grain, a common cargo, was measured in lasts.

Y

township	That part of the land enclosed by a head-dyke, containing the arable land and dwellings of the tenants.
truck system	The system embodying an agreement between merchants and customers whereby the merchant supplied the customer with credit, usually in kind, usually on the understanding that the customer dealt at the merchant's shop. It applied in Shetland to the disposal of the fishermen's fish, the buying of shop goods by the tenants, fitting out of crews for the Greenland whaling, and in the knitwear trade.
udal	A system of land tenure without feudal superior, dating from the Scandinavian settlement of Orkney and Shetland.
vent-jager	Literally, a *wind-hunter*. A fast sailing vessel used in the Dutch herring fishing of the 17th and 18th centuries to transport cargoes of herring, caught early in the season, direct to Holland. These herring fetched high prices which justified the extra expense.
voar	The spring; seed-time.
voe	A derivative of the Old Norse, *vágr*, a term applied in Orkney and Shetland to inlets of the sea, generally relatively narrow and sheltered from the open sea.
wadmel	A coarse, woollen cloth, woven in Orkney and Shetland, especially prior to the 17th century. Used in rent payment. See *wadmel measure*.
wadmel measure	Wadmel was measured in cuttells, and used as a money of account in the computation of rents. The cuttell was practically equivalent to an ell, or rather more than a yard. With the conversion of payment of rent into money in the early 17th century, six cuttells were equated with one gulden, or *shilling*, q.v., which was equal to 24s Scots, so that a shilling of wadmel meant six cuttells. The wadmel measure was subject to change in the 1570s, increasing by 25 per cent from 6 to 8 shillings per cuttell.
well smack	A *smack*, q.v., with a compartment built in above the bottom amidships, with holes through the bottom permitting circulation of sea-water within the well. The well was used for storage of fresh bait on outward voyages to cod fishing grounds, and also for keeping live cod, particularly during the final voyage of the season, when the smacks sometimes proceeded direct to the fresh fish market of Granton or the Humber ports. Although the English smacks were equipped with wells before the mid-19th century, there was only one such belonging to Shetland in 1860, and they were not acquired in appreciable numbers until the 1870s, as the fresh fish markets began to increase in importance.
West Coast herring fishing	A Shetland colloquial term for the herring fishing in the Minches, based mainly on Stornoway and Ullapool, in which Shetland boats participated, particularly after the advent of steam drifters and motor boats.
West Side	A Shetland colloquial term for the land and sea areas of West Mainland, St. Magnus Bay, and the bay of islands in the Scalloway area.
wherry	A decked fishing boat used by the cod fishers of Ireland and south-west Scotland in the Shetland area in the 1750s and 1760s.

wooden flake drying See *flakes*.

yager A small rowing boat used to travel between the shore and a fishing boat or trading vessel at anchor; a fishing vessel's boat. Sometimes used as a diminutive of *vent-jager*, q.v.

yard (croft) A stone enclosure built round a *croft* steading, used for storing corn, growing vegetables, stacking peats, and to provide shelter.

yard (ship) 1. A spar slung at its centre from, and forward of, a mast, and serving to support and extend a square sail.
2. Sometimes used indiscriminately for a gaff, particularly a large gaff, as on a *herring boat*, q.v.

yarn Spun woollen thread.

yoal See *'Ness yoal*.

zopindale A German coin, probably of silver, of uncertain value, in use in the Shetland trade with the German merchants in the late 16th century.

zulu A straight-stemmed hull form, with a steeply raked after stem, in contrast to the straight stern post of the *fifie*, q.v. Common, particularly among the larger class of herring boat acquired from the 1890s onwards.

Bibliography

MANUSCRIPT RECORDS

Shetland Archives

Bruce of Sumburgh Papers

Bruce of Symbister Papers

E. S. Reid Tait Collection

Hay of Laxfirth MSS

Tom Henderson Collection: Wreck Records compiled by R. Stuart Bruce; Miscellaneous Records

Irvine of Midbrake Papers

Lerwick Fishery Office, Records of

Lerwick Outport Records: Letter Books, Collector to Board, 1791-1890; Miscellaneous records

Lerwick Sheriff Court, Records of

Minutes of the Commissioners of Supply, 1753-1889 (incomplete)

Day Book of Thomas Gifford

G. M. Nelson Collection

Neven of Windhouse Papers

Scottish Record Office

Board of Trustees for Fisheries and Manufactures in Scotland, Records of

British Fishery Society, Letter Books

Court of Session Records: Petitions for sequestration and discharge of William Hay and Charles Ogilvy, and related papers

Department of Agriculture and Fisheries for Scotland, Records. Includes the records of the former Fishery Board for Scotland, and of the Board of Agriculture for Scotland

Exchequer Records: The Declared Accounts of Geo. McKenzie of Stonehyve and related papers; Customs Books, 2nd Ser., Orkney, Caithness and Shetland, 1669-1673

Crown Rentals: rental of Shetland, 1628

Morton Papers

Orkney and Shetland Papers

Papers of Alexander Piper of Newgrange, merchant in Edinburgh and Montrose

Scottish Board of Customs' Cash Accounts:
   Collectors' Incident Accounts, Port of Lerwick
   Minute Books
   Quarterly Returns for the Port of Lerwick, 1742-1830

Supplementary Parliamentary Papers

Treasury Records Accounts Scotland

National Library of Scotland

Chalmers MSS

Letter Book concerning the Earl of Morton's affairs in Zetland

Liston MSS

Melville Papers

Sibbald MSS. Small bound volume, nd., signed M.T.V., containing geographical descriptions of Shetland

Yester MSS

Library of the University of Edinburgh

Laing MSS

Public Record Office

Abstracts of Imports under Ports, Lerwick, 1873-1899. Customs 23

Abstracts of Exports under Ports, Lerwick, 1882-1899. Customs 24

Company Records

Hay & Company (Lerwick) Limited, Records

North of Scotland, Orkney and Shetland Shipping Company Limited, Records

Royal Bank of Scotland, Minutes of the Directors

Private Collections

Gardie Papers

Dr. Frances J. Shaw: Extracts from Commissary Court Records, Scottish Record Office

Dr. J. W. G. Wills: Extracts compiled from Thomas Mouat's Book of Zetland Product, Gardie Papers

PRINTED RECORDS

Parliamentary and Official Papers

Acts of the Parliaments of Scotland, eds. C. Innes, T. Thomson, A. Anderson (1814-1875)

Statutes at Large
Public General Statutes
Public General Acts

Calendar of State Papers relating to Scotland and Mary, Queen of Scots

Calendar of State Papers, Domestic Series

Calendar of Treasury Books and Papers

Calendar of Home Office Papers, George III

The Exchequer Rolls of Scotland

Register of the Privy Council of Scotland

Reports on the state of certain parishes in Scotland made to his Majesty's Commissioners for plantations of Kirks, etc. in pursuance of their ordinance date April 12th, 1627. The Parish of Nesting, by John Adamsone

Report by Thomas Tucker upon the settlement of revenues of Excise and Customs in Scotland, 1656. *Misc. Scott. Burgh Records Soc.* (1881)

Third Report from the Committee, appointed to enquire into the State of the British Fisheries, and into the most effectual means of their improvement and extension. Reports for Committees of the House of Commons, Vol. 10 (1785)

Minutes of Evidence taken before the Poor Law Enquiry Commission for Scotland (1843)

Report of the Commissioners appointed to enquire into the Sea Fisheries of the United Kingdom (1866)

Report of the Commissioners appointed to enquire into the Truck System (1871)

Report of the Commissioners appointed to enquire into the Truck System (Shetland) (1872)

Report of Her Majesty's Commissioners appointed to enquire into the conditions of the crofters and cottars in the Highlands and Islands of Scotland (1884)

Report of the Scottish Departmental Committee on the North Sea Fishing Industry (1914)

Report to the Board of Agriculture for Scotland on Home Industries in the Highlands and Islands (1914)

Annual Reports of the Fishery Board for Scotland (1882-1914)

Annual Statements of Trade and Navigation of the United Kingdom (1855-1914)

Newspapers and Periodicals

The Orkney and Zetland Chronicle (1825)
The Shetland Journal (1837)

The Orkney and Shetland Journal (1838)

The Orkney and Shetland Journal and Fisherman's Magazine (1838-39)

The Shetland Advertiser (1862-63)

The Shetland Times (1872-1914)

The Shetland News (1885-1914)

Manson's Shetland Alamanac (1891-1914)

Miscellaneous Printed Records

Anon, 'Acts and Statutes within the Lawting &c., within Orkney and Shetland, 1602-1640', *Maitland Club, 51, Misc., 2,* Part I (Edinburgh, 1840)

Balfour, David, 'Oppressions of the Sixteenth Century in the Islands of Orkney and Shetland', *Abbotsford and Maitland Clubs, 31* (Edinburgh, 1859)

Bang, Nina Ellinger, and Korst, Knud, *Tabeller over Skibsfart og Varestransport gennem Øresund, 1497-1783* (København og Leipzig, 1907-53)

Barclay, R. S., *The Court Book of Orkney and Shetland, 1612-1613* (Kirkwall, 1962)

Barclay, R. S., *The Court Book of Orkney and Shetland, 1614-1615,* Scott. Hist. Soc., 4th Ser., Vol. 4 (Edinburgh, 1967)

Donaldson, Gordon, *The Court Book of Shetland, 1602-1604* (Edinburgh, 1954)

Ferguson, James, *Papers illustrating the History of the Scots Brigade in the Service of the United Netherlands, 1572-1872,* Scott. Hist. Soc. (Edinburgh, 1899)

Firth, C. H., *Scotland and the Commonwealth,* Scott. Hist. Soc. (Edinburgh, 1895)

Firth, C. H., *Scotland and the Protectorate,* Scott. Hist. Soc. (Edinburgh, 1899)

Goudie, Gilbert, *The Diary of the Reverend John Mill, Minister of the Parishes of Dunrossness, Sandwick and Cunningsburgh in Shetland, 1740-1803,* Scott. Hist. Soc. (Edinburgh, 1889)

Johnston, A. W. & A., *Orkney and Shetland Records* (Edinburgh, 1907-42)

MacGillivray, Evan, 'Description of Shetland, Orkney and the Highlands of Scotland, By Richard James', *Orkney Misc., 1* (1958), 48-56

Marwick, J. D. *Extracts of the Records of the Convention of Royal Burghs of Scotland* (Edinburgh, 1870-78)

Millar, A. H., *The Compt Buik of David Wedderburne, merchant of Dundee, 1557-1630, together with the Shipping Lists of Dundee, 1580-1618,* Scott. Hist. Soc. (Edinburgh, 1898)

Renwick, R. (ed.), 'Extracts from the Records of the Royal Burgh of Stirling, A.D. 1519-1666', *The Glasgow, Stirlingshire and Sons of the Rock Society* (1887)

Terry, C. Sanford, *The Cromwellian Union,* Scott. Hist. Soc. (Edinburgh, 1902)

SECONDARY SOURCES

Literature: Shetland

Anderson, Arthur, *Striking Instance of Corn-Law Oppression* (London, 1844)

Anderson, Arthur, *Letters between Arthur Anderson and the Fishery Board* (N.P., 1845)

Anderson, Peter F., *Robert Stewart, Earl of Orkney and Lord of Shetland* (Edinburgh, 1982)

Aston University Sub-aqua Club, *The wreck of the 'Kennemerland'* (Birmingham, 1974)

Baldwin, J. R. (ed.), *Scandinavian Shetland: an ongoing tradition?* (Edinburgh, 1978)

Ball, Ronald G., 'The Shetland garrison, 1665-1668', *J. Soc. Army Hist. Res.*, 43 (173) (1965), 5-25

Barclay, R. S., 'The population of the parishes and islands of Shetland, 1755-1961'. *In* Cluness, A. T. (ed.), *The Shetland Book* (Lerwick, 1967), 44-56

Bax, A., Martin, C. J. M., '"De Liefde", a Dutch Indiaman lost on the Out Skerries, Shetland, in 1711', *Int. J. Naut. Archaeol.*, 3 (1974), 81-90

Beenhakker, A. J. *Hollanders in Shetland* (Lerwick, 1973)

Berry, R. J., Johnston, J. L., *The natural history of Shetland* (London, 1980)

Boud, R. C., 'Samuel Hibbert and the early geological mapping of the Shetland Islands', *Cartographic J.*, 14 (1978), 81-88

Brand, Rev. John., *A brief description of Orkney, Shetland, Pightland Firth and Caithness* (Edinburgh, 1701)

Brill, E. V. K., 'Whalsay and the Bremen connection', *Shetland Life, No. 17* (1982), 10-17

Brill, E. V. K., 'More Bremen connections with Shetland', *Shetland Life, No. 30* (1983), 34-37, 45

Bruce, R. Stuart, 'Some old-time Shetlandic wrecks', *Old Lore Misc. of Orkney, Shetland, Caithness and Sutherland* (1907-12), 1, 35-42, 123-128, 176-178, 217-220, 281-284, 308-309; 2, 31-33, 101-104; 3, 34-35, 164-165; 5, 20-24, 73-78

Bruce, R. Stuart, 'Glimpses of Shetland life, 1718-1753', *Old Lore Misc. of Orkney, Shetland, Caithness and Sutherland* (1912-13), 5, 156-159; 6, 31-37, 92-101, 129-135

Bruce, R. Stuart, 'The sixern of Shetland', *The Mariners' Mirror*, 4 (1914), 289-300

Bruce, R. Stuart, 'The haaf fishing and Shetland trading', *The Mariners' Mirror*, 8 (1922), 48-52; 17 (1931), 356-376

Catton, Rev. James, *The history and description of the Shetland Islands* (London, 1838)

Cluness, A. T. (ed.), *The Shetland Book* (Lerwick, 1967)

Cohen, A. P., 'The Whalsay croft: traditional work and customary identity in modern times'. *In* Wallman, S. (ed.), *Social anthropology of work* (London, 1979), 1-15

Coull, J. R., 'A comparison of demographic trends in the Faroe and Shetland Islands', *Trans. Inst. Br. Geogr.* 41 (1967), 159-166

Coull, J. R., 'The herring fishery in Shetland in the first half of the nineteenth century', *Northern Scotland*, 6 (1983), 123-40

Coull, J. R., 'Shetland's herring fishery — economic boom a century ago', *Shetland Life 33* (1983), 26-29

Cowie, Robert, *Shetland: descriptive and historical*, 2nd ed. (Edinburgh, 1874)

Crawford, Barbara E., 'The Earldom of Orkney and Lordship of Shetland; a re-interpretation of their pledging to Scotland, 1468-70', *Saga Book of the Viking Club*, 17 (1967-68), 156-176

Crawford, Barbara E., 'The pawning of Orkney and Shetland; a re-consideration of the events of 1460-9', *Scott. Hist. Rev.*, 48 (1969), 35-53

Crawford, Barbara E., 'Sir David Sinclair of Sumburgh: 'Foud' of Shetland and Governor of Bergen Castle'. *In* Baldwin, J. R. (ed.), *Scandinavian Shetland: an ongoing tradition?* (Edinburgh, 1978), 1-11

Crawford, Barbara E., 'The fifteenth century "Genealogy of the Earls of Orkney" and its reflection of the contemporary political and cultural situation in the earldom', *Mediaeval Scandinavia 10* (1978), 156-178

Crawford, Barbara E., 'The pledging of the islands in 1469: the historical background'. *In* Withrington, Donald J., *Shetland and the outside world, 1469-1969* (Oxford, 1983), 32-48

Crawford, Rev. James, *The parish of Lerwick, 1701-1901* (Lerwick, 1901)

Donald, Stuart B., 'Economic changes since 1946'. *In* Withrington, Donald J. (ed.), *Shetland and the outside world, 1469-1969* (Oxford, 1983), 198-215

Donaldson, Gordon, *Shetland life under Earl Patrick* (Edinburgh, 1958)

Donaldson, Gordon, *Northwards by Sea.* 2nd Edition (Edinburgh, 1978)

Donaldson, Gordon, 'The Scots settlement in Shetland'. *In* Withrington, Donald J. (ed.), *Shetland and the outside world, 1469-1969* (Oxford, 1983), 8-19

Duncan, W. R. *Directory to Zetland* (Aberdeen, 1854)

Duncan, W. R. *Zetland Directory and Guide. 2nd Edition* (Edinburgh, 1861)

Edmondston, Arthur, *A view of the ancient and present state of the Zetland Islands* (Edinburgh, 1809)

Edmondston, Arthur, *On the nature of the cod fishing carried on off the coasts of Zetland* (Edinburgh, 1820)

Espeland, Anton, 'Norsk samband med Orknøy og Hjaltland', *Norsk Aarbok, 9* (1928), 39-54

Eunson, J., *The shipwrecks of Fair Isle* (Fair Isle, n.d.)

Evershed, Henry, 'On the agriculture of the islands of Shetland', *Trans. Highland and Agric. Soc. Scot.*, 4th Ser., 4 (1874), 186-228

Farrell, R. T., Milne, P. H., 'Underwater surveying at Gulber Wick in Shetland', *Int. J. Naut. Archaeol.* 2 (1) (1973), 168-176

Fea, James, *The present state of the Orkney Islands considered, and an account of the new method of fishing on the coasts of Shetland, with observations* (Edinburgh, 1775)

Fenton, A., *The Northern Isles: Orkney and Shetland* (Edinburgh, 1978)

Flinn, Derek, 'Coastal and submarine features round the Shetland Islands', *Proc. Geol. Ass. 75* (1964), 321-339

Forster, W. A., Higgs, K. B., 'The "Kennemerland" 1971', *Int. J. Naut. Archaeol.* 2 (1973), 291-300

Friedland, K., 'Der Hansische Shetlandhandel'. In *Stadt und Land in der Geschichte des Ostseeraums* (Lübeck, 1973), 66-79

Gifford, Thomas, *Historical description of the Zetland Islands in the year 1733* (Edinburgh, 1879)

Goodier, R. (ed.), *The Natural environment of Shetland* (Edinburgh, 1974)

Goodlad, C. A., *Shetland fishing saga* (Lerwick, 1971)

Goudie, Gilbert, *The Celtic and Scandinavian antiquities of Shetland* (London, 1904)

Graeme, P. N. S., 'The Parliamentary representation of Orkney and Shetland, 1754-1900', *Orkney Misc.*, 1 (1953), 64-104

Graham, John J., 'The Weisdale evictions', *The New Shetlander, 130* (1979), 29-31

Graham, John J., 'Social changes during the Quincentennium'. *In* Withrington, Donald J. (ed.), *Shetland and the outside world, 1469-1969* (Oxford, 1983), 216-233

Grant, Francis J., *The County Families of the Zetland Islands* (Lerwick, 1893)

Gregson, Keith, 'Seamanship and Kinship: one Shetland Family's connection with the North East of England', *Northern Studies, 16* (1981), 29-37

Halcrow, A., *The Sail Fishermen of Shetland* (Lerwick, 1950)

Heineberg, H., *Wirtschaftsgeographie Strukturwandlungen auf den Shetland-Inseln* (Paderborn, 1969)

Henderson, T., 'Daughter of the dragon', *The Trident 7* (1945), 75

Henderson, T., 'The half deckers: a story of success and failure'. *In* Graham, J. J., Tait, J. (eds.), *Shetland Folk Book, 7* (Lerwick, 1980)

Henderson, T., 'Shetland's first steamship and first Parliamentary election', *Shetland Life No. 20* (1982), 8-10

Hibbert, Samuel, *A description of the Shetland Islands* (Edinburgh, 1822)

Jameson, Robert, *An outline of the mineralogy of the Shetland Islands and the Island of Arran* (Edinburgh, 1798)

Johnston, A. W., 'Rentals of the Crown Lands and revenues of the Lordship of Shetland c. 1507-1513 - c. 1832', *Old Lore Misc. of Orkney, Shetland, Caithness and Sutherland, 10* (1935-46), 262-286

Johnston, L. G., *Laurence Williamson* (Lerwick, 1971)

Johnston, Robert L., *A Shetland country merchant* (Lerwick, 1979)

Kranenburg, H. A. H. Boelmans, 'The Netherlands Fisheries and the Shetland Islands'. *In* Withrington, Donald J. (ed.), *Shetland and the outside world, 1469-1969* (Oxford, 1983), 96-106

Laurenson, J. J., 'Owre da hills ta Urie', *The New Shetlander No. 58* (1961), 21-23

Low, Rev. George, *A tour through the islands of Orkney and Schetland in 1774* (Edinburgh, 1879)

Mackay, J., *Shetland* (Dumfries, 1979)

Martin, C. J. M., *Full fathom Five: wrecks of the Spanish Armada* (London, 1975)

Miller, John A., Flinn, Derek, 'A survey of the age relations of Shetland rocks'. *Lpool. Manchr. Geol. J., 5* (1966), 95-116

Mowat, J. C., 'Inhabitants of Northmavine, Shetland, 18th and 19th century', *Scot. Geneal., 17,* (1970), 91-104

Muckelroy, K., 'The integration of historical and archaeological data concerning an historic wreck site: the "Kennemerland"', *World Archaeology 7* (1976), 280-290

Native of Zetland, A, 'On the State of the fisheries in the islands of Zetland, 1786', *Prize Essays and Trans. of the Highland Soc. of Scot., 1* (1799), 275-293

Neill, Patrick, *A tour through some of the islands of Orkney and Shetland* (Edinburgh, 1806)

The New Statistical Account of Scotland: The Shetland Islands (N.P., 1841)

Nicolaisen, W. F. H., 'The post-Norse place-names of Shetland'. *In* Withrington, Donald J., *Shetland and the outside world, 1469-1969* (Oxford, 1983), 69-85.

Nicolson, James R., *Lerwick Harbour* (Lerwick, 1975)

Nicolson, James R., *Shetland's fishing vessels* (Lerwick, 1981)

Nicolson, James R., *Hay & Company: merchants in Shetland* (Lerwick, 1982)

Nicolson, John, *Arthur Anderson: a founder of the P & O Company* (Lerwick, 1932)

O'Dell, Andrew C., *The historical geography of the Shetland Islands* (Lerwick, 1939)

O'Dell, Andrew C., 'The Shetland Islands' wreck rose', *The Mariners' Mirror, 19* (1939), 137-145

Osler, Adrian G., *Open boats of Shetland: South Mainland and Fair Isle*, National Maritime Museum, Monographs and Reports No. 58 (London, 1983)

Peterkin, Alexander, *Notes on Orkney and Zetland* (Edinburgh, 1822)

Ployen, Christian, *Reminiscences of a voyage to Shetland, Orkney and Scotland in the summer of 1839* (Lerwick, 1894)

Price, R., 'The 1974 expedition to the Dutch wrecks of Out Skerries', *Int. J. Naut. Archaeol., 4* (1975), 388

Price, R., Muckelroy, K., 'The second season of work on the "Kennemerland" site 1973. An interim report', *Int. J. Naut. Archaeol., 3* (1974), 257-268

Price, R., Muckelroy, K., 'The "Kennemerland" site: the third and fourth seasons 1974 and 1976. An interim report', *Int. J. Naut. Archaeol., 6* (1977), 187-218

Price, R., Muckelroy, K., 'The "Kennemerland" site: the fifth season 1978. An interim report', *Int. J. Naut. Archaeol., 8* (1979), 311-320

Price, R., Muckelroy, K., Willies, L., 'The "Kennemerland" site: a report on the lead ingots', *Int. J. Naut. Archaeol., 9* (1) (1980), 7-25

Robson, A., *The saga of a ship* (Lerwick, 1982)

Saint-Clair, Roland W., *The Saint-Clairs of the Isles* (Auckland, N.Z., 1898)

Sandison, C., *The sixareen and her racing descendants* (Lerwick, 1954)

Sandison, William, *A Shetland merchant's daybook in 1762* (Lerwick, 1934)

Shand, J., 'Foreign coin in Shetland', *Old Lore Misc. of Orkney, Shetland, Caithness and Sutherland, 6* (1913), 37-40

Shaw, Frances J., *The Northern and Western Islands of Scotland: their economy and society in the seventeenth century* (Edinburgh, 1980)

Shirreff, John, *General view of the agriculture of the Shetland Islands* (Edinburgh, 1814)

Sibbald, Sir Robert, *Description of the Isles of Orkney and Zetland* (Edinburgh, 1711)

Simpson, John M., 'The discovery of Shetland from *The Pirate* to the Tourist Board'. *In* Withrington, Donald J. (ed.), *Shetland and the outside world, 1469-1969* (Oxford, 1983), 136-149

Sinclair, Sir John, *Report of the Committee of the Highland Society of Scotland, to whom the subject of Shetland wool was referred* (Edinburgh,1790)

Sinclair, Sir John, *The Statistical Account of Scotland* (Edinburgh, 1791-99)

Skirving, R. S., 'On the agriculture of the islands of Shetland', *Trans. Highland and Agric. Soc., 4th Ser., 4* (1874), 229-263

Small, Alan, 'The distribution of settlement in Shetland and Faroe in Viking times', *Saga Book of the Viking Club, 17* (1967-68), 145-155

Small, A., 'Shetland: location the key to historical geography', *Scott. Geog. Mag., 85* (3) (1969), 155-161

Small, A., *The Norse building tradition in Shetland* (Stavanger, 1981)

Smith, Brian, Introduction (to facsimile reprint of 'An historical description of the Zetland Islands by Thomas Gifford, Esq.') (Sandwick, 1976), 8pp.

Smith, Brian, 'Shetland archives and sources of Shetland history', *History Workshop* (1977), 203-214

Smith, Brian, 'Scotsmen in Shetland, 1500-1700: a re-interpretation' (mimeo, n.d.)

Smith, Brian, '"Lairds" and "Improvement" in 17th and 18th century Shetland'. *In* Devine, T. M. (ed.), *Lairds and improvement in the Scotland of the Enlightenment*, Scott. Hist. Soc. (Edinburgh, 1979), 11-20

Smith, Brian, 'Stock Stove houses'. *In* Graham, J. J., Tait, J. (eds.), *Shetland Folk Book 7* (Lerwick, 1980)

Smith, Captain John, *England's improvement revived, Vol. VI* (1662). Section dealing with Shetland reprinted in *MacFarlane's Geographical Collections, Vol. III*, 60-65, Scott. Hist. Soc. (Edinburgh, 1908)

Smith, Hance D., 'The development of Shetland fisheries and fishing communities'. *In* Fricke, P. H. (ed.), *Seafarer and community* (London, 1973), 8-29

Smith, Hance, D., *The making of modern Shetland* (Lerwick, 1977)

Smith, Hance D., Introduction (to facsimile reprint of the Report of the Commissioners appointed to enquire into the Truck System (Shetland) (Sandwick, 1978)

Smith, Hance D., 'The Scandinavian influence in the making of modern Shetland'. *In* Baldwin, John R. (ed.), *Scandinavian Shetland: an ongoing tradition?* (Edinburgh, 1978), 23-35

Smout, T. C., 'An old scheme for Shetland. Opposition to the Hansa', *The Shetland News*, 11th November, 1958

Standen, Edward, *A paper on the Shetland Islands* (Oxford, 1845)

Stenuit, R., 'Early relics of the VOC trade from Shetland: the wreck of the flute "Lastdrager" lost off Yell, 1653', *Int. J. Naut. Archaeol.*, 3 (1974), 213-256

Stenuit, R., 'The wreck of the pink "Evstafi": a transport of the Imperial Russian Navy, lost off Shetland in 1780', *Int. J. Naut. Archaeol.*, 5 (3) (1976), 222-243; (4), 317-331

Stenuit, R., 'The wreck of the "Curacao": a Dutch warship lost off Shetland in 1729 while convoying a fleet of returning East Indiamen: an interim report', *Int. J. Naut. Archaeol.*, 6 (2) (1977), 101-125

Tait, E. S. Reid, 'Minutes of the Scalloway Road Subscription Committee', *Hjaltland Misc.*, 4 (1946), 18-79

Tait, E. S. Reid, 'The mussel scaap in Bressay Sound', *Hjaltland Misc.*, 4 (1947), 87-91

Tait, E. S. Reid, *Some notes on the Shetland Hanseatic trade* (Lerwick, 1955)

The Editor, 'Norway-Shetland trade in 1627', *The Shetland News*, 8th May, 1947

Thompson, Paul, Wailey, Tony, and Lummis, Trevor, *Living the fishing* (London, 1983)

Thomson, W. P. L., 'Funzie, Fetlar a Shetland runrig township in the nineteenth century', *Scot. Geog. Mag.*, 86 (3) (1970), 170-185

Thomson, W. P. L., 'Population and depopulation'. *In* Withrington, Donald J. (ed.), *Shetland and the outside world, 1469-1969* (Oxford, 1983), 150-180

Tonkin, J. W., 'Two Hanseatic houses in the Shetlands', *Hansische Geschichtsblätter, 94* (1976), 81-82

Thowsen, Atle, 'The Norwegian export of boats to Shetland and its influence upon Shetland boatbuilding and usage', *Sjøfartshistorisk Arbok, 1969, 1969*, 145-208

Tudor, John R., *The Orkneys and Shetland* (London, 1883)

Wills, J. W. G., Of laird and tenant, Ph.D. thesis, unpubl. (University of Edinburgh, 1975)

Withrington, Donald J. (ed.), *Shetland and the outside world, 1469-1969* (Oxford, 1983)

Young, Margaret D., 'Shetland history in the Scottish records'. *In* Withrington, Donald J. (ed.), *Shetland and the outside world, 1469-1969* (Oxford, 1983), 119-135

Literature: General

Abel, W., *Agricultural fluctuations in Europe: from the 13th to the 20th centuries* (London, 1980)

Ackerman, E. A., 'Where is a research frontier?', *Annals Ass. Amer. Geogr. 53* (1963), 429-440

Adams, I. H., 'The salt industry of the Forth Basin', *Scott. Geog. Mag., 81* (1965), 153-162

Adams, Ian H., *Directory of former Scottish commonties*, Scott. Record Soc. New Ser. 2 (Edinburgh, 1971)

Baasch, Ernst, 'Hamburgs Seeschiffahrt und Waarenhandel vom Ende des 16.bis zur Mitte des 17. Jahrhunderts', *Zeits. des Vereins für Hamburgische Gesch., 9* (1889), 295-420

Baetens, R., 'The organisation and effects of Flemish privateering in the seventeenth century', *Acta Historiae Nederlandicae, 9* (1976), 48-75

Beaujon, A., *The history of the Dutch sea fisheries*, International Fisheries Exhibition Literature Vol. 9, Part I (London, 1883)

Berend, I. T., Ránki, G., *The European periphery and industrialization: 1780-1914* (Cambridge, 1982)

Bridbury, A. R., *England and the salt trade* (Cambridge, 1955)

Brøgger, A. W., *Ancient emigrants* (Oxford, 1929)

Bugge, A., *Den Norske traelasthandels historie* (Skien, 1925)

Checkland, S. G., *Scottish banking: a history, 1695-1973* (Glasgow, 1975)

Coull, J. R., 'Fisheries in Scotland in the 16th, 17th, and 18th centuries: the evidence in MacFarlane's Geographical Collections', *Scott. Geog. Mag., 93* (1) (1977), 5-14

Day, J. P., *Public administration in the Highlands and Islands of Scotland* (London, 1918)

Dollinger, Philippe, *The German Hansa* (London, 1970)

Ehrenberg, R., 'Aus der hamburgischen Handelsgeschichte', *Zeits. des Vereins für Hamburgische Gesch., 10* (1899), 1-40

Entholt, Herman, and Beutin, Ludwig, 'Bremen und Europa', *Quellen und Forschungen zur bremischen Handelsgeschichte, Heft. 1* (Weimar, 1937), 16-19, 58-62

Flinn, M. W. (ed.), *Scottish population history from the seventeenth century to the 1930s* (Cambridge, 1977)

Findlay, J. R., *A history of Peterhead* (Peterhead, 1933)

Fulton, T. W., *The sovereignty of the sea* (London, 1911)

Gade, J. A., *The Hanseatic control of Norwegian commerce in the Late Middle Ages* (Leiden, 1951)

Galbraith, J. K., *The age of uncertainty* (London, 1977)

Galtung, J., Rudeng, E., Heistad, T., 'On the last 2,500 years in Western history, and some remarks on the coming 500'. *In* Burke, P. (ed.), *The New Cambridge Modern History, 13: Companion Volume* (Cambridge, 1979), 318-361

Gillett, E., MacMahon, K. A., *A history of Hull* (Oxford, 1980)

Graham, G. S., 'The ascendancy of the sailing ship, 1850-1885', *Ec. Hist. Rev.*, 2 (1956-57), 74-88

Grassie, James, *Highland experiment: the story of the Highlands and Islands Development Board* (Aberdeen, 1983)

Gray, Malcolm, 'The consolidation of the crofting system', *Agric. Hist. Rev.*, 5 (1957), 31-47

Gray, Malcolm, *The Highland economy, 1750-1850* (Edinburgh, 1957)

Gray, Malcolm, 'Organisation and growth in the East Coast herring fishery', 1800-1885'. *In* Payne, P. L. (ed.), *Studies in Scottish Business History* (London, 1967), 187-216

Gray, Malcolm, *The fishing industries of Scotland, 1790-1914: a study in regional adaptation* (Oxford, 1978)

Hoel, A. F., Werenskiold, W., 'Glaciers and snowfields in Norway', *Norsk Polarinstitutt Skrifter, IV* (114), (Oslo, 1962)

Jackson, G., *The British whaling trade* (London, 1978)

Lamb, H. H., *Climate: history and the modern world* (London, 1982)

Lane, F. C., 'Tonnages: medieval and modern', *Ec. Hist. Rev., 2nd Ser.*, 17 (1964-65), 213-233

Lawton, R., 'Historical geography from the coming of the Anglo-Saxons to the Industrial Revolution'. *In* Watson, J. Wreford, Sissons, J. B. (eds.), *The British Isles: a systematic geography* (London, 1964)

Lenman, Bruce, *From Esk to Tweed: harbours, ships and men of the East Coast of Scotland* (Glasgow, 1975)

Lythe, S. G. E., *The economy of Scotland, 1550-1625* (Edinburgh, 1960)

Lythe, S. G. E., 'The Dundee whale fishery', *Scott. J. Pol. Econ.*, 11 (1964), 158-169

MacLeod, I. (ed.), *To the Greenland whaling: Alexander Trotter's Journal of the voyage of the 'Enterprise' in 1856 from Fraserburgh and Lerwick* (Stornoway, 1979)

March, E. J., *Inshore craft of Britain in the days of sail and oar* (Newton Abbot, 1970)

Marwick, Hugh, *Merchant lairds of long ago* (Kirkwall, 1936-39)

Mason, John, *A history of Scottish experiments in rural education from the 18th century to the present day* (London, 1936)

Michell, A. R., 'The European fisheries in early modern history'. *In* Rich, E. E., Wilson, C. H. (eds.), *Cambridge Economic History of Europe, Vol. V: The economic organisation of early modern Europe* (Cambridge, 1977), 133-184

Michie, R. C., 'North East Scotland and the Northern Whale Fishing, 1752-1893', *Northern Scotland 3* (1) (1979)

Muckelroy, K., 'A systematic approach to scattered wreck sites', *Int. J. Naut. Archaeol.*, 4 (1975), 173-190

Muckelroy, K., 'Historic wreck sites in Britain and their environment', *Int. J. Naut. Archaeol.*, 6 (1) (1977), 47-59

Munn, C. W., *The Scottish provincial banking companies, 1747-1864* (Edinburgh, 1981)

Munro, W., *Scottish lighthouses* (Stornoway, 1979)

Naess, And., 'Skottehandelen på Sunnhordland', *Sunnhordland Tidss.*, 7 (1920), 7-85

Nicolaisen, W. F. H., *Scottish place-names: their study and significance* (London, 1976)

Nicolaysen, N., 'Skrifter og optegnelser angaaende Norge og Forfattede efter Reformationen', *Norsk Magasin, II* (Christiania, 1868)

Ouren, T., 'The Norwegian ice trade'. *In* Proctor, D. V. (ed.), *Ice-carrying trade at sea*, National Maritime Museum. Maritime Monographs and Reports No. 49 (London, 1981), 31-42

Pollard, S., *Peaceful conquest: the industrialisation of Europe 1760-1970* (Oxford, 1981)

Pollard, S., *The integration of the European economy since 1815* (London, 1981)

Rostow, W. W., *The stages of economic growth: a non-communist manifesto* (Cambridge, 1960)

Rymer, L., 'The Scottish kelp industry', *Scott. Geog. Mag.*, 90 (3) (1974), 142-152

Seton-Watson, Hugh, *Nations and states: an inquiry into the origins of nations and the politics of nationalism* (London, 1977)

Smith, C. E., *From the deep of the sea* (London, 1922)

Smout, T. C., *Scottish trade on the eve of Union, 1660-1707* (Edinburgh, 1963)

Smout, T. C., 'Scottish landowners and economic growth, 1650-1850', *Scott. J. Pol. Econ.*, 11 (1964), 214-234

Sperling, J., 'The international payments mechanism in the seventeenth and eighteenth centuries', *Ec. Hist. Rev.*, Ser. 2, 14 (1961-62), 446-468

Supple, B. E., 'Currency and commerce in the early seventeenth century', *Ec. Hist. Rev.*, Ser. 2, 10 (1957), 239-245

Stewart, J. Innes, 'The Scottish herring fishing industry and the factors which affect the market for current herring', *Scott. Geog. Mag.*, 47 (1930), 219-227

Thomas, H., *An unfinished history of the world* (London, 1979)

Thompson, D'Arcy W., *On whales landed at the Scottish whaling stations during the years 1908-14 and 1920-27*, Fishery Board for Scotland, Scientific Investigations, 1928, III (Edinburgh)

Thomson, W. P. L., *Kelp-making in Orkney* (Kirkwall, 1983)

Thowsen, Atle, 'Bergen — a Norwegian seafaring town', *Maritime Hist.*, 3 (1) (1973), 3-34

Trebilcock, C., *The industrialisation of the continental powers, 1780-1914* (London, 1981)

Turnock, D., *The Historical Geography of Scotland since 1707* (Cambridge, 1982)

Tveite, Stein, *Engelsk-Norsk trelasthandel, 1640-1710* (Oslo, 1961)

Unger, Richard W., *The ship in the medieval economy, 600-1600* (London, 1980)

Utterström, G., 'Climatic fluctuations and population problems in early modern history', *Sc. Ec. Hist. Rev.*, 3 (1) (1955), 1-47

Vamplew, Wray, *Salvesen of Leith* (London, 1975)

Vilar, Pierre, *La Catalogne dans l'Espagne Moderne: Recherches sur les Fondements Economiques des Structures Nationales* (Paris, 1963)

Vives, Jaime Vincens, *An economic history of Spain* (Princeton, N.J., 1969)

Wallerstein, I., 'Dutch hegemony in the seventeenth century world economy'. *In* Aymard, M. (ed.), *Dutch capitalism, world capitalism* (Cambridge, 1981), Ch. 2, 93-145

Willis, Douglas, P., The changing cultural landscape of Orkney, M. Litt. Thesis, Unpubl. (University of Aberdeen, 1967)

Index

z

Garriock, Peter, 105
Garthspool, 123, 221, 222
Genoa, 72, 237
George, C. J., of Nyholm, 100
George Rose, 112-113
German Empire, herring market, 172, 173
German market, dried fish, 67, 70; herring, 172-173
German merchants, 10-20, 77, 80, 94, 213, 226, 228, 284, 285, 286; duties on, 38-39; end of trade, 11, 38-39; exports by, 19-20; imports to Shetland, 18-19; landowners, 16; location, 13; 'moscopes', 12; operation, 15; trade points, 14; tenants, 17; timespan, 36
Germany, 74, 174, 197, 226, 235, 249
Gibraltar, 72, 238
Gifford, Patrick, 63
Gifford, Robert, 227
Gifford, Thomas of Busta, 24, 38, 44, 56, 61-62, 63, 70, 76, 80, 82, 84, 86, 88, 227, 235; Daybook, 56
gin, 60, 76, 80, 81, 96, 97, 98, 99, 100, 101, 102-104; gin and tea shops, 60
Girlsta, 117, 118, 216; laird of, 62
Glasgow, 65, 84, 141, 142, 156, 165, 170, 179, 188, 232, 235, 236, 238, 239, 244, 260, 261, 272
Gluss Voe, 13, 14, 16, 21
Godøysund, 33, 34, 234
Good Friend, 279
Gothenburg, 81, 99, 173, 234, 266, 271, 272, 274
Goudie, Gilbert, 288
Grace, 16
Grangemouth, 188, 198, 239, 272
Granton, 165, 198, 255, 260, 272
great boats, 223
Great Britain *see* Britain
Great Yarmouth, 208, 237, 238, 240, 252, 275
Greenland, 271, 272; fleet, 85; whaling, 88-89, 94, 96, 101, 128, 143, 158, 202; whalers, 123, 152, 274
Greenock, 65, 231, 235, 237, 243, 244
Greig, James, 105
Greig of Sandsound, 120
Grierson of Quendale, 127
Grimista, 222
Grimsby, 198, 231, 232, 272
Grimstad, 238
Grutness, 23, 53, 122, 193, 273; Voe, 13, 41, 81
Gulberwick, 27, 273
Gunnister Voe, 13, 14, 15, 16
Gutcher, 183

haaf fishery, 46-55; boats, 46-48; curing, 49; fishing grounds, 50, 52; improvements in,

85; land interests, 51, 54; method of fishing, 48; migration of labour, 51, 54; stations, 48-49, 50, 52-53; time span, 94, 107, 109, 165
Haaf Gruney, 118
haddock fishery, beginnings, 112, 168-169; boats, 179; location, 191, 192; trawlers, 197
half deck boats, 107, 113
halibut, 169
Halle, 173
Ham (Bressay), 122
Hamar Voe, 193, 194
Hamburg, 9, 11, 172, 197, 227, 229, 233, 234, 235, 236, 237, 238, 242, 250, 264, 271, 272, 280, 286; first contacts, 8, 10; 17th century, 20, 37, 59, 62, 65; 18th century market, 71, 72, 74, 75; 18th century imports from, 76, 78, 80, 83, 94, 97, 133, 135
Hamburg merchants, 39
Hamefarin, 285
Hamnavoe (Burra), 120, 122, 124, 191, 193, 228
Hamnavoe (Northmavine), 96
Hannover, 173
Hanoverian Succession, 84
Hanseatic League, 7-8, 9, 226; town, 289
Hansetag, 11
Haroldswick, 122, 273, 275, 280
Harriestede, Simon, 15
harrowbills, 80
harvest failures, 43-44, 82-83, 84, 107, 109, 136-137, 159, 182-184
Hay and Company, 104, 109, 112, 124, 169, 170, 179, 201, 246, 257, 260
Hay, James, 97, 99-100, 106, 110, 112, 227, 228
Hay of Laxfirth, 96, 100, 120
Hay and Ogilvy, 105, 106, 107, 109, 113, 118, 119, 124, 140, 142, 151, 159, 196, 229, 239-240, 257, 282, 285
Hay, William, 99, 104, 105, 106, 107, 114, 115, 123, 140-141, 216
Hayfield, 117
Hay's Dock, 107, 222, 240
hazel cuts, 80
Helliness, 271, 273
Helmsdale, 250
hemp, 86
Henderson, William, of Bardister, 95
Henderson of Gardie, 61; William, 61, 279; Magnus, 61; James, 64
herring curers, 174
herring fishing, 86, 94, 104, 105-106; early 19th century, 112-115, 120, 122-123; 1880-1914, 170-182, 192-197, 257-258; Herring Industry Board, 282, 285
herring luggers, 170; stations, 108, 115, 120, 122-123, 180, 192-194, 250; trade, 20, 75, 84, 94, 134-136, 160, 166, 172-179, 240, 242, 245, 256, 259